John Bradshawe

FROM 24/11/2010.
Richard L. Bradshaw
5 Tiburon Court
Manhattan Beach.
C.A. 90266

GOD'S BATTLEAXE

THE LIFE OF LORD PRESIDENT JOHN BRADSHAWE
(1603-1659)

Thou art my battleaxe and weapon of war:
For with thee will I break in pieces the Nations
And with thee I will destroy Kingdoms.
Jeremiah 51:20

RICHARD LEE BRADSHAW
Manhattan Beach, California
2010

Copyright © 2010 by Richard Lee Bradshaw.

Library of Congress Control Number: 2010914181
ISBN: Hardcover   978-1-4535-8393-7
               Softcover   978-1-4535-8392-0
               Ebook   978-1-4535-8394-4

All rights reserved. No part of this book may be reproduced or transmitted in any form or by any means, electronic or mechanical, including photocopying, recording, or by any information storage and retrieval system, without permission in writing from the copyright owner.

This book was printed in the United States of America.

To order additional copies of this book, contact:
Xlibris Corporation
1-888-795-4274
www.Xlibris.com
Orders@Xlibris.com
84720

CONTENTS

Introduction 11
Chapter One: The Bradshaw Family 23
Chapter Two: Up to London and Gray's Inn 49
Chapter Three: Every Subject Worse than a Turkish Slave. 64
Chapter Four: The Influence of Edward Coke,
    William Prynne, and John Lilburne 87
Chapter Five: Back to the High Peak Forest 99
Chapter Six: The Slide Toward War—Country Versus Court 141
Chapter Seven: The Committeeman 171
Chapter Eight: Time of Trial 193
Chapter Nine: Judgment Day 212
Chapter Ten: Execution 233
Chapter Eleven: Keeping the Lid on Chaos 245
Chapter Twelve: King Charles II Invades England 283
Chapter Thirteen: Subduing the Colonies, Breaking Bradshawe 311
Chapter Fourteen: The Wilderness Years 329
Chapter Fifteen: Bradshawe's Homes 356
Chapter Sixteen: Death and Resurrection 368
Chapter Seventeen: Remains and Remembrance 386
Appendices 393

ILLUSTRATIONS

Figure 1.	Wyberslegh Hall, near Disley, Cheshire	27
Figure 2.	"The Place", Stockport, Cheshire	28
Figure 3.	Catherine Winnington Bradshawe, from the stained glass at Marple Hall	29
Figure 4.	John Bradshawe's birth registers	30
Figure 5.	Minstrels at Tutbury Fair	34
Figure 6.	Ruins of Bradshaw Hall, Eyam, Derbyshire, about 1850	36
Figure 7.	Middleton Old Grammar School	42
Figure 8.	Brass of Henry Bradshaw at Halton, Bucks	50
Figure 9.	The Common Hall, Gray's Inn, London	52
Figure 10.	Sir Edward Coke confronting King James	89
Figure 11.	King Charles First	151
Figure 12.	Bradshawe's armored hat at the Ashmolean Museum	204
Figure 13.	Plaque set in Westminster Hall marking the site of King Charles' trial	207
Figure 14.	The King's Trial in Westminster Hall	214
Figure 15.	John Bradshawe, seated right center, faces King Charles standing left	215
Figure 16.	Lord President John Bradshawe	222
Figure 17.	The execution of King Charles	237
Figure 18.	Halford's drawing of King Charles's severed head	241
Figure 19.	Coin of King Charles (left) and coin of the Commonwealth (right)	259
Figure 20.	Free Born John Lilburne	270
Figure 21.	Eikon Basilke	272
Figure 22.	Eilkonoklates, Milton's answer to Eikon Basilke	273
Figure 23.	Sir Henry Ireton	289
Figure 24.	The Dunbar Medal	291
Figure 25.	Cromwell dissolves Parliament	325

Figure 26. John Milton 335
Figure 27. Andrew Marvell 336
Figure 28. Bradshawe's House in Congleton 356
Figure 29. Somer Hill, Kent 359
Figure 30. The Dean's House at Westminster Abbey 360
Figure 31. Remains of the hearth in Bradshawe's room 361
Figure 32. Bradshawe's Study rooms built on top
 the southwest tower, Westminster Abbey 362
Figure 33. Cromwell's mumified head 381
Figure 34. Plaque at Sidney Sussex College, Cambridge 382

AN ACKNOWLEDGEMENT

FOR MORE THAN twenty years, I have enjoyed the privileges of possessing a reader's pass from one of the world's most inspiring libraries—at first called the Library of the British Museum, then, simply, the British Library. There was never a more comforting place to spend a winter afternoon than among the softly worn blue green leather-topped desks of the old round reading room in the British Museum, knowing I was in the presence of the ghosts of Conrad, Wilde, Browning, Churchill, Hardy, and a thousand other authors whose books now stood quietly on the shelves encompassing me and rising high above my head up to the glass dome. Somewhere on those shelves lay the seed of every book that ever was, or ever will be, written. It was there I found the seed of this book.

The soft rumble of the book cart coming to deliver my chosen item, mingled with an occasional muffled cough, provided just the right music for serious study. There was a smell of leather, paper, wax, and wood. Out of the corner of my eye, now and then, I caught sight of a fellow reader sitting at a nearby desk: an eccentrically dressed unknown individual who would have been perfectly at ease in Disreali's world—a "gent" in a proper city suit, a captain of industry, Antonia Frasier, Dirk Bogarde, Professor Blair Worden, Sean Kelsey, Margaret Drabble, Paul Scofield, or Martin Amis. A nod was acceptable, but one never spoke, of course; that was not the reason we were all there. It was bad form to sneak a peek at the notes being taken or the book title being consulted.

Through an opening in the north wall of bookcases and across an access hallway, a small low room housed rare books and manuscripts. A special pink reader's ticket was needed to enter that sanctuary of precious paper and parchment. By the intercession of my dear late friend, Dr. Ronald Scott-Thorne Wilkinson, I obtained one of those pink tickets.

The London Library in St. James Square, the Library of the Society of Genealogists in Charterhouse Buildings, the Library of the Institute of Historical Research at the Senate House, and the Library of the National Maritime Museum at Greenwich were my other haunts and hideaways. I liked the old Public Record Office in Chancery Lane, but the round room at the British Museum was special. When the imposing new red-brick British Library began to rise in Euston Road, I wasn't sure my studies could ever be so peaceful again. The old round room closed, and the venerable furniture was sold. In its place the bright and airy Great Court of the British Museum was born. The British Museum Library was closed, and in the byways near Great Portland Street, it was said, clumps of sullen-eyed readers could be seen wandering aimlessly.

The new British Library opened in June 1998. The architect, Sir Colin St. John Wilson, presented a stunning design of soaring sunlit galleries, overhanging balconies, and the historic King's Library of books rising up in a crystal cube many stories high. It is a cathedral to the written word. The fourteen million items in the collection were safe, and there was room for the three million new items to be added each year. There had been no need for me to worry.

I've reached the age of eighty now. I am back to live in my native country, the USA, and my reader's pass has expired. I may never again walk through the doors of the British Library, but let me say to the people of the United Kingdom and all the staff of all their libraries, from myself and all those who will walk there, thank you for this priceless gift.

My personal thanks go to the loyal supporters of this book. Mr. Christopher Godber of Northamptonshire never lost faith in the project. Mr. Neil Ayres of Australia patiently read the manuscript and caught many errors. Professor Maurice Wright of Bradshaw Hall in Chapel-en-le-Frith kindly tolerated my intrusions on his private home and made Bradshaw relatives and me welcome. Major General Adrian John Bradshaw CB OBE, Sir Neville Purvis KCB, Sir Brian Harrison, and many others provided details and encouragement. Mr. and Mrs. John Cole, the late Mr. Alan Carr and Mrs. Judy Carr, Mrs. Trudy Stanford, Mr. and Mrs. John Richardson, Mr. and Mrs. Roger Bradshaw, Mr. and Mrs. John Bradshaw of Tipperary Town, and other friends who made my wife and me feel at home and lovingly guided us through some of the gentle complexities of life in the UK and Ireland.

Most particular thanks to my wife, Carolee, whom I have loved, and who has loved me, for more than half a century.

INTRODUCTION

*The race is not to the swift
nor the battle to the strong
neither bread to the wise
Nor riches to the men of understanding
Nor favor to men of skill,
But time and chance happens to them all.*
Ecclesiastes 9, 11

EXTRAORDINARY THINGS SOMETIME happen to ordinary men. John Bradshawe was an ordinary man who, extraordinarily, became one of the most renowned men of the seventeenth century. He sat in judgment of his lord and master, King Charles I, and sentenced him to death. He was Lord President of the Council of State from 1649 to 1653, and "by his office was in some measure the first man of the nation. He was to receive foreign ambassadors, and to represent, in his own person, upon occasions of public solemnity, the executive government of the Commonwealth of England."[1] The record of his tireless public activity is abundant and clear but scattered throughout the official records.

His influence in seventeenth century Anglo-American political thought has been largely ignored. Few modern scholars have felt compelled to examine Bradshawe's policies or motives, let alone undertake his biography. Two biographies were attempted, one in the eighteenth century and one in the nineteenth, but neither has been published. Only one or two writers have made him the subject of a play, a poem, or a novel.

This book is an attempt to make some historical sense out of the myth and confusion surrounding the story of his life. It is not revisionist history. My object is neither to demonize nor eulogize John Bradshawe. For that reason, as well as my own lack of capability, I have avoided the rhetoric of historical forms. In Francis Bacon's definitions of perfect history, this cannot be called a history of lives or a history of times. The earlier manuscript biographies are the starting point for this biography, updated in light of modern discoveries, and augmented with information that was not publicly catalogued before the twentieth century. Historians will find much of this work familiar and uncontroversial, but they may find a few previously overlooked references worth discussing. "In humane studies there are times when a new error is more life-giving than an old truth, a fertile error than a sterile accuracy."[2]

The first unpublished biography of Bradshawe was written in 1779 by the respected antiquary Rev. John Watson. His manuscript *Memoirs of the Family of Bradshaw of Marple in Cheshire* rests in the Bodleian Library. Several writers have consulted Watson's work and made liberal use of it. In 1801 Britton and Brayley quoted portions of the manuscript, verbatim, in their *Beauties of England and Wales*, but they gave no acknowledgement to Watson. Omerod's *East Cheshire* mentions the *Beauties of England* material as the most authentic memorial of John Bradshawe but does not repeat it. Foss's *The Judges of England* repeated the same information, and the author of the summary in the Dictionary of National Biography used the same source. There are several other short articles on Bradshawe, more or less accurate, more or less impartial, but all incomplete. Lord Campbell's *Lives of the Chief Justices* and Worthington Barlow's *Cheshire Biographies* are examples.

About 1850, Hugh Bellot, a barrister and author, discovered an early transcript of Watson's manuscript among his late father's papers. Struck by what he believed to be the impartiality of the biography, he proposed to publish it. He wrote an introduction announcing that *The Memoirs of John Bradshaw* (as written by Bellot, without the final e) is now published here for the first time as they left the pen of their reverend author. Bellot's introduction and transcript of Watson's biography is held in the John Rylands Library at Manchester.[3] Bellot was sufficiently captivated by the subject to write his own biography of Bradshawe. He hoped this would be published under the title *John Bradshaw, Regicide*. It also rests in the Rylands Library.[4] The publication of Bellot's biography was anticipated in a document of the Bradshawe family written in about 1850: "Bradshaw of Marple, a detailed account of the descent of the Marple branch of this family has been avoided here, as a Memoir of the Lord President with his descent, and notice of his ancestors, is in contemplation in which his character will be shown from his own Letters, Speeches, & c., &c. in a new and unprejudiced light, indeed we cannot help feeling inclined almost in spite of ourselves to prefer the fortitude and virtue 'worthy of an ancient Roman' and the utter disregard of self holding his course straight on in what he considered the service of his Country and leaving his reward to posterity regardless alike of the threats or daggers of his enemies which were the distinguished feature of the Character of England's greatest Republican Jno' Bradshaw . . ."[5]

Bellot gave the reason, he felt, that no Bradshawe biography had ever been published, and then he argued that the reason was basically prejudiced. Whole generations of eighteenth—and nineteenth-century men, whether Whig or Tory, had dismissed Bradshawe's historical importance because Bradshawe's contemporary critics, lead by Edward Hyde Earl of Clarendon, were so successful in depicting Bradshawe as an unknown provincial lawyer who became the insignificant tool of more powerful forces and blindly acted as their unprincipled puppet in the traitorous business of murdering the king and attempting to destroy the monarchy and then, having become arrogant with his newfound importance, used his position to enrich himself unjustly until Cromwell put him in his place and sent him back to the oblivion he deserved. This was a convenient fiction containing elements that allowed Bradshawe to be dismissed by Royalists, Parliamentarians, and Cromwellians alike. Bellot missed the point that this fiction was based on a misreading of Clarendon. Clarendon had his prejudices, and he was a political propagandist, but he could, however reluctantly, deliver fair judgment of his enemies as when he called Bradshawe a gentleman and when he said of Cromwell, "He was one of those whom his very enemies could not condemn." Christopher Hill has written, "No explanation of the English Revolution will do which starts by assuming that the people who made it were knaves, or fools, puppets or automata." Francis Bacon argued that, in history, "the workmanship of God often suspends the greatest weight on the smallest wires."

Yet, even in the middle of the last century, H. N. Brailsford maintained, "It was not the revolutionary tribunal over which Bradshaw presided that condemned King Charles to death. What it did was to put into legal language the verdict the Army had pronounced."[6]

Bradshawe was a revolutionary Republican and a hero to only the tiny and almost invisible band of strict Republicans and Independents of his time. To all others, then as now, he was the antihero who could never be glorified officially. His tributes were the insults of his enemies. He was branded a traitor on the margin of his birth register. He was posthumously hanged and beheaded. His headless corpse was flung, nameless, into an unmarked pit. In the public perception, Bradshawe achieves his highest political honor when his decapitated head is elevated, between those of Cromwell and Ireton, atop Westminster Hall.[7]

Robert Wright, alias Villers, alias Danvers, who styled himself Viscount Purbeck, disagreed with the public perception. Just at the time of the Restoration, he was expelled from the House of Lords and committed to prison for having the temerity to publicly say: *"Rather than Charles first want one to cut his head off, he would do it himself and that Bradshawe was a gallant man, and preserver of our liberties."* [8]

Capt. Laurence Moyer of Low Leighton county Essex, warden of Trinity House, was another who disagreed. About the time of Bradshawe's death, Moyer declared: *"The murder of the late King (was) the best piece of heroic justice, and Bradshawe the best patriot that ever lived."* [9] Moyer was prosecuted for this statement after the Restoration.

Throughout the Restoration and into the first quarter of the eighteenth century, the monarchy was so popular that it continued to be dangerous to challenge the accepted depiction of Bradshawe. It appears that most of Bradshawe's writings were being carelessly handled or purposely destroyed. We have none of his letters to wife or family—no private diaries—and only a few sparse personal statements of conviction. We have only scraps, many secondhand, of his philosophical thought. Less has been written of his personal life and feelings than almost any other public figure of the time.

There were nearly a hundred letters to and from Henry Bradshawe, John's brother, extant in the eighteenth century, but not all of them can be accounted for now. Watson was able to take copies of them about 1770. Very few of them are from John Bradshawe. We know more about Henry from his extant diary than we do of John. In 1862, A. Craig Gibson published *Original Correspondence of the Lord President Bradshawe*, in the *Transactions of the Historical Society of Lancs and Cheshire*, quoting from original documents in the hands of A. Rowson Lindgard, Esq. Of the twenty-seven items, one is a draft of a letter to the parishioners of Feltham, one a letter to an unnamed friend in Cheshire respecting government interference in the election, and one a letter to Henry Cromwell respecting interference in the judicial process in Cheshire. The rest are items of business or government.

As early 1661, Dr. George Bate wrote of Bradshawe, "And now I even tremble to think how I saw him the day of the Kings Tryal in Scarlet, with a heart and conscience as deep dyed as his gown, most devilishly and in humanely staining that white innocence of the Kings Majesty with approbation and wicked language, which I dare not mention in this place, unless I give occasion of making that sad wound to bleed afresh in the sight of all tender, and truly pious Christians."[10] To Dr. Bate, John Bradshawe was a "viper of hell, unawed by divine or human justice."[11]

Bellot argues that this prejudice against Bradshawe was solidly set before Watson wrote his biography in 1770. Clarendon succeeded in his role of royal propagandist, and there emerged in other writings the myth of the Martyred King versus the Bloodthirsty Regicides. Clarendon's *History of the Rebellion* was not published until 1702 to 1704. Whigs secretly ridiculed it as a Tory history, but it was dangerous to do so publicly while Clarendon's granddaughter, Queen Anne, was on the throne. Antony Wood, though a Tory and a High Churchman, had criticized Clarendon, and for that he was prosecuted in the vice-chancellor's court and expelled from the University of Oxford. Bellot may not have countenanced the unprecedented popularity of the monarchy as it was developing about the young Queen Victoria in his own time. An age is best known for what it chooses to believe; and the Victorians chose to believe, wholeheartedly, in the Monarchy and a Loyal Parliament. There was little interest in republicanism. Bellot's Bradshawe biography of 1850 would not have been assured a popular reception even if it had come to publication despite Thomas Babington Macaulay's nearly concurrent recasting of Clarendon's myth into that of King Charles the Tyrant versus the Patriots.[12]

Watson's timing should have been better than Bellot's, and yet, strangely, it was no more successful. If ever there had been a time when Bradshawe's republican sentiments could have been examined with a degree of impartiality, the 1770s seem ideal when the prestige of the monarchy was sinking toward the nadir it would reach under the sons of George III.

Republican government had been tried, and it had failed in England—a brief four-year experiment between the execution of King

Charles and the Protectorate of Oliver Cromwell. It can be debated whether this was fully Republican in form and substance. It was, certainly, experimental; and it was neither a monarchy nor, before Cromwell's Protectorate, a dictatorship. Bradshawe, Sir Henry Vane, and Admiral Blake, who developed the use of sea power to further imperialist objectives, had fostered the Navigation Acts and had physically attacked Dutch domination of the seas. They had achieved the sovereignty of Parliament and the Common Law, the control of Justices of the Peace and town corporations, and the abolition of Feudal tenures. Bradshawe subdued incipient rebellion in the Caribbean and American colonies. Before Cromwell seized power, the people of England had already seen the end of monopolies, prerogative courts, and arbitrary taxation. It was Cromwell who quelled resistance in Ireland, established diplomatic relations with Europe, and settled English religious policy. Christopher Hill has written, "These were the lasting achievements of the years 1640-60, though some were not finally confirmed until 1688." Bradshawe received no credit for the republican experiment in England and it was never again tried in his home country.

By the last quarter of the eighteenth century, the American Colonies were alive with Republican sentiment, and there John Bradshawe was being seen as more than just a rebellious murderer of his sovereign. He was being portrayed as a patriot.

J. A. St. John, after describing the grisly treatment of Bradshawe's corpse that had taken place in 1661,[13] adds, "To show, however, the different estimation in which the same name may be held by different persons, I will here introduce that eloquent and startling epitaph, written by an American on Bradshawe before the war of independence. It is said to have been dated from Annapolis, June 21st, 1773, and to have been engraven on a cannon, whence copies were taken and hung up in almost every house in the continent of America.

> Stranger,
> Ere thou pass, contemplate this cannon,
> Nor regardless be told
> That near its base lies deposited the dust
> of John Bradshaw;
> Who, nobly superior to selfish regards,
> Despising alike the pageantry of courtly splendor,
> The blast of calumny,

And the terror of royal vengeance,
Presided in the illustrious band of Heroes and Patriots.
Who fairly and openly adjudged
Charles Stuart,
Tyrant of England,
To a public and exemplary death:
Thereby presenting to the amazed world,
And transmitting down through applauding ages
The most glorious example
Of unshaken virtue,
Love of freedom,
And impartial justice,
Ever exhibited on the blood-stained theatre
Of human actions.
Oh, Reader.
Pass not on, till thou hast blest his memory!
And never, never forget,
That Rebellion to Tyrants
Is obedience to God."

This inscription was printed in the *Essex Gazette* (Salem, Massachusetts) for January 11, 1776, where it is described as being taken from cannon near Martha's Brae, Jamaica, "three years ago." Bryan Edwards in *History of the British West Indies* said there never was such a cannon. Thomas Hollis said in his *Memoirs*, 1780, that he had often seen this inscription posted up in the houses in North America, remarking, "It throws some light upon the principles of the people, and may in some measure account for the asperity of the war carrying on against them." The same epitaph is printed in the *Gentleman's Magazine* for 1784, as taken from the second volume of Hollis's *Memoirs*. Thomas Jefferson could have read the epitaph before he drafted the Declaration of Independence. A copy of the epitaph in Thomas Jefferson's handwriting and dated 1776 was presented to Lafayette upon his return visit to America in 1824. On that copy, Jefferson wrote, "From many circumstances there is reason to believe there does not exist any such inscription as the above, and that it was written by Dr. (Benjamin) Franklin, in whose hands it was first seen."

A correspondent sent a strange story to *Gentleman's Magazine* regarding Bradshaw: "During Sir Charles Hardy's government in New York, a person came from Connecticut (a province to which many fugitive Regicides and Republicans fled when they left Britain), on account of some dispute which was necessary to be heard before the Governor and Council of New York. His name being asked, he desired to know if it is necessary that he should give his real name, as his family went by the name of Smith, but the real name was Bradshaw.—'Bradshaw!' says a Gentleman of the Council (one who had much of the old leaven about him) that, Sir, is a venerable name; pray, Sir, sit down; bring the Gentleman an elbow chair; why did you change that name?—Why, Sir, my grandfather was the president Bradshaw; who, to save his life, fled, and came to Connecticut, where he lived under the name of Smith, in a retired place, near a wood, on the bank of the river Connecticut; keeping himself from society, and was generally known by the appellation the old man of the wood; and when he died, was buried in East Hadham Churchyard, in which neighborhood our family has since lived'.—If this story be erroneous, it may easily be discovered, as there are many curious and scientific men in that province, who would take pleasure in elucidating the matter. Dixwell, one of the Regicides, is in the New Haven Churchyard, in that province, with a coarse unhewn Barrstone at his head marked I.D."[14]

The most effusive contemporary praise of Bradshawe had been written in 1654 by John Milton: "John Bradshaw—a name which Liberty herself, in every country where her power is acknowledged, hath consecrated to immortal renown—was descended, as is well known, from a distinguished family. The early part of his life was devoted to the study of the laws of his country, having become a profound lawyer, an eloquent advocate, and a zealous asserter of the rights of the people; he was employed in important state affairs, and frequently discharged with unimpeachable integrity the duties of a Judge. When at length selected by the Parliament to reside at the trial of the King, he did not decline this most dangerous task; to the science of the law, he had brought a liberal disposition, a lofty spirit, sincere and unoffending manners; thus qualified, he supported that great and unprecedented fearful office, exposed to the threats and the dangers of innumerable assassins, with such firmness, such gravity of demeanor, such presence and dignity of mind that he seemed to have been formed and appointed immediately by the Deity himself, for the performance of that deed which the Divine Providence had long before decreed to be accomplished by this nation; and so far he exceeded the glory of all former tyrannicides, as it is more humane, more just, more noble, to pass a lawful sentence upon a tyrant, than to put him to death like a wild beast. Ever eager to discover merit, he is equally munificent in rewarding it. Delighted to dwell on the praises of others, he studiously suppresses his own."[15]

Silas Neville noted in his diary, *Sun Jun 29—1769, Mr. Hollis is possessed of land in Leicestershire which belonged to Lord Pres. Bradshaw. Fear of offending my friend prevented me saying 'If the land were mine I erect a monument to his memory.'*

I need to make clear the manner of spelling John Bradshawe's name, complete, with the final *e* which he invariably appended. Consistency in spelling is a modern affection, and Bradshawe's contemporaries did not always end his name with *e*. For purposes of clarity, I have chosen to do so, except when quoting from other sources, and there I spell the name as it is given. To do otherwise would corrupt the source and perhaps overlook the origin of some of the confusion that will become apparent.

There is the problem of all the other contemporary John Bradshaws with whom the regicide has been, and continues to be, confused. The early seventeenth century Registers of Gray's Inn contains the names of five other John Bradshaws in addition to John Bradshawe the regicide.

Other contemporary records reveal another six: John Bradshaw, Master of the Science of Defense, was paid to demonstrate his skill with weapons before the King of Denmark and the court of King James in 1603 and 1615,[16] John Bradshaw confessed that he had been employed by Lord Stanley "beyond the seas in plots" and was "hired to kill the King (James I) with pocket dags" in about 1615; John Bradshawe was killed in Gray's Inn Fields, 1623;[17] John Bradshaw, deputy chamberlain of the Exchequer from 1613 to 1633, Rouge Croix Pursivant and Windsor Herald of the College of Arms, planned and recorded the form of the Coronation of King Charles I in 1625;[18] John Bradshaw was nominated attorney general for Cheshire and Northern Wales on June 7, 1637; and John Bradshaw of Bradshaw in the county of Lancashire, Esq., was high sheriff of Lancashire from February 10, 1644, for four successive years in contravention of the Act of 28 Edward III. None of these men were John Bradshawe the regicide.

One of the most confusing records concerns the trial of three witches at Chester in October 1656. John Bradshawe and Thomas Fell were the judges. Representing the prosecution was John Bradshaw, attorney general for Cheshire. The three witches were convicted and hanged at Boughton, Cheshire.

Notes to the Introduction

1. William Godwin, *History of the Commonwealth of England from the Commencement to the Restoration of Charles II,* 4 Vols, (1824-1828),
2. Professor Hugh Trevor-Roper.
3. John Rylands Library, *English Manuscripts # 745a (R.72934),* Manchester.
4. John Rylands Library, *English Manuscripts # 746 (R.72934),* Manchester.
5. British Library, *Manuscript # 51022a, fol 5,*.
6. H. N. Brailsford, *The Levelers and the English Revolution,* (1961). 455,
7. Christopher Bradshaw-Isherwood, *Kathleen and Frank,* (New York, 1971)
8. *Parliamentary History of England, 1763, xxii,* 360-363, 382-384 *Gentleman's Magazine, ccxix,* 357.
9. *Calendar of State Papers, Domestic, Chas II 1660-1661*
10. George Bate, *The Lives Actions and Executions of the Prime Actors and principall Contrivers of that horrid murder of our late pious and Sacred Sovereigne King Charles the first,* (copy at British Library, 1661) 53-54
11. Rev. Mark Noble, *Lives of the Regicides.*
12. Thomas Babington Macaulay, *Edinburgh Review,* and *History of England from the Accession of James II,* (1848)
13. J.A. St.John, ed., *Milton's Prose Works,* (1848) vol I, 266-8, footnote
14. British Library, *Stowe Mss 185, fol 205,* A623 is peculiar narrative, written about 1741, that John Dixwell, alias John Davis, confessed to acting as the Executioner of King Charles I.
15. John Milton, *Second Defense of the People of England.*
16. *Chamber Accounts, 1605-06, MSC, vi, pg 44;* "To John Matthews and John Bradshawe upon the Council Warrant dated at the Court of Whitehall Vto. (Sept 1606) for the charges and pains of themselves and divers others Named in a schedule and annexed to the said warrant being sent for by Commandment from divers places within the realm to play and to shewe Skill in several weapons for the delight and pleasure of the Kinge of Denmarke at the Court of Grenewich and by way of showing his majesty's Reward the sum of C li." T. Pape, *Newcastle-under-Lyme (Staffs) in Tudor and Early Stuart Times,* (Manchester Univ Press, 1938)—"John Bradshawe of London, 'Fencer' bought a tenement in the iron market in tenure of Thomas Bruck, next adjoining the said iron hall, for vjd." *Chamber Accounts, pg 60-1615-16,* "To John Bradshaw, Daniel Carter and others Master of the Science of Defense upon the Councils Warrant dated at

Whitehall xiij Jan 1615 for their charges and pains in representing their skill before his Majesty and the King of Denmark at his last being here l li." R. D. Sayles, *Lord Mayors Pageants of the Merchant-Taylors in the 15th and 16th Centuries,* (1931) 112,—"Itm—Sir John Gore, Ld Mayor Paid to John Bradshaw, Mr (Master) of the noble science of Defense for Sixteen fencers wch did serve with handswords and for theire breakfast upon the triumph vij li."

17. *Middlesex Sessions Rolls, G.D.R., 4 Sept, 20 James I (1623),* "Recognizances, taken before Francis Williamson esq, J.P. of George Wirthinge and Peter Akar, both of St. Andrewes in Holborn, gentlemen, and John Barbar of New Inne, Midd. Gentleman, all three in the sum of Forty pounds each; For the said George Wirthinge's appearance at the Next session of . . . . For Middlesex "to answere to all such matters as shall bee objected against him, tuchinge the killinge of one John Bradshawe this yesterday in Grayes Inne Fields."

18. British Library, *Cotton Mss 6297, f.282. 330; 5756, f.258.*

CHAPTER ONE

The Bradshaw Family

The manor of Bradshaw, near Bolton-Ie-Moors, County of Lancashire, has given name to a family which, when we consider its extreme antiquity, its eminence, or its nobility of descent, is equaled by but few of the equestrian order of the kingdom.
**A Selection of Arms Authorized by the Laws of Heraldry,
Sir Bernard Burke**

☥

JOHN BRADSHAWE "WAS a gentleman of an ancient family in Cheshire and Lancashire but of a fortune of his own making," said the Royalist historian Lord Clarendon. This was more than faint praise. It was accepted that the Englishman so designated must be entitled, by the strict rule of the College of Arms, to bear the coat of arms of his family.

Oliver Cromwell clearly recognized the ancient dignities and told Parliament that he was by birth a gentleman, neither of any considerable height, nor yet any obscurity. Even the radical Leveler John Lilburne refused to plead when brought to court and identified as a yeoman. He insisted, "*I am the Sonne of a Gentleman, and my Friends are of rancke and quality in the Countrie (county) where they live.*" "The upward limit of gentility extended to the monarch, for whatever the dictionary might say, Elizabethan and Jacobean writers tended to group nobles and gentles together, distinguishing them from the great masses below.[1] All the people which be in our countrie be either gentlemen or of the commonalty . . . Therefore whether I use the terme of nobilitie hereafter or of gentilitie, the matter is all one. Whatever else he was, the gentleman was not a citizen, not soiled by trade—or so he liked to maintain."[2] The commitment to social distinctions was not confined to just the followers of the king; it carried through most of the Parliamentary gentlemen. The leader of the Presbyterian party, Denzil Holles, decried his Independent party foes in the Long Parliament as bloodsuckers who hatred of all gentlemen. He despised Cromwell's New Model Army and described them as "a mercenary army raised by the Parliament, all of them from the General (Cromwell) to the meanest centinal not able to make a thousand pounds a year in lands, most of the colonels and officers mean tradesmen, brewers, tailors, goldsmiths, shoemakers, and the like, a notable dunghill, if one would rake into it, to find their several pedigrees . . ."

Social elevation through the dignities and honors available to gentlemen was not necessarily a matter of wealth, but more importantly, the source of his wealth. Holles evidently felt the right to govern belonged only to those who had a minimum of £1,000 per year in rents from land. It was King James I who had introduced the sale of baronetages to gentlemen who had that minimum as a means of raising the revenue he desperately needed in May 1611. John Chamberlain felt that King James was so fond of knighting his faithful subjects that soon there would be no simple gentlemen or yeomen left in England.[3] The king, however, made his own distinctions and said John Lilburne and his Levelers were endeavoring to "cast down and level the enclosures of nobility, gentry and propriety, to make us all even, so that every Jack shall vie with a gentleman and every gentleman shall be made a Jack."[4]

So even to acknowledge Bradshawe as a gentleman was a concession that few Royalists could stomach. They preferred to think of Bradshawe and all the rest of his companions as base-born usurpers and common murderers of their king. Symonds[5] inaccurately says that Bradshawe was the son of a collar maker in Chester. Royalists knew how difficult it would be to sort truth and fiction about any man once a disreputable popular legend became firmly enshrined.

Nevertheless, John Bradshawe did bear, and stamped in his seal alongside his signature to the death warrant of King Charles I, the ancient coat of arms of Bradshaw—two black bendlets on a silver field with marks of cadence as a cadet branch of the ancient family and as the second son of his own family. Lord Clarendon probably knew the history of John Bradshawe's family nearly as well as Bradshaw himself. Distant members of Clarendon's own family were related by marriage to John Bradshawe, a connection which Clarendon used to encourage defection from Bradshawe and the Parliamentary party[6] but which he never revealed in his histories.

The success of the House of Commons Parliamentary party lay in the social structure of family and landowning. Most English landowners were commoners and therefore able to sit in the House of Commons. English titles descended singularly on the eldest son, and many an untitled commoner regarded himself the social equal of a duke, who might be his brother, his father, his grandfather, or even his son. William of Orange asked Sir Edward Seymour if he was a member of the Duke of Somerset's family, to which Seymour replied, *"Pardon me, sir, the Duke of Somerset is of my family."*

As with the names of so many other ancient and loyal families of England, the name of the family Bradshaw crops up regularly in the king's records. Robert de Bradesea (sic) died under the walls at Acre about 1189 during the Crusades of King Richard I. Nicholas Bradshaw, who was never knighted, was king's esquire to Henry IV and fought at his side in France in the fourteenth century. Sir William Bradshaw served King Henry V in France and died at Honfleur before the Battle of Agincourt.[7] Henry Bradshaw was attorney general to King Henry VIII and chief baron of the Exchequer to Edward VI in 1553. Laurence Bradshaw was chief surveyor of the king's works throughout the reigns of Henry VIII, Edward VI, Mary Tudor, and into the reign of Elizabeth I. Richard and Thomas Bradshaw were sergeants-at-arms to Queen Elizabeth I, and Canon Roger Bradshaw of Hereford Cathedral was chaplain to King James I. Peregrine Bradshaw was esquire to the body of King Charles I and page to Queen Ann.[8] Other Bradshaws achieved no special eminence, but by first half of the seventeenth century, they had spread over Lancashire, Cheshire, Derbyshire, Staffordshire, Warwickshire, and London as manorial lords, mariners, merchants, landed squires, stewards, priests, preachers, teachers, yeomen, and players.

At the time of John Bradshawe's birth, there were seven major branches of the Bradshaw family all recognizing their descent from the senior house of Bradshaw of Bradshaw near Bolton in Lancashire by bearing the Bradshaw of Bradshaw coat of arms with slight variations. Wooten's Baronetage says that all Bradshaws in England down to 1647 are descended from one Bradshaw of Bradshaw near Bolton who was living at the time of the Norman Conquest. Lineal descendants of Uchtred de Bradesea (Bradsha, Bradeschagh, Bradshagh, Bradshaghe), whose ancestor was a Saxon thane, occupied Bradshaw Hall near Bolton for twenty-four generations without interruption down to the late seventeenth century. Local tradition holds that the first Bradshaw Hall was built there AD 1074. Despite several rebuilds over the years, the old hall was in a ruinous state by the middle of this century, and it was demolished about 1949. The site is now covered in a development of new homes called Bradshaw Hall, and only the porch of the ancient hall is preserved adjacent to the main gate.

Another Bradshaw Hall was owned, until 1963, by lineal descendants of a Derbyshire man named John Bradshaw (circa 1332) and stands on the outskirts of Chapel-en-le-Frith, Derbyshire. It was rebuilt about 1620 out of the fabric of an older hall by Francis Bradshaw (1576-1635), a second cousin of John Bradshawe the regicide. Their common great-grandfather, William Bradshawe of Marple (d; ca 1562), had acquired the property in 1543 from his impoverished nephew and added it to the sizeable amount of property he already owned at Bowden and in the Coombs Valley near Chapel-en-le-Frith. Bradshaws had been living there since the thirteenth century, so the branching from the Bradshaws of Lancashire, if indeed that was the case, must have been very early.[9] Richard de Bradshaw had a house in the King's Forest of the High Peak about AD 1240, and John Bradshaw was master forester of the High Peak Forest in 1425.[10] Subsequent descendants acquired estates in Duffield, Belper, Foolow, Abney, Eyam, and just over the Derbyshire border into Cheshire at Marple Township, Parish of Stockport, about eight miles away. Marple Township lay within the Royal Forest of Macclesfield, and the manor of Marple was held by service of free forestry. The manors of Sutton, Disley, Taxall, and many others were held by the same service.

Figure 1. Wyberslegh Hall, near Disley, Cheshire

Two halls that stood within the Forest of Macclesfield, Stockport parish, Cheshire, are significant to this narrative: Wyberslegh Hall and Marple Hall. The Marple and Wyberslegh halls standing in the seventeenth century were probably built in the fifteenth century on the site of earlier buildings. Although the manor of Marple is omitted from the Domesday Survey reference to the manors of "Merpull and Wiburslegh" occur in the records of the thirteenth century.[11] Wyberslegh, the smaller and less imposing of the two, stood on a ridge of hills overlooking the village of High Lane about half a mile from Disley and two miles from Marple village. Marple Hall was much larger and expansive, giving the impression of a country estate surrounded by its own parklands. It was here that John Bradshawe's grandfather settled and where, as already noted, his great-grandfather William Bradshawe (d; prior to 1562) was living as early as 1533.

In 1606, seventy-one-year-old Henry Bradshawe (1535-1619) bought both halls and a "close commonly called the Place" from Edward Stanley of Tonge Castle, Salop, for £270. The Stanley family had been the hereditary high stewards of the Forest of Macclesfield since 1461. Henry Bradshaw had been living at Marple, perhaps at "the Place," and sharing the tenancy of lands in the township of Marple since 1578 when he was first entered in the manorial Court Rolls. In the purchase indenture, he is styled Henry Bradshawe, the elder, and is titled a yeoman. Henry's son, another Henry Bradshawe—styled the Younger—is mentioned as tenant at Wyberslegh Hall, and later he would be titled gentleman.[12]

The chief purchaser of other lands in Marple Township at that time was Henry's son-in-law Thomas Hibbert.[13] Henry, the elder, needed an estate of his own because he was a landless second son, and his brother, Godfrey (1531-1607), had inherited the Bradshaw Hall estate at Chapel-en-le-Frith, Derbyshire.

Figure 2. "The Place", Stockport, Cheshire

Another brother, Anthony Bradshawe (1545-1614), a scholar of Oxford, a London lawyer, and an accomplished poet, had obtained lands in Crich and Holbrook, the manor of Duffield, Duffield Mill, and a high post in Derbyshire. He wrote: "being in the 38 Elizabeth's reign (1596) by the Honourable Gilbert, Earl of Shrewsbury, Her Majesty's High Steward of the Honour of Tutbury, charged trusted and deputed to be under steward there, and also having spent above 30 years time partly in the Inner Temple and partly in the p'thonotaries office in the Court of Common Pleas at Westminster, where I also practised above 20 years as attorney . . . for the better instructing & advocating of my sons . . . I collected certain little books . . . concerning my service . . . in the said courts." His curious monument can still be seen in Duffield church.

Henry, the elder, of Marple married Dorothy Bagshawe of Ridge Hall in Derbyshire, who survived him. He died in 1619 and left an only son and heir, Henry the Younger (d: 1654), and a daughter, Sarah (or Elizabeth). Some early authorities stated that Sarah married the father of John Milton the poet, but subsequent research discovered that her husband was Thomas Hibbert.

Henry Bradshawe, the younger, and his wife Catherine Winnington were the parents of (1) William, who died in infancy; (2) Henry, the future Parliamentary colonel; (3) John, the future regicide; (4) Francis; (5) Dorothy; and (6) Anne. Catherine Winnington Bradshawe died, probably in childbirth of her fourth son, and was buried at Stockport on January 18, 1604, leaving her husband with five small children who all grew up without mother or stepmother. After his father died in 1619, Henry, the younger, moved from Wyberslegh Hall to Marple Hall with those of his children still living at home.

Figure 3. Catherine Winnington Bradshawe, from the stained glass at Marple Hall

John Bradshawe had been born in the winter of 1602 and baptized at St. Mary's, Stockport parish, in "December: 1602 John the sonne of Henrye Bradshaw of Marple was baptized the 10th." Alongside the entry of his birth in the Stockport parish register, someone other than the parish clerk has written the single word "traitor." Queen Elizabeth died the following year.

Figure 4. John Bradshawe's birth registers

Henry purchased land in Torkington from his brother-in-law, Lawrence Wright, Esq., of Offerton, in 1639. He took no part in the Civil Wars and lived a quiet unnoticed life at Marple where he died in August 1654 at eighty years of age or more. How he must have marveled at the activities of his second surviving son! Wyberslegh Hall remained his possession, and he gave it to his eldest son, Col. Henry Bradshawe, in 1630.

Both Marple and Wyberslegh were within Stockport parish, and Wyberslegh had always been linked to Marple. John Bradshawe's father was a tenant at Wyberslegh but perhaps not actually resident in the hall before 1606. Based on the register entry, it is not possible to determine exactly where he was born—"the Place," Marple Hall, Wyberslegh Hall, or even Bradshaw Hall at Chapel-en-le-Frith eight miles away. Most likely, however, it would have been at "the Place" [14] in Marple. Henry Bradshaw, the elder, did not complete purchase of Marple and Wybersley Halls until four years after John's birth.

Kathleen Bradshaw-Isherwood, who had lived at both Halls in the early 1900s, sincerely believed, on no apparent evidence, that Bradshawe was born at Marple in a room that had become known as the Bradshawe Room.[15] She collected notes on the history of Wyberslegh and Marple, the life of John Bradshawe, family trees of the Bradshawe and Isherwood family, and copied out extracts from the diary of Rev. Charles Bellairs who had visited John and Elizabeth Bradshaw-Isherwood at Marple in the summer of 1838. It seems Kathleen shared her great-grandmother's fascination with family history.

Bellairs said he took the train from Liverpool to Manchester and went to the Royal Hotel where he was collected by a "high spare antique chariot of the color of mustard," its doors almost covered by an enormous coat of arms and the crests of the Bradshaws and the Isherwoods. At Marple Hall he was impressed by "the ample Elizabethan mansion without any modern additions, the sort of a house you would expect for an oldfashioned gentleman." The next morning his host showed him around the house and explained that one small apartment was "vulgarly called by my wife 'King Charles's Closet.' I do not at all approve of it myself, but I have to put up with many things which I disapprove of . . . My wife is of a very romantic turn and it frequently leads her to excess. That extraordinary and indeed ludicrous figure on its knees in the centre is intended for the Martyr King Charles I, and he is supposed to be kneeling before that little table, perusing his death warrant. You are perhaps not aware that Judge Bradshaw who presided at his trial was born in this house, and that I am descended from his eldest brother. I am not proud of the connection, Sir, though I believe he left considerable wealth to the family, but my wife considered that it ought to be illustrated by that ridiculous figure before you. She selected several pieces of old armour from the collection in the hall[16] and had a kneeling block made on which they fitted. The hair, (which flows over the shoulders from beneath the helmet) was cut off her own head when she had a fever. The purple velvet bag breeches were made from the skirt of a worn-out dress, and the leathern jack-boots were made by a neighbouring shoemaker, and as the figure is kneeling you can see at once that the soles have never been used. I do not like to remove it, Sir, as it would cause discord in the house, but I assure you, Sir, I am ashamed of it."

If it was Elizabeth who framed the tradition of Bradshawe's birth at Marple, she may have failed to note that the house she knew was not the house of 1602. It had been heavily rebuilt and encased in brick about 1660. Only a gable of the original timber-framed Cheshire country house was visible in one of the upper rooms. Among the furniture of the hall was a bedstead brought from Wyberslegh, supposed to have belonged to John Bradshawe, carved with emblematic devices and mottoes: "He that is unmerciful, mercy shall miss; but he shall have mercy that merciful is," and "Love God not gold; Sleep not until U consider how U have spent the time; if well thank God; if not, repent." These mottoes also appear in a carved ceiling at Bradshaw Hall in Chapel-en-le-Frith. Inscribed in the glass of one window at Marple was the familiar verse which has been traditionally attributed to Bradshawe:

> *My brother Harry must heir the land,*
> *My brother Frank must be at his command,*
> *While I, poor Jack, will do that,*
> *That all the world shall wonder at!*

On panels, adjacent to the fireplace, were painted these verses;
Though thou be for thy pedigree accounted as ancient as Satan, in wisdom as wise as Solomon, in power as mighty as Alexander, in wealth as rich as Croesus, or for thy beauty as Flora, yet if thou be careless of thy religion and of thy God, thou art a wretch most vile and miserable. My son hear the instruction of thy Father, and forsake not the law of thy Mother, they shall be an ornament of grace unto thy head, and chains about thy neck. Long life and peace shall they add to thee. Remember true wisdom is the principal thing, and good conscience the best estate.

It's impossible to know whether these were painted before the hall was rebuilt in 1658/1660. As a consequence, we don't know if John Bradshawe ever saw them. They seem to echo his religious beliefs though no one accused him of being as fanatical as Oliver Cromwell.

Bradshawe spent his early years with his father at Wyberslegh Hall and with his grandfather at Marple. In the second or third year of his life, the plague struck Manchester, and then Stockport, with horrid consequences; nearly a third of the population was swept away. Those who had other places where they might be welcomed fled the area. The Bradshawes could, and probably did, flee to the refuge of their relatives at Chapel-en-le-Frith or elsewhere in the open air of Derbyshire. Bradshawe's mother died about this time either from the effects of the plague, childbirth, or a combination of both.

Any feminine influence on John's early life probably came from his grandmother Dorothy, his aunt Sarah (or Elizabeth) Hibbert, his cousin Barbara Davenport Bradshaw at Chapel-en-le-Frith, and his sisters who were three and four years older. There is evidence that Bernard Wells and his wife Barbara, later of Holme Hall near Bakewell, were longtime friends of John's grandfather at Marple. Young John and his brother Henry often visited with the Wells family, and Henry would marry Bernard's daughter in 1630. Apart from mothering, there was little a woman could influence in the upbringing of a young seventeenth century gentleman.

John would have received more formative influence from the men of his own family, the parish vicar, and the local gentry. To be mastered were the considerable arts and skills—hawking, hunting, horsemanship and swordsmanship, gaming, and managing servants—expected of every gentleman's son before he was allowed abroad alone. There were the recreations of bullbaiting and bearbaiting, but Puritan churchmen frowned upon these cruel pastimes and, consequently, local authorities began suppressing them at more urbane city and town fairs. If there was sufficient money, he might have indulged in some exercise in firearms, but largely with long-gun fowling pieces; the pistol was not yet a gentleman's weapon. The Bradshawes of Marple and Chapel-en-le-Frith were subject to Forest Law and pursued the proud and independent life of the Macclesfield and High Peak Foresters. The few remaining deer that could occasionally be taken in the old High Peak Forest of Derbyshire were still killed with arrows fired from English longbows by men who bore the ancient offices of Forester-of-Fee, Bow Bearer, or Axe Bearer.

It was the Foresters of Lancashire, Cheshire, and Derbyshire that turned the tide against the French two hundred years before. Among King Henry V's archers at the Battle of Agincourt was Ralph Bradshaw in the muster of Lord Grey of Codnor, Oliver Bradshaw, John of Marple, and Thomas Wybbersley in the muster of Peter Leche of Chatsworth. John Bradshawe's grandfather and his grand uncles, Godfrey of Chapel-en-le-Frith and Anthony of Duffield, could tell stories from their firsthand knowledge of ancient Forest Law and how King Henry VIII encouraged every Englishman to apply himself in his recreation at the practice of archery. Bowling and other games were forbidden as leading to the decay of archery.[17] By 1600, the practice of archery in urban areas continued only as a gentleman's sport. In the forests of Derbyshire, practical use of the bow survived much longer. The Privy Council had decreed in 1595 that bows should never again be issued as weapons of war, but as late as 1621, the Archbishop of Canterbury aimed his crossbow at a buck and accidently killed a gamekeeper.

Chapel-en-le-Frith, the capital of the High Peak, was a *fridd* (or piece of forest) cleared of occupants by the king's verderers after the Conquest and divided into three wards: *Campana* (or Champion), Longendale, and *Hope Dale* (or Edale). To the Norman conquerors, a forest never implied a densely wooded country but simply a land set aside by law for the king's pleasure of hunting. Deer and wild boar were the principal objects of the chase, and wolves lingered there until the start of the sixteenth century.

The King's Forest of the High Peak included the whole northwest corner of Derbyshire. Within this forest lay the parishes of Glossop, Castleton, Hope, Chapel-en-le-Frith, a large part of Tideswell, and some of Bakewell and Hathersage. Overriding the ecclesiastical authorities in these parishes were the governmental powers of the chancellor and Council of the Duchy of Lancaster and the manorial administrations of the Steward of the Honor of Tutbury. Tutbury Honor included twelve Derbyshire manors with which the Bradshaw family name was anciently linked: Appletree Hundred, Alderwasley, Barton-Blount, Chapel-en-le-Frith, Duffield, Glossop, High Peak, Osmaston, Radbourne, Windley, Wingfield, and Wirksworth.

Figure 5. Minstrels at Tutbury Fair

One of the most alluring attractions for young John Bradshawe and his contemporaries was the annual Tutbury Fair. The Bradshawes of Derbyshire, Staffordshire, Leicestershire, and Nottinghamshire would certainly have attended. Each year on the "morrow after the Feast of the Assumption," the Castle, Priory, and town of Tutbury in Staffordshire played host to the King of the Minstrels and his court. Minstrels from throughout the Honor were called to Tutbury to prove their talent, revel, feast, and elect a king for the ensuing year. All the king's Foresters were also assembled at Lydgate Field and rode, with the minstrels going before, to the high cross in town and then to the church. One of the Foresters bore the head of a freshly killed buck "garnished about with a rope of peas," and all the other Foresters carried green boughs in their hands. At the church the buck's head was offered up, and a great banquet was held to welcome the new King of the Minstrels. The outgoing King of the Minstrels paraded between the steward and the bailiff.

After the ceremonies and dinner, all the minstrels went to a barn near town where a maddened bull was to be released for them. The bull had his horns sawn off, his ears cropped, and his tail cut off at the stump. Just before his release he was smeared all over with soap and pounded pepper was blown up his nose. The steward read out a proclamation. The bull was to be captured before sunset within the county of Staffordshire by the minstrels at their own peril. Only minstrels were allowed to come within forty feet of the beast. The enraged bull was then released. The chase was on! The captor, if there was such a man, cut a small tuft of hair from the bull and delivered it to the market cross as proof of his success. The bull was brought to the bailiff's house where a rope and collar were fastened on, and he was taken to the bullring in the high street and baited by dogs. The minstrels could then sell, kill, or divide him among themselves. Later it was decreed that the bull could be captured in Derbyshire as well, and sometimes he got as far as Sudbury or Hoon. If the bull was not captured before sunset, he reverted to his donor, who had been the Prior before the dissolution but was the Duke of Devonshire in later times.

This fabulous fair, instituted by John of Gaunt in 1381, was tolerated for nearly four centuries; and during John Bradshawe's time, it was presided over by the Earl of Shrewsbury, Steward of Tutbury Honor, from the 1590s to 1616, and by the Earl of Arundel for the next twenty years. Both Shrewsbury and Arundel were patrons of the Bradshawes. Anthony Bradshawe of Duffield was for a while the Deputy Steward of Tutbury and may have presided in the absence of Shrewsbury.

Robin Hood, the freebooter of Sherwood, was said to have indulged himself in an excursive ramble to the famous Tutbury Minstrel's Fair and returned home with a bride, Clorinda, the queen of the festival. Clorinda's irresistible charm seems to have been the skillful way she killed a deer.

Imbued with tales of the forest families, young Bradshawe may have ventured into Hathersage church to see the tombs of his ancestors, the Eyres of Moor Seats and North Lees.[18] John Bradshawe would not have missed a peep at the mighty bow of Robin Hood's companion, Little John. In a manuscript of Elias Ashmole, dated 1625, is this note: "Little John lyes buried in Hathersceeh Churchyard... they say a part of his bow hangs up in the church. The bow was one of the treasures of Hathersage, along with Little John's cap, but in the eighteenth century they were carried away to Cannon Hall near Barnsley."[19] It seems they have since disappeared, but Little John's grave is still pointed out in Hathersage churchyard. From there Bradshawe could have walked or ridden his saddle horse the four miles across bleak Abney Moor and Foolow to Eyam where his cousin, Francis of Chapel (1576-1635), owned another Bradshaw Hall.

Figure 6. Ruins of Bradshaw Hall, Eyam, Derbyshire, about 1850

The Bradshawes of Marple were anti-Catholic and Calvinist in their belief of predestination. The Church of England also believed in predestination from about 1560 until 1625. The Bradshawes were Presbyterian or Independent[20] in their resistance to church government of the bishops. This overlapping of religious conviction was typical of the period, but the Bradshawes of the time would have seen themselves as religious conservatives and antirevolutionaries; in their eyes it was the king and his bishops who were making revolutionary religious change. Before 1620, the term *Puritan* was ambiguous.[21] After that, it was used as a derogatory term, largely to encompass all those who opposed the bishops; it would be some time before it took on all the political and religious connotations with which we associate the term today.

In the ancient manors surrounding Manchester and northward, the powerful Catholic community survived with obstinate durability. Right down to 1640, many people were not sure that Protestantism had come to stay in England. In the 1620s and 1630s, the outlook was perhaps more pessimistic than the two generations before. The paranoiac fear of Popery was intensified in the minds of many Englishmen by the suspicion that the Catholic church intended to impose absolute monarchy as a form of government upon the whole world. Always in the back of the Englishman's mind was the reign of Bloody Mary. In the five-year-reign of the last Catholic monarch, nearly three hundred protestant men and women had gone to the stake. However, the Bradshawes could not quite associate the memory of this persecution with their good Catholic relatives, nearby neighbors, and close friends, who had refused to swear allegiance to the Protestant Queen Elizabeth.

There had been a real threat to Queen Elizabeth's throne, and it came, largely, from the Spanish king. The Armada had failed to smash England in 1588; but Father Robert Parsons, the Derbyshire-born head of the Jesuit mission to England, encouraged King Philip to prepare another attack. Parsons firmly believed that England could only be brought back to the Pope by force of arms. In a proclamation of November 29, 1591, Elizabeth denounced these preparations and specially mentioned a schoolman named Parsons arrogating to himself the name of the Catholic King's Confessor. Parsons replied with *Responsio ad Edictum Elizabethae* in which he declared that the right of the Pope to depose monarchs was an article of faith. Three years later he followed up with his inflammatory *Conference about the Next Succession*. He propounded a genealogical argument pointing to the Infanta of Spain as the best successor to Elizabeth, and a legal and historical argument that the people of England had the right to alter the line of succession for just causes, especially for religion. With this one book he alienated much of the English Catholic community. Oddly, however, two subsequent events were urged from the arguments contained in the book: King James I endeavored to arrange marriage between the Infanta of Spain and his son (the future Charles I) to defuse the succession contention, and Judge John Bradshawe would cite Parsons's arguments, during the trial of King Charles, maintaining that the English people had an historical and legal right to alter the line of royal succession for just cause.

In the 1600s, the anti-Catholic laws were stringently administered for only brief periods, 1605 to 1607 in the wake of the Gunpowder Plot, 1629 to 1637 under Charles I, and in the 1640s when Parliament passed strict edicts against papists. Witnesses were so reluctant to come forward and juries so hesitant to convict that these stringent laws became self-defeating. Under James I, twenty-five Catholics were executed (twenty were priests or lay brothers). Only one perished under Charles I from 1625 to 1640. Under the Long Parliament up to 1646, the victims numbered nineteen, and of that number no layman was executed for sheltering or converting. Under Parliament, Lord President John Bradshawe, the New Model Army, and Lord Protector Cromwell, only two priests were executed between 1646 and the Restoration of 1660.

The Rector of St. Mary's Parish church in Stockport was Richard Gerard in 1602 when John Bradshawe was born. The first church on the site was in existence about 1190, but very little remains of this structure. A much larger church replaced the original structure about the year 1310, and of this the chancel remains covered by a fine single-framed roof erected between 1306 and 1334. This was the church the Bradshawe family would have known, not the remodeled church of 1812-14 which now exists. For the convenience of the Bradshaws of Marple Hall, a small barnlike timber-framed chapel existed on Marple Ridge from about 1580, and a curate from St. Mary's Stockport would have journeyed out to conduct service there. Marple chapel gained its own preacher after the 1625 split developed between those who held to Calvinism and those who held with the king's bishops and Arminianism. The first name on the extant list of incumbents is Samuel Newman, who was there about 1630. He was dead within four years. John Jones followed as preacher, and through his influence, and that of the Bradshawe's of Marple, Presbyterianism was advanced in the neighborhood.

When it came time to select a place of education for young John Bradshaw, one of two local grammar schools, Marple or Stockport, would have been the logical choice. Marple Grammar was new, having been endowed in 1603 with contributions from the neighborhood. The curate was the headmaster, but little is known about him from

1603 to 1630. John Bradshawe makes no mention of having attended Marple School. The Goldsmith's Grammar School at Stockport had been founded by Sir Edmond Shaa, Lord Mayor of London in 1482. In 1601, controversy arose over the Goldsmith's appointment of a new headmaster. He was rejected at the request of the bishop of Chester and the local rector. The townspeople rejected the next headmaster and forced him to resign in 1603. It was a year before a successor was named, but within three years new controversy arose, and that master was dismissed in 1608/09. Luke Mason was headmaster in 1609, Walter Pott succeeded him in 1612. Bradshawe may have attended Stockport school for a short time before going on to his next.[22]

In his last will and testament, John Bradshawe mentions just two schools where his father sent him for a part of his education: the grammar schools at Bunbury in Cheshire, and at Middleton in Lancashire. Henry Bradshawe chose these schools for some reason, and the most obvious would be the religious conviction of their benefactors and headmasters.

Which school did Bradshawe attend first, Bunbury or Middleton? Probably Bunbury first and then Middleton. That is the order in which he mentioned them in his last will. I've found no other clue.

Thomas Aldersey, member of an old Cheshire family at Spurstow, purchased the rectory and old college at Bunbury about 1594. He leased to tithes to Ralph Egerton of Ridley who was an uncle to Mary Marbury, the future wife of John Bradshawe. Aldersley was a wealthy member of the Haberdasher's Company of London, and with their assistance he founded, at Bunbury, what he thought would become a classical school. Aldersey's Bunbury School continued the work of Sir Hugh Calveley's monastic college, originally founded in the fourteenth century. The school was free to all children, with priority given to those born in Bunbury Parish. Girls could attend up to age nine or until they learned to read English. Mary Marbury may well have attended Bunbury.

The London livery companies had come under the influence of powerful city Puritans, and the Haberdashers Company were sponsoring lectureships for such city preachers as Thomas Gataker[23] and John Downham.[24] In 1634, Archbishop Neville complained to the king that Bunbury was a gross example of the evil of lectureships. The charities of the Haberdasher's Company found this parish of Bunbury a stronghold of godliness, largely because of a Calvinist Puritan who lived nearby, John Bruen (1560-1625), the "embodiment of the puritan ideal of a pious layman." Bruen's house at Bruen Stapleford was called, for the power and practice of religion, the very topsail of England. Bruen had grown up as country gentleman and remembered his childhood when "the Holy Sabbaths of the Lord were wholly spent in all places about us, in May Games and Maypoles, pipings and dancings, for it was a rare thing to hear a preacher, or to have one sermon in a year." When he reached manhood, he abandoned all those pleasures and gave himself entirely to his godly pursuits, spending the whole of every Sunday at church. His home was opened to all: the poor and hungry were fed, clothed, and travelers passing through Cheshire on the way to Ireland would spend the night in order that they might continue on their journey all the better for "having seen his face and having heard his voice." Some gentlemen of the area placed their sons as boarders at Stapleford to hear Bruen's teachings and benefit from his fellowship. He had an implicit belief in special providences, judgments, and witchcraft. William Hinde (Hynde), the second preacher of Bunbury from 1602 until his death in 1629, wrote *A Faithful Remonstrance; of the Holy Life and Happy Death of John Bruen of Bruen-Stapleford, in the County of Chester, Esquire*, published in London and dated 1641. Henry Bradshawe of Marple must have known the fame of John Bruen, Thomas Aldersey, and William Hinde. These were men to mold young John Bradshawe.

A typical sixteenth century curriculum at Bunbury was largely an oral education and would have changed very little by John Bradshawe's time in the first and second decade of the seventeenth century. Rhythm and rhetoric, which included histrionics, were taught as a part of the necessary intellectual accomplishments of a gentleman who would be expected to ride and fight with a sword, be self-reliant and businesslike, express his ideas clearly and aesthetically, disclaim and write verses, and sing, recite, and dance. Masters taught reading, writing, and penning of the English, Latin, and Greek tongue in both prose and verse. The master had some choice of texts, but Caesar, Cicero, Terence, Mantuanus, and Virgil were the most recommended. School began with prayers and scripture reading which was rendered in English from Greek and Latin texts. In the evening, a further chapter of the Bible was read, prayers said, and a psalm sung. The master and the usher were to catechize their pupils weekly. Scholars were to practice the manly sport of archery and "eschew all bowling, carding, dicing, quoitiong, and all other unlawful games, upon pain of extreme punishment, to be done by the schoolmaster."[25] The beautiful *court hand* style of handwriting, as taught in the ancient monastic cloisters, lingered on as a part of education until about Bradshawe's time, and his writings of later life show signs that he practiced that style. Records of the early headmasters of Bunbury are sketchy, but John Glover was named as teaching there in 1578 and continued until well past Bradshawe's time.

Aldersey chose Christopher Harvey as his first preacher at Bunbury, whose verses are quoted in Isaak Walton's *Compleat Angler*. Walton says of Harvey, "he hath writ of our Book of Common Prayer; which I know you will like the better, because he is a friend of mine, and, I am sure, no enemy to angling.

> *What? Pray'r by th' book? and common?*
> *Yes, why not?*
> *The spirit of grace and supplication*
> *It is not left free alone For time and place,*
> *But manner too: to read, or speak by rote*
> *Is all alike to him, that prays*
> *In's heart, what with his mouth he says."*

When Harvey died in 1601, the Haberdasher's Company chose William Hinde who, with the influence of John Bruen, became a central figure among Cheshire nonconformists. The company often interceded with Bishop Thomas Morton of Chester on Hinde's behalf. Hinde objected to the wearing of surplices, making the sign of the cross at baptism, and kneeling at communion.

A subsequent headmaster of Bunbury school, and possibly a fellow scholar with Bradshawe, Edward Burghall, whose *Diary* contains frequent mention of Bunbury, wrote: "There was a remarkable judgment fell upon a wretched, debauched fellow in Bunbury, one Robinson a bearward, who followed that unlawful calling, whereby God is much dishonoured (especially at those parish festivals called wakes) was cruelly rent to pieces by a bear and so died fearfully. That worthy man Mr. Hind(e), who then preached at Bunbury, had, not without cause, much inveighed against these disorders which were usually at Bunbury wakes, and had threatened God's judgments against the same." Bearbaiting at Bunbury continued well into the nineteenth century.

From Bunbury school, Bradshawe progressed to Queen Elizabeth's Free Grammar School at Middleton, north of Manchester and not far from the ancient manor of Bradshaw. The schoolmaster of Middleton

Grammar was Robert Walkenden. His name appears from 1591 to 97, and in 1613 he is called curate. In 1623, he is called curate and schoolmaster.

Figure 7. Middleton Old Grammar School

Middleton accommodated about two hundred pupils and supported thirteen scholarships at Brasenose College, Oxford. The school had been re-endowed in 1572 from an older chantry by a former pupil and native of Lancashire Alexander Nowell (1507-1602), who became Dean of St. Paul's Cathedral in London. Nowell was born at Read Hall in Whalley. He inclined toward Calvinism in doctrine and Puritanism (Presbyterian) in matters of order. He was a keen enthusiast of angling and another friend of Izaak Walton. Alexander Bradshaw was a personal servant of Dean Nowell, and his name occurs frequently in the latter pages of the Towneley Manuscript[26] as a witness to gifts made out of the trust of Nowell's brother. Alexander Bradshaw[27] was still the dean's servant in 1592 when the Dean made his will by which Alexander Bradshaw was to have a legacy of five marks.

With the level of preparatory education John Bradshawe received at Bunbury and Middleton, one would expect his next school to be one of the colleges of Oxford or Cambridge. It seems unlikely that he spent any sizeable periods of time at either Wyberslegh or Marple Halls after 1615.

On the slimmest of evidence, Hugh Bellott and W. B. Stephens [28] stated that Bradshawe was articled to an attorney's office in Congleton from about 1618. Foss, in his *Judges of England*, was more cautious and said, "I know nothing of his career till I find him a barrister of Gray's Inn."

John Peile, author of the *Biographical Register of Christ's College Cambridge*, lists a John Bradshaw who matriculated pensioner in April 1620, but notes, "I do not know any proof that John Bradshaw of Marple, the well-known regicide, studied at Cambridge; he was baptized 10 Dec 1602—which would suit our man, and he was admitted Gray's Inn (John, son of Henry, of Marple) 26 May 1620, which is also compatible. But each date suits equally well a John Bradshaw matriculated sizar at Emmanuel 8 July 1619; and there's a tradition (not mentioned in the D.N.B.) that the regicide was at that College. Henry Bradshaw, his nephew, was admitted at Christ's 1651." Christ's College was one of the two prominent Cambridge colleges for puritan and evangelical preachers.

John Bradshaw, son and heir of Henry Bradshaw of Marple, of Cheshire, gent,[29] was admitted to Gray's Inn, aged seventeen years, five months, and sixteen days.

Notes to Chapter One

1. Marcia Vale, *The Gentleman's Recreations*, (London, 1997).
2. Richard Mulcaster, *Positions wherein those primitive circumstances be examined which are necessarie for the training up of children*, (London 1581)
3. N. E. McClure, ed., *The Letters of John Chamberlain*, (Memoirs of American Philosophical Soc., vol XII, 1939).
4. *Mercurius Politicus*, (16 Nov 1647-1648)
5. Richard Symonds, *Church Notes,* British Library.
6. *The Cheshire Sheaf*, 3rd Series, (Aug 1921), 68, quoting Earwaker's Mss of Royal Pardon dated 19 August 1651;—"Charles (II) by the Grace of God King of England Scotland France and Ireland defender of the Fayth etc. whereas we are certefyd yt ye psons hereafter named, vizt; Thomas Marbury (of Marbury), Edward Hyde (of Norbury), John Crewe (of Crewe), and Henry Brooke (of Norton) are willing to return to their Allegeance and to act in our service under our right trusty . . . Earle of Darby . . . We doe therefore . . . pardon them . . . all forfeiture of life and Estate"—Thomas Marbury was John Bradshawe's brother-in-law. Brooke and Hyde were Marbury's brothers-in-law. All were strong supporters of Parliament at the beginning of the Civil Wars. The King's supporter Edward Hyde, later Lord Clarendon, was a distant cousin of Edward Hyde of Norbury. It seems probable that Clarendon contacted and offered secret pardon to win them away from supporting John Bradshawe and Parliament.
7. Sir Harris Nicolas. *History of the Battle of Agincourt*. King Henry V's jewels were handed to his followers as security for wages. There was pledged to "John Pilkington and William Bradshagh (Pilkington was his step-father) a little tablet of gold, garnished with the arms of England and France, and a gold chain, wrought with letters, crowns, &c.". The jewels were not redeemed until 1431, (10 Henry VI), sixteen years after William Bradshagh's death, as is shown by the *Kalendars and Inventories of the Treasury of the Exchequer of 9 and 10 Henry the Sixth*: "Pilkington and William Bradshagh restored by me Oliver Chorley, on the 3rd December, 10 Henry VI, to the Lord Treasurer and Chamberlain, one tablet of gold, with the arms of England and France, with a chain of gold made of letters . . . and crowns; with one bracelet with a fetterlock of gold; together weighing by the troy weight 8- ounces, and in which the gold was value of 28s. to the ounce." See also Lt Col John Pilkington, *History of the Pilkington Family*

of Lancashire, (privately printed Liverpool,1912),. William Bradshaw had also fought for the King at Shrewsbury, in 1403, where he was wounded. He received a grant of 6s. per year "for good service at Shrewsbury" *Chester Jour of Architectural, Archealogical, and Historic Soc.*, Part XII, Div I, 1883, 353.

8. Rev G. E. Jeans, *A List of the Existing Sepulchral Brasses in Lincolnshire*, (Horncastle, 1895), 61, 110.
9. C. E. Bradshaw Bowles, Bradshaw Hall and the Bradshaws, *Jour of the Derbyshire Arch. & Nat. Hist. Soc.*, Vol XXV. (1903), and British Library, *Add'l Mss 51822a,*
10. Marguerite A. Life Bellhouse. *The Story of Coombs My Valley,* (privately printed). J. Tilley, *Old Halls, Manors, and Families of Derbyshire,* (1892) Vol I. Pym Yeatman, *Feudal History of Derbyshire,* Section VI,
11. Marple and Wyberslegh were part of the Honor of Tutbury and within the pouralee of the Forest of Macclesfield. When the Earldom of Chester came into the King's hands the Forest of Macclesfield became a Royal Forest, and the residents held their lands "in capite" of the King. Sir George Vernon of Haddon Hall, Marple, Wyberslegh (and many other manors) died without male heirs and his possession were divided between two daughters; Margaret and the famous Dorothy Vernon, the wife of Sir John Manners. Margaret died about 1596 and her son Sir Edward Stanley of Tonge, inherited Marple and Wyberslegh which he held of the Queen, as Countess of Cheshire, by knight's service, and by the service of finding one Forester in the Forest of Macclesfield *Cheshire Inquisitions.*
12. The purchase deed of Marple was witnessed by Peter Bradshawe "merchant of London" (d; 1625), nephew of Henry Bradshawe the elder. "one messuage and tenement and the lands belonging or appertaining situate in Marple, and now or late in the tenure or occupation of the said Henry Bradshawe the elder, or Henry Bradshawe the younger . . . and one other messuage or tenement and lands situate in Marple of Wibbersley . . . heretofore in the tenure or occupation of one Lawrence Stafford, gent., deceased and now or late in the tenure of Henry Bradshawe the younger (this was probably Wyberslegh) . . . and one close commonly called The Place with its appurtenances' . . . dated 7 July 1606"
13. H Heginbotham,.*Stockport, Ancient and Modern*, vol ii (1892), 185. Thomas Hibbert was the eldest son of Nicholas Hibbert who died at Stockport in 1597. Thomas's grandson, Henry Hibbert, gained high position in the church and became chaplain to Sir Orlando Bridgeman. The Hibbert family and the Bradshaw family probably knew each other in

Derbyshire before arriving at Marple. Thomas Hibbert, who died in 1676, gave £60, "the interest thereof being £3, to be applied annually for the purpose of binding a poor child a parish apprentice, and to be paid to the overseers of the poor of the townships near Chapel-en-le-Frith," Samuel Bagshaw *History, Gazetteer and Directory of Derbyshire,*. (1846)

14. "The Place" became known as "Peace Farm" (possibly corrupted from "the Piece"). This ancient farmhouse and its adjoining barn were demolished in a local "slum clearance" in 1936. Ann Hearle, *The Archive Photographs Series; Marple and Mellor*, (1997), 17.
15. *Kathleen and Frank*, Christopher Isherwood, (New York, 1971), 292,
16. Ibid, 322. When Henry (Bradshaw-Isherwood) inherited Marple (in 1924), he didn't consider settling down in it. In 1929 he sold off most of the furniture that had any value. (The suits of armor in the entrance hall were subsequently rented to film company and used, appropriately enough, in Rene Clair's film, *The Ghost Goes West,* starring Robert Donat). The sale was conducted by auction on 30th and 31st July 1930. A 31-page catalogue detailed all 378 lots, at the first day of the auction Mr. Brady, the auctioneer, advised that the family portraits and pictures listed in the catalogue had been withdrawn from the sale. There were about a dozen of these. Their whereabouts today is unknown.
17. On May 26 1568 a pardon was granted to a Peter Bradshaw for causing the death of Francis Fulwood, aged 18, at Lubstrope, county of Leicestershire. "Bradshaw while practicing archery with others by misadventure shot Fulwood so that he died there 14 Nov." *Acts P.C.* On June 29, 1590 at Manchester in Lancashire Richard Bradshaw of Turton, yeoman, Thomas Jepson of Ardewicke, labourer, Hugh Chetham of Entwysle, husbandman, Thomas Horrockes of Edgeworth, tailor, Ralph Hey of Darwyn, waller, and John Romesbothome alias Crappe of Tottington, husbandman, were called to answer because the "played at Bowls"—*Remains Historical & Literary, Chetham Society*, Vol 77, New Ser. (1917), 3,
18. Henry Bradshawe, great-great-grandfather of John the regicide, married Elizabeth daughter of Robert Eyre who was the second son of William Eyre of North Lees, near Hathersage. Hunter, *Familiae Minorum Gentium*, (Harle. Soc), Vol ii, 544.
19. J. C. Cox, *The Churches of Derbyshire*, (London, 1877), Vol II, 579,. John Pendleton, *History of Derbyshire*, (London, 1886), 176., Dr. Spencer Hall, *The Peak and Plain*, 30-36.
20. "Presbyterian" as John Kenyon has observed, is "almost as difficult a word to construe as "Puritan." In its original sense it was applied to a member of

a Church which was governed by elders, or presbyters (Greek presbuteros), and in which no higher order, such as a bishop was recognized. Adopted in Scotland in 1560, it never found many converts in England although by the Solemn League and National Covenant of 1643 Parliament rather ambiguously introduced Presbyterianism into the English Church. The Presbyterian Church was never completely established anywhere other than London and Lancashire. Presbyterians sought as their goal an all-embracing national church—a state like Calvin's in Geneva—in which the Magistrate would be a faithful member of the church who could punish ecclesiastical transgression as defined by the church elders. Until that goal was achieved they denied the right of any Magistrate to interfere with their churches. Opposed to the Presbyterians were the Independents, who rejected both elders and bishops, and who advocated the autonomy of local church congregations—*Cavaliers and Roundheads*, Christopher Hibbert, 1993, pg 180.—They taught that a church was a body of Christians assembled in one place appointed for their worship and that each such body was complete in itself, with the right to draw up the maxims by which they thought proper to be regulated. No man who was not a member of their assembly, and no body of men, was entitled to interfere with their proceedings. John Selden and Bulstrode Whitlocke favored as a more extreme of Independency as expounded by Thomas Erastus, a 16th century German physician. Erastians believed that religion was an affair between man and his creator, in which no other man or society of men was entitled to interpose. Erastians were, for the most part, lawyers who resented the Ecclesiastical courts power to fine, punish, or excommunicate. Although they were fundamentally different in belief, the Presbyterians, the Independents, and the extreme sects maintained a loose confederacy under the term "Puritan" as long as they were united in the fight against Anglican Bishops, Catholics, and the Stuarts.

21. More than one author tried to define the term Puritan. Definitions varied from the pure in heart seeking purity in religion to a nickname for religious hypocrisy. At the time John Bradshawe came to London the followers of Calvin believed in the doctrine of predestination, the cult of God's elect, and individual interpretation of scripture. They denied the apostolic succession of the bishops and sought to bring each individual close to God without the intervention of ritual of ceremony. Slowly they became more at odds with the bishops and insisted on simplicity of worship; condemned kneeling, bowing, crossing, ornaments, the wearing of surplices, and pictures as "Roman" or "Popish." They rejected transubstantiation and

took Communion bread and wine as purely symbolic. In some people's mind the term Puritan covered the extreme sects which social disorder had brought into being.

22. *Dictionary of Nat'l Biography,*—John Bradshawe (1603-1659)
23. *Dictionary of Nat'l Biography,*—Thomas Gataker (1574-1654), Puritan divine, critic, and biographer of William Bradshaw (1571-1618). Gataker and Bradshaw shared a room at Sidney Sussex College, and Gataker preached Bradshaw's funeral sermon at Chelsea old church in 1618.
24. John Downham was brother-in-law to Roger Bradshaw of Aspull (d; 1625). His brother, George Downham, was Bishop of Derry. They were sons of Wm Downham, Bishop of Chester.
25. Joan Beck, Tudor Cheshire, J.J. Bagley, ed., *History of Cheshire*, Vol 7 quoting the rules of St. Helen's school, Northwich.
26. Rev. Alexander B. Grosart, *The Spending of the Money of Robert Nowell of Reade Hall, Lancashire,* (privately printed, 1877), quoting the manuscripts of Towneley Hall.
27. Alexander Bradshaw became servant to Dr. Overall, successor to Dean Nowell as Dean of St. Paul. Alexander Bradshaw died in 1603. *Wills at Chelmsford Essex.* 143 BW 6
28. W. B. Stephens, *History of Congleton*, (Manchester Univ. Press).
29. John Foster, *Register of Admissions Gray's Inn, 1582-1889*, (London, 1889).

CHAPTER TWO

Up to London and Gray's Inn

*The sweet harmony between all the worthy members
Of this honourable Society has been the music
That to me was ever the most pleasing . . .
all the other Inns of Court are not able
to meet you on equal terms in the lists of honour*
Sir John Finch, upon leaving Gray's Inn, 1634.

✠

JOHN BRADSHAWE'S GREAT-GRANDFATHER, William Bradshawe of Marple, died before 1562., John's grandfather, old Henry Bradshawe of Marple, died in 1619/20, aged nearly eighty. John's father, another Henry who would live to nearly one hundred, succeeded to the estates. This last Henry, who lived a widower for sixteen years, arranged for his second son to study the law at one of the Inns of Court in London. Henry's uncle Anthony and his cousins had been at the Inner Temple before 1600, but Gray's Inn was chosen for his son. Gray's Inn was more inclined toward Calvinism than the Inner Temple just then. On a Spring day in May 1620, John Bradshawe packed his belongings, saddled his horse, bade his father and brothers good-bye, and rode off on the four—or five-day journey to London. His father would have sent a servant, perhaps two, to accompany young John on the journey. Down to the Goyt River, crossing at Whaley Bridge and into Derbyshire, he might have stayed the first night with his cousin Francis at the ancient Bradshaw Hall in Chapel-en-le-Frith to see the rebuilding going on there. Perhaps he ventured a bit further to Bradshaw Hall in Eyam. The next day he could have easily reached Crich, Belper, or Duffield where he could find a welcome from other relatives. Passing through Derby,

Coventry, and Banbury, he reached Oxford. From Oxford, a short diversion could have taken him through Thame and past Aylesbury to the little church at Halton near Weston Turville where a simple brass plaque commemorated Henry Bradshaw, the famous Attorney General and Baron of the Exchequer to King Henry VIII (See Appendix 1.).

Figure 8. Brass of Henry Bradshaw at Halton, Bucks

It was about thirty miles to Barnet where, from the heights, he caught the wondrous sight of the spires of old St. Paul's and Westminster Abbey. Past the green fields on the outskirts of London above Holborn, he turned his horse off the dusty lane onto the paving of Gray's Inn Lane and turned once again, at the iron-bound tree, through the venerable gateway into the Inn that would be his home for the next seven years.

"No English institutions are more distinctly English than the Inns of Court . . . Unchartered, underprivileged, unendowed, and without remembered founders, these groups of lawyers formed themselves and in course of time evolved a scheme of legal education, an academic scheme of the mediaeval sort, oral and disputatious What is distinctive of mediaeval England is not Parliament, for we may everywhere see assemblies of Estates, nor trial by jury, for this was but slowly suppressed in France; but the Inns of Court and the Year Books that were read therein, we shall hardly find their like elsewhere."[1] The extant records of Gray's Inn begin in 1569, although its origins are much older. In the last half of the sixteenth century, members of the Inn held power at the heart of Queen Elizabeth's court: William Cecil (later Lord Burghly), Francis Walsingham, Sir Nicholas Bacon, and Sir Gilbert Gerard. Other famous members adorned her glorious reign: Lord Howard of Effingham (who commanded the fleet against the Spanish Armada), Sir Philip Sidney, Edward Stanhope, and Francis Bacon. In the first year of his reign, King James specified that only gentlemen of certain rank were to be admitted to Gray's Inn.

All the Inns of Court were rigorously selective in their admissions policy, but the professional discipline was most strict at Gray's. John Bradshawe's Derbyshire relatives had previously entered the Inner Temple,[2] but he was admitted at Gray's perhaps through the influence of Sir Humphrey Davenport who was Reader there in 1613. Sir Humphrey's family resided at Bramhall in Cheshire and were well acquainted with the Bradshawes of Marple and Wyberslegh (which lay just a few miles away).[3] Additional influence may have been exerted In Bradshawe's behalf by his distant cousin, Peter Bradshawe,[4] who had made a tremendous fortune out of *Manchester goods* in London and Ireland. Peter's warehouse lay "at the sign of the Antelope" in St. Augustine's parish, Watling Street, London.

As a newly admitted student, Bradshawe joined a society of about three hundred fellows composed of young students and graduates, barristers, and eminent men of the court. Most lodged within the Inn, and a new member was not admitted until a chamber for his lodging was available. They took their meals together in the common hall and paid a fee to belong to the master's mess. An exception was made for students who were admitted after a course of study at one of the subservient Inns of Chancery: Staples Inn and Barnard's Inn. These students might pay reduced fees and take their meals at the clerk's mess in the common hall, waiting on the rest of the company as sizars did at university. Cooking and eating in the chambers was forbidden, although there were constant complaints about oyster shells being thrown out chamber windows, until finally orders were issued to the butler that no oysters were to be served in chambers. Attendance at chapel and acceptance of communion in conformity to the established church was compulsory, but there were members, such as Robert Rich, the second Earl of Warwick, and Dr. Richard Sibbes, preacher of the Gray's Inn Chapel, whose attitude on religious matters was decidedly nonconformist. Secretary of State Conway wrote to Archbishop Laud, "the Earl of Warwick (Robert Rich) is the temporal head of the Puritans and the Earl of Holland (Henry Rich his brother) is their spiritual head."

Figure 9. The Common Hall, Gray's Inn, London

The king's royal court was alive with commercial, cultural, religious, and political excitement when John Bradshawe arrived, excitement in which some members of the wide-ranging family of Bradshaw were personally involved. King James VI of Scotland had been on the throne of England, as King James I of Great Britain,[5] for seventeen years. It was secretly muttered that Queen Elizabeth, a woman who ruled like a man, had been replaced by King James, a man who ruled like a woman. All attempts to locate survivors of Sir Walter Ralegh's 1585 Roanoke colony in Virginia had failed(See Appendix 2.). In 1603, Gosnold,

Gilbert, Archer, and John Brereton[6] stepped ashore at Cape Cod—the first spot in New England ever trodden by English feet. The first four voyages of the East India Company had been concluded before 1610.[7] The old Globe Theatre had burned down in 1613 and was rebuilt the following year. King James, who was fond of granting monopolies, granted a monopoly for twenty-one years of the manufacture of delftware to Edmund Bradshawe in 1613.[8] Arbella Stuart died in the Tower of London in 1615 under suspicion of mothering a child who could be an heir to the throne.[9] Shakespeare had been dead four years, and the first folio of his works would be published in 1623. Pocahontas died and was interred at Gravesend in 1617 after being entertained at court in London.[10] King James's *Book of Sports* had been propagated in Lancashire that year and was introduced throughout the kingdom the following year.[11] The new King James version of the Bible was being placed in the pulpits of all churches.[12] John Donne was presiding as Dean of the old St. Paul's and preacher at Lincoln's Inn, (See Appendix 3.). Sir Walter Ralegh(See Appendix 4.) was beheaded in October 1618, and King James's queen died the following March. On May 6, 1621, the *Mayflower* sailed back into London carrying news of the successful Pilgrim landing in New England. Sir Francis Bacon was coming to the end of his chancellorship and in 1621 would return to his chambers in Gray's Inn. In the middle of that year, two parties were beginning to form, one for the king and another for the people, that gave rise to the names Whigs and Tories. In the following spring, King James dissolved the parliament, maintaining that the House of Commons had no other privileges except those concessions granted by the king and his predecessors; it was within his power to revoke them if he was given just cause. The House, on the other hand, maintained they enjoyed these privileges by ancient and undoubted right, and it was not within the king's power to withdraw them. The Puritans sided with the Commons; the Arminians declared for the king(See Appendix 5.). There was ample fodder to feed the vociferous debates and endless discussions between John Bradshawe and his fellow members of Gray's Inn.

    The road through Gray's Inn to becoming a legitimate practitioner of the law was long and arduous. Students arrived from university or, as mentioned, through one of the Inns of Chancery to which they might have come directly from grammar school. Study was not reading books nor sitting written examinations. Knowledge came from listening, was achieved by actual practice, and proven by the spoken word. The teaching method had two central features: readings and moot courts. Reading terms began twice yearly on the first Monday in Lent and the first Monday in August. At 8:00 a.m. on the appointed day, the reader came into the common hall, and there, in front of the whole company assembled, he read an act or statute on which he would base his reading for the whole term. He would then "declare such inconveniences and mischiefs as were unprovided for and now by the same statute be redressed, and then reciteth certain doubts and questions which he hath devised that may grow upon that statute, and declareth his judgement therein." One of the younger utter barristers challenged a question raised by the Reader and argued that the Reader's opinion was contrary to law. For the following two hours, the other readers and utter barristers gave their judgment on the same question, and the Reader who had introduced the question countered the objections and defended his initial proposal. Then any Judge or Serjeant-at-Law present declared his opinion. Apparently these were not joyless or boring affairs for "the Justices intervene occasionally to give a ruling, to tell a story . . . to quote the Bible, the classics or a continental brocard. And the Serjeants are quite as ready tongued. They all have the resources of the highest culture of the Middle Age to draw upon and in that Hall . . . the most highly cultured life of the Middle Age is finding its fullest expression in argument and repartee, in illustration and criticism, in apt quotation, in gibe and sarcasm . . ."[13] Readings continued daily throughout the term.

 Moot courts were held each evening after supper. The reader and two benchers would argue a doubtful case put to them by one of the utter barristers, and two inner barristers would put forth an imagined case, in the traditional French spoken at English law courts. That case was then criticized by the utter barristers and benchers. Between reading terms, other moot courts and less formal *bolts* were held for the junior students. After five years as an *inner barrister,* the junior student at the Inn might become an *utter* or *outer barrister,* but he would still have two years of hard study and practice before he could come before any bar at Westminster Hall to plead or set his name to any plea. Even then, only four members of Gray's Inn could be called to the bar each year: two in Easter term and two in Michaelmas term. These four were to be "the fittest for their learning and honest conversation and well given." It is obvious that not all students admitted intended to complete the full course and become practicing barristers. In the year that John Bradshawe came to Gray's Inn, another 118 students were also admitted.

On May 26, 1620, when John Bradshawe was admitted, another student was also admitted: Henry Cromwell who was Oliver Cromwell's cousin and the brother-in-law of John Hampden, Edward Whalley, Valentine Walton, and John Desborough. Among the other members of Gray's Inn that year were Robert Bradshaw of Overton in Lancashire; John Cook, the future solicitor general at the trial of King Charles; George Fleetwood, the elder brother of Charles, the future parliamentary general; Humphrey Mackworth who would serve in the parliamentary Army with John Bradshawe's brother; Tom May, the future controversial parliamentary author; Theophilus Clinton who became Earl of Lincoln; Thomas Wentworth, the future ill-fated Earl Strafford; Walter Steward, one of the gentlemen of the Privy Chamber; Charles Lord Lambert; Christopher Hatton; Simon Mayne; Denzil Holles; and Roger Downes.

In June 1620, Peter Brererton, fourth son of William Brereton of Ashley in the county of Chester, was admitted. The Brereton family hall at Ashley was not far from Bunbury School, and Peter may have been a schoolmate with Bradshawe there. If Bradshawe visited Peter and his father at Ashley Hall during his Bunbury School years or on holidays from Gray's Inn, it is there he could have met his future wife, Mary Marbury, of nearby Marbury Hall. Mary was Peter Brereton's cousin. She was eight years older than her future husband, and as with his mother, her mother had died during Mary's infancy. William Brereton of Ashley assisted in the care and upbringing of his young niece. He might have encouraged her to attend Bunbury School. Within the following year or two, the new members included Sir Robert Carr, one of the gentlemen of the Privy Chamber to Prince Charles and treasurer of the Privy Chamber.

The turbulent period in which gentlemen of Gray's Inn regularly engaged in furious street fights against the gentlemen of the Lincoln's Inn had come to an end before 1620, but spirited high jinks and "witty ribaldry which made the company merry" continued to characterize the Christmas revels. On Twelfth Night in 1623/24, the revels ended at Gray's Inn in a mad prank. The young gentlemen had broken in the royal armory at the Tower of London and carried off four cartloads of small cannon from which they proceeded to fire one deafening cannonade in the middle of the night. King James, "awakened by this noise, started out of his bed and cried 'Treason! Treason!' and the City was in an uproar; in such sort . . . that the whole court was raised and almost in arms."

The fledgling lawyers' pranks were not always so innocent. From *Grayes Inne the First Day of the Terme* (probably Easter term, 1623), Sir Peter Legh of Lyme, Cheshire, received a letter filled with the latest London news.[14] The writer commences with a narrative of his own family concerns and his breach of the rules of the Inn.

Concerning my letter to my father I will only say this much. What fruit that father may expect to come to his son's studies, that willingly doth suppress the instrument of his labours and willingly keep in fetters the freedom of his mind? For neglecting the exercises of the house, it is a frivolous objection. Himself hath been satisfied in it and Mr. Damport[15] *will justify me, knowing I never neglected but one exercise of my own, which was to argue a case, which according unto course another should have done for me at my first caning to this house, & I by feeing the Butler did of purpose neglect it, only deferring the time, that after I had been here a while, I might plead the case for myself.*

After relating the news of Prince Charles and the Duke Buckingham's voyage to Spain, he says:

To conclude all my relations, I will tell you of one mad prank that happened within these two nights. Sir Thomas Bartley was arrested hard by Gray's Inn, for 4000 £ debt, & carried to the higher end of Holborn, & committed under custody; About twelve of the clock at night, some Gentlemen of our house & of Lincoln's Inn, met together for his rescue, broke down the house, took him away with them, beat the Constables sergeants & Watchmen, & though St. Giles was raised & almost all Holborn, yet they with their swords & pistols kept them off, & brought him along to Gray's Inn, there were divers hurt with Halberds, and about 200 swords drawn, & at least 2000 people, There are 5 or 6 gents taken & sent to Newgate, & we hear that the names of above 60 gents are given up to the King, What will be done about it, we shall know in time. There are more murders drownings, death & villainies, than hath been known in London of long time before.

The letter is signed Jo: Bradshawe. In 1916, Lady Newton quoted this letter in her book *The House of Lyme* and concluded, on what evidence she didn't say, it had been written by John Bradshawe the regicide. Another John Bradshaw "of Westminster, gent"[16] had entered Gray's Inn on August 12, 1622. Not without reason, John Bradshawe and his doublegangers confused many contemporary writers and continue to perplex some today.

In 1622, the Herald of the College of Arms made his official visitation of Cheshire when the gentlemen and esquires of the county were called upon to enter their descent and show their claim to the arms they bore. Henry Bradshawe of Marple did not obey the summons. Staunch Calvinist that he was, he might have felt contempt for territorial distinctions, accomplishments, dignities, and the King's Herald. By contrast, John Bradshaw of Bradshaw, in Lancashire, attended the Royal Herald, entered his descents, and produced a precious letter from Henry Percy, the first Earl of Northumberland, to his "well-beloved friende" John Bradshaw, who had fought at Chevy Chase and elsewhere during the reign of King Richard II, as further proof of the right to bear the honorable distinction of arms.

Early in 1623, the news of a horrible massacre at the Jamestown colony reached London. Indians had unexpectedly fallen upon the tiny colony of Virginia and nearly succeeded in obliterating all there. As John Bradshawe read the lists of the living and dead, he would have seen the names of Giles Bradshaw with his wife and children among those killed at the ironworks at Falling Creek on the James River. Also killed was John Rolfe, Pocahontas's husband.

At Gray's Inn, John Bradshawe made acquaintance with two young students who would be his lifelong companions: William Brereton of Hanforth in the county of Chester who was admitted in January 1622/23, and Thomas Fell of Ulverstone in Lancashire who arrived some nine months later.

Brereton was a young gentleman with a sizeable fortune who would be created a baronet in 1626/27. He was not admitted to the bar. In 1634-1635, he travelled throughout England and Ireland then crossed over the English Channel into Holland and the United Provinces. His surviving diaries reveal that he visited all the "swarming" denominations in the Dutch cities, including a Jewish synagogue, and much admired the Dutch principle "no man persecuted for religion nor scoffed at be he ever so zealous." His bias toward Puritanism was further confirmed by his marriage to Susanna, daughter of Sir George Booth of Dunham Massey, and his close association with Colonel Dukinfield of Dukinfield and Henry Bradshawe of Marple.

Thomas Fell was admitted to the bar, and in 1645, he and John Bradshawe were called to the Grand Company of Ancients of Gray's Inn. In the early days of the Civil War he served on the King's Bench with Bradshawe in Chester and Wales. He married Margaret Askew, a powerfully independent woman who would, some years after Thomas Fell's death, marry George Fox, the founder of the Society of Friends, as her second husband, and become styled by some as the Mother of Quakerism.[17] It was through her that John Bradshawe would come into contact with the Quakers and become convinced of religious toleration for their beliefs.

Toleration was not evident in London in 1623. Three hundred Catholics were gathered in Shakespeare's old Blackfriars Theatre to hear an address by Mr. Drury, "a Jesuit." As the priest warmed to his message, the floor beams gave way and the building collapsed. Almost one hundred people were killed. Puritans of London welcomed this as a sign that God's vengeance would be visited on all their enemies.

Notes to Chapter Two

1. *The English Law and the Renaissance*, F. W. Maitland, London, 1901
2. Anthony Bradshaw (1545-1614), grand-uncle of John Bradshawe the regicide, was of the Inner Temple and the Court of Common Pleas at Westminster for more than 30 years during the reign of Elizabeth I. Anthony's grand-nephew, Francis Bradshawe (1576-1635) was of London in 1610 and an indenture bearing that date describes him as of the Inner Temple. In his last will Francis left 5 £ to Henry Bradshawe of Marple and 20 shillings to John Bradshawe for a mourning ring (PCC 43 Sadler). Francis Bradshawe (1576-1635) was the last Bradshaw to live at Bradshaw Hall in Chapel-in-le-Frith, His brother George Bradshaw succeeded and took residence at Bradshaw Hall in Eyam and in his will dated 17 June 1646 he named his kinsman John Bradshawe the regicide as one of his executors. *Notes From a Peakland Parish*, Wm. Porter Smith, Sheffield, 1923, P3 45. George's son married the daughter and co-heir of John Bradshawe's old classmate at Gray's Inn, John Vesey of Brampton, Yorks.
3. In 1610 Francis Bradshawe (1576-1635) married Barbara Davenport daughter of Sir John Davenport. Francis was High Sheriff of Derbyshire in 1631. Sir John Davenport was High Sheriff of Cheshire in 1617. Davenport was a distant relative of Sir William Davenport (15351640) of Bramhall and his brother Sir Humphrey Davenport (1566-1644) of Gray's Inn. In 1642 Sir Humphrey's son wrote John Bradshawe the regicide and therein addressed him as "my very loving Cousin." In 1644 Sir Humphrey Davenport's wife wrote a letter which she directed to Bradshawe as "My very Worthy good cousin."
4. Peter Bradshawe (?-1629), uncle of the previously mentioned Francis (note 3), witnessed the purchase deeds of Marple and Wybersley in 1606. He petitioned Robert Cecil, Lord Salisbury, concerning an extended lease of a farm in Chinley, Derbyshire, Cal of State Papers, 2 July 1609—much to the displeasure of the Earl of Shrewsbury whose manor of Glossop was adjoining. In that petition he styled himself Sir Peter Bradshawe bt.—there is no other evidence that he was ever knighted. He was granted a lease in 1616, after Shrewsbury had died. Wolley Charters, fo1227. Peter Bradshawe was granted the manor of Litton near Eyam, Derbyshire, 3 Nov 1620, and devised it in his will to his sons, Edward, Peter, Francis, Paul, Thomas, and William. The tithes and the tithe barn of the manor were devised to Peter Bradshawe by Walter Curle, Dean of St. Chad in Lichfield,

30 Oct, 1624. Edward, son and heir of Peter, espoused the Royalist cause and leased the manor (probably under duress) to "John Bradshawe and William Ellis of Gray's Inn" Wolley Charters, xi 8.

5. *6th Report, Historical Manuscripts Commission*, pg 672. One of the first Royal Ordinances that King James issued was the appointment of William Bradshawe to be one of the two Pages to the ill-fated royal heir Henry, Prince of Wales (1593-1612), and to his sister Princes Elizabeth.

6. *Dictionary of National Biography.* John Brereton (b: 1603) was probably a relative of John Bradshawe's friend Sir William Brereton q.v. DNB—who was himself, later, interested in New England settlement. He sailed from Falmouth on the "Concord" with 24 gentlemen and eight sailors, twelve of them intending to settle in New England. The voyage was sanctioned by Sir Walter Ralegh who had an exclusive crown grant of the whole coast. They stayed at Elizabeth's Island for some weeks until abandoning their plan and returning to England. Brereton wrote *A Briefe Relation of the Description of Elizabeth's Isle. and some others toward the North Part of Virginia* . . . written by John Brierton, one of the Voyage. Captain John Smith in his Adventures and Discourses speaks of "Master John Brereton and his account of his voyage" as fairly turning his brains and impelling him to make the voyage which results in planting the Jamestown colony in 1607.

7. Samuel Purchas, *Hakluytus Posthumus or Purchas his Pilgrimes*, (Hakluyt Society, 1905/06). Samuel Bradshaw sailed out to the East Indies on the fourth voyage of the Honourable East India Company (1609). He wrote a long letter narrative of the voyage. He took command of the ship as it limped homeward and valiantly tried to reach England. The ship was wrecked on the coast of Brittany and Bradshaw was not among the survivors. Other Bradshaws were involved with the India company; Ellis Bradshawe employed as a company officer at Deptford and Blackwall from 1603; Philip Bradshawe as a surgeon at Bantam (present day Indonesia) from 1620 but in 1623 he was accused of being such a "continual drunkard that nothing can reclaim him so that though he have reasonable skill, that beastlike vice overthrows all his other good parts." In 1626 the company gave a gratuity of 20 s, to Philip Bradshawe "who had been a physician in the Indies," to clear him out of Marshalsea Prison. Cal of State Papers East Indies, 27 August 1628. In his later years John Bradshawe the regicide reviewed these records looking for background material on the treaties with the Dutch.

8. *Research Volume of the Surrey Archaeological Society*, No.11972; Edmund Bradshaw, a London merchant and trader in North Africa, was granted a monopoly to manufacture "all manner of Fiansa earthen vessels being

work not heretofore put in use within this kingdom" having, for payment of £100, relinquished to the King his prior monopoly of the manufacture of gold and silver thread. In 1612 he established a pottery in Montague Close on the north wall of St. Savior's church (now Southwark Cathedral) then the parish church of William Shakespeare and many of his associates of the nearby Globe Theatre. He took Hugh Cressy, another London merchant, as his Partner but was not involved in the Partnership after 1614. He became embroiled in an attempts to free Englishmen enslaved by the Barbary pirates (See Chapter III) and had the primary role in negotiations between the London merchants, the English crown, and the King of Morocco—Cal of State Papers Domestic, 1636. He was, so it appears, dead before 1650. His widow, Surehope Bradshaw, had dealing with John Bradshawe the regicide and the Council of State in 1652.

9. Ann Bradshawe, daughter-in-law of Anthony Bradshaw (1545-1614) of Duffield was lady-in-waiting and fellow prisoner in the Tower with Lady Arbella Stuart

10. John Rolfe and Pocahontas were married at Jamestown. Pocahontas was instructed in Christianity and baptized at Henrico in the Virginia colony by Alexander Whiitaker (1585"1616/17), the "Apostle of Virginia" who was son of William Whitaker (1548"1595) the celebrated Puritan master of St. John's College, Cambridge, by his wife, a daughter of Nicholas Culverwell. Alexander's grandmother was a sister of Alexander Nowell Dean of St Paul's and patron of Middleton School where John Bradshawe the regicide had been a student. Alexander Whitaker drowned in the James River of Virginia about 1617.

11. In the autumn of 1617 King James had made a Royal Progress through Lancashire and while being entertained at Houghton Tower he was presented with a petition principally signed by Lancashire peasants, tradesmen, and servants, representing that they were debarred from lawful recreations upon Sunday, after evening prayers, and on holidays. The petition asked that these restrictions imposed in 1579 by the Earl of Derby, the Earl of Huntingdon, William Downham Bishop of Chester and other high commissioners, might be removed. The King patronized "the lawful recreations and honest exercises" so much valued by his "good people within the county of Lancaster" and he agreed to their return for Lancashire. On May 24 1618 The *Book of Sports* was published by royal command allowing dancing, archery, vaulting, May Games, Whitsun ales, and May-poles to be enjoyed after divine service. The bishops were ordered to publish and read the book in all the parish churches throughout

the kingdom. This caused offense to many in the clergy and the puritan element refused, point blank, to obey.

12. Nicholas Tyacke,.Puritanism, Arminisnism, and Counter-Revolution, Conrad Russell, ed. *The Origins of the English Civil War: Problems in Focus Series,* Section 2, Part 4 (London, 1975) "The Geneva annotated version of the bible, with a bound-in catechism expressing the idea of predestination, was the most important vehicle of Calvinist thought before 1611. The Lancashire town of Bolton where the Bradshaws of Bradshaw manor worshipped was known as "the Geneva of the North," so strong was the acceptance there of the Calvinist creed. While not endorsing an absolute doctrine of tyrannicide, the Calvinist commentators admitted the legitimacy of resistance to magistrates, particularly in issues of religious freedom. The annotation for *Ecclesiastes, vii.3.* was glossed as "withdraw not thyself lightly from the obedience of the prince." King James insisted that his new 1611 Authorized translation of the bible should contain no marginal notations at all, except variant readings and cross-references.

13. Wm. Bolland, *Manual of Year Book Studies,* (London 1925)

14. Lady Newton, *The House of Lyme,* (London, 1917), 121._

15. Sir Humphrey Davenport (1566-1644) of Gray's Inn, whose surname was often spelled "Damport" in contemporary documents; called to the bar 21 Nov 1590, Reader in Lent 1613, Sergeant-at-Law 26 June 1623, knighted 17 June 1624, Bencher of Gray's Inn and Judge of the Common Pleas 1630, Lord Chief Baron of the Exchequer 1631, Impeached by Parliament in 1641, died at his estate of Sutton near Macclesfield. He adhered to the Royalist cause during the Civil Wars. The power over life and death of felons seized within the Forest of Macclesfield was vested, anciently, in the Davenports and none of the subordinate Foresters could exercise this power. J. P. Earwaker, *East Cheshire,* Vol 11, 532,.

16. John Bradshawe "of Westminster" could be the John Bradshaw who matriculated from Christ's, Cambridge, April 1620. John Peile, *Biographical Register, Christ's College, Cambridge 1505-1905*; John Bradshaw born about 1602 second son of Roger Bradshaw of Aspull, Lancs., and grandson of Wm Downham, Bishop of Chester; nephew of the Puritan preacher John Downham; legal agent for Sir Peter Leigh of Lyme; Attorney General for Chester and Flintshire: married at Prestbury 16 Sept 1625 to Dorothy daughter of John Davenport of Woodford. He and his elder brother, William, were disowned and excluded from their father's will (1625) (*Harle Mss 1987* f.48b) and the inheritance passed to Roger Bradshaw's sons by his second wife (Margaret Hindley daughter of Roger Hindley of Aspull). Those sons

and heirs were Edward Bradshaw (1606-1671) sometimes Mayor and M.P. of Chester, and Richard Bradshaw of Pennington & Aspull (1610-1685) the Commonwealth Ambassador to Hamburg and Russia.

17. Isabel Ross, *Margaret Fell: Mother of Quakerism,* (London 1949). In the 1600s one of the most radical ideas propounded by George Fox was his insistence that women were equal to men in religion, and that a woman had the obligation to leave her unbelieving husband if he would not be convinced of the *Truth*. Margaret Fell had become convinced by George Fox as early as 1652 but Thomas Fell, while sympathetic, was never totally convinced—at least publicly. In *George Fox's Journal,* abridged by Percy Livingstone Parker (London 1903), Fox said Judge Fell "sometimes wished that I were a while with Judge Bradshaw to discourse with him."

CHAPTER THREE

Every Subject Worse than a Turkish Slave.

The most civilized and enlightened nation is that whose industry can pour upon the world the greatest proportion of the best and most valuable commodities in the shortest time.
"The Industry of the British Nation"

✠

NEARLY A HALF century of building expansion had left Gray's Inn a mixture of rosy Jacobean brickwork and Elizabethan timber, but all over the Inn, buildings of new brick and mortar were replacing the irregular huddle of "weakly built and much decayed" half-timbered hanging buildings. The gardens and paths where Sir Walter Ralegh and Sir Francis Bacon had strolled, deep in conversation about the planned last voyage, were being replanted. The offices the Star Chamber Office and the Duchy of Lancaster lay within the precincts of the Inn, and negotiations were in progress to reassure the tenants of their future accommodations. The office of the Chancellor of the Duchy, worth £8,000, was vacant in 1618, and Lionel Cranfield offered £800 for the post. Ultimately he offered to Duke of Buckingham £4,000 in gold, but Sir Humphrey May outstripped all the rivals for the office. Gossip attributed his success to his having a pretty young and, perhaps, obliging wife—a charge that was proposed at the attempted impeachment of Buckingham. Over the duchy office adjoining the Commons Hall, William Gerard had built a little rooftop chamber for his son, Gilbert, who was Clerk to the Duchy.[1] West of the hall, Humphrey Davenport was demolishing old chambers and rebuilding them in the new style. Sir Richard Osbaldestone, King's Attorney for Ireland and a bencher at Gray's Inn, was planning and erecting a long range of chambers from the side of the gatehouse and running behind the chapel into the south court. With the exception of the Hall and portions of the chapel and library, the Gray's Inn we see today contains few remains of the Tudor, Elizabethan, Jacobean, or Caroline Inn.

On April 23, 1627, John Bradshawe, Mark Shaftoe, and John Keyte were ushered into the Hall, and there, in the presence of Sir Richard Osbaldestone, William Denny, Peter Phesant, and eleven benchers, they were called to the bar. It was an auspicious and challenging time for ambitious young barristers who hoped to build their fortunes in royal patronage, parliamentary politics, ecclesiastical preference, or mercantile adventuring. The next two decades would see the victory of lawyers and English common law, the defeat of the king and princely prerogative courts. Puritan gentlemen of the time were not expected to shun prosperity; Richard Sibbes, preacher of Gray's Inn, instructed Bradshawe and his fellows: "Worldly things are good in themselves and given to sweeten our passage to Heaven and to sweeten our Profession of Religion."

The head-on clash between government and national aspiration was still fifteen years into the future, but for some time, discord had been growing. The discord, which would blossom into the civil wars, has been variously described as a constitutional contention between the House of Commons and King, a religious struggle between bishop and presbytery, and a political chasm between Royalist and Republican. Historians have credited these high-sounding principles as some of the reasons for war. No doubt strong elements of each moved men to die for laudable causes on great occasions; but behind the pretensions of principle, most men, then as now, live and work for their own material interest all the time. When high-sounding principle confronts reality, it is most assuredly not reality that gives way. Men and nations must, first and foremost, live. Thomas Mun recognized that livelihood is the basis of most human activity when he wrote: "The love and service of our country consisteth not so much in the knowledge of those duties which are to be Performed by others, as in the skilful practice of what is to be done by ourselves;[2] . . . for the Merchant is worthily called the Steward of the kingdom's stock, by way of commerce with other nations; a work of no less Reputation than Trust, which ought to be Performed with great skill and conscience, that so the private gain may ever accompany the publique good . . . If we duly consider England's Largeness, Beauty, Fertility, Strength, both in sea and Land, in multitude of Warlike People, Horses, Ships, Ammunition, advantagious situation for Defense and Trade, number of Seaports and Harbours, which are of difficult access to enemies, and of easie outlet to the Inhabitants, wealth by excellent Fleece wools, Iron, Lead, Tynn, saffron, Corn, Victuals, Hides, Wax, and other natural endowments, we shall find this Kingdome capable to sit as master of a Monarchy. For what greater glory and advantage can any Nation have than to be thus richly and naturally possesses of all things needful for Food, Rayment, war, and Peace not only for its own plentiful use, but to supply the wants of other Nations, in such measure, that money may be thereby gotten yearly, to make our happiness compleat."

When John Bradshawe came to London in 1620, the great questions of grievances, the Spanish marriage, monopolies, and money scarcity were occupying the House of Commons. In a speech to the Commons, Sir Edward Coke[3] enumerated seven causes for the scarcity of money: (1) the turning of money into plate; (2) the use of gold folia in gilding; (3) the undervalue of silver; (4) the East India company, who intercept the *dollars*[4] and other moneys that would otherwise come into the kingdom, and bring in for it nothing but toys and trifles; (5) the excess of imports over exports; (6) the French merchants who carry forth £80,000 per annum and bring in nothing but wine and lace and such trifles; (7) the patent (monopoly) for gold and silver lace and thread, which wastes our bullion and coin, and hinders the bringing of it into the kingdom. Edmund Bradshaw,[5] a merchant of London trading in the Barbary coast since the start of the seventeenth century, owned the famous gold and silver thread monopoly until he surrendered it to King James in 1612. From the time of Elizabeth, the Crown had found that it could provide itself with a source of revenue outside cannon's control by granting monopolies for the production or distribution of individual commodities to courtiers willing to pay for the privilege and give the king a portion of the profit. Sir Walter Ralegh had the monopoly of playing cards and the monopoly of selling wine.[6] Monopolies were defended as a legitimate device for the protection of a developing industry or product; sort of an early-day exclusive patent. The consuming public was incensed because monopolists were responsible for higher prices and restraint of their liberties in "habitations, trades, and other interests."

When Parliament met on January 30, 1621, a cry was raised against monopolies in general and the monopoly in the manufacture of gold and silver thread in particular. Sir Edward Villiers, Master of the Mint, MP for Westminster, and half brother of George Villiers (Duke of Buckingham), was excluded from the May parliament for attempting to speak on the question of a monopoly in which he had a personal stake—the old Bradshaw monopoly of gold and silver thread, in which Villiers had invested £4,000 and from which he derived a pension £500 annually after the monopoly was once again taken into the king's hands in 1618. Buckingham's younger brother, Christopher, had been promised pension of £800 annually out of the same monopoly but actually received only £150 during the whole of its existence. Parliament ruled the monopoly oppressive and illegal. Worse, from their point of view, it placed money in the hands of two brothers of the despised duke. Even more infuriating, Sir Giles Mompesson, Buckingham's brother-in-law, possessed the badly abused monopoly of licensing alehouses and the strange monopoly of collecting the fines that were levied against those who infringed on his brother-in-law's gold and silver thread monopoly. Sir Giles fled the country. Buckingham attempted to clear himself of involment by implicating his brothers in their other monopolies as well as that of gold and silver thread. Sir Henry Yelverton, the deposed attorney general,[7] challenged Buckingham, but it soon became apparent that a quarrel with Buckingham was tantamount to a quarrel with the king. King James had said: *"You may be sure that I love . . . Buckingham more than anyone else . . . Christ had his John and I have my George."* In the same year, Francis Bacon was disgraced and returned to lodgings at Gray's Inn. The charges against Edward and Christopher Villiers were dropped, monopolies were outlawed in 1624, but King James and his successor continued to grant monopolies not to individuals, which was technically banned by Parliament, but to companies. There was a growing feeling that all Stuart kings would be bad for mercantile expansion, overseas trade, and foreign colonization.

Sir Walter Ralegh recognized that seapower, trade, and overseas expansion went together. He wrote, "This was Themistocles's opinion long since, and it is true, That hee that commands the sea, commands the trade, and He that is Lord of the trade of the world is lord of the wealth of the world." Unfortunately, a year after Ralegh's death, a royal commission reported that out of the total of forty-three English ships of war, nearly half were unserviceable and kept from sinking only with great difficulty.

The civil wars were as much due to a quarrel between Stuart kings and England's merchants as to many other principles. The Crown was also impassive to merchant adventurers and New World colonial acquisition unless it filled the royal purse with ready cash in the form of gold or silver. It was only on a hunger for gold that James agreed to Ralegh's last voyage. Queen Elizabeth had from time to time pried money out of her long-distance trading companies, but she had repaid them by being faithful to their interests. James had not protected them from either the Spanish or the Dutch. James and his court were notoriously under the hand of Count Gondanar, the Spanish plenipotentiary in London who paid bribes and pensions to them. Gondanar intrigued to obtain the execution of Ralegh and forward Prince Charles into marriage with the Spanish Infanta. An epigram, composed in France at this time ran:

Tandis qu' Elizabeth fut Roy, L'Anglois fut d'Espagne l'effroy.
Naintenant, devise et caquette, Regi par la Reine Jaquette.

In English:

Whilst Elizabeth was King,
The English were of Spain the Terror.
But now, governed by Queen Jaquet, They only talk and prattle.

Spain was suspected of a tacit understanding with the Dutch, working against English mercantile interests. Most of the Spanish New World treasure was carried in Dutch warships. The Dutch obtained a favorable treaty from King James, and they felt so confident they did not even honor the liberal terms of that treaty, crippling the English East India Company. King Charles followed his father in robbing English merchants both of their trading privileges and of their capital while failing to give their trade any adequate protection abroad. The massacre at Amboyna[8] was one of many acts of Dutch violence against the English Grocers Company trading in the East Indies. It was an insult that sunk deep into Englishmen's memory; they could no longer trust their government. Had the attacks taken place in Elizabeth's reign, Amsterdam would have been besieged.

King James died on March 27, 1625. Almost immediately, Charles authorized Buckingham to negotiate a loan of £300,000 from the Dutch on security of the Crown jewels, which were to be sent to Amsterdam. Four years later he sold four thousand tons of English iron cannons to the Dutch in order to redeem the jewels. The situation worsened for the English East India Company; the Dutch cut down their nutmeg plantations, King Charles forced the company to sell him saltpeter at his own valuation, raised the customs on pepper to 75 percent of its value, and chartered privateers whose actions got the company into difficulties. Then, surprisingly, Charles gave his support to a second India trading company organized by Endymion Porter,[9] one of his Gentlemen of the Royal Bedchamber and John Bradshawe's fellow member at Gray's Inn. It was financed by Sir William Courteen,[10] and by its rivalry and mismanagement, all the East India trade for England was nearly ruined. Charles pledged £10,000 to the Courteen Company in return for a share of the profit but was never, as with most of his pledges, required to stump up the cash. The East India Company was so injured by Dutch actions and by Courteen's rivalry that it could not raise the necessary capital for a new voyage, yet "notwithstanding the order in Councill." Mr. Courteen was fitting out ships from England, and establishing factories in the East Indies."

Commencing with the coronation of King Charles,[11] and for the next three years, Buckingham was virtually King of England. Abruptly, Parliament issued challenges to the new king of a kind unknown throughout the previous reign. They voted him the income from tonnage and poundage for one year only, instead of the traditional lifetime grant. The limitation was moved on the argument that tonnage and poundage duties were designed to guard the seas, and the king should not have them until he guarded the sea against pirates. Also at issue was the contention that customs duties could not be levied except by consent of Parliament. Charles argued that he had to live, and that without this item, the single largest of his income, *I neither may nor can subsist.* Parliament had voted two subsidies amounting to about £140,000; Charles was probably expecting ten times that amount. He summoned the Parliament to Oxford and demanded a new subsidy. Sir Edward Coke, the deposed Chief Justice, in a highly influential speech denied there was any need for granting more subsidy—subsidies were for exceptional circumstances, and no such circumstances had been established. Trade was in depression, and the king's subjects could bear no heavier load. The Crown's ordinary expenses should be borne out of income from lands and revenues. He argued for a complete reform of the administration. So long as the king was led by corrupt advisors, there should be no encouragement. The question that Coke and Parliament were asking was why, if the crown was so poor, it could afford to pay Buckingham, the royal favorite, so much.

Apart from untold royal gifts, Buckingham demanded payment from every person who desired his assistance in obtaining royal patronage. Buckingham chose Sir John Coke (no relation to Sir Edward Coke) to voice support of the crown in Parliament; unfortunately, John Coke believed in absolute monarchy and was the only man among the government officials who had incurred the positive dislike of the opposition leaders of the Commons.

Later that year, John Coke was appointed one of the king's principal secretaries of state. Buckingham, Lord High Admiral and Commander of the Army, reversed the late king's policy and went to war with Spain, honoring the compromise he had reached with Parliament the previous year. This popular war brought Parliament to the realization that they must vote huge sums of money to the war in addition to paying off the king's debts of £666,666. They appropriated new subsidies in such a way that Buckingham could not get his hands on them and the king could not use them to pay off his debts. Buckingham attacked Spain, and while that campaign was going badly, he picked a quarrel with France as well. The parliamentary opposition believed he had lost command of his senses and should never be trusted with power in future.

The 1625 expedition against Cadiz, Spain, and another against La Rochelle, France, were both disastrous. None of the king's sailors or soldiers were being paid, and those survivors returning from the Cadiz expedition were being illegally billeted in private homes. Desertion was rife. Every able-bodied English yeoman was in constant danger of being press-ganged. Count Mansfield embarked an English army of twelve thousand men for the Palatine but landed in Zealand with only a third that number who quickly disbanded; the other eight thousand had died of plague onboard the transport ships. Survivors simply wandered aimlessly over Holland and northern Europe.

The king coerced loans from his subjects, merchants, and the trading companies supposedly to finance the wars, but in reality, to fund his own extravagance. Charles was a connoisseur. He had already begun to build the collection of paintings that would amaze Rubens, whom he engaged to paint the ceiling of the new Banqueting Hall at Whitehall. Van Dyke was engaged to paint the royal family. Charles outbid Cardinal Richelieu to obtain the Mantuan Collection, and he bargained with Cardinal Barberini to import treasures from Italy. The merchants, old aristocracy, the city of London, and country squires abhorred paying taxes to fund the pleasures of the court and its parasites.

Parliament moved impeachment against Buckingham in 1626, but they had not countenanced the new king's loyalty to his late father's favorite. By the following year, opposition leaders were taking seriously the king's threat to dispense with Parliament altogether. It would later be claimed that beginning with the accession of Charles, there had been a grand conspiracy to change the government and religion of England. C. V. Wedgwood has perceptively written: "The King's ideals were clear from the first. He wanted his subjects . . . to accept his absolute authority with unquestioning obedience . . . This was the only just basis of government as he saw it; this once achieved he would—of his own good will, and not by any legal obligation—protect their traditional rights and freedoms within the framework of the laws, and ensure equal justice."[12]

A mutiny broke out at Plymouth in March 1628 while about one hundred men were being press-ganged. The whole army of the south was put under martial law. The commander of Plymouth Fort, Sir Ferdinando Gorges, had been regularly appealing to the Privy Council for food, stores, gunpowder, and money, but now he wrote Buckingham an amazingly enlightened letter stating he presumed "to write plainly what (he) finds to be the heart-burning and cause of the grief of the sailors; 1. They say they are used like dogs; not suffered to come ashore 2. They have no means to put clothes on their backs, much less to relieve their wives and children 3. When sick they have no allowance of fresh victuals 4. The sick when put ashore are suffered to perish for want of being looked to 5. some of their provisions are neither fit or wholesome 6. They has a lief be hanged as to be dealt withal as they are." Gorges concluded that if the Buckingham could reform of these abuses he would gain the hearts of those he must make use of and satisfy the world of his care but, "if there be delay in the reformation, there will be ruin in the conclusion."[13] Buckingham prepared to sail in relief of La Rochelle aboard the ship *Swiftsure*. The captain of the *Swiftsure* was John Pennington(See Appendix 6.).

Buckingham was assassinated at the house of Capt. John Mason in Portsmouth on August 23 following.[14] King Charles wished to have the assassin, Lt. John Felton, tortured on the rack, but the Privy Council and the Chief Justices advised against it; Felton was quickly executed and his body publicly exhibited in chains.

With the hated royal courtier now out of the way, some opponents believed the king would reach an accommodation with Parliament. MPs had impeached a priest for expressing absolutist views, passed the Petition of Right, insisted that taxation could only be imposed with the common consent in Parliament, and forwarded a number of resolutions against religious innovation and the collection of customs while delaying dissolution by holding the speaker, Sir John Finch, down in his chair. For all that, six months after Buckingham's death, the king still had the arbitrary powers of imprisonment and taxation, impositions, and tonnage and poundage. Sommerville said, "Under James, men had feared for the future. Under his son it was the present which terrified them." Secretary of State Coke accused the parliamentary opposition of attacking not only the abuses of royal power but the power itself and warned them the wrath of a king was like a roaring lion. Charles succeeded in raising his income, without Parliamentary consent, to such a point that he was sufficiently solvent to dispense with Parliament altogether. He did exactly that in 1629. No Parliament was called for the next eleven years. The period of the king's personal rule began. In the 1630s, he succeeded in raising his annual income from about £600,000 to £1 million without a single vote of Parliament.

John Bradshawe's friend and future patron, twenty-three-year-old Sir William Brereton, Bt., was MP for Cheshire in the final Parliament. If Bradshawe, just completing his second year of law practice in the courts of Westminster Hall, had expected to join his friend in Parliament, his hopes were now dashed. "It is impossible," wrote Sir John Oglander, "for a mere country gentleman to grow rich or raise his house. He must have some other vocation with his inheritance, as to be a courtier, lawyer, merchant, or some other vocation. If he hath no other vocation, let him get a ship and judiciously manage her, or buy some auditor's place, or be vice-admiral in his county." Hugh R. Trevor-Roper has said, "It was no accident that the first thirty years of the seventeenth century saw an unprecedented scramble for office, an unprecedented and rising market in office, a desire to make office hereditary, as in France; and that, in the 1630s when the parsimonious government of Charles I cut down the opportunities at court, there was an unprecedented emigration of the gentry to North America. Nor is it an accident that the gentry, who thus embarked on colonial schemes, were Puritans and became leaders of the Independents." Throughout the 1620s, Puritan lawyers, judges, and MPs believed that they were making compromises and accommodations that preserved the king's prerogatives while saving the ancient rights of the subjects from the encroachment of avarious royal councilors like Buckingham. By degrees, however, they were having to make these accommodations by stealth and by craft because they were hoping to restrain the king himself, not just his royal courtiers. When the king dissolved Parliament, he took away their only effective means of open restraint; they could conform, they could flee, or they could fight. As yet, they were unprepared for a fight. The Puritans, who could not bring themselves to conform, planned to emigrate.

Of crucial importance was the organization of the Providence Island Company, whose animator was Robert Rich, Earl of Warwick (See Appendix 7.). The announced purpose of the company was to establish a colony and a government on a West Indies island, but it also provided cover for opposition political meetings. Sir William Brereton, John Pym, Lord Saye and Sele, Lord Brooke, John Hampden, and Arthur Haselrig seriously considered the idea of settling in New England. The king published a proclamation forbidding any person to depart the kingdom without license (July 1635) and two years later made it more specific by forbidding Presbyterians to go and settle in America. The Privy Council backed this final proclamation by issuing an order against transporting them. Rapin's *History of England* said that Oliver Cromwell was actually embarked for America when this order stayed his ship. Whether John Bradshawe determined to emigrate we do not know. Other members of the Bradshaw family did.[15]

Meanwhile Barbary pirates were continuing to seize English sailors at sea and even taking captives from English coastal towns. From Sallee,[16] the Moroccan home port of the Barbary pirates, the raiding ships would venture forth and take their fill of English prisoners, then return to port and sell the captives in the slave markets. It was reported that the pirates wintered in lowlands of Holland where their needs were supplied. An estimated 466 English ships had been taken before 1616, and losses were continuing. Conrad Russell said, "The government's complete failure to deal with the pirates perhaps did more to disgrace it in the eyes of its subjects than almost anything else."[17] This judgment applied equally to the reigns of King James and Charles.

Infuriated at the economic losses of ships and crews, English merchants and ship owners had offered King James the sum of £40,000 in

1617 to finance an all-out attack on the pirates. James and Buckingham dithered on for three years until a yearlong expedition ventured out but achieved nothing. Under these circumstances, the merchants did not favor a proposal in May 1622 that there should be another expedition. Some ship owners refused to pay their share of the promised sums due for the first expedition and were duely summoned to answer to the king's officers.[18] By this time, many merchants favored negotiations with Abdallah al-Manoun, ruler of Morocco at Fez, or failing that, an embargo and reprisals. Al-Mamoun died in 1623 and was succeeded by his son Abd-el-Malik, but in the climate of anarchy, he ruled for only three years. According to a report made in March 1626, there were about 1,400 English captives in Sallee, almost all taken in the English channel within twenty or thirty miles of Dartmouth, Falmouth, or even as far away as Plymouth. Peter Mathew, merchant of London, homeward bound from Portugal, was captured and taken to Sallee where he was sold for the equivalent of £140. He was bound with an iron chain and forced to grind like a horse at a millstone. He was fed on little bread and water and tortured in an attempt to make him convert to Mohammedism. A great ransom was established for his release. John Temple, master of a small ship of London, was captured and taken to Sallee where he was so abused that he died within eight days. One of his crew was murdered, and his cabin boy was forced to be circumcised and turn Turk.[21] Robert Ensome was captured off Scilly, lost his whole estate, and was taken to Sallee where he was sold as a slave. He wrote that he was *cruelly misused to make him forsake Christ and serve Mahamet.* His ransom was set at £250, which neither he nor his wife could procure.[20] Henry Young, master and part owner of the *Delight* of London, was surprised by three pirate's ships in the Straits of Gibralter. Young and his crew resolved to die fighting rather than submit. The pirates set fire to the ship, and Young, along with seventeen crew members, died clinging to the masts. Trinity House records are filled with such narratives.

John Harrison, the English agent in Morocco, ransomed some prisoners in 1627; he simply handed over guns and powder to the pirates in exchange for about 190 English captives. This angered the Moroccan ruler and did nothing to curtail the piratical acts.

At least one English sea captain took action. The Lords of the Admiralty sent to Sir Henry Marten, Judge of the High Court of the Admiralty, notice that "John Maddock, mariner, in a voyage from London to St. Lucar, being master of the William & John, took a ship that belonged to Sallee and carried her and the men that were therein to Calles (Calais) and there sold them." On hearing this, the pirates of Sallee gave order to take all the English ships at sea that could be conquered and to imprison all English merchants in Sallee. John Harrison called Maddock's "a mad act." The Admiralty lords recommended Henry Marten send for the Barbary merchants, as also Captain (Edmund) Bradshaw.[21] In 1631, Turkish pirates landed in Baltimore, Ireland, sacked the town, and carried away 109 of the residents. Capt. Francis Hooke was accused of negligence. The crew of his ship became embroiled with foot soldiers at Ballyhack, and they killed Lieutenant Polton from Lord Esmond's regiment. In 1632, fifteen of Hooke's officers and crew were found guilty of the murder. The lord justices and council at Dublin Castle, recognizing the shortage of sailors, wrote to Hooke, *Feb. 16 1632—Dublin Castle . . . we cannot dimish the crew of so many. Nevertheless we must make an example of some. You shall therefore deliver up to the sheriff of the Co. Wexford, Richard Tanner, a trumpeter, John Pimcell, William Prescott, Richard Bradshaw, William Thomas, Daniel Battye, John Filbrris, and John wells, those being the fittest to be delivered up to justice.* They authorized Hooke to press-gang replacements.

For those poor captives who managed to escape the pirates, there was cold comfort on their return to England. Local Parish registers of the time detail encounters with *Turkey Slaves*, and it is apparent that many a local Rector had to decide whether to give the wanderer alms or have him *whipped out of the Parish*—local poor laws required each parish see only to their own indigents. There were no pensions for sailors, and ship owners were not obliged to pay wages to captains or crews who returned without ship or cargo intact. Even those who arrived back with a prize of war in hand were often deprived of their possessions. Thomas Duffield, Hendrick Henderson, and three other English sailors petitioned Buckingham, explaining they had been captive onboard the Sallee pirate ship, *Heart's Desire*, but they mutinied and killed sixty-two of the Turks. In 1626, they brought the ship into Crookhaven, Ireland, where Capt. John Mason,[22] treasurer of the army, and officers of the king's fleet took the ship from them and sent them away with only the clothes on their backs. The prayed for compensation but, apparently, received none. John Mason wrote the secretary of the Admiralty and asked for the *Heart's Desire* in lieu of pay due him.[23] It appears the Admiralty was pleased when officers of the king were satisfied to accept the prizes in lieu of their pay, which was sadly in arrears.

A group of London merchants trading in Morocco undertook to collect funds for redeeming captives, and they reported receipt of £942 14s. 4d. from which they disbursed £424 14s. 4d. to buy presents for the embattled ruler of Morocco, sherif Mulay Zidan (sometimes called Emperor or King of Morocco), but Capt. Edmund Bradshaw alleged that the presents were things unlikely to be acceptable to the sherif. It was, therefore, ordered that the unsuitable presents be sold at the best available price, and in the future, only gifts deemed suitable by Captain Bradshaw and Sir William Courteen were to be purchased. It was Courteen's rival, Indies trading company, which had nearly ruined the chartered East India Company. The lords of the Privy Council conceived it a prerequisite that *a fit person* should be sent to entreat with the emperor for release of the captives, and they recommended Capt. Edmund Bradshaw to King Charles for that assignment. Armed with the king's commission, Bradshaw made his way back to Morocco early in 1636. The senior William Courteen died that year, and his son, another William, succeeded.[24]

In May, about 150 English mariners were captured, eight of whom were forcibly circumcised and tortured in an attempt to make them *turn Moors*; the rest were threatened. Captain Bradshaw reported that he had discovered a disturbing element in the matter: the emperor believed some four or five English merchants were trading with Moroccan rebels and pirates. In a petition to the Privy Council, Bradshaw mentioned the money that had been collected and reveals it had been delivered to the very merchants who were trading with the rebels. The King of Morocco was not going to assist the English captives or pay any debts (Bradshaw was owed £5,965) until trade with the rebels was prohibited.

Courteen's company was trading with the rebels, but it seems unlikely that King Charles would prohibit a trade from which he personally stood to profit. Courteen later justified that trade on the basis that all other Barbary merchants did the same.

Whatever negotiations Bradshaw had with sherif Zidan were sabotaged by a pirate raid staged that summer. Ever more daring and totally out of sheriff Zidan's control, the pirates landed near Bristol and Cardiff, taking women and children captive. Questions were raised in the Privy Council concerning Bradshaw's competence and authority. Bradshaw responded angrily: "7 November 1636 Petition of Capt. Edmund Bradshaw to the King Petitioner was sent with your Majesty's letter, as also with orders from the Council, to treat with the King of

Morocco for peace, freedom and trade, and liberty of your subjects in captivity. All of which I performed. And if I have not carried myself [free] from offense to all men, let all the punishments that can be inflicted on a man be done unto me. Notwithstanding, upon false accusation of Robert Blake that I was not sent from the State but had counterfeited your letter, the business of the State was altogether hindered, petitioner defamed, his life subject at the will of the King, and he was also hindered the recovery of a great sum of money, Prays reference for examination of the Councill."

Blake sensed that Bradshaw might not be redeemed so he petitioned to be given the mission to the Moroccan ruler for himself. Capt. Giles Penn, grandfather of the Pennsylvania founder, petitioned the secretary of the Admiralty, urging his own employment as ambassador, messenger, and supervisor (over those trying to negotiate with Morocco), and that the Lords of the Admiralty would allow him past expenses "out, of the moneys collected for captives in Barbary many years past, the remainder being in the hands of Sir William Becher (a clerk of the Privy Council) whereof £150 was given to Capt. Edmund Bradshaw . . . being of small consequence" for the King of Morocco "can never command his rebels . . . to give up one Christian without money. Only they will give him good words and delude him." Giles Penn was appointed English counsel to Sallee in 1637. Penn's daughter-in-law was Rachel, the daughter of Ralph Bradshaw of Pendleton and Manchester. Francis Bradshaw and William Bradshaw of Gloucestershire had been associated with Giles Penn's father. There is no immediate evidence to link this family association with Penn's petition against Edmund Bradshaw, but the coincidence is interesting.

Robert Blake (sometimes mistakenly identified as the great Commonwealth admiral) William Cloberry (a factor for the London merchants), and Sir Brian Janson increased the pressure on Bradshaw in front of the Council of Trade. Blake's accusations included a charge that Bradshaw had come into disgrace with the King of Morocco by using chemistry and conversing with witches. Bradshaw disputed the accusations, and as to the practice of chemistry, he explained that a chemical powder which he had while in Morocco was a medicine taken by Blake himself and by the Queen of Morocco. Blake was thereby cured of the flux, and the queen received so much benefit that the King of Morocco sent Bradshaw a Barbary horse in reward and later asked for more powder. He denied all communication with witches, whom he has ever abhorred, but stated that some of the most learned people of that country came to him to confer about the powder and other experiments in chemical art. Sloane manuscript number 739 at the British Library is a small volume of hand-written formulas entitled *Collectanea Medica* and dated 1649. On page 55 b is the formula for Captain Bradshaw's alchymical powder. It seems a murderous mixture of salt, mercury, green vitrol, vinegar, and gold—perhaps a byproduct derived from a salt glaze Bradshaw discovered while involved in his monopoly of pottery making.

Robert Blake and Sir William Courteen's company succeeded in destroying Edmund Bradshaw's Moroccan trading venture. Bradshaw was locked away in Fleet prison *for aspersions cast on Blake*. Blake obtained the royal monopoly of the Barbary trade for William Cloberry's company in 1638. That was taken away by William Courteen the younger who lost it when he was bankrupt.

One of Bradshaw's last petitions to the Council is dated 1638 from Fleet Prison. He says that he had negotiated the affairs of the Crown of Morocco and taken away the obstacle of the "first making and detaining the English captives by this present King's father," and that under orders of His Majesty and the Council, he negotiated peace and liberty for the captives. He claimed that this was affirmed by a letter that he brought from the King of Morocco, dated May 27, 1637, which is not different from a letter that the king's ambassador brought in September. "Petitioner prays the Council to take him into their consideration in regard that in this negotiation he has spent much money, besides long time and travel, receiving no return but trouble, sickness, and disgrace."

The King of Moroco's letter to King Charles[25] was: *to crave his aide . . . (p)ardon mee this is not to instruct for I know I speak to one of a clearer and quicker sight than myself, but (I) speake this because God hath please to grant me happie victory over some Part of rebellious pirate(s) that have long molested the peaceful trade of Europe and hath presented further occasion to root out the generation of those that have been so (acrimtious?) to the good of our nations and I mean that since it hath pleased God to see (antious?) to our beginning in the conquest of Sallee.* He then asks for English sea forces to support his land forces and concludes, *I doubt not but the Lord of Hosts will protect and assist those that fight in see glorious a cause nor ought you to think this strange that I so much reverencinge the Peace and accord of nations should first exhort A warr (.) Your great Prophett Jesus Christ was the Lyon of the Tribe of Juda as well as the Lord and lover of Peace which may signifie unto you that hee who is a lover & mayntyner of peace must always appear in the terror of his sword & wadeinge through seas of blood arrive to tranquility.* Surehope Bradshaw, widow of Edmund Bradshaw, petitioned the Council of State in 1652 while John Bradshawe was the Lord President. Bradshawe and the Council referred the petition to the Committee for Foreign Affairs, asking them to prepare a letter to the King of Morocco on her behalf, if they saw cause.

The haunting memory *Turkish pirates* was revived and used by William Prynne in 1642 when he urged resistance to the king's "popish depopulating cavaliers."[26] "Will not every common soldier . . . became . . . equal in monarchy to the great Turk himself . . . ? Either therefore this resistance must be granted . . . else every common soldier will become more than an absolute monarch, every subject worse than a Turkish slave."

Notes to Chapter Three

1. Gilbert Gerard followed his father William (d; 1608) as Clerk of the Duchy of Lancaster. Gilbert was born 1587, admitted Gray's Inn 1592, knighted 1624-5, baronet April 1630, M.P. (Mddlsx) five times from 1621 but excluded 1648, Treasurer of War 1642 & member Council of War 1643. In April 1648 appointed Chancellor of the Duchy of Lancaster and continued there until August 1649 when he was replaced by John Bradshawe. Thomas Fell, Bradshawe's old friend from Gray's Inn, was Vice-Chancellor. The Duchy jurisdiction lapsed in 1653 but the County Palatine continued to Jan. 1654 with John Bradshawe and Thomas Fell as Commissioners.
2. Thomas Mun, *England's Treasure by Forraign Trade*, 1630-1640. (First printed in 1664 but written, probably about 1630). President John F. Kennedy paraphrased Mun's first sentiment as "Ask not what your country can do for you; Ask what you can do for your country."
3. Dictionary of Natl Biography, Sir Edward Coke,
4. *Dollar,*—a 17th century English term for Spanish "pieces of eight."
5. *Cal. State Papers. Domestic Series.* "Captain" Edmund Bradshaw Bradshaw," was a merchant of London trading in the Barbary Coast as early as 1607. He possessed the monopoly of making of gold and silver thread but surrendered it to King James in 1612 in exchange for £ 100 and a replacement monopoly; "the sole privilege of making all manner of Fiansa earthen vessels being work not heretofore put in use within this kingdom perfected the art and brought it into the kingdom." Bradshaw and Cressy's pottery works were established in Montagu Close, adjoining St. Saviour and St. Mary Overie (now Southwark cathedral). He was not involved in the pottery after 1614. Two years later he engaged in the Barbary coast trade and obtained the Privy Council's intercession on his behalf in a dispute over stolen cargo. In 1625 he made complaint in Star Chamber against Sir John Price and obtained warrant for Price's apprehension. Price fled overseas. Six years later Price was back "in Wales endeavouring an accord with his lady and rectifying his estate." He employed Thomas Newton to sue for his pardon. Newton spread the story that Bradshaw had boasted "he had lain with Sir John's Lady" and said that was why Price originally fled the country.
6. Sir Walter Ralegh licensed John Keymer to sell wines in Cambridge about 1584. Acts of the Privy Council, 1591; "Letter to Sir John Paiton,

Alexander Balam, John Ripse, Robert Gatherel. Whereas complaint hath been made unto us by one Geoffrey Bradshaw of Wisbridge in the Isle of Ely, vintener, That there is injuriously detained from him by one William Fletcher, a license granted to him by Sir Walter Raughley (Ralegh), knight, for the selling of wine."

7. In 1621 Sir Henry Yelverton, the King's Attorney General, was accused, in the Star Chamber, of passing some clauses in the City Charter not agreeable to the King. After a hearing which lasted for three days he was fined £4000 and sent to the Tower. Sir Edward Coke had recommended a fine of £ 6000. This was not the first £ 4000 the King had obtained from his Attorney General. In a conversation with his friend Sir James Whitlock, Yelverton revealed that he had not paid Buckingham "nor any other subject in the kingdom on[e] farthing" for the post of Attorney General, but, when the appointment was made he had gone privately to the King and had given him £4000 "readye money. The King took him in his armes, thanked him, and commended him mutche for it, and tolde him he had need of it, for it must serve even to buy him dishes, and hurried him off with it to the Privy Purse, for fear perhaps that Buckingham should intercept it." John Southerden Burn, *Liber Famerlicus*, (London 1870), 57. One of Buckingham's servants told Yelverton that Sir James Lee had offered £ 10,000 to Buckingham for the post of Attorney General.

8. In 1623 the English representatives of the Honourable East India Company at Amboyna, in the East Indies, were falsely accused of a plot to capture the fort there. Captain Towerson and nine of his men were cruelly tortured and then shot.

9. Rev J. Granger, *A Biographical History of England* etc. Vol 11, (1779), and D.N.B.—Endymion Porter was a favorite of both King James and King Charles. Porter used this acceptance to become the prince of contact men. He actively undertook secret services for the king during the Civil wars and died abroad, in the court of Charles II. He respected learned men in general, but loved poets. His friend Robert Herrick addressed several poems to Porter and one to "Mrs Katherine Bradshawe, the lovely that crowned him with laurel." "Mrs," was a 17th century contraction of "Mistress." Katherine Bradshawe was daughter of John Bradshaw, Windsor Herald of the College of Arms and a Deputy Chamberlain of the Exchequer. Bradshaw and Porter were among those named for installation in the first initiation of the Royal Academy. 10. D.N.B.—William Courteen (Courten or Curteene) (1572-1636) and his brother Peter entered into Partnership with their brother-in-law John to form the wealthy London

firm. William was operating in London and Peter was agent in Holland. He had agents in Zeeland where Barbary pirates were said to winter. Courteen was prosecuted in the star Chamber, 1619, for illegally exporting gold coin. Courteen built a fleet of twenty vessels and traded Portugal, Spain, Guinea, and the West Indies. In 1624 one of his ships discovered the island of Barbados. Over the next four years he colonized the island and organized speculation in the endeavor. In 1631 his capital was estimated at £150,000. He and his associate, Sir Paul Pindar, lent money to King James and King Charles. Their joint loans ultimately amounted to £200,000. He died early in 1636.

11. Sir Francis Palgrave, *The Antient Kalendars & Inventories of the Treasury of His Majesty's Exchequer,* (London, 1836) Vol III. A certain John Bradshaw of Southolt, county Suffolk, was one of the Deputy Chamberlains of the Exchequer 1613 to 1633, custodian of the Domesday Book, Windsor Herald, and Rouge Croix Pursuivant of the College of Arms. In February 1626 he prepared "The form of the coronation taken by Mr. [John] Bradshaw Herald of Arms." The same year he was one of 84 Persons nominated for the first institution of The Royal Academy—*Archaelogia, Soc. of Antiquaries*, Vol 32, 132. In 1627 he received an additional £ 10 over his ordinary pay for "sorting, ordering, and digesting his Majesty's Records . . . . remaining in his Majesty's Treasuries at Westminster." His co-Deputy of the Exchequer was Scipio le Squire who became a member of Gray's Inn on August 10, 1627 while John Bradshawe, the regicide, was member there. John Bradshaw the Deputy Chamberlain prepared a transcript of the Norfolk manors listed in the Domesday Book for Thomas Howard Earl of Arundel at about the same that Arundel appointed John Bradshawe, the regicide, to the post of Glossop Manor Steward. John Bradshaw the Deputy Chamberlain died in 1633 leaving three sons; John, William, & Thomas, and a daughter, Katherine. British Library *Mss* 19,119.

12. C. V. Wedgwood, *The King's Peace, 1637-1641,* (1966), 60-61.

13. D.N.B.—Gorges, Ferdinado (1566-1647) and Calendar of State Papers Domestic, 1628-29, HMSO, P 37.Sir Ferdinado Gorges "father of English colonization in America" commanded the *Great Neptune,* Perhaps his own ship, one of those which the King Charles and Buckingham agreed to place at the disposal of the King Louis XIII of France in 1625. Admiral John Pennington commanded the Vanguard in that fleet—D.N.B. *Pennington, John (1568-1646)*. Much to their chagrin Gorges and Pennington learned the French King planned to use the ships against rebellious Huguenot

Protestants at La Rochelle. Gorges used certain pretexts to hang onto the *Great Neptune* and return her safely to England. English sailors refused to serve and returned home. On August 3 1625 Pennington handed over the *Vanguard* and seven hired merchants ships but retained the *Gorge* (or *George*). By April 1627 King Charles determined to go to war with France and opened talks with the leading French protestant, Duke Rohan. Buckingham sailed for France with an English expedition but upon being refused landing at the protestant stronghold of La Rochelle he descended on the nearby Isle of Rhe and attacked the French fort of St. Martin. In November, having lost about 5,000 men, he abandoned the expedition and returned to England. The King of France besieged La Rochelle and only then did the Protestants there plead for English aid. The Earl of Denbigh led an unsuccessful attempt to relieve La Rochelle in May. Buckingham was preparing a second attempt when he was murdered. Robert Bertie, Earl of Lindsey took command of the fleet and appeared before the French blockade of La Rochelle on September 20. English attempts to breach the blockade were ineffectual and La Rochelle surrendered to King Louis on 20 October.

14. *Calendar State Papers, Domestic,* 1628-29 pp 277, 325. August 29, 1628, An examination was made of "John Foord, of Dover. Being at Bradshaw's house, there was a health, begun by Bates to John Waller, of Dover to Lt. Felton. Waller drank the health to Bradshaw, and so did the rest of the company, Bradshaw said he could not tell whose health he had drunk. Bates and Waller said together, it was to him who killed the Duke. Bates said he thought he would be pitifully tortured. Waller answered that they could do nothing to him but hanging." Two days later Walter Roades was examined "in confirmation, and partly in explanation, of the statement of John Foard respecting the drinking the health of Felton, at the sign of the Ship at the pier in that town." On September 9 Thomas Plummer of New Ranney was examined "respecting the drinking of Felton's health, at Bradshaw's house in Dover, by himself, John Waller, Bradshaw, and others." No further identification of this Bradshaw is mentioned

15. King Charles granted a charter to his Chief Justice of the Common Pleas, Sir Robert Heath, for a new colony to be named *Carolina*. Heath quickly turned it over to Sir George Berkley. sir William Boswell and Samuel Vassall, a London merchant, agreed with Berkley to provide ships, equipment, men, and money. In September 1632 Vassall's agent went to Virginia and then traveled southward as far as St. Helena River. The next year Edward Kingswell accepted, from Vassall, the Governorship of Carolina. Kingwell

sailed with his wife, family, and *attorney* William Bradshaw on the ship *Mayflower* which had been formerly named the *Christopher and Mary*. Peter Andrews was captain. The group waited at Jamestown for the promised equipment and money. It never carne and Kingswell returned to confront Vassall in London leaving William Bradshaw behind to collect debts in Accomack and Northampton counties, Virginia. When Kingswell died in London, 1636, he bequeathed to William Bradshaw his "cloth suit and cloake, the Doublet whereof is lyned with Orange tawney taffety, together with the Orange tawney silk stockings." His executors were instructed to recompense Bradshaw well "for his paynes in business between mee and Mr. Vassal." Roger Wingate, Kingswell's son-in-law, inherited rights to Kingswell's Virginia property and he returned to Virginia where he served as the colony's treasurer and on the Council in 1639. By that time Bradshaw was dead in Virginia.

16. The port of Sallee (Sale), near present-day Rabat on the western coast of Morocco, occupied a commanding position over early shipping lanes. In 1609 a fiercely Islamic group of Moors were expelled out of Hornachos in the Estrernadura district of Spain from where they had been raiding the Straits of Gibralter for decades. Bringing their weapons and gold they moved into Sallee, repaired and garrisoned the old Kasba, and gained the encouragement from Mulay Zidan (d; 1618) the ruling sherif at Marrakech. They became known as Homacheros and were largely engaged in piracy. They allied themselves with a rebellious champion of Holy War, the mujahedin Sidi al-Ayachi. In 1627 the Hornacheros and Sidi al-Ayachi expelled Mulay Zidan's governor and negotiated directly with King Charles's agent John Harrison. For a short Period there was an uneasy peace. Then Maddock's action infurated the pirates. Merchantmen making their way south to the Canary Islands, or the East Indies, passed this way. Just a few leagues above sallee lay the entrance to the Straits of Gibralter where trading ships passed on their way to Seville, Tripoli, the Levant, Italy, Venice, and Turkey. Sailing light, fast, and maneuverable ships the Barbary pirates were more than a match for the English merchant ships; they could not so easily overpower the more heavily armed Spanish and Dutch East Indiamen. For this reason, and others, the Dutch and Spanish gave tacit approval of the pirate's activities. There were also pirates of Turkey, Tripoli, and Spain all falling within the broad terms Barbary, Turkey, or Sallee pirates. Even some English captains joined the pirates as privateers against Spanish and Dutch ships, or joined the Mulay Zidan in an attempt to suppress the trade with his rebels and pirates.

17. Conrad Russell, ed, Parliament and the King's Finances, *The Origins of the Civil War, Problems in Focus series*, (London 1973).
18. G.G. Harris, *Trinity House Transactions, 1609-1635*, (London 1983). The corporation of Trinity House, Deptford, was responsible for collecting the money from their shipowner Brethern who were to pay a share of the costs for the first expedition against the pirates. Ships that traded to the south paid more while those which traded to Germany and Greenland contributed less. Trinity House agreed to fees of about £ 1,000 yearly but double that rate was imposed by the Privy Council before 1620. Captain Thomas Best, Master of Trinity House in 1621/22, protested to the Duke of Buckingham and persuaded him to induce the King to reduce the contribution. Buckingham later stated that the reduced fee was only temporary but the Brethren of the corporation stood firm and their disobedience was reported to the Privy Council. When the Council finally got around hearing the matter they quickly issued a warrant for the arrest of Captain Best and Captain Chester; strangely they didn't attempt the arrest of Captain Robert Bradshaw, who was Master of Trinity House for 1622/23
19. Ibid
20. Ibid
21. (See Note 5).
22. It was at Captain John Mason's house in Portsmouth that the Duke of Buckingham was assassinated in 1628. Two months after Buckingham's death the Privy Council issued £150 to Mason, "treasurer of his majesty's formerly employed in his majesty's service." Robert Rich earl of Warwick, Sir Ferdinado Gorges, and captain John Mason possessed controlling interests in the Council for New England and after the fighting in France and Spain ceased they revitalized the Council between November 1629 and July 1632, making 20 grants of lands north of the Merrick in North America. Warwick continued to attend Council meetings until November 1631 when a dispute arose with the Massachusetts Bay Company and an order was issued requiring all patents to be brought in for examination and confirmation. A grant, dated 4 November 1631, gave to Captain Richard Bradshaw 1500 acres "above the head of the Pahippscot (Pejepscot or Peckipscot River) on the north side thereof" the consideration being the expense that Bradshaw incurred "in his living there some years before" and that he now purported to "settle there with other his friends and servants." Due to unfortunate circumstances captain Richard Bradshaw was unable to settle in his land grant. see Cal. State Papers, Dom., 1633-36, various

notations, Peter Coldham, *English Adventurers and Emigrants,* 30, 37. Henry S. Burrage, *Beginnings of Colonial Maine*, 209. Wilbur D. Spencer, *Pioneers on Maine Rivers*, 245, and Dorothy O. Shilton & Richard Holworthy, *High Court of the Admiralty Examinations, 1637-1638*,. Sir Ferdinado Gorges was made *Lord Palatine of Maine* in 1639 though he never crossed the ocean to his Palatine kingdom. He spent some of his later years attempting to have the Massachusetts Bay Company Charter expunged. He died 1647. Captain John Mason went on to be Governor of Nova Scotia.

23. *Cal. State Papers, Domestic Series,* 1625-26., HMSO, 246, 257
24. D.N.B. Sir William Courteen's son, William the younger, married Catherine Egerton the daughter of John the first earl of Bridgewater and succeeded to his father's business after 1636. He possessed the monopoly of trading in Barbary until 1638. The Dutch seized his East India trading ships in 1641 and he was driven into bankruptcy two years later.
25. British Library, *Harle Mss;2104*, folio 291 (old), Pencil numbered 35. It appears to be a near-contemporary undated copy
26. William Prynne, *The Third Part of the Soveraigne Power of Parliaments and Kingdomes* (1643), 3, 70, 84.

CHAPTER FOUR

The Influence of Edward Coke, William Prynne, and John Lilburne

✠

THE LITTLE WE know about young John Bradshawe gives no inkling he was anxious to join in armed rebellion against his king, but as a Calvinist and a member of a great society of lawyers, he must have agreed with the developing and revolutionary ideas of curbing princely prerogative and resisting absolute sovereign power. Calvinism was not yet in total opposition to the Crown; it was at war with Arminianism and the Bishops. Committed Royalists believed that God spoke, by example, in explicit support of nonresistible monarchy as a form of government, and that loyalty to the Crown should be intellectually unquestioned. They devised the term *polarchy* to describe and ridicule all other forms of government. On the reason why England had come to a somewhat mixed system of government, Royalists favored the proposition that the *imperium absolutum* established by William the Conqueror after the Norman Conquest had gradually evolved because successive kings had graciously granted revocable concessions that self limited the manner in which they chose to administer sovereign power. The Magna Carta, the Charter of the Forest, and the king's undertaking not to legislate without Parliament's consent were viewed, by the Royalists, as princely gifts which were not to be understood as returning any part of sovereign power to the English people (which, it was said, they never had) or placing any enforceable limits on the king's power. For Royalists, Charles I's title dated from William's conquest in 1066, but with the dissolution of Parliament in 1629, even some Royalists recognized a threat, inherent in Charles's period of personal rule, to the system of mixed government.

King James I had played a dangerous ideological game in a search for moral support of his efforts to favor a Dutch Republic. In a letter to Bishop Abbott, he asked the clergy to give their judgments as to *how far a Christian and protestant king may concur to assist his neighbors to shake off their obedience to their own sovereign upon account of oppression.* In response, Convocation at Canterbury in 1606 drew up three books of canons and constitutions relating to civil government, with a statement of principles upon which they were grounded. They were not propagated because James refused to sanction the first book on the basis of the doctrine laid down in canon xxviii which, while absolutely denying subjects the right of resistance, nevertheless affirmed that new forms of government originating from successful rebellion have divine authority. James thought this canon struck at his own title, as merely *de facto* and not *de jure*; and further, that it gave the stamp of divine authority to proceedings that, in themselves, were evil (See Appendix 8.) Moderates like Charles Dallison insisted that sovereignty remained with the king while statue law making belonged to the king, Commons, and Lords acting in unison; determining the validity and interpretation of the law belonged to the judges. Thus, the people are governed by the king, and the king's government is directed by established law "of which the king is not judge, nor can he by himself alter the law." King James disagreed. Flattered by Archbishop Bancroft's notions of princely prerogative, he gave strong support to the argument that ecclesiastical courts should have coordinate jurisdiction with secular courts, both their powers being merely delegations from the king. Sir Edward Coke, then Chief Justice of the Common Pleas, sensed the danger of extending the royal and ecclesiastical authority. The king summoned the judges and told them that, as he was informed, he might take what cases he pleased away from the judges, who were but his delegates, and determine them himself. Coke told him that it was not the law. Coke recounted the ensuing confrontation in his own *Reports*: "Then the king said that he thought the law was founded upon reason, and that he and others had reason as well as the judges. To which it was answered by me, that true it was that God had endowed his majesty with excellent science and great endowments of nature, but his majesty was not learned in laws of this realm of England, and causes which concern the life, or inheritance, or goods, or fortunes of his subjects, they are not to be decided by natural reason, but by the artificial reason and judgment of the law, which law is an act which requires long study and experience before a man can attain to the cognizance of it; and that the law was the golden met-wand and measure to try the causes of the subjects; and which protected his majesty in safety and in peace; with which the king was greatly offended, and said that then he should be under the law, which was treason to affirm, . . ."

Figure 10. Sir Edward Coke confronting King James, pictured on the door of the U.S. Supreme Court Chambers

Parliamentarians propounded thoughts that the English community had originally established by immemorial laws combined with the natural law of self-defense—a pluralist constitution that required the cooperation of monarchy, Commons, and Lords for its normal functioning. To subvert this *fundamental law* was to transform this mixed monarchy into an absolute monarchy. *Fundamental law*, however, was an ill-defined term during the sixteenth and seventeenth centuries, and it appeared in both parliamentary and Royalist writings. Among the various definitions, normal English usage seems to have been one denoting immemorial customary law. Martyn P. Thompson[1] has said, "J. G. A. Pocock's[2] study of seventeenth century legal and historiographical thought has considerably sharpened appreciation of normal usage; it was Edward Coke's; (See Appendix 9.) it arose during Elizabeth's reign; it identified fundamental law with a body of traditional rights deriving supposedly from time immemorial . . . What made fundamental law fundamental was precisely its antiquity and character as an ancient custom . . ." But it was not the only understanding. When Francis Bacon first used the term *fundamental law* in 1596, he stated very clearly that he was referring not to immemorial, customary, law but to the specific laws of King Edward I. John Selden felt that every law was "a Contract betwixt the Prince and the people and therefore to be kept." Custom itself was a contract to be kept. Judge John Bradshawe would, in 1649, maintain that King Charles had broken a contract with the English people and therefore violated fundamental law.

In 1628, King Charles introduced his controversial forced loans. Roger Manwaring, a local clergyman, responded to Bishop Laud's call for the church to support the forced loans with such enthusiasm that even the Archbishop of Canterbury was shocked. Manwaring said that taxes were due the king by divine right no matter what authority imposed them and that there could be no justice between the king and his subjects because they were too unequal. John Pym and his stepbrother Francis Rous resisted, declaring the subject was protected from taxes and loans not "introduced by any statute, or any charter or sanction of princes, which was the ancient and fundamental law, issuing from the first frame and constitution of the kingdom." Sir John Coke, one of the principal secretaries of state and chief apologist for the government, confessed to the Commons that the king had broken the law but urged that it had been done out of necessity. He advised Parliament to petition the king not to repeat it. In answer to an earlier remonstrance from Parliament, the king bade the Commons to rely on his word. Sir Edward Coke (no relation of Sir John Coke), having been deposed from the judicial bench and now member of Parliament for Buckinghamshire, took up the point of the king's admonishment: *"Was it ever known,"* he told the House of Commons *"that general words were a sufficient satisfaction to particular grievances? . . . The king must speak by a record and in Particulars, and not in general. Let us have a conference with the lords and join in a petition of right to the king for our particular grievances . . . not that I distrust the king, but because we cannot take his trust but in a parliamentary way."* The subsequent alteration made to the petition by the lords, the saving of the words king's *sovereign power*, was strongly resisted by Edward Coke. This *sovereign power*, he said, was a new and dangerous phrase, unknown to Magna Carta and other statutes of freedom. *"Take we heed what we yield unto; Magna Carta is such a fellow that he will have no sovereign."* Edward Coke was now in his seventy-eighth year. His life had been devoted to veneration of the law—its technicalities as well as for its substance—and a belief that the liberties of England were dependent upon rigorous maintenance of the law and the following of legal precedents. "Possessed with this one idea he exercised a great and beneficial restraint on two of the most dangerous and unwise English kings . . . From the fragments of his parliamentary speeches which survive, we can still understand how, with all their grim Pedantry, they stirred the blood of those who listened to them." This strength of resistance must have made a lasting impression on John Bradshawe who, if not personally present to hear, most certainly would have received first-hand ringing reports of Coke's speeches

Other men joined the resistance, including many members of the Society of Gray's Inn where John Bradshawe lodged. A new term, *patriot*, was proudly worn by the king's opposition. Dryden scoffed, *"gulled by a Patriots name, whose Modern sense is one that would by Law supplant his Prince."*

The next Parliament impeached Roger Manwaring. John Pym echoed his stepbrother's opinion when he addressed the House: *"those commonwealths have been the most durable and perpetual which have often reformed and recomposed themselves according to their first institution and ordinance; for by this means they repair the breaches and counterwork the ordinary and natural effects of time."* Many MPs harkened back to this idea of *first institution* of the Commonwealth as precedents for fundamental law and mixed monarchy. Writers such as William Prynne, Charles Herle, William Bridge, Jeremiah Burroughs, Henry Parker, and Philip Hunton dealt exhaustively with these ideas. William Prynne was the most influential on the fledgling lawyer John Bradshawe.

A year after John Bradshawe was called to the bar, William Prynne, a lawyer of Lincoln's Inn, published one of the first of his lifetime's output of two hundred books and pamphlets. Antony Wood calculated that Prynne wrote a sheet for every day of his adult life. He was one of the most militant Calvinists and devoted intense study of theology, ecclesiastical antiquities, and the law. He took upon himself the job of censoring everything in his sight: the manners, fashions, follies, politics, and religion of his age. *Health's Sickness* and *The Unloveliness of Lovelocks*, published in 1628, were treatises intended to prove that the custom of drinking healths was sinful and that it was "mannish, unnatural, imprudent, and unchristian" for women to cut their hair short, while for men to wear their hair long was "unlawful unto Christians." John Bradshawe did not subscribe to Prynne's pronouncements and wore his hair long all his life. Neither did King Charles who wore a lovelock, which was considerably longer than the rest of his hair, on the left side of his head. It appears that Charles cut off his lovelock in 1646.

Most writers who attacked the government in those days were not interested in the principle of freedom of expression but only in expressing their own version of truth. Prynne had no real objection to royal supremacy and in fact became one of its chief defenders, but he stoutly maintained that no subject should obey a command to sin. He was as appalled that the government permitted the publication of what he wished censored as he was that the government censored that which he wished to publish. By contrast, printers had vested interests in freedom of the press; and Michael Sparke, Prynne's printer, raised that issue, claiming that the Star Chamber decree on which censorship was based had no legal authority since it was not established by any Act of Parliament or Common Law. In spite of strict censorship, Catholic, sectarian, and Anabaptist books were illicitly available at London in the 1620s. As William Laud was successively promoted to Bishop of London and then Archbishop of Canterbury, he was given the two sees which controlled censorship of London printers. Cambridge press was already controlled by Arminians, and with Laud's election as Chancellor of Oxford in 1631, they gained control of the last non-Arminian press in the country. During the rest of the 1630s, almost all works licensed for publication were Arminian.

In February 1630, Alexander Leighton, the father of Archbishop Leighton, was fined £10,000 by the court of the Star Chamber for two books: *Zion's Plea* and *The Looking Glass of the Holy War*. He was then transferred to the ecclesiastical High Commission Court to be deprived of his ministry; then he was to be whipped, pilloried, lose both his ears, his nose slit, his face branded with a double SS (sower of sedition), and lastly sent to Fleet prison for life. Archbishop Laud removed his cap and gave thanks to God as the sentence was read. The horrid sentence was carried out on the frosty and snowy days of November 16 and 23; according to the terms of the sentence, he was to be publicly exposed and punished twice. He lay in Fleet prison for more than ten years.

Archbishop Laud, later at his own trial, insisted that he had not violated the canon which forbids a clergyman to have anything to do with a sentence affecting life or member. He said, "to take away an ear is not a loss of hearing, and so no member is lost; so for burning the face, or whipping, no loss of life or member."

One last Puritan attack had slipped through Archbishop Laud's net. William Prynne obtained a license, May 31, 1630, to print his attack on stage plays entitled *Histriomastix*, a huge volume of more than a thousand pages published in November 1632. Plays were unlawful encouragements to immorality, female actors were whores, and audiences were sinful, Prynne contented. He made pointed reference to tyrants such as Nero and argued that magistrates should suppress plays. It may have been sheer coincidence that the queen and her ladies took part in a stage play, in the presence of the king and court, in January 1633. Archbishop Laud portrayed *Histriomastix* as a specific attack upon the king and queen.

A particular scandal broke about this time. Mervin Touchet, nineth Lord Audley and second Earl Castlehaven, was convicted of sodomy and assisting the rape of his own wife, for which he was beheaded in April 1631. Two of his servants were hanged. His unfortunate wife was a daughter of the Earl of Derby. Audley's sister had been married to Sir Francis Bacon, Audley's two aunts had been married to Lancashire gentlemen, Anne's husband was Thomas Brooke of Norton, Elizabeth's first husband had been John Bradshaw of Haigh (died before 1601), her second George Legh of High Legh (died 1616/17). Lord President John Bradshawe would come to possess, as a gift from Parliament, Audley's magnificent country estate, Fonthill-Gifford in Wiltshire.

King Charles issued a proclamation in June 1632 that all lords and gentlemen must depart from London and return to their country estates. To further ensure their departure, another royal proclamation forbade any building of houses on new foundations in London. Perhaps this was a plan to clear the troublesome Parliamentarians out of London and back to the countryside while King Charles took his planned royal progress to Scotland. More likely, the king hoped most people would not obey his Proclamations because the fines generated would add money to his empty coffers. In the Star Chamber three years later, charges were brought against several hundred people for residing in London in defiance of the king's proclamation. All of the accused were allowed to compound for their offense, i.e. pay an amount of money to avoid prosecution and pay again each time prosecution was threatened. A new royal proclamation was issued commanding all persons to gain the king's license before departing the kingdom. There was, of course, a fee to be paid for the king's license and a sentence to be pronounced in the Star Chamber on those who obstinately refused to obey the proclamation.

During the periods of their personal rule, the first two Stuart kings relied heavily upon the famous *proclamation statute* (31 Hen. VIII, c.8). The preamble recites the justification for the Act as being the disobedience to proclamations touching matters religious and civil owing to the absence of legal power to enforce them—the occasional need of urgent action by the executive and the king's indisposition to stretch his prerogative. The Act empowered the king, with the assent of the majority of the council, to issue proclamations which are to have the force of Acts of Parliament so long as those proclamations do not prejudice life or property nor repeal existing laws. The sheriffs are to publish any such proclamation in four market towns or six towns and villages. Offenders, upon conviction before the council in the Star Chamber, shall incur the penalties specified in the proclamations, if the proclamation was published in the shire where the offender dwells. It then appointed twenty-six judges, whose offices are set out,[3] to hear the case "in the Starr Chamber at Westminster or elsewhere, or at least before halfe the number afore rehersed" (i.e., thirteen judges formed a quorum). This constituted a special tribunal, not specifically the Court of the Star Chamber, to try the particular offence of disobeying a royal proclamation. From this tribunal, the king would grow his powerful Court of the Star Chamber.

The Court of the Star Chamber was a creature of the king's prerogative and claimed its jurisdiction from the statute *pro Camera Stellata* (3 Henry VI c.1—1488), although it was not founded by Act of Parliament during that reign. There had been earlier examples, as early as Henry III, of proceedings before the "King and Council sitting in a room called the Star Chamber," but they were not proceedings of the Court of the Star Chamber. A resolution prior to Henry VII, in the twenty-eighth Book of Assize, page 51, that *Coram Nobis et Concilio resolved to be Coram Rege et Concilio in Camera Stellat* was cited as affirming that the king was to be supreme judge of all, sitting in his throne of majesty surrounded by his wise men and sages, distributing justice in his royal person. The argument went that as the king or his council found themselves overburdened, the king had committed pleas to the Crown to certain judges (the King's Bench), matters of common right to other justices (the Common Pleas), and affairs of the revenue to others (the Exchequer). All these, however, before they were distributed to others, were more properly determinable before the king and his council. Britton's treatise on the law, written in the time of Edward I, concluded in the king's name, "we will that our own Jurisdiction be above all Jurisdictions in all cases real and personal."

The main offenses punished in the Star Chamber were largely unknown to the common law: forgery, perjury, libel, fraud, conspiracy, riot, and maintenance. Under the comprehensive definition of "contempts of the King's Authority," all offenses against the state were included in the time of King James. In so doing, the Star Chamber permanently enlarged the limits of English criminal law. Cases in the Star Chamber were not, of necessity, brought by the king's Attorney General. In fact, they could be brought by one of the very judges of the court. It appears, also, that the accused was seldom accorded the right to defense counsel. John Bradshawe and his fellow common lawyers attacked the jurisdiction and proceedings of the Star Chamber, but without success as long as the council kept to its proper business and steered clear of politics. As the crown began to use the Star Chamber to strike at political opponents, then the lawyers joined with the Parliament; the Star Chamber was finished. Afterward, the King's Bench, without much difficulty, adopted the Star Chamber jurisdiction.

Prynne was conveyed before the court of the Star Chamber, at the insistence of Archbishop Laud, on charges of publishing the seditious libel *Histriomastix*. He was fined £5,000, imprisoned in the Tower of London for a year, and after another hearing, newly sentenced to life imprisonment, mutilation by having both his ears cut off in the pillory, and degradation by the loss of his university degree and expulsion from Lincoln's Inn. He stood in the pillory for three days in May 1634 while the bloody business of butchering his ears took place, but by June he was sufficiently recovered to address a letter to Archbishop Laud, charging him with injustice and illegality. From prison, Prynne continued to pen a flood of anonymous tracts against the Sabbath breakers, bishops, and prelates in general. The discovery that he authored of one of these brought him, once again, to the Star Chamber in June 1637. He was sentenced to have his nose slit, lose the rest of his ears, be branded on the cheeks with a hot iron, and suffer continued life imprisonment. In company with two other convicted and sentenced libelers, Henry Burton and

Dr. John Bastwick, he bore his punishment with defiant courage. The executioner botched the job and cut away a sizeable chunk of Prynne's cheek; he severed Burton's temporal artery. Faithful followers mopped the blood from around the base of the pillory and preserved their gory kerchiefs as relics—a scene that would be repeated at the execution of King Charles. It would be Prynne's thinking, enhanced and moved to centre stage, that would lead to the trial of the king.

John Lilburne, twenty-three-year-old London apprentice, had involved himself in clandestine printing and distribution of Bastwick's *Litany* and Prynne's *News from Ipswich*. Archbishop Laud moved against him in the Star Chamber where Lilburne obstructed the trial by refusing to take the oath, the lawfulness of which, he said, he doubted. At this there was much amazement; the Star Chamber oath had never before been refused. Lilburne claimed all the protection of the laws of the land and holy writ as a freeborn Englishman. His defense failed, and in April 1638, he was tied to the tail of a cart and smartly whipt from the Fleet to Westminster. The executioner told Lilburne, *"I have whipped many a rogue before, but now I shall whip an honest man."*[4] It appeared the authorities were determined to leave him in King's Bench prison to die, but throughout London, the news spread that John Lilburne had stood on his rights as a freeborn Englishman, and he promptly earned the lifelong affection and loyalty of his fellow citizens along with a permanent nickname: Freeborn John. Lilburne's uncle, Humphrey Hixon, must have watched nervously from Greenwich Place where he occupied the post of Royal Keeper of the King's Wardrobe. Lilburne's aunt, Mary Bradshaw Hixon, was the daughter of John Bradshaw of Bradshaw manor. Lilburne, Prynne, Burton, and Bastwick languished in prison until the returned Parliament of 1640 obtained their release. Six years later, John Bradshawe (the regicide) acted as counsel in John Lilburne's hearing before the House of Lords. By this time, however, a rift was developing between Bradshawe and Lilburne who, with the Levelers, had moved on from a concern for fundamental and traditional rights to the rational abstractions of natural rights. John Bradshawe was residing, primarily it seems, at Congleton in Cheshire throughout the 1630s, so unless he visited London at the time, he would have witnessed none of the sufferings of Prynne and Lilburne.

In 1630, at the age of twenty-seven, Bradshawe had been appointed to a prestigious post: steward of the Manor of Glossop in Derbyshire. This was not, in all probability, a random appointment, nor necessarily an appointment made solely on merit. Like all Jacobean patronage, it would have been made because of influence, in reward for long-term loyalties, or through close family ties. John Bradshawe counted royal courtiers, gentry, merchants, lawyers, and men with close connections to noble households among his relatives. The motives which moved kinsmen to perform favors varied from affection and gratitude to a sense of obligation or expectation of reciprocal favors at some time in the future. Clearly John Bradshawe was a rising young gentleman and well worth an investment.

Notes to Chapter Four

1. Martyn P. Thompson, The History of Fundamental Law, *Am. Historical Rev.* vol 91, 1119.
2. J. G. A. Pocock, *Ancient Constitution*,
3. The 26 Judges were; the King, the Archbishop of Canterbury, the Lord Treasurer, the President of the Privy Council, the Lord Privy Seal, the Lord Chamberlain, the Lord Admiral, the Lord Steward (or Grand Master), the Lord Chamberlain of the King's Household, two other Bishops from the King's Council, the Secretary, Treasurer, and Controller of the King's Household, the Master of the Horse, the two Chief Judges, the Master of the Rolls, the Chancellor of Augmentations, the Chancellor of the Duchy of Lancaster, the Chief Baron of the Exchequer, the two general surveyors, the Chancellor of the Exchequer, the Under-Treasurer of the Exchequer, and the Treasurer of the King's Chamber. In the minimum quorum of thirteen, two of the following had to be present; Lord Chancellor, Lord Treasurer, Lord President of the P. C., Lord Chamberlain, Lord Admiral, and the Chief Judges.
4. Pauline Gregg, *Free-born John, A biography of John Lilburne*, (London 1961), 64.

CHAPTER FIVE

Back to the High Peak Forest

> *In forests I, at liberty and free,*
> *Liv'd in such pleasure as the world ne'er knew*
> *Till this last age, those beastly men forth brought,*
> *That all those great and goodly woods destroyed.*
> **Michael Drayton, 10th Nymphall, C. Brett (ed.),**
> **Minor Poems, Oxford Univ. Press, 1970**

> *In ancient times, no matter where,*
> *A nation lived of wise men . . .*
> *Who made good laws to guard a hare,*
> *A Partridge or a pheasant;*
> *But left the poor to nature's cares*
> *Say was not this right pleasant?*
>
> *Who to this country, would not run,*
> *Where only freedom's got at?*
> *Where birds escape the fatal gun,*
> *And men alone are shot at?*
> **Anon, London Magazine, 1776, in R. H. Lonsdale,**
> **New Oxford Book of 18th Century Verse**

☖

"OF KINFOLKES ESTEEM the company of them most that be rich, honest and discreet and use them in your causes before others. If they be poorer and yet of good conscience and humble regard them well."[1] If John Bradshawe's appointment as Glossop

Manor steward was finessed with the influence of concerned relatives, and that seems the plausible method, then it was a step along the usual path followed by other aspiring young Jacobean and Carolinian courtiers—from the notice of a nobleman, to the notice of the court, to the notice of the king from whom all honors flowed. The gentry of Derbyshire, Lancashire, and Cheshire had always sought the patronage of some powerful noble. Their favor was the surest way to high office in government, so the ablest and most ambitious men were drawn into their service. Such service was often service to the king in disguise. The earls Arundel and Pembroke, sons-in-law of the Earl of Shrewsbury, had at their disposal not only the sizeable patronage in their own heritable manorial lordships but also patronage and power which they could dispense, as royal officials, from the offices of Chief Justice of the Forest, keepers of the royal forests, constables of royal castles, and stewards of royal honors. Drawing upon their own resources to enforce these royal commissions, and dependent upon the goodwill of their own retainers, they chose deputies or associates to reinforce the principle that the sovereign authority must act through the local medium; it cannot itself take in hand the business of local government. King James and his son did not subscribe to this principle. Nor would they support Fortescue's axiom that the king exists for the kingdom, not the kingdom for the king, "for the preservation of the laws of his subjects, of their persons and goods, he is set up, and for this purpose, he has power derived from the people so that he may not govern his people by any other power."

It must be reiterated that the three centuries leading up to the 1630s were characterized by the homogeny of powerful local English families—i.e., all those of common surname. In the counties Palatine of Cheshire and Lancashire, the High Peak Forest of Derbyshire and farther north, especially strong kinship groups continued longer than elsewhere, guaranteeing protection of their members and occasionally resorting to feuds against enemies. In 1604, the warden of the West Marches complained that the law was powerless in the face of surname loyalty coupled with frequent intermarriage among strong families. Younger sons of old families married well and established stronger cadet branches. In Lancashire particularly, it was said the second rank of the gentry consisted mainly of cadet branches of leading families. That was certainly true of the 1630s Bradshaws of Lancashire, Derbyshire, and Cheshire, again remembering that they all bore the same coat of arms with marks of cadence for cadet branches.

It would have been simply inconceivable that John Bradshawe would not have known how the wider Bradshaw family had served the great nobles and the kingdom and proudly made that service known to his associates, his vicar, his master, the king's advisors, and (if he could) to the king himself. Yet we, today, lack a systematic study of the liveried retainers, stewards, foresters, esquires, knights, and yeomen who played such a decisive part from the reign of Edward II through the reign of Richard II. They formed the beginnings of offensive military and administrative structure, replacing the old feudal system of baron's and knight's service, (See Appendix 10.) predating the county muster of the Tudors and the standing army of the Stuarts. These servants and allies of some great noble house formed a sort of literate and intellectual personal bodyguard, occupying strategic places in government, effectively limiting the power of the greater barons, ecclesiastical aristocracy, and the Crown. The Bradshaw family provides a most revealing example of these servants, exemplified by Nicholas Bradshaw (d; ca 1415) (See Appendix 11.) who loyally served three earls and three kings throughout his life, became king's esquire to Henry IV, and was rewarded with annuities, pensions, privileges, and life grants of manors—not with a heritable peerage, heritable lands, or even a knighthood. Gradually the Tudors began to fill the Commons of parliament with royal servants. As a result, the Crown retained effectual control of the Commons and strengthened the Crown at the expense of the nobility and the clergy. It would have been as inconceivable for the greater barons to exact a Magna Carta from Henry VIII as it was for the clergy to resist his dissolution of the monasteries or the commons to limit his income. This is the sort of Commons that King Charles would have preferred. Unfortunately, Parliament was now out of the control of royal servants and in the control of lawyers and the law. When Charles found he could not control his Parliament, he dismissed it.

Charles's assumption of personal rule despoiled John Bradshawe's chance to carry the Bradshaw name into Parliament once again.[2] Instead, he entered the service of a noble lord. A deed engrossed in Latin appointing John Bradshawe Steward of the Manor of Glossop—signed by Thomas Howard, Earl of Arundel and Surrey, Earl Marshall of England, High Steward of the Honor of Tutbury, High Steward of the Royal Forest of the High Peak, and lord of the manor of Glossop—was in the possession of A. Rowson Lingard about 1861. It was endorsed in Bradshawe's handwriting, *Patent for the Stewardship of Glossop*, which was clearly visible, but otherwise it was described as being in imperfect condition much mutilated by vermin.³

The manor of Glossop, thirty miles in circumference, was a parcel of the Royal Forest of the High Peak within the ward of Longendale, lying about eleven miles east of Manchester. Its outer boundaries were within a few miles of Chapel-en-le-Frith and Marple. It encompassed the seven hamlets of Glossop Township in Glossop Dale.

In 1537, King Henry VIII had taken the manor away from the Cistercian Abbey of Basingwerk and granted it to the premier earl of England: Francis Talbot, fifth Earl of Shrewsbury. Shrewsbury became lord of the manor over tenants who had formerly belonged to the abbey. Some tenants would cause Shrewsbury trouble, particularly when he arbitrarily raised their rents.

In July 1541, Shrewsbury wrote to the Earl of Southampton acknowledging an order for twenty bucks to be taken from the King's Forest and delivered to Hatfield a day or two before the king (Henry VIII) arrived there. Shrewsbury says that his servant, Robert Bradshaw, (See Appendix 12.) will deliver the venison and discuss matters with Southampton, reassuring him that the king would be welcome to come to the earl's "poor house" at Wingfield and hunt in Duffield Firth when he visited Nottingham.⁴ Robert Bradshaa (sic) wrote to Shrewsbury from Worksop manor—on the edge of Sherwood Forest in Nottinghamshire—on December 5 (no year but before 1566) about wine, fish, pasties, venison, pheasants, etc., to be sent to Chelsea and to the earl's favorite seat at Sheffield for Christmas.⁵

The fifth Earl of Shrewsbury died before 1566 and was succeeded by his thirty-eight-year-old son and heir, George (1528?-1590), the sixth earl. He had been present with his father at the coronation of Edward VI where they would surely have met another man with Derbyshire connections: Henry Bradshaw, the king's Attorney General.⁶ Like so many of the old aristocracy, George was thought to be *half a Catholic,* but if that was true, his later anti-Catholic actions disguised his convictions.⁷

In April 1565, Godfrey Bradshawe⁸ "of Bradshawe" made an indenture with Robert Eyre of Edale that his son and heir, Francis Bradshawe (1555/6-1619?), would marry Eyre's ward, Anne Stafford, coheiress to lands and a hall in Eyam.⁹ Francis could not have been more than ten years old when the marriage took place, probably on May 4, 1565, which is the date of a receipt for "three score and ten pounds" which Godfrey paid to Robert Eyre. In compliance with the indenture,

Godfrey released all his goods and chattel to "Francis his son and heir and Anne (Stafford) his wife and to Leonard and Amita Bradshaw, children of the said Godfrey." This would have been a normal sort of marriage settlement since Shrewsbury was lord of the manor of Eyam and Stafford's lands would be subservient to the manor; and furthermore, it was Shrewsbury who originally held the wardship and custody of the young heiress before he had bargained it away to Robert Eyre. About this time, Shrewsbury married Bess of Hardwick but soon began to quarrel with her over her extravagant penchant for house building, and later he expended much of his health and money in serving as custodian of Mary Queen of Scots.

Nicholas Garlick, the Catholic martyr who was born in Glossop, said in 1584 he hoped *"ere it be long to have all things in the old order, for the whole country about them were Catholics, and very desirous of priests, wherof there are a great store in the High Peak."* Shrewsbury conducted a raid on the private Catholic chapel of Sir Thomas Fitzherbert at Padley and there seized Garlick and Robert Ludlam, another priest. Ludlam, Garlick, and a third priest, Richard Simpson, were hanged, drawn, and quartered at Derby.

On the September 10, 1569, Shrewsbury, lord of the manor of Eyam, made an order binding Godfrey Bradshawe "to assure to his eldest son Francis all his lands after his death to him and his heirs male," certain arrangements being made with respect to the lands that Francis had acquired from his wife. Godfrey undertook, by memorandum[10] to Shrewsbury dated September 10, 12 Elizabeth (1570), that he would entail his lands upon his eldest son, Francis Bradshawe, and that such lands in Eyam as should come to Francis in right of his wife's inheritance from her late father, Humphrey Stafford, would be exchanged with the earl for other lands in Derbyshire. No such exchange took place.

Despite continuing troubles with the tenants of the manor of Glossop, Shrewsbury once again secured the queen's favor just three years before his death and was allowed to purchase a part of the High Peak Forest, which was formally disafforested for that purpose. There was a huge strip of the forest between Glossop and Chapel-en-le-Frith known as Bowden Middlescale that encompassed the hamlets of Beard, Ollersett, Whittle, Thornsett, Great Hamlet, Phoeside, Kinder, Bugsworth, and Chinley. A large map of the time charted the whole forest. At some unknown time, this huge map was cut into four pieces: three are preserved in the Public Record Office and one piece is missing.

Near Glossop it is stated on the map that the greater part of the forest there was then held by the Earl of Shrewsbury. A rectangular patch, more to the west of the Longdendale division, is described: "The herbage of Chynly otherwise called Maidstonfield. God(frey) Bradshawe and other farmes." Shrewsbury may have thought Chinley was a part of his purchase, but the Bradshaws would dispute that. An indenture from the Duchy of Lancaster, dated November 15, 1568, granted Chinley to one Lawrence Minter for thirty-one years at a yearly rent of £14 13s. 4d. as soon as the lease of the same to George Grimesdich expired. The very day that Minter obtained the lease, he sold it to Richard Celey, who sold it on October 2 to Godfrey Bradshaw, "who has now sold to Anthony Bradshaw his brother, and to Leonard and Francis (sons of Godfrey)."

In 1596, there were serious riots at Chinley, near Chapel-en-le-Frith, about Godfrey Bradshawe's enclosure of these formerly common lands; Godfrey had been roughly handled and forced to take proceedings in the Star Chamber against several persons for breach of the peace.[11] Later this land would cause more serious troubles between Shrewsbury and Peter Bradshawe, the son of Godfrey.

Gilbert Talbot (1553-1616) succeeded to the earldom upon his father's death in 1590. This seventh Earl of Shrewsbury had known of the Bradshaws in Derbyshire since his youth. He was married, at age fifteen, to Mary Cavendish, the daughter of Bess of Hardwick; within a year, Bess had become his stepmother as well as his mother-in-law. From 1570 until 1572, he was sent away to university in Padua. He sided with his mother-in-law/stepmother during his father's life, but as soon as the old earl was dead, he engaged in disagreements with his queen, his tenants, and nearly all his family.

The seventh Earl of Shrewsbury's honors included the hereditary offices enjoyed by his father—steward of the Honor of Tutbury, chief justice of the forest courts north of the Trent, and high steward of the Forest of the High Peak. The high steward (sometimes called the Master Forester) of the High Peak held appointment from the Crown by letters patent. His position drew a fee from the proceeds of the forest, and his power was unassailable by any common law; he answered only to the king for his actions. He was independent of, and not amenable to, the king's chief justiciar. All forests were, at first, considered outside the common law or right of the kingdom; they were not liable to be visited by the ordinary judges of the *curia regis* but only by special commission and by special royal officials—i.e., one of the two Chief Justices of the

Forest Courts, one north of the Trent River and one south. The forests had customs and laws peculiarly their own, circumscribed by the Charter of the Forest, and these were drawn up rather to ensure the peace of the beasts than that of the king's subjects.

A legal entity with specific boundaries, not a term implying merely physical characteristics, the forest was said to have been placed under a distinct code of laws before the reign of King Canute, who in AD 1016 supposedly promulgated the *Constitutiones de Foresta*. By these laws, the supreme jurisdiction of the forests of England was committed to four *thegenes* (thanes, or principal barons). Inferior authority was delegated to four *lesthegenes* (lesser barons), and immediate custody of each forest was entrusted to two *tinemen* (minuti hanines) whose office it was to guard, in nightly watches, the king's vert or venison. The penalties of the Saxon code were chiefly pecuniary except for two offenses, for which the free man forfeited his liberty and the slave or serf lost his life: (1) having offered violence against one of the four great thanes, and (2) having killed a royal beast. The ancient ancestor of the Bradshaws, Ughtred, is called one of the king's thanes.

Some authorities believe that the *Constitutiones de Foresta* was no Saxon code but a Norman forgery devised to reinforce the idea that their own strict forest law had earlier precedents. In any case, a fundamental alteration took place in the government of the forests with the coming of the Normans. The first clause of Henry II's Assize of Woodstock in 1184, which attempted to formulate the rules of the forest law, announced that even a free man who trespassed against the king's venison would be mutilated and blinded. During the reigns of Henry II and his son, Richard the Lionheart, these penalties were liberally inflicted, making nonsense of the story that the legendary Robin Hood harbored any affection for King Richard. Whole populations were forcibly removed to create new forests, and only the king's officers and those of the king's subjects who submitted the forest laws and accepted that their transgressions would be judged by the king only as pleas of the forest were allowed to inhabit there by royal consent. Strictly speaking they belonged to no parish, diocese, hundred, or county. About one third of England was counted royal forest by the end of King Richard's reign.

Forest law was cruel, oppressive, and administered solely at the king's prerogative. One contemporary official described the law, with unconscious humor, as being not absolutely but only reasonably just. Under this system it was criminal for the landholder in the forest to cut holly or to fell an oak tree on his own property and more criminal to kill a stag than to murder a man. He could not disturb the beasts of the chace even if they broke down his fences and destroyed his crops. If accused of an offense, the forest dweller had no more protection from English common law than from the law of a foreign land. Frequent fines and extortions reduced the common forest dweller to poverty; if he failed to attend one of the many courts or name a poacher he paid a fine, if he kept dogs which had not been expatiated he paid a fine, if he sold or took away timber he paid a fine, if bow or arrow were found in his keeping he paid a fine (only foresters were allowed bow and arrows—lesser officials carried a small ax, and crossbows were forbidden altogether). Greyhounds and mastiffs were banned from the forest. With this in hand, searches for illegal weapons, dogs, or venison could be undertaken in all forest dwellers homes. As if that were not bad enough, the law was often flaunted by the forest officers themselves who might freely impose fines and extortions of a purely illegal nature or grant privileges in return for payment from ordinary forest dwellers. With license from the king, Foresters of Fee might be allowed to take lesser animals such as hare and rabbit or birds, take a certain kind of wood for fuel and house building, and fatten pigs on fallen acorns. In the time of King Edward the First, Hugh Stratford, who paid a bribe to be a forest officer, extorted from the township of Denshanger a quarter of their wheat plus a goose and a hen from every house yearly for sharing in the privilege of fencing their fields and collecting dead firewood. Foresters could not be questioned for the killing of a trespasser in the forest. Ministers of the forest were not to be put on assizes, juries, or inquests taken outside the forest.

    The chief barons demanded and received at Runnymeade the Magna Carta and the Charter of the Forest from King John before he died in 1216. Earl Marshall, as regent of the ten-year-old King Henry III, reconfirmed the Magna Carta and reissued a separate Charter of the Forest in 1217.[12] The penalties of mutilation, blinding, and death were abolished, all afforestations made at the expense of private persons since 1135 were cancelled, and some of the more oppressive restraints upon owners of land lying within the forest were removed; but the forests and their inhabitants would continue, over the ensuing centuries, outside the process by which the rest of England came to be assimilated into a uniform law of the land. This would be the root of future evils. That all free men should be subject to the common law alone and that this law should be applied without respect of persons or places was not yet the aspiration of the majority of the king's subjects, particularly if the common law were seen to be corrupt but efficiently administered and the forest law equally corrupt but easily flaunted. Most forest dwellers, wealthy or poor, depended upon customary, hereditary, and traditional rights, not on written evidence. Hereditary rights of purpresture and assart, in some instances going back four centuries, established land tenures for the established forest dweller. Traditional rights to collect fuel, fruits and berries from the waste, honey from the forest, to pasture cattle and beasts on the commons, to glean after harvest, meant the difference between a viable life and starvation to cottagers who had no assets but their own labor. Anthony Bradshawe had put himself at the head of a movement to maintain forest law in Duffield, not because he was dependent upon traditional rights for his livelihood, but because customary liberties of the forest rather than the authority of the common law formed his political environment and supplied his political ideas. Christopher Hill has said,[13] "until the absolute rights of private property in land—or as it is polite to call them these days, the doctrine of possessive individualism—were established during the revolutionary decades by the abolition of feudal tenures and Star Chamber, and the subordination of forest courts to the common law . . . until then kings and their favorites could override the customary property rights—or what were believed to be rights—of even powerful landowners."

One burdensome obligation of the early strict interpretation of forest laws, apart from severity, lay in them making it imperative on every freeholder to attend many of the courts of the forest at the expense of tending his own crops and animals. The justice seat met once every three years, swainmote courts three times a year, other woodmote courts every forty days. This burden was counterbalanced for the Foresters of Fee by their participation, however slight, in the maintenance of the liberties of the forest. In later practice it was sufficient that four men and the resident forest official attend subordinate courts and represent each of the four adjoining villages. By the time of the Stuart kings, freeholders of the forest commonly leased, sold, and bargained their lands. When they took on tenants, they became landlords, but not always as lords of the manor. They could not claim the old system of feudal tenure; it had always been good feudal law that no one was bound to answer in any court but the court of his own lord. These tenants, unlike their forest landlords, began to resort to the courts of the common law, and soon justices of the Common Pleas began to accept their entreaties. A general ameliorating process of the justice system and progress of civilization lessened the harshness of the forest law by the time of John Bradshawe.

Subservient to the high steward, there were various sorts of Foresters; some such foresters are foresters in fee and have the same office to them and their heirs, paying unto the king a certain fee farm or rent for the same,(See Appendix 13.) "and there are some other foresters of the king that have their office but for term of their life only; and again there are some Foresters of the King that have their office by letters patent from the king . . . durante bene placito,"

In *The Canterbury Tales*, Chaucer describes a forester:

> *And he was clad in a coat and hood of green;*
> *A sheaf of peacock arrows bright and keen*
> *Under his belt he wore full thriftily,*
> *Well knew he how to dress his tackle yeomanly*
> *His arrows drooped not with feathers low,*
> *And in his hand he bares a mighty bow;*
> *A not-hed had he with brown visage*
> *Of wood-crafte knew he well all usage*
> *Upon his arm he bore a gay bracer*
> *And by his side a sword and buckler*
> *A Christopher on his breast of silver sheen*
> *A horn he bore, the baudrick was of green*
> *A Forester was he sothily, as I guess.*

By grants of land made at various times by the sovereign, the Foresters of Fee became tenants in capite and held the land granted to themselves and their heirs in perpetuity, by hereditary service, of guarding the king's forest. *The Great Coucher Book* of the duchy of Lancashire explained, "And all the foresters offices be to walk in the forests, and to see that the king's wood and deer be not destroyed, and they shall present all these trespasses within their offices and they have no fee of the king, but hold their lands by that service . . . And these be the foresters of the fee in Duffield Frith; the heirs of Stone, of Brockshawe, John Bradborne, Nicholas Kniveton, and the heirs of John Bradshawe . . . These claim the same liberties in Duffield Frith; the Abbot of Darley, the parson of Duffield, the parson of Mugginton, the heirs of Peter Nevill, the heirs of Cordell, the heirs of Bradbourn, the heirs of Knyveton of Mercaston, the heirs of Coterowe, the heirs of Ranston, the heirs of Burton, the heirs of

Bradshawe, the heirs of William Pim, and have used the same liberties time out of mind.[14] Also inhabitants of Duffield and Needwood have common in the king's forest chaces at all times of the year for all manner of beasts of their own rearing, except beasts not commonable—as goats, sheep, and beasts of merchandise, and stoned horses that are above one year old and under the value of 10s." By 1225, the foresters were gaining royal warrants for house building (pupresture) and cultivation (assart) in the High Peak Forest at Bradshaw Edge, Coombes Valley, Bowden Edge, and in Macclesfield Forest.

It seems the first house built on the site of the present Bradshaw Hall near Chapel-en-le-Frith (the Chapel in the Forest) must have gone up between 1215 and 1225. It lay within the Forest of the High Peak and the ancient honor of Tutbury. The foresters built a small chapel about this same time and dedicated it to Thomas a Becket who, as a militant archbishop, had defied the English king and become a popular saint. The parish church of Chapel-en-le-Frith stands on the site of the forester's ancient chapel, and there Bradshawe's ancestors were buried.

For the murder of Thomas a Becket, King Henry II submitted himself to physical punishment, pronounced by an ecclesiastical court, on charge and conviction for failing to protect one of his own subjects from himself. Some would maintain this established the principle that the king was not above the law, i. e., there was no sovereign immunity. On this principle John Bradshawe would sit in trial of Charles the First in 1649.

Troubles had arisen at the adjoining manor of Glossop during the days of the sixth Earl Shrewsbury who, like his son, was lord of the manor which he held in capite as the High Peak steward. He also had rent-paying tenants on his manors. Apparently without sufficient justification, and in ancient feudal style, he abruptly raised the land rents. He probably presumed he could handle any protests in his own manor court, or at least forestall complaints in the forest courts. The tenants of Glossop manor, however, rebelled, and some even armed themselves. They organized protests, uttered threats, and marched as far as Sheffield, Barnet, and on to London where they planned to lay their case before the queen and her court.

George Scargill and Richard Roberts had written to the sixth Earl of Shrewsbury on the October 4, 1579, to inform him that most of the Glossop tenants had agreed to the rent increases, but the tenants at Sinmondley were resisting. Black Harry Botham refused to pay and threatened he would kill anyone who tried to evict him. He was set on the stocks at Glossop. Under this coercion, his father, old Harry Botham, agreed. Black Harry ended up in a London prison.

In the months that followed, the lords of the Privy Council wrote Shrewsbury from Greenwich urging him clemency for four tenants of Glossopdale threatened with eviction. This feud was still simmering when the sixth Earl died in 1590 and his son succeeded. Robert Kidman wrote to him, October 28, 1593, in the matter of Glossopdale, Cecil (Earl of Salisbury and the Queen's secretary of state) told him. though the queen favored the tenants in the sixth earl's time, "your cases were much different." Despite this, the queen advised Shrewsbury to ease his tenant's hardships. Tenants of Shrewsbury's other manors were also dissatisfied. William Knyveton wrote in 1594 "about the court and town of Belper which the Earl farmed under the crown, and the discontent of the tenants . . . recommends (Anthony?) Bradshawe for the posts of coroner and steward of Belper." Shrewsbury continued to pressure his tenants, and he was put under arrest at royal command, not allowed to come to court in the latter half of 1595. The following year he was restored to royal favor and sent to Rouen conveying the Garter for King Henri IV.

That year, Anthony Bradshawe, great uncle of the regicide, was deputized by Shrewsbury to serve as understeward of the honor of Tutbury. The ancient honor was a noble kind of lordship held of the king, having many lordships of manors dependent upon it, and at the time of Shrewsbury's stewardship it encompassed two hundred thirty-six towns and hamlets in Derbyshire, eighty in Staffordshire, thirty in Leicestershire, and nine in Warwickshire, including the manor of Glossop, Chapel-en-le-Frith, the Forest of the High Peak, and Duffield Forest and manor. Anthony Bradshawe was quite a different steward from Shrewsbury.

Anthony was expert in forest law and wrote extensively about the laws and customs of Duffield Forest, notably a fifty-four-stanza poem, stanzas ten through fifteen read;

> 10. *This forest hath it four brave woods in midst of it they lie*
> *Holland Duffield Colebrook Belper the sure castle fast by Fine*
> *thicks and lands they do contain and herbage good they yield*
> *And stirred with so sweet asserth as ever man beheld*
> 11. *All which in order good to keep such forest laws as need Are*
> *executed duely there at woodmote courts with speed The pawnage*

>   Tackrents and duties thereof with customs raise Collectors four
>   receive and pay at the audit times always
> 12. This forest small environed is with six Parks yet remaining Morley
>   Belper Posterne and Shottle and Ravensdale appertaining All
>   which are farmed at this time and yield no deer at all save only
>   Mansell Park hath game and yet but very small
> 13. Wherefore those Keep's names shall pass, their officers and
>   their fees Though heretofore they were esteemed each one there
>   degrees In Shottle and Posterne tennants had herbage at easy
>   rates Of which they are now quite debarred and shut out of
>   those gates
> 14. This forest hath foresters of fee which partly hold their land
>   By services there in to do, as I understand Their names be
>   Bradborne, Bradshaw, Bruckshaw and the heirs of Stone All
>   which at forest courts must be with others many a one
> 15. Curzon esq lieutenant is to keep these things in order and under
>   him the keepers walk and watch in every border Which officers
>   offenders all against vert should present And for the King in
>   forest courts are sworn to that intent

Anthony, as deputy steward, held woodmote courts in 1598, 1600, and 1604 where the fines imposed were almost exclusively for taking firewood and coppice (poles). In speaking about Shottle and Postern Parks, he refers to King James's unpopular policy of allowing enclosure of common lands upon which the old tenants had formerly depended for the privilege of cultivation, foraging and pasturing their animals, digging coal, and free passage for their horses and carts. The royal forests had always been a potentially profitable source of money for the king's personal purse, and the fines, rents, and fees collected there were outside the control of Parliament or the common law. In reality, much of the money was often diverted by the master forester of his subofficers. The Crown could gain the greatest amount of money by selling forest lands. When a royal forest was disafforested, the deer were destroyed, and one third of the common lands were sold to noblemen for enclosure as private land. As recompense for the loss of common foraging and pasture, the other two thirds were to be rented to the old commoners on condition that they also enclose their new parcels. In fact, the old residents seldom received any benefit from the policy, and they "were compelled by force and terror to submit thereto." Anthony Bradshawe did much to sustain the privileges of the tenants of Duffield Forest by pleading the forest laws when the king would have preferred to forget them.

Anthony also wrote an odd sort of question and answer account of the visit between himself and an unidentified distinguished visitor, May 1, 1603. He refers to his visitor as W.N. and himself as A.B. The preamble begins: "W.N. of C. in the Countie of Suffolk, gent. an ancient Scholar and companion of the said A.B. above 40 years past in the Universitie of Oxford (there proceeding graduates together) & afterward divers years fellow student and practice with the said A.B. in the Inner Temple London . . . took pains to repose himself for a few days with the said A.B. at his house aforesaid whence he went to Buxton well & so to Bradshaugh (sic) Hall in Bradshaugh Edge a little there beguiled where the said A.B. was born and his ancestors whither the said A.B. very willingly accompanied him & the better occasioned to visit his brother & friends there sc, &C."

W.N. (question)—"And what is that which you call Bradshaugh Edge wherein your brother now dwelleth. A.B. (answer)—Sir I take that to be a certain part of the parish of chapel de la Frith which the King of England in time past gave unto one of my ancestors for service done as partly apperth in some evidences of my brothers which are without date, afore the Conquest of England . . . though my former ancestors were of like unthriftie and have in tymes past sold away most of the same, and so my brother hath but a little rernayndr therein . . ."[15] Whatever these evidences were, they have long since disappeared.

"And I being (in 38 Elizabeth Rine and nunc illustris sime) by the v, Honble Gilbert Earle of Shrewsbury her Majesty's High steward of the aforesaid Honour of Tutbury (whereunto the said firth and the manor therein belong and are parcel of) charged trusted & deputed to be understeward there, & also having spent above thirty years time partly in the Inner Temple London partly in the prothonotary's office of the Court of Common Pleas at Westminster where I also practiced above 20 years as Attorney was so careful to discharge my dutie in that place and office as that both for my better service to his majesty and my better standing of country and multitude to whom it appertained—and also for the better and more upright & easy performances of my duty in that place & the better understanding instructing & advocating of my sonnes and clerks which I employed under me in that office I, out of my own small study reading & experience & with the help of the notable & profitable books of Cowither[16] & Customarie[17] &

Cher of Duffield Frith, the booke of Entries & Abridgements of the Statutes & of some learned readings of Forest lawes Devised & as time would permit, collected certain little books for precedents for the proceedings processes & entries concerning my service doing in the said courts—As namely one littel book of such points & learning of the forest laws as I supposed to be convenient & sufficient to be dealt in touching this forest or chase. One other little book of precedents of such processes of sundrie sorts as lye and are to be used in the same court and of fees of the court & of officers & of their duties which I have drawn into a mixed form agreeable to custom & the course of common Law so nearly as by my often conference with learned councel in the laws & good court keepers I could contrive. One other called a Lantern for copyholders—Two other books of the Leet charge & of the court keeps Baron charge with good note the articles of both the said charges and divers other points necessary to be observed sc, One other little book showing how carefully orderly and upright juries ought to carry themselves in such service there and how & in what actions costs & damages are allowed. One other little book containing such material pains ordinance and by-laws continuans to be generally and respectively observed in the whole Residency in the said firth from time to time agreed on and as it were enacted by the Leet Juries for common weale and good governance sake there and how bylaws bind and how they may be repealed which I do use to bring to every Leet both that the Leet Juries may consider and present the defaul ts & breaches of any of them & also to keep their memories & save their labours to make the like or same again and double. And one other of precedents of formes of surrenders which I specially and carefully do keep proposing it shall remain continually in my house called Farley's Hall in the manor of Duffield aforesaid to the intent to ease pleasure all or any such of her Majesties tenants in the said Firth with the copies of any such surrender presentment or Inquisition of any lands or escheats as have passed or shall pass before me whilst I shall be in my said office by the calendar and Folio or leaf of which Register the partie taking a copy of the same may easily find the Record thereof enrolled with the Auditor in the castle of Tutbury aforesaid [which may do good if any casualty erasure alteration or imbeasling (sic—embezzling ?) or removing of such record should chance without any intention to make any gain to myself or to my posterity by the same Register (though I have taken some pains in the making thereof nore than other stewards do ordinarily use to do).[18] Only this charges I impose & devise & hope it will not offend, that where I have erected a little Almeshouse for harbouring of a few poor folks in the town of Duffield aforesaid [as the poor widow offered her mite) & have established for the same poore but thirtie shillings yearly to buy them some simple cloth for coats; I say I have ordered the ancient of the same poor for the time being shall keep the key of the box wherein the same book of Register shall lie in my said house. And that every such Person as shall need and desireth to have a copy of any surrender or thing entered in the same book shall cause that poor Person which so keepth the said key in the said poor Almshouse to come & bring the same key to me or my successor or posterity inhabiting at my said house to have a search sc, and shall give to such bringer of the said key sixpence toward buying of some fuel for the said poor. And then upon such search, the Party requiring to have a copy of anything in the same book to be had paying the clerk some small thing for the writing thereof. And Sir because you say your occasions elsewhere will not suffer you to make longer abroad with me here to propose my said small books neither are they worthy of such your pains [they being both rude & rashly penned & as yet were but Partly to be applied to this frith & the courts & places & purposes abovesaid & not generally to other manors and courts I will at your instances & out of my love to you upon our old acquaintance lend & deliver the same little books to you to take with you for the space of two months to propose them (if so you will vouchsafe) & then to return them safely unto me, syth (?) some of mine may happily hereafter make some use of the same and of the promises."

"W.N.—Truly sir I thank you and shall take it for such an exceptionary courtesy, as I know not how to reacquit and I will return and restore them to you safely and as speedilly as I can. And thus for this time farewell must be our conclusion with this that I must ever acknowledge myself to dep't more in debt to you both for my entertainment and for our conference this while had then I can recompense and I must truly report that I have not known (though I have been employed in many countries & courts) any Steward of your rank that hath bestowed such pains and care in his place as you have done in yours and as by your acts and books is manifested all of them being collected and written in your own time and most of them in your own hand. And the same so being extant it cannot be justly said that you have hid your candle under a bushel but have so left it as may happily light your posterity and to good to your neighbors of the frith and manors in case they will take the pains and care to peruse and observe the said customs and notes and effects of your travel. God keep you Finnis"

From this it appears Anthony Bradshawe revered the Forest Charter and took, literally, the king's promise made in the reissued charter of 1219: "neither we nor our heirs will procure anything whereby the liberties contained in this Charter shall be infringed or weakened; and if anything contrary to this is procured from anyone, it shall avail nothing and be held for nought."

Yet the forest system had never been completely popular with any class in the community. It was unpopular with the landowner because it fettered his rights over his land. Demands to limit the forest's boundaries had been granted in the forest charter as reissued in 1217 and 1219. A statute of 1327 finally fixed the boundaries, and they remained so until Henry VIII afforested the land around Hampton Court. Such complaints were made by the inhabitants of the adjoining parishes that it was disafforested after Henry's death. It was unpopular with the cottager because of the heavy-handed powers of the forest officers. These arbitrary powers, especially those of the foresters, led as previously mentioned to abusive practices, extortion, and malicious attachments. Other branches of the law began to encroach upon the jurisdiction of forest courts. Sir Edward Coke (1552-1633), Attorney General to Queen Elizabeth and Chief Justice of England to King James, who was a member of the Inner Temple with Anthony Bradshawe, laid it down in the time of Elizabeth that, generally, the forest law is "allowed and bounded by the common laws of this realm." Thus it became possible for a man who was unlawfully imprisoned by a forest officer to get his release by habeas corpus from the King's Bench on a point of law. If injustice was done at the Forest Justice Seat, the case could be removed by *certorari* into the King's Bench; however, the King's Bench might decline to hear a case that ought properly to be decided by the forest law.

The destruction of timber throughout Duffield Frith was excessive during Queen Elizabeth's reign. A survey taken in 1560 found that there were a total of 111,968 trees, of which 59,412 were large oaks, 32,820 small oaks, and 19,736 dottard oaks only suitable for fuel. A similar survey of 1587 found only 2,764 large oaks and 3,032 small oaks. In 1581, a commission called to view and report on Duffield Frith came to the conclusion that "there is a woodward and collector or forester-in-fee of each ward," and until recently there had been other foresters-in-fee, bow-bearers, "and such like," but since the "game is utterlie destroyed," they did not examine the grants for those offices. They suggested that the queen might gain advantage by selling off leases in the undergrowth and setting up "*bloweng*" mills for melting lead ore on Hulland brook and Blackbrook in Chevin ward (one of the wards of Duffield Frith, near Belper). The population, numbering 1,800 men, women, and children, petitioned the queen not to carry out the leasing of the underwood as they had from time beyond memory been accustomed to crop and browse these woods for their pigs and cattle, paying a price for the privilege at the end of winter. If the leasing were carried out, they considered they would be debarred from this as well as from their customary rights of fuel wood and wood for the repairs of their houses and hedges, and that they would be "utterly impoverished thereby and constrayned to seek dwellings other where."[19]

John Manwood wrote and published a treatise on forest law in 1598, and it would be interesting to know whether he had read Anthony Bradshawe's *little books*. In 1573, Roger Manwood, a cousin of John Manwood the author, was a member of the Inner Temple with Anthony Bradshawe and Edward Coke. Manwood complained that "Forest laws are gone clean out of knowledge in most; places in this land and they are grown into contempt with many inhabitants in the forest." It was the lack of consistent administration that was leading to the demise of the system, and the main cause was the decay of the court of the justice seat. Subordinate forest courts could do very little except present the criminal to the justice seat—it was there that they were punished—so the whole execution of forest law depended upon the regular holding, every three years, of the justice seat. In a second printing of his treatise, issued after Queen Elizabeth's death, Manwood says, "But now of late within these hundred years there have been very seldom any Justice seats at all kept for Forests. And when there is any kept the same is slenderly performed, that there is very little or no good at all done thereby . . . for the records of the proceedings of the Forest matters are not orderly kept or returned into his Majesty's court of Exchequer . . . whereby the rents growing due unto his Majesty . . . with the fines that are assessed and not paid, and all bonds that are forfeited unto the king for any matter concerning the Forest, might, in due course of law, be levied and gathered to the King's use: for, nowdays, if it do that a Justice Seat be kept for one forest, the same is seldom or never finished . . . and some few fines, and perhaps none at all, for any offense paid. And then, when the Justice in Eyre of the Forest doth chance to die, the records of the Forest remaining in some private man's hands, and not returned into the court of Exchequer, by some means or other they are smothered, so that they never do come to light . . . but if that Justices of the Forest would duly hold their Justice Seats, and cause Perfect records thereof to be kept; or else they would cause the records of their proceedings to be returned into His Majesty's Court of Exchequer, whereby there might be execution of their proceedings . . . then the laws of the Forest would be better known, and also more regarded than they are now at this day."

Anthony Bradshawe had addressed these very points and set about protecting the ancient liberties of the forest, at least as far as Duffield Firth was concerned, by preserving a copy of all his proceedings. A full and formal forest court was held at Chevin House[20] on December 19, 1598, before Anthony Bradshawe, deputy steward. The foresters John Curzon,[21] William Kniveton, William Bradburne (esquires), and John Brockshaw (gentleman) appeared, and the names of the agisters, parkers, and ward collectors were set forth. Henry Butler held the joint sinecure offices of bow bearer and axe bearer while Richard Clark was the ranger. No offenses against venison were presented, but a large number of vert trespassers were fined for taking away horseloads, sleighloads, and back burdens of wood, bark, and undergrowth. Bradshawe held another court at the same location eighty-two days later; John Curzon was named lieutenant as well as forester, (See Appendix 14), and Sir Humphrey Ferrers was added to the foresters. Two parkers were fined for nonappearance, and no less than 123 vert trespassers were fined. *Waynelodes (wagon loads)* are mentioned among the accounts of illegal wood taken.

Bradshawe's next court, held July 8, 1600, assigned two trees to the town of Duffield toward repair of their bridge. A heavy fine of 10s. was assessed on Richard Feme; not only did he cut two cartloads of greenwood but he had the effrontery to sell them in the market at Derby.

Among his first acts upon coming to the throne in 1603, King James appointed Gilbert, Earl of Shrewsbury, to the post of Chief Justice in Eyre of the forest north of the Trent. Other than retaining him as a Privy Counsellor, this was the only honor the king bestowed upon Shrewsbury, the premier earl of England; and the insult did not go unnoticed in Shrewsbury's mind, nor in the mind of his stepmother, Bess of Hardwick.

There is record of a Duffield Frith court held in 1604 and another in July 1605 to which Sir Edward Cokayne, keeper of Mansell Park, sent his deputy William Jesson to report that there remained seventy-six deer at Mansell and that four or five had died in the last winter. Henry Butler, the bow bearer and axe bearer, did not appear and pleaded for relief from the duty of being called to "woodpryses." Anthony Bradshawe wrote to Thomas Coke at Sheffield Lodge from Duffield, December 26, 1607, stating that under Shrewsbury's warrant he and George Curzon had held a woodmote court and charged a jury, but he doubted its impartiality and urged Shrewsbury to hold a "swainmote" at Tutbury Castle, as his father did, in order to obtain reliable information as to trespasses against the woods and soil of the forest and frith of Duffield. This would indicate that no swainmote had been held for Duffield or the High Peak Forest since long before 1590. Two days prior to this letter, Bradshawe had written Shrewsbury about the holding of a woodmote court according to the Earl's warrant and enclosing notes taken from the custom book. He asked that the king's tenants at Duffield be permitted to buy the ollers (alderwood) to be sold by a commission from the king at 8d. per load, or alternatively, that they might be used in the earl's iron works at Hopping Mill. On the reverse, he wrote a second letter stating that his cousin Peter Bradshawe would sell the lease of Cutthorp House to the earl, and he included a list of candidates for the bailiwick of the Peak.[22] In 1606, Godfrey Bradshawe and Peter Bradshawe were high Peak receivers and bailiffs.

The old Shrewsbury vs. Bradshawe contest over the herbage at Chinley had resurfaced late in 1606. Anthony's nephew Peter Bradshawe was attempting to gain Chinley in freehold, and Shrewsbury was determined to add it to the manor of Glossop. "This Bradshaw is a Perilous busy companion and seeketh to cross me in everything he can," he wrote his servant, John Hercy, and instructed Hercy to take the matter to the personal attention of the Earl of Salisbury, if necessary, to frustrate Bradshawe. Shrewsbury was godfather to Salisbury's eldest daughter. Unfortunately, Shrewsbury didn't seem to know that Bradshawe was already dealing closely with Salisbury.

Peter Bradshawe was an influential merchant tailor of London who had amassed a fortune trading in *Manchester goods*.[23] A grant of the manor of Southrop, Gloucestershire, was made by the king to Peter Bradshawe in 1605. This grant seems to have been surreptitiously suppressed because in 1607 the manor was granted in fee to the Earl of Salisbury, who sold it to Sir Thomas Roe in 1608. Some twenty years later, after Salisbury's death, charges were made that Salisbury had plotted a fraudulent transaction and enlisted Bradshawe in order to deceive the king(See Appendix 15.).

John Hercy wrote to the Shrewsbury about a suit before the chancellor of the Duchy of Lancaster (Sir Thomas Parry) between (Anthony?) Bradshawe and Staynerood concerning the perquisites of the court of the High Peak in February 1608. In March, the Earl of Shrewsbury dismissed Anthony Bradshawe as his understeward and named Sir John Bentley as successor. Bradshawe wrote to Shrewsbury protesting his removal from office and asking whether he was to proceed with the approaching court leet.

There is a petition in the Calendar of State Papers, dated July 2, 1609, from "*Sir*" Peter Bradshawe and others to Salisbury requesting a stay in extention of the lease of their farm in Chinley, alias Maystonfield, which he purchased. There is no other evidence that he was ever knighted. He did, finally, obtain a lease of Chinley but only in the year that Shrewsbury died, 1616.

In 1609, Peter Bradshawe and Francis Bradshawe, the younger, were bailiffs of the liberty in the High Peak, or as the office was also called, County Bailiffs.

Shrewsbury's reason for dismissing Anthony Bradshawe has not been discovered, if indeed he ever committed it to paper. As already noted, there was trouble between Shrewsbury and Bradshawe's nephew Peter over the herbage at Chinley. More troublesome may have been the association of Anthony's daughter-in-law and Shrewsbury's neice Lady Arbella Stuart. Sometime during 1603, Lady Arbella Stuart retained Anne Bradshawe as her lady-in-waiting. Anne is often referred to simply as Mrs. Bradshaw, and the record identifies her as the wife of Exuperie Bradshawe of Duffield in Derbyshire. Exuperie was the son of Anthony Bradshawe. Anne was the daughter of John Lisley of Moxhull in Warwickshire by his wife Dorothy, the daughter of George Willoughby.

Lady Arbella, a niece of Mary Queen of Scots, was born at old Chatsworth house and grew up in the care of her maternal grandmother Bess of Hardwick, the Countess of Shrewsbury. Bess had carefully avoided political entanglements all during the reign of Queen Elizabeth despite her position as a hugely wealthy woman, probably second only to the queen. Bess's fourth husband, George Talbot, sixth Earl of Shrewsbury, had been commanded to guard, house, and care for the deposed Mary Queen of Scots—it nearly destroyed him both physically and financially.

Shrewsbury housed the Scots queen at Tutbury castle in 1567 and 1568, then Wingfield Manor for a year, back to Tutbury for a year, Chatsworth for the year 1570, and Sheffield castle for the next fourteen years. While he was thus engaged, Bess embarked on one of the most ambitious projects of house building ever undertaken outside the royal family. She built the first Chatsworth house, the still magnificent Hardwick Hall, and several others. Just outside the main gate of Hardwick Hall stood an inn known as *Bradshaws* where Bess often housed the overflow of her visitors. John Hardwick of Hardwick, Bess's father or grandfather, served on jury panels with most of the Derbyshire gentry, including Henry Bradshaw of Bradshaw in 1494/5.[24]

All this extravagance further put an unbearable strain on Shrewsbury's finances, or so he said, although Bess maintained she was spending only her own money and the money he owed her as a part of her marriage settlement. She was determined to establish a dynasty for the sons she had mothered by her second husband, Sir William Cavendish. She was also determined that her granddaughter Arbella should have her rightful place and estate in succession to the throne. By the time of the Scots queen's execution, Bess had become painfully estranged from Shrewsbury, and Arbella had become equally estranged from the royal court.

Sir Robert Cecil had mounted a close watch on Lady Arbella because of rumors that a clandestine marriage was being arranged between Arbella and Lord Hertford's eldest son, William Seymour. Such a marriage would challenge the royal succession when Queen Elizabeth died, and it seemed the queen was not far from death. Letters written on behalf of Lady Arbella by Bridget Shorland were being intercepted. In a letter of January 1603 to Mr. Brawshawe (sic), Bridget speaks of Arbella's restraint from liberty and her sense of being forsaken by all her friends. Arbella asks that a letter be carried to her aunt Mary Talbot, wife of Gilbert, seventh Earl of Shrewsbury. This letter had obviously been intercepted, and an appended note states, *The messenger that was to have carried the abovesaid letter returned with a feigned answer by word that Mr. Bradshawe was not at home.* Again, Shorland wrote to Mr. Bradshawe: *My Lady would entreat you ride post to the Court and deliver this letter that is enclosed to Sir Henry Brouncher.*"[25] The note appended says, *"the messenger that was to have carried the abovesaid letter returned a feigned answer by word that Mrs. Bradshawe would send Sir Henry Brunker's letter to her husband to be carried with all speed.* Mrs. Bradshawe of Bridget

Shorland's letters must be Anne, the wife of Exuperie Bradshawe. She was under suspicion at this early date.

Queen Elizabeth died in March 1603 without an heir or any formalized order for the succession. Of the fourteen candidates with genealogical links to the throne, only four were seriously considered: the Spanish Infanta, Lord Hertford, Lady Arbella Stuart, and King James VI of Scotland. The Infanta's claim was based on a shadowy connection to John of Gaunt, and Hertford's had the semblance of being the heir-at-law. Both these gradually faded away, and the contest narrowed to the two great-grandchildren of Margaret Tudor. James represented the elder branch, but there appeared to be an historical impediment; under feudal law, no alien could inherit English land. On this thin restriction, Arbella's fragile claim was forwarde and had she been a more enterprising woman, she might have made an effective bid for the crown. As it appears, she was trying to find any excuse to escape her grandmother's care, and her attempt to marry Hertford's eldest son was probably motivated by that desire. The throne of England descended upon Lady Arbella's cousin, James Stuart King of Scotland, the son of Mary Queen of Scots. Camden's history represented Salisbury and Northampton as *the two prime wheels* which drove James's *triumphant chariot*. The two countries were united, and James Stuart became King James I of the United Kingdom of England, Scotland, Ireland, and France.

Some Englishmen feared James's alliances with Catholic Spain, and a conspiracy to place Arbella Stuart on the throne was formed by Henry Lord Cobham, his brother George Brooke, Sir Walter Ralegh, Sir Griffith Markham, and others. Cobham and George Brooke were brothers-in-law to Robert Cecil, Earl of Salisbury. It does not appear that Arbella was directly involved in the plot, nor is it clear that she would have willingly cooperated with the conspirators had they been successful. The plot was quickly suppressed, and Raleigh was put on trial at the indictment of Attorney General Sir Edward Coke. Cobham accused Ralegh of being the animator of the conspiracy, and his guilt was taken for granted. Chief Justice Popham, presiding, ruled that the evidence of one person, whom it was not necessary to produce in open court, was sufficient in cases of treason. Popham was not twisting the law against Ralegh but merely stating an interpretation universally placed upon the law of treason, as it was supposed to have been modified by Statute 1 and 2 Philip and Mary.

On the heels of this conspiracy followed another: the infamous gunpowder plot. English Jesuits, particularly Father Henry Garnet, were blamed. Accusations were leveled against Gilbert seventh Earl of Shrewsbury, Arbella's uncle, who was thought to be *half a Catholic*. John Clay of Crich, gentleman, made slanderous allegations that Shrewsbury had been forewarned of the plot and absented himself from the Parliament under cover of his *unhappy gout*. Clay further alleged that Shrewsbury warned Sir John Harpur, knight of the Shire for Derbyshire, to be absent from Parliament and told Sir Charles Cavendish to stay away from London.[26] Shrewsbury was not charged.

The Earl of Arundel informed Shrewsbury, his father-in-law,[27] that the tenants of Glossop manor were to be heard in a special meeting of the Privy Council. He asked that some knowledgeable person be sent to London to represent Shrewsbury's interests. Sadly Shrewsbury had dismissed his most knowledgeable representative, Anthony Bradshawe, although given Bradshawe's commitment to upholding the forest law and laws of tenancy, he might well have sided with the tenants rather than with Shrewsbury.[28]

Bess of Hardwick, Dowager Countess of Shrewsbury, died in February 1608 at Hardwick Hall. She had been suspected of being involved in the Ralegh conspiracy. In her final years she had lost her close affection for Arbella, although they never totally severed their relationship. Bess built dynasties in the descendants of her second and third sons: the dukes of Devonshire and Newcastle. From her daughter Frances descended the dukes of Kingston. From her eldest son descended the Barons Waterpark, children of Sir Henry Cavendish and his wife Sarah (nee Bradshaw), first Baroness Waterpark.

In June 1610, Lady Arbella Stuart finally succeeded in marrying Sir William Seymour without the king's knowledge or permission. The marriage was arranged in secret, and a minister of Crayford performed the ceremony in the presence of ladies-in-waiting Mrs. Biron and Mrs. Anne Bradshawe, Gentleman Usher Hugh Crompton, Edward Rodney, Edward Kirton, and Mr. Reeves. In September, Arbella believed herself pregnant. The threat of a potential male heir to the throne was a worry to King James, and the unapproved marriage had already angered him. William Seymour was confined to the Tower, and Arbella was placed in custody of Sir Thomas Parry, chancellor of the Duchy of Lancaster, at Lambeth. Arbella's income from the Crown was severely curtailed. It was determined that Arbella would be sent to

Durham and delivered into the care of the bishop there. Arbella and Seymour made an abortive attempt to escape, and they involved Anne Bradshaw (See Appendix 16) in their plot. With dumb luck Seymour made it to Ostend. Arbella and Anne were captured and returned to London for imprisonment. As they were lead through traitor's gate at the Tower of London, Arbella and Anne must have realized that they might never have hope of release or pardon for their crime. But of what crime? They had not been charged, although James could have charged Arbella under the Act of 1535 forbidding her marriage without royal approval. He did not do so; that she had not faithfully supported him was treason enough in his eyes. Anyone connected with the escape attempt was shut away for questioning and potential punishment. Countess Mary, wife of the Earl of Shrewsbury, was already imprisoned for assisting the escape plot. The contemporary scribbled list of those arrested and their places of confinement will be found in Harleian manuscript 7003, folio 143, at the British Library.

Robert Cecil, Earl of Salisbury, died of cancer on May 24, 1612, aged just forty-nine. King James lost his best councilor and the one most likely to recommend mercy for Lady Arbella. In June, the case of Mary Countess of Shrewsbury was brought to the Star Chamber, not to determine her guilt but simply to add up her punishment. Sir Francis Bacon demanded and obtained a heavy penalty: a £20,000 fine and confinement during the king's pleasure, which meant an indefinite sentence. Mary was allowed home in November 1613 to nurse her sick husband, but only for two days! During the year that followed, Anne Bradshawe may have been released, but Lady Arbella petitioned to be allowed the services of Anne Bradshawe, Mrs. Chaworth, and three other servants to attend her in the Tower. That petition was granted, and then Arbella was once again forgotten by the king. In July 1613, Hugh Crompton had been released from imprisonment; in September 1614, Arbella's loyal and devoted Anne Bradshawe left, perhaps due to ill health, to return to her husband in Duffield. Anne's father-in-law, Anthony Bradshawe, died that year and was buried in the curious tomb he had built for himself in Duffield Church. No doubt twelve-year-old John Bradshawe was present at the elaborate funeral.

Lady Arbella Stuart died on September 25 of the next year. Sir William Seymour heard the news in his place of exile. Lady Arbella had been in touch with him during her imprisonment and had even sent him small amounts of money from her own meager resources.[29]

The day after Arbella died, Sir Ralph Winwood, secretary of state, commissioned an autopsy. It was found that she died from "a chronic and long illness . . . her negligence as by refusal of remedies . . . a confirmed unhealthiness of liver, and extreme leaness." Arbella had starved herself to death. With little ceremony, her body was placed in the vault of Mary, Queen of Scots, at Westminster Abbey on September 27. Seymour returned from exile in January, obtained the king's pardon, was created Knight of the Bath, and served the Royalist cause with distinction during the civil wars. He took a second wife, and they named one of their daughters Arbella. King Charles II restored to him his great-grandfather's[30] title—Duke of Somerset. Just weeks after obtaining the title in 1660, William Seymour died.

In February 1617, the results of a Privy Council examination just concluded was given, and it stated that whereas "a reporte was given out amongst divers persons that lady Arbella Seymoure late wife of William Seymoure, knight, daughter of Charles Stewarde (sic), and grandchild to Matthew, Earle of Lennox, had a child during her confinement at Sir Thos. Parrie's house at Lambeth, in the yeare of our Lorde 1610." The king commanded Secretary of State Sir Francis Bacon and others to make inquiry. Seymour was called to testify but said he could offer no evidence; he suggested that the council interview "Mrs. Ann Bradshawe, wife to Exuperie Bradshawe, a gentlewoman attending at the time neere the person of the said Ladie Arbella and best able to clear that doubte." It was discovered that Anne had a "weakness and indisposition of boddie" and could not undertake a trip to London without danger to her life. Mr. Edmondes, one of the clerks of the Privy Council,[31] went to Duffield to interview Anne on January 21, 1617.

Anne said that she had heard those reports that there was a child, but she knew they were lies. She further said that she had served Lady Arbella from 1603 until a year or a little more of her death, and that while Arbella had suffered from a swelling that required her clothes to be let out, there was subsequently an effusion of blood that proved her to be without pregnancy.

In the same year, Winwood procured Sir Walter Ralegh's release from the Tower and permission for him to undertake his last voyage to Guiana.

After their release from confinement, Hugh Crompton and Edward Kirton joined the household of Sir William Seymour and were members of Parliament in the 1620s; Crompton died in 1645, Kirton in 1654.

Mary, Countess of Shrewsbury, had petitioned for release and was given her freedom on Christmas Day 1615. Her husband died in May the following year. She refused to cooperate with the enquiry about Arabella's alleged child and was put back in the Tower. The old £20,000 fine, which had never been collected, was revived, and the Shrewsbury manor of Worksop was seized by the Crown. Mary remained in the queen's lodgings, probably three or four rooms, at the Tower until November 1623; she died in 1632 leaving three daughters as her coheiresses. Alethea, the third daughter, married Thomas Howard, second Earl of Arundel(See Appendix 17.) who, in 1630, appointed John Bradshawe as steward of Glossop Manor.

The following year, Francis Bradshawe (1576-1635), "the younger" of Chapel-en-le-Frith, was High Sheriff of Derbyshire. His father, Francis the Elder (1555/6-1619/20?), qualified as a justice of the peace in 1615. Francis the younger, also a justice of the peace, was a member of the Inner Temple,[32] the same Inn of Court as his great-uncle Anthony Bradshawe. In the year that John Bradshawe, the regicide, first journeyed up to Gray's Inn, Francis had completed a total rebuild of Bradshaw Hall in Chapel on the thirteenth century foundations of the previous half-timbered hall.

In order to assume the office of High Sheriff, Francis assigned his lifetime appointment as High Peak bailiff, which he had held for six years, to George Halley. He also had to incur quite a lot of expense attendant to the grand display of High Sheriff. There were expenses connected with the courts, the trial and execution of prisoners, the feeding, lodging, and entertainment of judges and juries, and the wages of the sheriff's escort, for which the High Sheriff was responsible. At the expiration of his year in office, he was empowered to deliver a *bill of cravings* to the treasury.[33] His lengthy bill for the two summer Derby assizes states that he paid three shillings for five men that "attended the prisoners with halberds at the Execution—3 shillings and 4 pence to Mr. Pym for burying the executed prisoners, 18 pence for tolling the bell, 4 shillings for two gallons of 'carrot wine and white', 3 pounds 8 shillings for baking venison pies, and more than £11 for beer." Sheriff Bradshawe was required to attend the high and mighty circuit judges, who represented the king in person, from the moment they crossed the border into Derbyshire until he handed them onto the sheriff of the next county, although it appears that Bradshawe went as far as Leceister city to meet his judges. His traveling retinue of twenty-five men would have included two trumpeters and twenty-one javelin men. He was a wealthy and powerful man, and he should have been knighted. The Crown could demand he pay a fee if he refused knighthood.

Sheriff Bradshaw would probably have journeyed down to Tutbury Fair on the morrow after the Feast of the Assumption accompanied, perhaps, by John Bradshawe the future regicide. In 1630, when John Bradshawe first became Arundel's steward of Glossop Manor, orders were issued "for the better ordering and governing of His Majesty's court called the Minstrel's Court, yearly holden at Tutbury . . . and of the musicians and minstrels within the counties of Stafford and Derby who owe suit to the same court." Among other things, it was ordered that no one exercise the art and science of music for gain unless he completed seven years training and was admitted by the steward and jury of the minstrel's court. In 1636, the festival was deferred from the fifteenth to August 23 because King Charles came to Tutbury castle for five nights. As the minstrel's court fell into disuse, a mixed multitude of drunken and brawling participants joined in the dangerous chase and, in 1778, the practice was ended although a bull was baited on the same day for many years thereafter.

During the days of King Charles's personal rule, the loss of parliamentary taxation led the royal counselors to *fiscal fuedalism*. They revived medieval princely prerogative which, though archaic, were in theory legal. Two of the most annoying were knighthood fines and forest law fines.

According to the Act of 1227, all men who had lands or rents to the value of £40 a year were required to attend the king's coronation and be knighted; in 1630, Attorney General William Noy suggested to King Charles that he could fine all men worth over £40 who had neglected to attend the coronation five years earlier. No allowance was made for the diminished value of money over the four-hundred-year interim. Noy was said to have the ability to make law, "which all men else thought not to be so." Noy himself had written that "all liberties are derived from the crown. A liberty is a royal privilege in the hands of a subject." Within five years he had collected £173,537 from knighthood fines. One victim of the fines bitterly said the law was just "an old skulking statute long since out of use, though not out of force." A ballad was circulated;

> *Come all you farmers out of the country carters,*
> *Ploughmen, hedgers and all.*
> *Honour invites you to delights,*
> *come to Court and be all made knights.*

The next potential source of money lay in a sudden and revolutionary resurrection of forest law. In theory, the courts of two royal Chief Justices of the Forest centrally controlled the revenues of the royal forests in the name of the king. They appointed officials, maintained boundaries, verified land tenures, assessed fines for violations of vert and venison, and issued warrants for casual puchases of timber and minerals among other things. As early as 1547, however, Henry VIII had taken the management of forest timber from the justices of the forest and given to the Exchequer. Crown woods were sold by Exchequer warrant, and forest offenders were prosecuted in the court of the Exchequer instead of at the justice seat. In fact, as Manwood said in 1598, the courts of the forest eyre (justice seat) had been nearly nonexistent for decades, leaving the way open for corrupt or lazy subofficials to allow almost unchecked encroachments. Cases were heard by subordinate forest courts which could convict offenders, even in absentia. These subordinate courts, woodmote and swainmote, could assess only small fines for minor offenses, and these were ineffectual against powerful nobles and landowners. Illegally taking wood, timber, and agisting sheep or cattle, then paying a fine to the woodmote, was easier and probably cheaper than obtaining a court or Exchequer warrant for the purposes. A roll of presentment showing the names and a summary of the more serious encroachments was supposed to be drawn up by the subordinate court awaiting the pleasure of court of forest in Eyre whenever it was held. The Forest Eyre could then pronounce sentence on this roll alone. Judicial fines had once formed a major portion of the royal forest revenue, but by the second decade of the seventeenth century, the brothers-in-law Arundel and Pembroke, chief justices of the forests north and south of the Trent respectively, had held only intermittent courts of the forest in Eyre—and those chiefly in just two forests, Windsor and Waltham, both under Pembroke's jurisdiction. This slow relinquishing of authority reduced the crown revenues, but it also diminished the office of chief justice of the forest to little more than a ceremonial sinecure. Any revitalization of the ancient law would massively increase the work of the officials. To men like Arundel and Pembroke, their office of Chief Justice was just one of their many preferments. Neither pressure nor ambition could convince them to throw their energies into radical reform.

Manwood and his contemporaries, who spoke of the decline of forest law, lamented the reduction in forest revenues. Neither the proceeds of the rare justice seat nor the small fines collected in the occasional subordinate courts were reaching the king's Exchequer with any regularity, nor were the findings of encroachment within the royal forests. The forest law remained in use, but it had lost most of its terrors. A law originally intended to protect a royal privilege now safeguarded the local-level interests of the commoners. They had come to regard it as traditional, beneficial, and protective; it was the Crown which was finding it restrictive.

Under King James and King Charles, the Star Chamber and the Exchequer claimed royal prerogatives unknown under the Tudors, rejecting the idea of traditional, absolute, or unqualified rights for forest dwellers outside the common law. Challenges were launched against the tenure of lands in the forest and adjacent disafforested areas. Under strict forest law, all buildings, all ironworks, agriculture, and similar activities were illegal within the bounds of a royal forest. Crown officers seized lands or levied heavy fines when the tenant could not produce a recognized grant or copyhold documents. Peter Bradshawe was turned out of his troublesome Chinley farm in 1622. The Crown officers must have discovered a flaw in Bradshawe's lease. King James I, to whom it reverted, granted it to Edw Budbie and William Weltden of London for a considerable sum of money, and in the following year, they sold the property back to Peter and Francis Bradshawe. It was never the intention of the royal councilors to regain central control of the forest lands. Threat, seizure, and fines were merely the means to an end of raising royal revenue. The first two Stuart kings had developed a habit of using laws for purposes which were directly contradictory to those for which the laws had been framed. Gardiner, in his *History of England*, judged that "as a means of improving revenue the revival of forest law proved largely abortive . . . Charles . . . allowed himself for the sake of a few thousand pounds to be regarded as a greedy and litigious landlord rather than a just ruler or a national king."

James I was the last English king to be passionately fond of hunting, but he rarely moved outside the southeastern corner of England after his coronation. Natural resources and timber from the royal forests were becoming more valuable than the king's hunting privilege, and most of the outlying royal forests had been encroached upon.

In the Forest of Bowland, high in the Pennies on the borders of Lancashire and Yorkshire, there had been much small-scale enclosure and clearing in the sixteenth century leading to the creation of a landscape of small hedged or walled enclosures and isolated farmhouses. At first the king decreed they be built of timber and thatch, but by the beginning of the seventeenth century, they were of stone in a landscape from which timber trees had all but disappeared, From a survey made in 1652, we learn that the forest had been held from the Crown by several tenants on leases, "but now, for the moste part, the said landes are fee-farme, being sold to the respective tenants by King James and King Charles as appears by diverse letters patent."

Encroachments south of the Trent had been tolerated for centuries until the death of the William Herbert, Earl of Pembroke and chief justice of the forest court, in 1630. Earl Holland, the new chief justice south of the Trent, readily cooperated with Attorney General Noy to revive the forest courts to fine all who had trespassed on forest lands.[34] When Charles proclaimed new boundaries for the Forest of Essex, he in effect cancelled all the disafforestation promised by the Magna Carta and the Charter of the Forest, which the ancestors of the present holders had purchased at considerable expense and had enjoyed for generations. Many copyholders, unable to produce their own documents and stymied by the disappearance of many ancient forest court records, found themselves pushed out of their secure franchise into the position of leaseholders or tenants at will. Younger sons of peasants and yeomen were unable to obtain any land and were restricted from sharing the common, gathering, or hunting. Powerful local families who had land within purlieus (the circuit of ground surrounding the forest which had been disafforested) believed they were defending the ancient constitution when they called upon the king to protect their privileged hunting rights.[35] These customary and often conflicting rights, believed to be secured by the Charter of the Forest, had heretofore been respected or ignored by the Crown.

No concern for customary rights troubled King Charles when he ordered new forest creation or forest clearance and enclosure. Between 1630 and 1636, the Forest of Braden in Wiltshire was disafforested and enclosed. Of an area of a little over four thousand acres, in which no less than fourteen villages had the right to pasture their livestock from time immemorial, the Crown finally allotted only 390 acres as compensation for the loss of these rights of common. Richmond Park was created and the landholders evicted. The bounds of Rockingham Forest reexamined and enlarged from six to sixty miles. Fines for ancient encroachment totaling more than £50,000 were assessed on the earls of Salisbury and Westmoreland and Sir Christopher Hatton. In 1609, the Earl of Salisbury had, in order to better the Crown's finances, issued a commission to Sir Thomas Tyringham and Sir Robert Johnson to cut timber in the royal forest of Whittlewood, Northarnptonshire, and Buckinghamshire. Salisbury was prepared to recognize environmental factors. Only two in a hundred were to be felled, and Johnson was ordered to observe "What place they maie be spared without anie blemishe to the beautie of our forsaid Parkes Forests and Chaces," and he was to "have principall care to forbeare in the felling of anie trees or Faire tuftes soe neare the Scite or mansion howse (yf there be anie of anie note) as may disgrace the habitacon." Despite this kind of caution, at the Northamptonshire Forest Eyre for Rockingham Forest, which opened in 1635, the deceased Earl of Salisbury was convicted of having assorted 2,300 acres of Brigstock Parks in 1604, destroying the vert and a thousand deer and enclosing the parks. His heir was fined £20,000 even though his father had obtained a pardon from James I. Three years later the heir paid £3,000 for remission of the $20,000 fine and the recovery of his parks at Brigstock.

At Lord Holland's court of the Forest Eyre for Dean Forest in July 1634, juries were outrageously intimidated and threatened by Sir John Finch who had succeeded as attorney general upon the death of Noy. Fines worth £130,000 were assessed on eight hundred presentments, some of which referred to events that had been awaiting presentment to the justice seat for more than forty years! Earlier Elizabethan and Jacobean Dean Forest swainmote and attachment court rolls show small fines ranging from a few pence to £1, producing a total of between £15 and £40 per year.

In 1633, King Charles disaforrested one of the seven wards of Duffield Frith. His Council of the Duchy of Lancaster assigned to King Charles a third part of Belper ward in Duffield Frith. In September 1634, the king granted this third part to Sir Edward Sydenham at a yearly rent of 21s. 8d. At the same time, the Duchy council proposed to assign to the king a third part of Chevin ward to be chosen by the casting of lots. The other two parts of Chevin were to be granted to those who had formerly held it in common at 2s. per annum for each acre they promised to enclose in private fee farms. Nearly four hundred commoners of Chevin opposed the council's arbitrary proposal; only thirty-one agreed to it. Nevertheless, the proposal cleared the council, and the king's commissioners took what part they liked best without casting any lots. They took all the places where coal pits were dug. The king immediately granted this third to Sir Edward Sydenham for a yearly rent, and it was enclosed. The remaining two thirds were also enclosed, and only those thirty-one commoners who agreed to the proposal were admitted as tenants. The remaining majority of inhabitants threw open the enclosures in 1643 and "Had not the distraction by the late Warres prevented them, they had all joyned in a Bill of Reviewe to reverse the Decree made upon soe slender grounds and soe illegally without theire consent." All of the old forest thrown open by violent means in 1643 remained common until 1786. Local opposition to enclosure prevailed without violence in the larger ward of Duffield that included Shottle Park due—at least in part—to the forest court records maintained by Anthony Bradshawe (d; 1614), his heirs, and his relatives who held lands in Duffield at Chevin and Belper.

The High Peak Forest around Chapel-en-le-Frith remained a royal domain until 1641 when the inhabitants of the "district being desirous to be freed from the severity of the forest laws and customs and the incomodiousness of deer, lying and feeding in their corn and grass, and other inconveniences" petitioned King Charles for disafforestation. This seems more an excuse for expansion rather than a plea for relief. Almost all the deer had died in the dreadful blizzard of 1641. Because of Tudor domestic policy, the general move of population had been Northward. In 1589, at a court held in Chapel-en-le-Frith, twenty-one aggressors were fined for lopping trees, possibly for building shelters. An enquiry made as early as 1516 found; "No grass left for deer in the Forest . . . because of cattle and sheep." There was an attempt then to restrict sheep and cattle by slaughtering. The enclosure of the common lands in Chapel was deferred until the reign of Charles II as result of the civil wars.[36]

Notes to Chapter Five

1. Sir William Wentworth's advice to his son, 1604, quoted by Ralph A. Houlbrook, *The English Family, 1450-1700*, 2. Roger Bradshaw was M.P. for Derby in 1406 and for Stafford in 1416; Thomas Bradshaw of Rigge was Elector for Derby Borough 1447 and 1455; County Elector 1447, 1449; Thomas was M.P. for Derby Borough in 1450/51; Robert and John Bradshaw were Derby County Electors in 1467; John Bradshaw of Ludlow was M.P. 1545; John Bradshaw of St. Dogrnaels was M.P. for Radnor 1554; Joseph Bradshaw was M.P. for Westminister 1632/33—*Hist of Parl 1439-1509* Vol I, HMSO, Col Joshua Wedgwood.
3. A. Craig Gibson, Orig Correspondence of the Lord President Bradshaw; etc., *Trans of the Hist Soc of Lancs & Ches*, New Ser, Vol II, (1862), 43 et seq.
4. A calendar of the *Talbot Papers in the College of Arms*, Vol P, Folio 77. *Derbs Arch Soc Rec Ser*, Vol 4 f 1968.
5. A calendar of the *Shrewsbury Papers in the Lambeth Palace Library.*, Mss 705, folio 144—see also Mss 695, folio 82. *Derbs Arch Soc Rec Ser* Vol 1 for 1965.
6. Henry Bradshaw of the Inner Temple (b: ca. 1505, d: 1553), was appointed Solicitor-General to King Henry VIII in 1540; Attorney-General in 1545, and Chief Baron of the Exchequer to King Edward VI in 1553. In 1544 when the King became too ill to deal with day-to-day business Henry Bradshaw and eight courtiers were given a commission to sell manors and lands taken from monasteries and Catholic recusants. The King found signing documents so burdensome that nearly every petition to the Privy Council was being countersigned by Bradshaw. He approved the use of a "drie stamp" of the King's signature as a substitute for the actual signature. On the 24th September 1544 Bradshaw signed a grant of the manor of Erith, Kent "alias Leosnes, Kent which belonged to the late Queen Jane" to "Elizabeth countess of Shrewsbury"—*Ltrs & Papers, Foreign & Dom, Hen VIII, Vol XIX, Pt I, P 188*.—Elizabeth was the daughter and co-heiress of Sir Richard Walden of Erith and stepmother of Francis the 5th Earl of Shrewsbury—the "late Queen Jane" was Queen Jane Seymour who died in 1537. Henry Bradshaw's cousin was Robert Pursglove (ca. 1500-1579), Bishop of Hull, Suffragan to the Archbishop of York, and Archdeacon of Nottingham. Pursglove was born in Tiddeswell, Derbs, to Adam Pursglove and his wife Modwina (nee Bradshaw). He was consecrated as a protestant

bishop under Edward VI but became a fervent catholic under Queen Mary Tudor and refused the Oath of Suprermacy to Queen Elizabeth. He founded Grammar Schools in Tiddeswell and Gisburne, Yorks. Henry Bradshaw and his wife Joan sold a farm in Tiddeswell to Adam Pursglove and Adam conveyed the farm to the Tiddeswell Grammar School—*Jour Derbs Arch & Natl Hist Soc.,* Vol XXXII, (1910), 1-31.

7. The 6th Earl of Shrewsbury, as Lord Lieutenant of Derbyshire, made strenuous efforts against his Catholic recusant neighbors—J.C. Cox, *The Churches of Derbyshire,* Vol 1, 185-186, and Vol II, 249.
8. Godfrey Bradshawe was the elder brother of Lord President John Bradshawe's grandfather. Their younger brother was Anthony Bradshawe of Duffield.
9. C.E. Bradshaw Bowles, Bradshaw Hall and the Bradshaws, *Jour of Derbs Arch & Natl Hist Soc,* Vol XXV, (1903) and, On the Bradshaws and Staffords of Eyam, with a Notice of the Old Hall, *The Reliquary,* Vol 2, (1861-62), 219.—The engraving of Bradshaw old Hall at Eyam which accompanies the article in *The Reliquary* shows the hall in considerably better repair than it exists today. It continues to deteriorate. The ruin is said to be part of an elaborate Hall erected by George Bradshawe (1587-1646) about 1630 on the site of an earlier Hall of the Staffords. George was the brother and eventual heir of Francis Bradshawe of Bradshawe Hall in Chapel-en-le Frith who was High Sheriff in 1631. Uninformed local tradition has blackened Squire George Bradshawe's name by alleging that he was the only resident who fled the plague of 1666 which decimated Eyam; in fact he was dead long before then and his young widow had gone to live at Brampton. The allegation is repeated in William Wood's otherwise excellent *History & Antiquities of Eyam, 1865,* pg 148.—George was associated in business with his uncle Peter, of Watling Street London, and was constantly engaged in personally managing their plantations in Ulster, Ireland, which his uncle had bought. He made trips to Ireland in 1628 and 1629, after the Partnership with his uncle ended, and another trip in the interest of his widowed aunt after September 1630. In his will, made 17 June 1646, he names among his executors "Henry Bradshawe the younger (of Marple) and John Bradshawe, Esq., (the regicide) of Grayes Inn his brother." The will is endorsed with an acquittance by John Garland to John Bradshawe, Esq., for £200, bequeathed to Garland's wife Mary daughter of George Bradshawe. In 1626 George married Elizabeth, the young daughter of Sir Hugh Culham (Culme, Cullam) Provost.-Marshal of Cavan and Monaghan in Ireland. She died in 1677 and was buried at Treeton church, Yorks.

10. *Wooley Charters* XII 41
11. Enclosure Riots at Chinley, *Jour of Derbs Arch & Natl Hist Soc*, Vol XXI, (1899).—Chinley, just a few miles north of Bradshaw Hall at Chapel-en-le-Frith. Godfrey Bradshwe sold portions of it to his sons Leonard and Francis and his brother Anthony. Godfrey enclosed the lands and tried to prevent, his neighbors from trespassing upon it. His neighbors, including Edward Kirke, Thomas Bowden, Will Ridge, Thomas Rawlinson, and Richard Shower, were all accused of throwing down his enclosures and threatening to "kill, murder and maim the said Godfrey Bradshawe" and hire an arsonist to burn his house down. Edward Bradshawe was appointed to serve warrants on the offenders and arrest some of them at the town of Hayfield. Rawlinson and Bowden, on foot, and Ralph Mellor, on horseback, with a "great company" of others drew their weapons—"bowes, pitch forks, clubs, staves, swords, and daggers"—and chased the two Bradshawes out of town.
12. *De Houghton Deeds & Papers,* RR 964, ee362. One of the earliest grants made by King John, dated 9 October 1199 at Le Mans, was the confirmation of an original grant he had given ten years before, while he was Earl of Lancaster and Derby, to the knights, thegns, and free tenants dwelling in the forests of the honor of Lancashire that they might cultivate their woods and sell or give their herbage at will, hunt hares, foxes, and certain other beasts with their dogs, with quittance of inspection (rewardi) of forests without disturbance from the king's bailiffs. It appears that £200 and 10 chargers were paid for this confirmation—*Lancs Pipe Rolls*, Farrer, pg 418-9.—Despite the confirmation he went, to the trouble of punishing 'those who trespassed in his forests when he was on a progress through the north in 1201. Eight years later he ordered the hedges to be cut down and the ditches filled-in throughout the royal forests. King John was forced to sign the Magna Carta and the Charter of The Forest at Runnymeade on the 15th of June 1215 and he died the following year. Ten-year-old King Henry III was obligated by the Regent to issue a revised Magna Carta and a separate Forest Charter with the seals of Gualo, the Papal legate, and William Marshall, Earl of Pembroke. The young king had no seal of his own until the third year of his reign. The Council issued an ordinance declaring no grants in perpetuity should be made until the King was of full age. The ordinance was strictly observed; the reissued Magna Carta and the Forest Charter were the only charters made during his minority, neither of which he ever revoked. The 1217 Magna Carta was found among the archives of Gloucester Abbey and is now in the Bodleian Library. The

existence of the separate Forest Charter was surmised, but not proven, by Blackstone—Great *Charter,* p xlii—but shortly after he wrote, an original was found among the archives of Durham Cathedral—*Magna Carta,* pp 443-5, Thompson.—At age seventeen King Henry began to attest himself, even though still counted a minor, and on 11 February 1225 he reissued a Charter of the Forest. Early in 1227 he declared himself to be of full age—twenty-one. He issued an inspeximus and confirmation dated 21 March 1228/9 from Marlborough, of King John's old grant, made in 1199, to the Forest dwellers of Lancashire and Derbyshire—*De Houghton Deeds & Papers, S965,* ee 361,—*Lancs & Ches Rec Soc,* Vol 88, 259.

13. Christopher Hill, *Liberty Against the Law,* (Penguin Books edn, 1997)., 31.
14. A legal phrase *time immemorial,* which, in fact, does not bar every historical legal precedent but the citation of any legal precedent dating from before the coronation of King Richard I.
15. At the Assize of the Forest, Henry III, 1252 a.d., Robert Esseburn, the king's Constable of the High Peak, reported that eighteen years earlier he had detained Mathew de Schepley, Mathew de Scorches, Bate Bradule, Roger de Burton, and others, *with their boys,* who had come into the Forest and committed venison trespasses. He took them before Robert Ros who was then Justice of the Forests. Roger escaped and when Esseburn recaptured them he beheaded them on the spot. He let the boys go because they were *youthful.* Esseburn was fined 10 marks for allowing the escape but committed no offense by beheading his prisoners. Mathew de Schepley was fined 60 shillings and Mathew de Scorches was fined 20 shillings for his trespass. Richard de Bradshawe and many others provide bail for de Scorches. *Assize of the Forest before G. Langley,* Roll I, F.52, *P.R.O.* Duchy of Lancs.
16. *The Reliquary,* Vol 23, 1882-83, pg 137
17. Probably the *Great Book of Coucher for the Duchy of Lancs.* 8 Ed III
18. There are two transcripts in *Harleian Mss 5138, 568*—British Library., dating from about the end of the reign of Henry V, of the *Customary of the Honour of Tutbury* including Duffield Frith and the High Peak. *The History of the Castle, Priory, and Town of Tutbury,* Sir Oswald Mosley, London 1832—Appendices quoted historical manuscripts including much of Anthony Bradshawe's manuscript of about 1600, which is now lost. See also *Jour of Derbs Arch & Nat'l Hist Soc, Vol* XV, 1893, pg 69.
19. *Alderwasley and the Hurts,* (Vienna, 1909), 22. In 1575 three tenants of the manor of Alderwasley, representing all the other customary and

copyhold tenants, brought suit complaining that Edward Lowe, lord of the manor, infringed on their customary rights and neglected the keeping of court rolls, which it was alleged "used to be ingrossed in parchment by the Steward of the Manor 'and delivered to the Queen's majesties her noble and gentle officers of the castle of Tutbury where the copyholders of the manors might always at their pleasure have serches and copies of such things as to them be needful . . ." The suit was heard in the Court of Chancery before Lord Chancellor Sir Nicholas Bacon, father to Sir Francis Bacon.

20. "Every free man shall agist (i.e, to pasture domestic animals for a period of time) his wood which he has in the forest as he wishes and have his pannage (right to keep swine for foraging in the forest). We grant also that every free man can conduct his pigs through our demesne woods freely and without impediment to agist them in his woods or anywhere else he wishes. And if the pigs of any free man shall spend one night in our forest he shall not on that account be so prosecuted that he loses anything of his own,"—*Forest Charter, 1225, c.9.*—"Every free man may henceforth without being prosecuted make in his wood or in land he has in the forest a mill, a preserve, a pond, a marl-pit, a ditch, or arable outside the covert in arable land, on condition that it does not harm any neighbor" *c.12.* "Every free man shall have the eyries of hawks, sparrowhawks, falcons, eagles, and herons in his woods, and likewise honey found in his woods." *c.13*

21. Chevin, or "Chevinside," near Belper, Derbs, Chas Kerry, Court Rolls of the Manor of Holmesfield, *Jour of Derbs Arch and Natl Hist Soc,* Vol XX; (1891)—20 Oct 1600 "John Bullock, having lent £100 to Will. Bradshaw, sen, gent., and Anna his wife, Anthony Bradshaw, son of the said Willm. and Gertrude his wife, and Wm Bradshaw, bro of Anthony, . . . Bullock received as security for repayment 20 acres of Land at Chevynside near Belper.".

22. Probably Anthony's nephew, Peter Bradshawe. The term *cousin,* in 16th century usage, often encompassed many close family members. Cutthorp village lies about four miles northwest of Chesterfield. Presumably he included the names of his elder brother, Godfrey, and his nephew Peter. *Mss of the Marq of Salisbury, Hist Mss Comm*, Vol XVII, 328.

23. Peter Bradshawe (d; ca. 1630), citizen and Merchant Tailor of London, fourth son of Godfrey Bradshawe of Chapel-en-le-Frith and Marple. He owned the manor of Litton (Derbs.), a plantation in Ireland, and mills at Duffield, Bonsall, Castleton, Ferneley, Coombes, and Bentley. His London business was housed at the sign of 'The Antelope in Watling Street. He and

John Berry of Canterbury stood bond for the will of Frances Howard, widow of Henry Fitzgerald 12th Earl Kildare and wife (married after 1597) of *the wretched* Henry Brooke Lord Cobham. For their bond Bradshawe and Berry received the Mansion house called Deptford Strond and also the spiritualities of Lycale in Ireland. This seems to have been a device to protect the estate of the Frances, the Dowager Countess of Kildare, who was regretting her marriage to Henry Brooke. Brooke and his brother, George, were both convicted of plotting against the crown; Henry, the instigator of *Cobham's plot* to place Arbella Stuart on the throne, and George, implicated in *Bye's plot* on behalf of English catholics. The Brookes were brother-in-laws to Robert Cecil 1st Earl Salisbury and Henry was a close friend of Sir Walter Ralegh although he later betrayed Ralegh and blamed him, probably unjustly, for hatching the plot.

24. Hist Mss Commission, catalogue of Misc Mss,(1903), 36, 42, 49, 124, *Manuscript of Sir George Wombwell of Newburgh Abbey*, Narrative of Robert Pilkington about the struggle, begun in 1478, between himself and the Aynesworths for lands in Mellor, Derbyshire; " . . . on Thursday after St. Peter's Day (1494/5) two of Robert Pilkington's tenants, William Roubothum and William Beley, went, to the countie of Derby to enter their replegares (writ to recover property) but the county baillie was not there, yet the sherev (sheriff)cald mayster Robert Bradischawe entered thaym of his owne mynd and kyndness and amytted the said ij tenandesattorney." Appearing at Derby, as a jury panel concerning the matter; John Hardwick of Hardwick, Henry Bradshaw de Bradshaw, Rufus Olerschaw de Bradshaw Edge, John Stafford of Shawe, Nicholas Jodrell, gent., Thos. Samon of Anselywodhowse, gent., Nicholas Brown of Morchall, gent., Thomas Wodck of de Ronley, Christopher Hyde of Glossop, Thomas Molt of Ekules (Eccles), Thomas Gyre of Bolysorewodhws and Radulphus Whyttechurch. Pilkington thought these juries were "knawen (cousins or kindred?) and proved for the most parchell (partial) whest (?) that eyver passed at Derby that ane mon (man) couth thynke or herde tell." Pilkington wrote "another letter" to his cousin "Sir Perys (Peter) Bradishaw at that time chief chaplain to my lord Dean of Arches." William Roubothum traveled to London to appear with "Perys Bradishaw" at a hearing held in Bow Church, Cheapside.

25. Brouncker was assigned as Lady Arbella's jailer in 1603. Sir Henry Brouncker (d;1607) was President of Munster until 1605 when he was succeeded by Donough O'Brien 4th Earl of Thomond, Sir Henry was father of Sir William Brouncker, Vice Chamberlain to Prince Charles.

William's mother was Anne, daughter of (?) Lord Monteagle Parker,. *D.N.B.*

26. *Cal of Shrewsbury and Talbot Papers,* Vol II, P 283. The examination of John Dakin, 8 Jan (1605/06)touching certain slanderous speeches used by John Clay of Crich, gentleman.
27. *Cal of Shrewsbury Talbot Papers,* Vol III, m/475 30 Dec 1607—The Earl of Arundel to Earl of Shrewsbury from Whitehall.
28. Anthony Bradshawe's poem *A Friends Due Commendation of Duffield Frith, The Reliquary,* Vol 23, (1882-83), probably written about 1603-08, explained the different sort of copyhold land tenures and made strong representations about tenants rights:—
34. What more than this can reason wish to expect in Duffield Fee who this dislikes deserveth less and worser plant may be And touching laudable, freedoms & liberties Their Charter goods Customs book the same right well decrees
35. Which if they keep inviolate & well hold together A mighty man cannot then wrest with silver nor with gold But if the fagot bound on break & sticks fly to & fro Then Duffield Frith turns upside down, their wealth is overthrown
50. Now with good customs laudable if tenants keep them well I know few manors in the land which can this Frith excell which to preserve I wish, and warn that; men together hold Then them to hurt none can prevail & thereof be then bold
51. The better sort of Duffield men their customs understand And how they do concern themselves, their houses and their lands The poorer sort & ignorant which custom book have none By song may learn some customs now & memory alone."

Before 1603 Bradshawe had written manuscripts on precedents and forms of Land holding, which he described as "little books"—one particularly called *A Lantern for Copyholders.* I have been unable to determine if it or any other of his "little books" were printed.

29. David N. Durant, *Arbella Stuart, a Rival to the Queen,* Arbella may have sent Seymour the Book of Hours she inherited from Mary, Queen of Scots. She dedicated it "Your most unfortunate Arbella Stuart" The book was taken into Russia during the French Revolution and was last seen at the Hermitage Museum.
30. Edward Seymour, Earl of Hereford and Duke of Somerset., had been named Lord Protector of young King VI the questionable last will of King Henry VIII. Henry Bradshaw, the King's Attorney General, had consented to Henry's will, Edward's succession, and Seymour's Protectorship. A copy

of King Henry VIII's will in the British Library *Harle Mss 293—fol 71* bears the following note; "N.B.the original of this will under seale is in Mr. Bradshawe's Hands of the Taylie Office: whereby this coppie (which is neare as old as the Time) is examined." The second patent appointing Edward Seymour, Duke of Somerset, Protector of the young King Edward VI is signed by Henry Bradshaw—*Archaelogia, Soc of Antiquaries, Vol 30*, pg 474.—During his Protectorship Seymour proposed a redress of the evils of common lands enclosures and appointed a six-man commission including John Hales, M.P. for Preston, Lanes. Hales wrote to Seymour regarding the Commission, July 24 1548; "If the matter is handled as in the past in the exchequer, that the king's attorney" (Bradshaw) "and solicitor" (Griffin) "may put in and out, do and undo what they wish, your intent will be frustrated and our labors in vain"—*Cal State Papers, Ed VI, 1547-1553*.—After Northumberland's seizure of power, Bradshaw, as Attorney-General, saw to the confinement and execution of Seymour in November 1551. In 1549 Sir Edmund Molyneaux, king's Sgt-at-Law, and Henry Bradshaw, Attorney General, had reported on the prisoners lately committed to the Tower, including Hales and Seymour.

31. Perhaps the same Thomas Edmondes who conducted negotiations with Fr. Augustine Bradshaw (White) after the Gunpowder plot.
32. Francis Bradshawe the elder, of Eyam, wrote from the house of his relatives at Shalcross in 1614 to Sir George Manners, the father of the 8th Earl of Rutland, at Haddon Hall, returning him "he Council's letter and Orders concerning the eating of flesh meat and a warrant to the High Constable for affectuating the same" *Jour of Derbs Arch & Nat'l Hist Soc*, Vol XXVIII, 1906, pg 104.—In an Indenture, bearing the date 19 May 1610, Francis Bradshawe the younger is described as of the Inner Temple—*Bradshaw Hall and the Bradshaws,—Journal of Derbs Arch & Nat'l Hist Soc*, Vol x.xv, (1903). Francis followed his father as a Justice of the Peace. On the 22nd of July 1623, for the sum of £120 he received from William Stafford of Botham Hall (now called Bothomes) the assignment of a lease for 60 years of a shop in Bakewell held by John Manners of Bakewell—*Wolley Charters* xii, 76. 59 (44) Ibid, vol XXV
33. C.E.B.Bowles, *Expenses of the Shrievalty during the Summer Assize of 1631*, *Jour of Derbs Arch & Natural Hist Soc*, Vol XXVI, (1904), 23-40
34. G. Hammersley, The Revival of Forest Law, *History*, LXV (1960), 84-102
35. *C.S.P. Dom, 1625*, P 182—Vol DXXV, # 80 1626; "*Petition of Sir Gilbert Houghton, Sir John Bradshaw, and four other gentlemen of co, Lancaster, to the Council.* Many gents of good rank and quality, using hawking and hunting

for their recreation, are much prejudiced by persons of mean quality, who destroy much game of partridge and hare with greyhounds, setting dogs and nets. And though some of them are not inhibited by the statute to keep a greyhound, they ought not to destroy the game, same by storing their houses in unreasonable measure, and others by making common sale of the game to inns and alehouses. pray that warrant may be given to Mr. Ralph Robinson, one of the messengers of His Majesty's Chamber who knows the country, for suppressing the abuses." The statute of 13 Ric II, cap 13 decreed that "he who may hunt lawfully in any Pouralee (purlieu) ought to have woods or freehold land within the Pouralee to a yearly value of 40s." By statute of I Jac, cap 7 (1603) that was changed to "lands of inheritance with a yearly value of £ 10 . . . or be the son of a knight, baron, or person of a higher degree, or son & heir apparent of an esquire." Hunting was not allowed at night or on Sundays. Pouralee men could only hunt on his own land with his own servants, remembering that, any beasts that strayed or were pursued out of the royal forest onto his lands belonged to the king.

36. J. Charles Cox, *The Royal Forests of England*, (London 1905).

CHAPTER SIX

The Slide Toward War— Country Versus Court

*To know both when and where and in what cause our lives to lose,
Is a thing of greater skill than most men suppose.*
Joseph Rigby, Mayor of Wigan, 1649

☩

SOME MODERN HISTORIANS have seen the influence of *Country* versus *Court* in explaining the origins of the English civil war.[1] Definitions of country and court vary within that explanation but don't seem to prove the existence of an official country party or a band of country gentry with common political ideal or a practical platform of reforms. There is more evidence of a cohesive band of supporters about the king and his court. It was some time before John Pym and John Hampden,[2] the leaders of the Commons, began to appeal to the personal passions of the mob to sway power away from the king. As Conrad Russell has pointed out, the king did not have the physical power to force the major part of his subjects to perform actions they did not want to perform. Neither did he have the power to restrain them from performing actions he did not want them to perform.[3] He could only attempt to punish individuals, or small groups of individuals, after they had trangressed.

In John Bradshawe's native Cheshire and Derbyshire, the majority of the gentry had few contacts with King Charles's court, but they were distrustful of crown policies and the ways of central government. By the same token, they had little concern or contact with any organized country opposition party. William Davenport of Bramhall, a county squire of no national reputation,[4] kept a commonplace book in the years 1613-1642[5] detailing his political awareness and his sufferings during the civil wars, in which he tried to play a purely passive role. Sir Peter Legh of Lyme (1563-1636), *a gent of great antiquity and of great worth in the Counties of Cheshire and Lancashire*, regularly corresponded with his friends, Essex, Leicester, Buckingham, successive earls of Derby, Rutland, Lord Herbert of Cherbury, Viscount Savage, Elias Ashmole, Henry Lawes, Sir Peter Daniel of Over Tabley,[6] Henry Bradshawe of Marple,[7] and a certain John Bradshaw of Gray's Inn who would become his legal agent. (See Appendix 18). Sir Peter was a great Royalist, but his death, and the deaths of his three successive heirs, before the advent of war saved Lyme Hall from destruction, aided perhaps by the friendship of the Bradshawes of Marple. William Moreton of Little Moreton, who served as a parish provost with Congleton's Mayor John Bradshawe, received letters full of court intrigue from his son who lived as a private secretary with several noble families and became a king's ambassador.

One Cheshire landowner and MP (1627-8, 1631, 1640) did become a part organized opposition. He was Sir William Brereton of Handforth, Bt., old acquaintance and Gray's Inn colleague of John Bradshawe the future regicide. Brereton's landholdings were only moderate by Cheshire standards, but he had other financial interests including lands in New England.

Brereton came from the younger branch of a family whose mainline was Royalist. He came in conflict with the city of Chester in the 1630s but did not declare himself a political militant until later. He must have recognized a serious lack of militant Puritans among the seventy or more families of Cheshire gentry involved in county affairs. Nine families were prominent Puritans, Calvinist, Presbyterian, and Independent in the 1630s: John Bradshawe and his brother Henry Bradshawe of Marple, Peter Daniel of Over Tabley, Thomas Brooke of Norton, Jonathan Bruen of Stapleford, John Crewe of Utkinton, Robert Duckenfield of Duckenfield, Hamnet Hyde of Norbury, and John Legh of Booths. Under the leadership of Sir William Brereton, they were the militant faction inside the Cheshire Parliamentarian movement during the civil war.

Opposing Brereton and his adherents were the Royalist Stanleys of Alderley, Fittons of Gawsworth, and Leighs of Adlington. A high proportion of the civil war leaders and many regiments of the most enthusiatic troops on both sides came from the region of northeast Cheshire, John Bradshawe's birthplace.

The important River Dee seaport of Chester, with a population of less than six thousand, was the only town of significance in the eyes of the rest of the nation. The population of Macclesfield was about two thousand while that of Stockport and Congleton was well under that number. Congleton had but five streets. Chester, Macclesfield, Stockport, and Congleton elected mayors and aldermen, but with the exception of Chester, they were administratively treated as part of the county and occasionally made subject to interference of the king's Privy Council.

Congleton, on the London to Liverpool road, was a manor as well as a borough and in early times had been subject to the jurisdiction of the steward of the Honor of Halton and the Duchy of Lancaster. A charter granted to the borough by Queen Elizabeth I (1584) reconstructed the Congleton ruling body, and another charter of King James I (January 19, 1624-25) established the borough constitution in detail. James's charter reduced the power of Halton Honor Steward (the incumbent was Sir John Savage, Viscount Savage, d; 1635) and changed his role from an officer of the Duchy of Lancaster to an officer of the borough of Congleton.

In September 1628, the city of London accepted the manor and town corporate of Congleton from King Charles in part payment of a loan arranged by Edward Ditchfield.[8] Upon petition of the citizens, common council, and the mayor of London, Congleton was granted to Edward Ditchfield, John Highfield, Humphrey Clarke, and Francis Moss. Soon thereafter, William Bramhall bought it for about £400. Bramhall was called fee farmer of the manor.[9] This seems peculiar since King James's charter declared Congleton a free borough of itself, with a body corporate composed of the mayor, eight aldermen, sixteen capital burgesses, and a high steward who was "a person of high repute and special eminence to be elected by the corporation." Serving largely the role of legal representative and advisor to the corporation, the high steward made an official yearly visit to the town, which was celebrated with the presentation of gifts and a communal feast.

John Bradshawe was rapidly becoming a man of substance. He returned to Congleton about 1630 when he became Steward of Glossop and was appointed legal advisor or councilor to the corporation of Congleton. The honor of being a freeman of the town was conferred upon him—"Spent on Sacke and Beere at the makinge Mr Bradshaw a freeman, viis." In 1634, he had made a bond to pay Philip Antrobus (of Peover) the sizeable sum of £93.[10]

Bradshawe, now a well-known lawyer in Congleton and Earl Arundel's steward of Glossop for the prior seven years, became Mayor of Congleton in 1637;[11] and some years later, the same John Bradshawe, to the general satisfaction of most historians,[12] became high steward of Congleton. William Newton, probably a relative of Bradshawe's brother-in-law, was deputy mayor.

John Savage, Viscount Savage, son of the last Halton Honor steward, and *Mr. Bradshaw*, presumably the mayor, offered £900 to purchase, on behalf of the town and tenants, the manor of Congleton for the king in June 1639. The deal was not struck, and Henry Brooke of Norton acquired the manor of Congleton in 1650, then granted a part of it to Thomas Warburton in 1652. Both Brooke and Warburton were distantly related to John Bradshawe's wife.

For the purposes of religious government, Congleton was a part of the parish of Astbury and possessed a small wooden chapel in the town. The church ordinances required that "in the highest seat of the Chapel on the south side shall sit the Mayor of the town, and in the highest seat on the north side shall be the wife of the Mayor." The ancient chapel was taken down in 1740. The actual parish church, St. Mary Astbury, is about a mile southwest of Congleton. It is one of the most beautiful churches in the country.[13] The rector of Astbury from 1626 to 1649 was Dr. Thomas Dod, archdeacon of Richmond, dean of Ripon, chaplain-in-ordinary to James I and Charles I, as well as rector of Malpas. At the time, John Bradshawe was mayor of Congleton. The churchwardens were nominated by the eight parish provosts, popularly called the *Posts*. They were the Mayor of Congleton and the owners of Great Moreton Hall, Little Moreton Hall, Yeaton (now Eaton) Hall, Rode Hall, Davenport Hall, Somerford Hall, and Brereton Hall.[14]

The mayor of Congleton was required to live in the town for the whole time he was in office. Bradshawe arranged a seven-year lease for a house and lands in Congleton from Richard Greene in April 1637, but Bradshawe's lease was not to commence until Greene's grandmother and mother died. A fine timber-framed house is pictured in Stephens's *History of Congleton* and identified as John Bradshawe's house.[15] While waiting for the lease to come into effect, Greene built up a debt to Bradshawe.

It is possible that Bradshawe and his wife shared the house with the two elderly Greene women.

In May, all Congleton was mourning the death of Lady Brereton, the wife of Bradshawe's friend and patron, Sir William Brereton. Through this lady, Brereton was related to Richard Bradshaw, merchant and mayor of Chester in 1648. Richard's brother, Edward Bradshaw, was sheriff of Chester City in 1636 and mayor in 1647 and 1653. Their half brother, another John Bradshaw, was probably the attorney general of Cheshire from 1637 throughout the interregnum. In the 1630s, Brereton had been one of the busiest Cheshire magistrates. He was also a conscientious deputy lieutenant of the county.

By 1639, John Bradshawe was attempting to collect debts from Richard Greene and several kinsmen. Peter Daniel of Over-Tabley, MP for Chester (1625), county deputy controller for the Crown (feodary), and a strong supporter of Parliament, addressed a letter to his worthy friend:

John Bradshaw, Esq, at his house in Congleton—Being yesterday at Stapeley with my Daughter Greene she acquainted mee with some debts that were betwixt my sonne Greene and you and beinge about to depart came a letter as it seemed from you to my sonne Greene which in his absence she opened and read and acquainted mee with the contents. It seemeth by the letter that you have dealt favourable with him which he either slighteth or fourshoweth, for which he is blame worthie. my intention was to have conferred with him and my daughter about the debt and other business, but missinge him I pressed my daughter to send him to Tabley to resolve a course of satisfaction)

But seeing it is brought to that issue as your letter expresseth. Let me mediate for a little time longer, for if you have (as I am assured of it) granted the time past to Mrs Sneade (Sneyd?). Doe me the favour as bestow a little time upon mee and it shall not be longe. I crave but until the assize weeke, and though he and his waies faile yet I will not.

The truth is this, my sonne and I are to sell some Land to Dr. More; all things are agreed upon the fininshinge by fine and recovery you . . . . the assize must perfect, that being donne, I will see you payed with the Doctor's money.

This I hope will content you the rather at my desire and that all prosecution may be suspended till that time. I shall take it as especiall courtesie, at all times ready to requite, the interim an expression of an thankfulness.

Thus desiringe to receave your answere with a fiatt ut petitur my respects remembered to your self and my cosen (cousin) [16] *your wife, I remayne Yours to serve you Peter Daniel Tabley 6 7ber (October) 1639*

Daniel then took the opportunity to attach a PS, which seems to bear on Bradshawe's position as steward of the corporation of Congleton;

Sir I am to desire your advice in a business of importance at this assizes but your corporation and mine cannot agree yet I will find out a way to meete with you and instruct you if you condisend to pleasure me as to give meeting, at some place neere to you not hinderinge your occasions. My daughter Greene will this day send unto you to the like purpose be pleased to take notice of my request, and satisfie her that you have condisended, that her mind be not further troubled.

Peter Daniel's well-intentioned promise did not come true, and it was not until October 25, 1641, that Bradshawe became fully possessed of the Congleton lease. Because of the old debts, Greene gave Bradshawe security on other lands in Stapeley to guarantee that Bradshawe would "peaceably and without interrupcon injoy" the Congleton properties for seven years. While in residence, the former mayor and now high steward lived in considerable style. Thomas Parnell[17] and Samuel Roe[18] were taken into Bradshawe's service as clerks. Henry Bradshawe of Marple mentioned his brother's "five servants" in Congleton. Head, in his book *Congelton*, written about 1887, says, "During Bradshawe's mayoralty his personal attention was much given to the welfare of good government of the borough. Here in his old house of Elizabethan character, with its high painted gables, quaint windows, and black and white diapered walls, Bradshawe lived in no mean state; keeping an ample retinue of servants, and surrounded by such aristocratic appendages as the custom of the time required. It may be inferred, too, that at this early stage of his career, during the brief quietitude of his country life, the lofty domineering tendency of his nature began to evince itself. His shrewd knowledge of the law; the strict observance of all details attending municipal matters; his jealous extraction of the recognition of his superiority from those beneath him either in intellect or social status, begat among his small circle of Congletonian acquaintances sentiments of either esteem or fear. From these he extracted the homage due to his civic office as appears by the statues ordaining that 'Aldermen in the thire gownes, the rest of the comon councell in their cloakes, and the freemen with their halberts to attend the Maior for the tyme beinge att faires, &c'. And that four constables and five freemen 'shalbe be ready with theire sev'rall halberts to attende the Maior for the tyme beinge unto and from the Chapell every Sunday and other Holy Daie to divine service and sermons and at other convenient tymes and places as they shalbe thereunto required."

Other business was taking Bradshawe away from Congleton. Momentous things were taking place in London, and Bradshawe must have been there. King Charles had manipulated the Scottish Parliament, attempted to impose *The Book of Common Prayer* on the Scottish church, and had been routed by the Scots army at Berwick. At this point, John Bradshawe's old Gray's Inn colleague, Earl of Strafford (Thomas Wentworth), was called back from Ireland. Strafford was a determined king's minister, and he nearly exhausted his personal fortune raising an army of Irishmen with which to punish the Scots. "Never came a man to so mightily lost a business" was Strafford's comment. King Charles needed money to bring the Scots under subjection. Strafford had squeezed the Irish parliament for every penny they could manage. After eleven years of personal rule, King Charles agreed to summon an English Parliament in March 1640. The newly convened Parliament had other grievances to settle with the king than just his squabble with the Scots. In fact, many members of the Short Parliament were sympatric to the Scots.

William Brereton's candidature for parliament threw him into confederacy with some men who would soon become his worst enemies: Lord Strange (the future Earl of Derby), Viscount Savage, Lord Cholmondley, and Sir Thomas Aston.

Several authorities take the view that Bradshawe was judge of the London Sheriff's Court as early as 1640,[19] and that would not be inconsistent with the scant record we have of his whereabouts at the time.

In May, the king decided that Parliament had nothing to offer him, and he dissolved it. No sooner was this Short Parliament "dissolved than a general opposition to the war with Scotland surfaced. Lord Thomas Savile (first Viscount Savile of Castlebar), who entertained a fierce hatred of Earl Strafford, sent a messenger to Scotland bearing a hollow staff which enclosed a paper promising aid and encouragement to the defeat of Strafford. Saville had probably counterfeited the signatures of six great English lords (Bedford, Essex, Brooke, Warwick, Say and Sele, Mandeville,) and presumably their seals to the bottom of the document. These lords, mostly members of the Providence Company, agreed with

Savile in their hatred of Strafford but would have cautiously avoiding signing an incriminating paper.

The Scots, seizing the offensive, entered England in August and routed Earl Strafford's ill-equipped troops. From that moment, Strafford was doomed. He endeavored in vain to inspire his troops and intimidate the king's councilors who were asking for peace with Scotland. Lords Wharton and Howard attempted to present a petition for peace, but Strafford caused them to be arrested, stand courts-martial, and unsuccessfully demanded that they be shot at the head of the army as aiders and abettors of revolt. Strafford suggested an Irish army be brought over to England, or failing that, a French force. In October, the king, Hamilton, Strafford, Laud, Falkland, Holland, and Lord Strange met at York. The council urged that the king call a Parliament. Charles was profoundly dispirited. He was out of money with no means of raising more. His soldiers mutinied and deserted in whole regiments. His subjects were on the verge of resistance everywhere. Even though the son of a Scotsman himself, he had counted on the English displaying hatred to the Scots. No such public hatred developed. The Scots, ostensibly his enemies, were more favored by his subjects than his own court because of their stance against the bishops and *The Book of Common Prayer*.

He commissioned sixteen peers to open negotiations with the Scots and summoned the Parliament, which would become known as the *Long Parliament*, assembled on November 3. In vain he attempted to influence the Parliamentary elections, but his chosen candidates were largely rejected, and even Sir Thomas Gardiner whom the king wished to have as speaker was turned down.

The future Royalists—Culpepper, Digby, and others—were opposed to the king's policies and wished to remove Catholics from high office, separate the king from his "*evil-councillors*," impeach Archbishop Laud, have trennial Parliaments, and restore government according to law; but unlike the men of the Providence Company, they were unprepared to go to extreme lengths to achieve their goals. John Pym and the Providence Company men had already determined that the Earl Strafford, as representing one of the *king's evil councillors,* had to be executed.

On November 3, 1640, the new members gathered for the Parliament, which would outlive the king who summoned it. Nearly all the members were prepared to present some petition of grievance from their constituents. The root of all these grievances, said Digby, was "the want of Parliaments . . . The People of England cannot open their ears, their hearts, their mouths, nor their purses to his Majesty, but in Parliament." The members set about to determine "whether the king should be permitted to govern the people of England by his sole will and pleasure, as an absolute monarch, and without the assistance of Parliament, as he had lately done, or whether he should be compelled to admit the two houses of Parliament to a participation in the legislative authority with him, according to the constitution of England ever since the first institution of the House of Commons in the reign of Henry III." The decision was easily reached, the two houses were declared an integral part of the government of the kingdom, and any attempt to govern without them was an unconstitutional and arbitrary exercise of royal prerogative.

Before an Act for Perpetual Parliaments could be passed, the gathering was aroused by rumors of foreign armies sent to support the king, an Irish army sent over by Strafford, and the king's intention to forcibly secure the Tower of London. Now events escalated rapidly. Three days after the opening of Parliament, a member for Cambridge, Oliver Cromwell, rose to make his maiden speech and demand the release of freeborn John Lilburne. Two days later, the Commons impeached Strafford and demanded his immediate imprisonment. Within weeks, Parliament had released Lilburne, Prynne, and Burton. They reached London in late November and paraded through the streets of London in joy and triumph escorted by a hundred coaches, two thousand horsemen, and a vast crowd of well-wishers on foot. A week later, Bastwick was released from imprisonment and received a similar welcome. Strafford was impeached and charged with high treason. December 11, Archbishop Laud was accused of high treason. March 11, Laud was committed to the tower, and Strafford's trial began on the twenty-second. When the court failed to convict Strafford of high treason, Pym moved for a Parliamentary Bill of Attainder. Commons passed the bill by a majority of 204; the Lords majority was seven.

Strafford was convicted of treason, not by a court of law but by an act of Parliament. Strafford's life now depended on the king, who eventually persuaded himself that the safety of his queen and his son, the prince, required his submission. He signed the act. Strafford was beheaded on Tower Hill, May 12. At the same time, the king had put his signature to an historic bill, guaranteeing that Parliament could never be dissolved without its own consent.

An act was passed that declared the court of the Star Chamber an arbitrary and tyrannical tribunal, unknown to the ancient laws of the country and in violation of the provisions of Magna Carta. The Star Chamber court at Westminster and the same jurisdiction used in the Star Chamber of the Duchy of Lancaster were forever swept away on August 1, 1641. The king assented.

On the same day, the burgesses of Newcastle-under-Lyne, Staffordshire, elected John Bradshaw, esq., of Congleton to be their high steward. It is presumed that this is the regicide, but that is by no means certain.[20]

In August, the king went to Scotland. Pym, Mandeville, Fiennes, and Hampden realized that once in Edinburgh, the king might discover the fatal contents of Saville's letter inviting the Scots to invade England. For that and other reasons, both houses wanted to appoint commissioners to spy on the king but were unsure of how to appoint such a delegation without the king's assent. They revived a medieval practice of voting an ordinance but with a new innovation; in the Middle Ages, the king had issued an ordinance without the necessary assent of his Parliament, and now the Parliament declared an ordinance without the necessary knowledge or assent of the king. They drew upon the precedent of the *ordainers* of King Edward II's reign. From the general tenor of those ordinances, however, it was assumed that authority of Parliament resided in the baronetage. Lingard's *History of England* said of that time, "The Commons had nothing to do but to present petitions and to grant money."

In the amazing first year of the Long Parliament, Laud and Strafford had been removed without the king's approval, planting fear in all the other king's councilors, and Parliament had achieved an unprecedented degree of sovereignty and stability. Some thought the battle had been won. As John Pym and his followers had become ever more zealous and uncompromising, the more reasonable members of Parliament showed themselves increasingly prepared to defend the king and the bishops. Party names were attached to the opposing camps. King's supporters were *Cavaliers*. Parliament's supporters were *Roundheads*. At Whitehall Palace, the king had often been beset by petitioners. Those who aggressively expressed their discontent risked being beaten or wounded by disbanded soldiers who rallied around the king awaiting employment. The haughty carriage and flamboyant dress of this quasi-royal guard earned them the name of Cavaliers. The petitioners, mostly in plain attire and with their hair shorn of lovelocks, were called Roundheads.

Figure 11. King Charles First

The king had no time to gain any advantage from his newfound friends. A huge rebellion broke out in Ireland in October. Thousands of Scottish and English settlers were killed by the native Irish, now released from Strafford's oppressive rule. Pym blamed the king, or rather, the queen who had been in secret correspondence with the Irish Catholics.

Sir Simonds D'Ewes told the story of events in the House of Commons on November 30, 1641 in his journal.[21] Sir John Strangwayes rose in the Commons to say he had received information of a "plott or conspiracie for the distruction of some members of this howse which he conceived to bee little lesse than treason and said that hee was informed that some of the members of this howse were either contrivers of it or consenters to it." He asked for a select committee to examine the matter. The Commons called for Strangewayes to reveal his information. Strangewayes named no names but produced a paper telling of a discourse between an apprentice named Cole, his master Mr. Mansfield, and John Michelson, master of divinity. Cole had told them on Wednesday night, November 24, that Mansfield, who was a constable, had given him a sword and told him to go to Westminster Palace Yard where he would meet a thousand more armed men. Mansfield said they had been sent for by some Parliament men because a vote was likely to go against *the best affected partie*. The vote went well, however, and they all returned home. The Commons conceived that Strangewayes had made a larger accusation of treason than the paper warranted. Cole, Mansfield, Michelson, and Dr. Escot were summoned to the Commons. Mr. Kirton, another MP, said he could add some more particulars. John Pym said he had heard there was a conspiracy by some members to accuse other members of treason. Kirton produced a paper which was read by John Wilde, the clerk of the house. Captain Venn, an MP, was named in Kirton's paper: "That one Mr. Lavender a Cittizen of London being in the howse of Mr. Farlow in Woodstreete taking tobacco with some others . . . (when) there came word that a message was come from Captain Ven (who) desires him to come away speedily armed to the howse of Commons for swaords were there drawne . . . This relation was subscribed by Mr. Bradshaw[22] (of Grayes Inn), Mr. Lawrence Rudyerd, Mr. Farlow of Cambridge and Mr. Farlow of Woodstreete." Captain Venn offered to speak, but the house decided it was not "fitt till somewhat were proved against him." Warrants were issued for Lavender, Farlow, and others, including probably Bradshaw. Further enquires into the matter were apparently shelved, and Clarendon says, "they who offered to make proof . . . were appointed to attend many days, but . . . were never admitted to be heard."

Parliament assumed the prerogative of nominating the lord lieutenants and deputy lieutenants of the counties. Sir William Brereton and John Bradshaw[23] were among those nominated deputy lieutenants for the county of Lancashire, although other business prevented Brereton from assuming the role. Ashton, Shuttleworth, Rigby, and John Moore, members of Parliament, were sent to Lancashire to organise the militia; and Moore carried express instructions for Sir William Brereton MP, the newly appointed military commander of Cheshire, requiring him to transport the horse troops of Lancashire and Cheshire into Ireland for reinforcements of the English troops already there. Lord Newburgh, chancellor of the Duchy of Lancaster, was ordered to issue Commissions of the Peace to John Bradshaw,[24] Thomas Fell, and others.

There had been mobs in the London streets the whole year. The Parliament presented the Grand Remonstrance to the king in December. It was not at all the Christmas gift the royal family would have wished.

When a rumor that Parliament was planning to impeach the queen reached the king's ear, he ordered the imprisonment of Lord Mandeville and Pym, Hampden, Holles, Strode, and Haselrig of the Commons.[25] On January 4, when the Parliament reassembled, the king personally invaded the House of Commons and took the Speaker's chair to order their arrest. They were not there. The king pursued the *five members* to their sanctuary in the city of London and at the Guildhall in front of the Common Council demanded they be handed over. The council solemnly refused to answer the demand. The king cast his eye upon an ardent Presbyterian London sheriff and told him he would dine with him. The sheriff bowed, and when the assemblage rose, received the king into his house with all splendor and respect. If, as some authorities maintain, Bradshawe was judge of the London Sheriff's Court at this time, he would have been present.

The king left both London and Parliament dumbstruck with fear and anger, but more importantly, he left himself and his family unprotected. His Cavaliers had fled.

The Parliament convinced themselves that an enormous breach of privilege had taken place. It was agreed they could not sit in safety until reparation had been made and a trusty guard mounted to protect them from similar insults. They adjourned for six days. Every hour of those days, the city and the Parliament grew closer and mutually reinforced each other's courage. The aldermen pressured Mayor Richard Gurney to call out London's own private militia, the Trained Bands. The Royalist Gurney refused and was removed. The Trained Bands mustered anyway by someone's orders. The Puritan Issac Pennington[26] was put in Gurney's place. Within days, six thousand London citizens were under arms. They provided daily guards for Parliament—one hundred men to each house. They would become the backbone of the Parliamentary infantry, just as Cromwell's Ironsides became the strength of the cavalry.

John Bradshawe was at Issac Pennington's side in the city of London. Alone in Congleton, Mary (Marbury) Bradshawe took her husband's sister to task about an overdue debt of £100. Mary addressed her sister-in-law, Dorothy Newton:

Sister Newton I received a letter from you about the last day of November last, wherein you said Mr. Bradshaw hath given you longer time for the paiment (sic) of the 100£ which you owe him upon condition that you send the interest to mee within A fortnight after your messenger George Newton had him here, which he promised should bee performed; but some six or seven weeks after in stead of the money George newton promised should be sent mee you conveyed mee a letter without a messenger, not desiring any Answere to it, but requesting mee to forbeare the money untill Christmas, and then you would send it, but when Christmas came no monie came; tis just like the rest of your doings, for ever since I came here I have seene nothing but deceit and jugling in you, you are the most lawles woman that I ever knew, for you neither regard bond, promis, letter, mesage, or anie thing if you can pay your debts with sleights and tricks 1.) tis well for you my husband cannot paye those ingagements he is in for you and other of his kindred after that manner, but payes redy money; if you and some others of you that have land could manage your Affaires no better, how can you expect that hee which hath no land should paye your depts (sic), but indeed there is no shame in some of his kindred expectations from him, except people have A desire to ruine him. I never see the like of some of you. I have sent this bearer for the interest, or to know from you, if you can and will tell truth, when I shall have it you would not vouchsafe my husband an answere to his letter nor bee seen by his messenger; but I bid this messenger staye for and answere, the interest as I take it the 4th of April next comes to sixteen pound; and for 100£ his promise to give you longe day, being only conditional and broken of your part I conceive he is not bound, therefore if you will not give newe and sufficient securities for the payment of it uppon those days George Newton mentioned to my husband from you you must expect present suite, but if you will putt in good and sufficient securitie, and you shall have (sic; hand ?) in your olde bond when that is done, but you must first give me the names of two at least sufficient sureties all which being done you shall find me your loving sister, Mary Bradshawe—Congleton, 29th Januarie 1641 (1642 new style).

Just nineteen days before this letter was written, King Charles, accompanied only by his wife, his children, and some attendants, left London and the palace of Whitehall, to which he was destined never to return except on his way to trial and condemnation before Judge John Bradshawe. The Parliament passed the Militia Ordinance on January 31.

King Charles met the Prince of Wales at Greenwich, intending to withdraw northward. At Theobalds in Hertfordshire, twelve commissioners from the Commons overtook him and presented Parliament's demand that he return to London. Clearly Parliament intended to show they knew the king was on the run.

A week later at Newmarket, other Parliamentary commissioners presented petitions to the king demanding, among other things, that he deliver the authority over the kingdom's militia and the munitions in the Tower of London to Parliament. They presented the Militia Ordinance to the king for assent on February 22. The king refused.

Two days later, the queen gathered up the crown jewels and departed for Holland to solicit continental aid for her beleaguered husband. The Militia Ordinance was confirmed by both houses on March 5 without the king's assent. Parliament secured the Tower. The king rejected all entreaties and continued north to York.

From all over the kingdom, petitioners converged on York. John Bradshaw of Bradshaw (1583-1665/6), Warden of Manchester, and many other gentlemen of Lancashire journeyed to York to present their petition asking that the king return to his Parliament.

Negotiations went on, but it was no longer Parliament addressing the king or the king addressing Parliament. Both began to appeal directly to the whole kingdom through pamphlets, periodicals, and occasional journals.[27] Volunteer messengers sold them about the country, and the people crowded to buy and read them. At the heart of this novel appeal to public opinion lay the conflict of national sovereignty versus the divine right of kings, although the authors constantly professed that the laws, the statutes, the traditions, and the customs were the only legitimate criteria of the dispute. King Charles took advantage of this and published his views in the name of his council, claiming to speak for *Old England* and her laws. He aimed at exposing the illegality and pretensions of Parliament while remaining silent about his own secret despotic views and ultimate designs. Parliament attempted to suppress the Royalist publications while, in contrast, the king ordered the messages of Parliament to be printed side by side with his own answers. The Royalist faction in Parliament grew stronger and bolder, but a little-noticed member from Cambridgeshire, Oliver Cromwell, began to watch, denounce, and expose the Royalists. He, more than any other member, was already involved in the machinations of revolution. There was little doubt that war was eminent.

In April, the king and his party of three hundred horsemen were refused entrance in the city of Hull by the governor, Sir John Hotham. The king proclaimed Hotham and his followers traitors and addressed a message to Parliament demanding justice for such an outrage. James Stanley, Lord Strange urged that the Royal Standard should be raised at Warrington in Lancashire. The king agreed that it would be when the time came and appointed Strange the Royalist lord lieutenant of Lancashire and Cheshire. Strange handed the king a contribution of £40,000 and returned to put his his home counties in preparedness for the king.

Lancashire remained the strongest Catholic county. Since the time of the Reformation, Catholics who refused to take the oath of abjuration had been stigmatized as *recusants* and deprived of all their offensive weapons. King James and King Charles had levied heavy fines on the recusants throughout their reign. Now, espousing the desperate royal cause, a number of powerful Lancashire Catholics (Trafford, Townley, Anderton, Gerard, Clifton, Cansfield, William Bradshaw of Haigh,[28] and others) petitioned the king to have their weapons returned so that they might defend their king, country, and families. King Charles graciously agreed, more out of need than conviction. At the end of May, a number of Royalist Catholics and others assembled about seven miles from Lancaster armed in a warlike manner. The sheriff was called in to disarm them.

The Earl of Derby took Roger Bradshaw of Haigh (1628-1684), the fourteen-year-old Catholic heir to the estate at Wigan, into his care but arranged for him to be raised a Protestant. Parliament's reply to the king's proclamation of Hotham's treason was little short of a declaration of war. It was considered so by both sides.

June 9, 1642: "Votes and declaration of both Houses of Parliament. Whereas it appears that the King, seduced by wicked counsel, intends to make war against his Parliament: and in pursuance thereof; under pretense of a guard for his person, has actually begun to levy forces both of horse and foot, and sent out a summons throughout Yorkshire and other counties for calling together greater numbers . . . The Lords and the Commons do declare that it shall be lawful for anyone to contribute money, plate, arms, horses, and other supplies, to those persons whom the House shall appoint for the preservation of the public peace, and for the defense of the King and both Houses of Parliament from violence, and to uphold the power and privileges of Parliament. It is understood that whatsoever is brought in shall not at all be employed on any other occasion than the purposes specified; which are, to maintain the Protestant religion, the King's authority and his person in his royal dignity, the free course of justice, the laws of the land, the peace of the kingdom, and the privileges of Parliament against any force, which shall oppose them." At the urging of the London preachers, the citizens surrendered their plate, their money, and their jewels to Parliament. For ten days the Guildhall received such an influx of plate that there were neither enough men to receive it nor enough room to hold it. As judge of the Sheriff's Court at the Guildhall, Bradshawe would have assisted.

"Poor women brought in the weddings rings and their gold or silver hairpins. On the other side, the colleges of Oxford sent plate to the King and the colleges at Cambridge were prepared to follow suit until Cromwell prevented them."

Thirty-two Lords and sixty members of the Commons departed London to join the king at York. The departure of so many Royalists left the leaders of the revolution in undisputed possession of power in Whitehall. Lord Chancellor Littleton sent the great seal to the king and thereby produced a furor in London because government was generally considered to be inherent in the possessor of the seal. The house ordered Philip Wharton lord lieutenant of Lancashire, June 27, to deliver all the magazines of Lancashire for the use of Parliament. Lord Strange defied the order, took possession of magazines and arms for the king, and advanced on Manchester. Philip Wharton also moved toward Manchester. Lord Strange reached Manchester first, and there, on the afternoon of July 5, 1642, the first blood of the English Civil Wars was shed. Finding that those in charge of the Manchester garrison would not submit, Strange launched an attack. After losing twenty-seven (some say less) of his own men and killing eleven of the citizens, he was forced to withdraw. Parliament ordered that an account of the attack be printed in London: " . . . Wee expect daily, when the L. Strange will visit us again, but I hope the Lord will enable us against his coming. They give out many threatening speeches against us, and it is thought here, that he hath sent for many more forces toward York . . . This is the beginning of Civill Warre, being the first stroke, that hath been struck, and the first bullet that hath been shot; but God knowes, when the ending will be, or when the troubles of this Kingdome will grow to a period. Many thousands, I doubt, will lose their lives, before that this Kingdom will be settled in peace and unity, as it hath bein formerly; for no man knoweth the cruelty of warre, but those of us who have felt and tryed it; for when that time cometh, many a child will be fatherlesse, and many a poor wife husbandlesse." Cynical proposals for accommodation had been sent to the king in the middle of June, and Parliament received the answer they anticipated. Civil war was put to the Commons on July 9.

Parliament sent directions into every county for the immediate organization of the militia, ordered every citizen to disobey the king's Commission of Array, negotiated a loan from the city of London, and sent commissioners to report on the king's activities in York.

A group of Cavaliers invited Strange to a public entertainment in Manchester where the king's call to arms was read out. Four hundred Royalist troops were mustered. Manchester was still a Royalist town. Angered by the effrontery of this blatant act, two deputy lieutenants mustered their Roundhead countryside forces, entered town, and beat to arms. In the brawl, several of Lord Strange's men were wounded. A local weaver named Richard Percival was killed. A shot just missed Strange as he rode away toward Ordsall. Now under pressure from his supporters, the king issued a Commission of Array on July 10. Lord Strange assumed that he still possessed the king's promise that the Royal Standard would be raised at Warrington, and so in order to be ready, called every able-bodied Lancashire man to muster at one of the three places. This sort of feudal muster had not taken place since the threat of the Spanish Armada, yet at Bury Heath, Ormskirk Moor, and Preston Moor, groups of up to twenty thousand bewildered men and boys appeared carrying their best rusty swords, pikes, and muskets. Strange was proceeding into Chester and North Wales to conduct similar musters when he received the king's order to cease such noisy gatherings. The Privy Council whispered in the king's ear that it was unsafe to entrust so great a power to the young and ambitious Lord Strange. The king removed him from the lieutenacy of Cheshire. The king's promise to raise the Royal Standard at Warrington was withdrawn. John Savage, now newly created Earl Rivers, was appointed joint lord lieutenant of Lancashire to keep check on Lord Strange.

It was John Savage who had worked with John Bradshawe to attempt the purchase of Congleton some four of five years earlier.

War measures were adopted. The Earl of Essex was appointed general in chief of a Parliamentary army—twenty thousand infantry and forty-five hundred cavalry. Lord Kimbolton (later Earl of Manchester), Lord Brook, Sir John Merrick, John Hampden, Denzil Holles, and Oliver Cromwell received military commands. Parliament seized all the public revenues, ordered the counties to provide arms and ammunition, and dispatched the lord lieutenants and MPs to recruit in their home counties. In the counties, many of the gentry were still hoping to postpone or prevent armed conflict. In Nantwich, Cheshire, Royalists and their Catholic supporters paraded about the town, preventing Sir William Brereton from recruiting.

The Royal Standard was raised at Nottingham on July 22. The Royalist lord lieutenants were ordered to return to their counties and read the royal

Commission of Array. In Leicester, the Royalist mayor was forbidden to read the commission by the Puritan Lord Francis Willoughby of Parham, who had been sent by Parliament to proclaim the Militia Ordinance. In London, the mayor did read the king's Commission of Array but was soon thereafter clapped up in the tower. The attempts to read one of the two rival proclamations caused outbreaks of violence throughout the kingdom.

On September 16, Lord Strange was impeached for high treason by vote of the knights, citizens, and burgesses in parliament assembled. The sheriffs of Lancashire were ordered to apprehend Strange and bring him up to London. At this crisis, the king ordered Strange to assemble all his forces and join the royal army, which had moved through Chester and was now assembling at Shrewsbury. The men who had mustered in response to the Commission of Array in July and August had long since wandered back to their homes, unfed and unequipped, from their makeshift camps on the moor and heath.

Manchester was being fortified for Parliament. A Cavalier wrote, "Manchester is the very London of these parts, the liver that sends blood into all the counties there aboute, and until it is cleansed or obstructed, I cannot imagine that there can be any safety in this neighbourhood". At the headquarters of the royal army, the king hesitated on his plan to move toward London and decided that Manchester must first be shattered. On Sunday, September 24, Lord Strange arrived outside Manchester at the head of four thousand infantry, two hundred heavy dragoons, one hundred cavalry, and a company of artillery with seven field pieces.

In anticipation of such an assault, some wealthy townspeople and nearby countryside landowners had hired an experienced German soldier named Johann Rosworm, lately come from the Irish rebellion to place the city in a state of readiness for the Parliament party. He was guaranteed £30 by Henry Bradshawe of Marple; Richard Heyricke, the warden of Manchester; and twenty other gentlemen.[29] Rosworm wrote that the town was four-to-one for the king, and some Royalists publicly threatened to cut his throat if he attempted to keep Lord Strange from entering. Lord Strange sent two gentlemen to buy Rosworm's allegiance with a gift of £150. Rosworm indignantly refused and set about fortifying the town. He ordered mud barricades to be thrown up at crucial points. Chains were hung neck high between buildings and posts sunk into the streets to hinder cavalry charges. Four days before the arrival of Lord Strange's force, the church bells had been rung backward as a secret signal to the Parliament men of the countryside to bring their weapons and enter the town. Townspeople, perhaps under duress, were employed casting bullets night and day. Col. Ralph Asheton commanded the county militia. Mr. John Moore, Col. Richard Holland of Denton, Sir Thomas Stanley, Capt. JohnBradshaw of Bradshaw,[30] Mr. Holcroft of Holcroft, Mr. Hyde of Denton, Mr. Peter Egerton of Shaw, Mr. Erid of Denton, and Mr. Booth (brother to Sir William Brereton's late wife) commanded companies of musketeers and pikemen.

On Monday, the attack began in the midst of a pouring rainstorm. Rosworm's employment had been only to advise and direct, but he took fifty musketeers and stood firm at the weakest point, Salford Bridge. General Fairfax wrote in his memoirs:

The Earl of Derby (Lord Strange) began to play with his cannon about twelve o' clock upon Deansgate and Salford Bridge; and this afternoon the battle was hot on both sides; most of the towns-men constantly charged and discharged most resolutely, to the great admiration and terror of the enemy. While the battle raged, a number of soldiers were dispatched by Lord Strange to set fire to two barns which stood near the end of Deansgate (then extending only to the end of Black King Street) and the flames burst forth with so much fury, that, had not the wind changed at that critical moment, it is probable that the town would have been reduced to ashes. A shout of 'The town is ours, The town is ours' was now set up by the assailants, but, by the valour and energy of Captain Bradshaw and his band of militia, they were beaten back, and many of them slain in the assault.

Rosworm wrote in his own *Complaynt*;

I was necessitated to send 20 of my Muskettiers to Captain Bradshaw at Deansgate.

That afternoon, the assailants turned on the bridge where Rosworm and his remaining thirty men held out. On Tuesday, half his musketeers deserted, and Rosworm held the rest together under threat of his drawn sword. Other volunteers came to his aid, and his force finally numbered twenty-eight. Captain Bradshaw's command cannot have been much different. Lord Strange offered at least two terms of surrender, but the garrison was determined to "maintain their cause and their armes to the utmost drop of their blood." Thursday morning, a youth standing on the parapet was killed by a cannonball. The Royalist Captain Standish of Duxbury was killed by a sniper shooting from the tower of the collegiate church. That evening Lord Strange received word that his father, the 6th Earl of Derby, had died. A second message came from the king. Having heard that the parliamentarian army was moving out from London to met him, the king ordered the new 7th Earl of Derby to discontinue the siege of Manchester and bring his troops to Shrewsbury immediately! Prisoners were exchanged, and the dead were collected on Saturday morning. The six-day siege was lifted. The garrison of Manchester was down to their last barrel of powder and a few feet of match. According to Thomas Hawkins's eyewitness account, read in the House of Commons on October 2, the garrison lost only four men during the siege while the Royalists lost two hundred, including Sir Gilbert Gerrard. From afar, John Bradshawe anxiously awaited word from Manchester and his brother.

The king's Cavaliers clashed with the Earl Essex's Roundheads at Edgehill, near Kineton, Warkwickshire, in October. Neither side was sure of the outcome. King Charles moved through Reading toward London. Essex blocked the king at the battle of Turnham Green in November. John Venn and his Parliament troop commanded Windsor Castle. The people of Windsor were predominantly in favor of Parliament, and not without reason. The Crown had strictly enforced forest laws on the residents in Windsor Forest, punished poaching with vigor, and seized common lands for enclosure.

As all combatants moved their attention on London, the Royalists of Cheshire agreed a cessation of arms for a month. In Lancashire, the towns, villages, and even manors were garrisoned for either king or Parliament, and the skirmishes that were fought seemed more like family feuds than full-scale war. There were furious but short engagements.

Early in December, Captain Venables and Capt. Robert Bradshaw ventured out of Bolton with their Parliamentarian companies of cavalry toward Wigan where Royalist troops captured them. Robert Bradshaw was still prisoner in the following summer.

> *To the keeper of the Prison in Ludlow Castle—Whereas George Dodding esq, Ralph Arderne Esq, Francis Fitzhugh, George Tolson, and Robert Bradshaw have been committed to the Castle of Beaumorrice for levying war against his Majesty, which place in respect of the situation thereof is subject to danger and is therefore thought fitt that they bee removed from thence. These are therefore, in his Majstys name, to require you to receive the said prisoners into your custody in the Castle of Ludlow, & Them there to retain til you have received further orders or that shall be delivered according to lawe,—Chester, dated 5 June 1643*
>   *N. Byron (Nicholas Byron, Royalist Governor of Chester,*
>   *Col-General of Cheshire and Shropshire)*

Sir Thomas Fairfax moved his troops into Lancashire early in 1643, by which time even the Royalists were acknowledging the shire was a *lost country*. In September, Essex had pushed his Parliamentary forces into Reading and blocked the king's forces from reaching London. King Charles declared that the Lords and Commons were not a free Parliament and in effect denied their authority. They denied his. The government of archbishops and bishops had been denounced as evil and swept away by ordinance of Parliament. Charles, it appeared, was negotiating for an Irish army to be sent over to England. He was also pressing for more continental aid and reassuring the Scots of his good intentions.

Toward the end of 1643, John Pym and his supporters in the English Parliament were frantically negotiating a Scottish alliance. A covenanting army of twenty-one thousand under Earl Leven would be sent across the border into England to support Parliament. The price was money to support the Scots army and the signature of members of the English Parliament on the Scots Solemn League and National Covenant, which stated the Protestant religion should be maintained in Scotland, according to the form already established there, and reformation would be effected in England. John Pym had signed in September with supreme confidence that he could control the Scot Presbyterians as well as his own anti-Presbyterian faction in Parliament. The ever-pragmatic Cromwell considered it a political expedient to gain much-needed forces. Sir Henry Vane the younger, who was more religiously tolerant than Cromwell, was suspicious of its dour Calvinist Presbyterian content. He altered the English wording of the National Covenant in such a way that would it leave it open to wider, vaguer, and more liberal interpretation. John Pym, master propagandist, inspired organizer of civil demonstrations and the moving spirit of rebellion, died in December.

As a means of searching out Catholics, every officer or commander in service of Parliament was ordered to sign the National Covenant before February 5 or be discharged from his command and kept in custody. But it was not only Catholics who refused the covenant. Independents, Baptists, and followers of dissenting sects also refused. From this coercion to conform, or at least from about this time, emerged a parliamentary political group of Independents, distinct from those who were only religious Independents. Sir Arthur Haselrig, Thomas Harrison, Thomas Scott, Edmund Waller, Henry Vane, and John Bradshawe led the political Independents. They were also leaders of the Republicans.

Cromwell signed the National Covenant on the last possible day, February 5, was promoted to lieutenant general, and appointed second-in-command to Earl Manchester. Throughout 1643, Cromwell had been denying that any of his troops were members of the dreaded Anabaptists. In the spring of 1644, Major General Lawrence Crawford sparked a quarrel that would lead to bitter divisions between Cromwell and Manchester. Crawford, a die-hard Scottish Presbyterian, hated Baptists—as most Englishmen did at the time—and hated any Independents who would tolerate Baptists. Crawford arrested his own lieutenant colonel, Henry Warner, for refusing the covenant on the basis of his Baptist convictions. Cromwell concluded a long angry letter to Crawford: *take heed of being sharp . . . against those to whom you can object little but they square not with you in every opinion concerning religion.*

Cromwell had no desire to curry favor with Baptists or Independents, and he certainly didn't want to make enemies of the Presbyterians. He was a military leader with a serious lack of manpower. He would not be bothered, for the time being, with minor religious differences between otherwise well-effected fighting men. Papists were, of course, another matter altogether. Time enough to cleanse the Agean stables when the war was won, he thought.

After defeating the Parliamentarians at the Battle of Newark, Prince Rupert advanced toward Lancashire at the head of a powerful Royalist army. He quickly subdued Stockport, where he took hundreds of prisoners. His troops overran Marple Hall and Wybersleigh Hall, but Col. Henry Bradshawe of Marple and his family were probably in Manchester. The Manchester garrison, once again, withstood attack.

On May 28, 1644, Rupert launched a furious assault on the little town of Bolton, joined by the Earl of Derby who was newly returned from the Isle of Man. Bolton was the closest market town to the ancient Bradshaw manor. After the town fell, Prince Rupert refused to give quarter to the garrison. Twelve hundred Bolton defenders and four ministers were put to the sword. Farms and manors in the neighborhood were devastated. Parliamentary commanders were infuriated and determined upon revenge. That revenge would cost the Earl of Derby his head.

On July 2, 1644, the decisive battle of Marston Moor was fought. The Royalist army was split. Prince Rupert's whole army was pushed off the battlefield. Parliament forces shadowed Rupert's forces as they marched away to Cumberland and Westmoreland. The king withdrew into his headquarters at Oxford.

It was a war weary country that watched 1644 come to an end. The countryside had been ravaged, and food stores were nearing exhaustion. Country people were being bankrupted by the needs of soldiers billeted upon them. Much of the parliamentary army was reduced to a poorly equipped and poorly disciplined rabble.

On the other hand, King Charles's force, while greatly reduced, had relieved the siege of Donnington Castle and was on the way to take up winter quarters at Oxford behind the cannons recovered from Donnington. Charles was in Oxford on November 13. Queen Henrietta Maria had escaped from the seige of Exeter and had arrived in Paris "sufficiently recovered from her long illness to apply herself intermittently to business." On December 3, Charles drafted a letter to his queen:

I have sent bearer Mr. Talbot to try and procure me from Venice that w^h for the present I have most need of, Mony, for the speedy & hansome conueyance of part of w^h hither he will propose to thee somewhat wherein thou may assist.

If the king was successful in obtaining aid from the Continent, he could come back stronger in the spring.

Lieutenant General Cromwell was angrily accusing his superior, Earl Manchester, of failing to diligently prosecute the war—specifically for allowing Charles to escape Donnington. Essex suggested that Cromwell might be charged with being "an incendiary." Sir Henry Vane's Independent party in Parliament was attacked as the war party. Cromwell, also a member of Parliament, had no option but to side with the Independents. He rose in Parliament to speak. He acknowledged the many criticisms being voiced against certain MPs who were allegedly prolonging the war for their own self-interest because they *had great places* and military commands. He told the Commons he was openly expressing to them what others were saying in secret. He disclaimed any interest of his own to prolong the war. While he respected those commanders, members of both Lords and Commons still in power, meaning chiefly Manchester, "but if I may speak my conscience without reflection upon any, I do conceive if the Army be not put into another method, and the War more vigorously prosecuted, the People can bear the War no longer, and will enforce you to a dishonourable peace."

Denzil Holles's peace party and some Scots were already negotiating with the king.

John Bradshawe wrote to Colonel (John?) Moore relative to a refusal of Mr. Langton to be a judge and to explain the king's reaction to some proposals (1644, 4 Nov London);

If you please to nominate anew to my Lord Admiral (Robert Rich, the Puritan Earl of Warwick and Lord Admiral) you must pretend at least misfortune to the former . . . . The Parliament propositions were received with derision answered with a direction to J. Style thus 'tell the men that sent you I intend not to lose my friends, my Crown, my religion, for their pleasure' The Duke of Richmond and the Duke of Southampton are daily expected from the King with propositions.

The Commons overpowered the objections raised in the Lords in January, and almost without great notice, William Laud, King Charles's archbishop of Canterbury, was executed.

The Commons sought the consent of the Lords to pass the Self-denying Ordinance in December 1644. The idea of self-denial came from Cromwell's observation: "I hope we have such true English hearts, and zealous affections toward the general weal of our Mother Country, as no Members of either House will scruple to deny themselves, and their own private interest, for the public good." Under the ordinance, no member of either house of Parliament could hold a commission in the army. Forty days were allowed for the individual to decide his career—Parliament or army. Manchester, Essex, Waller, and many others did resign their commissions. Cromwell declared his willingness to resign because he said, until the whole army was *new-modeled*, there would be no notable success in defeating the Royalists.

Control of the army was taken from the hands of the Parliament and handed to the newly formed Committee for Both Kingdoms. Cromwell began organizational matters to make the New Model Army responsible to its commanders as opposed to a tool of Parliament. The forty days limit under ordinance came on April 17, but then came news that the king was planning to break out of Oxford. Ordinance or no, Cromwell was needed. He was given forty days extension from the terms of the ordinance. Denzil Holles accused Cromwell of juggling events and the ordinance to promote the purposes of the warlike Independents. The New Model Army officially took the field in May with all soldiers except the Cavalry in their buff leather jackets, dressed in red coats, and under command of Sir Thomas *Black Tom* Fairfax. The Royalist Lord Digby ridiculed them as the *New Noodle*. At the start of the same month, the king had marched forth from Oxford, heading north. Cromwell was given a further extension. The question was raised whether the king intended to relieve the siege of Chester.

Chester had been besieged by Sir William Brereton, and he proposed a plan for the king's destruction: Fairfax and Cromwell would link up in the king's rear while Brereton held on against the royal onslaught and finally join with the Scottish army descending from the north. He wrote to John Bradshawe:

If the Scottish forces be active themselves in the advance and part of Sir Thomas Fairfax in this pursuit upon the rear, I should have great encouragement to believe this should be the last game they should ever play.

In the end, the Committee for Both Kingdoms missed the opportunity and vetoed Brereton's plan. It was not until the Royalists capture and sack of Leicester city on June 1 that the committee realized the danger of letting the king's forces roam the Midlands. Fairfax successfully insisted that Cromwell be appointed lieutenant general of horse in the New Model Army.

The Battle of Naseby, June 14, 1645, was a resounding victory for Parliament, and it sealed the king's fate. Thousands of Royalist captives were paraded through the streets of London. The entire Royalist foot were killed, captured, or wounded. Charles's artillery train, his private baggage, and his private correspondence were captured. Naseby was a triumph for the Independents and the New Model Army. King Charles had neither the men nor the money to conquer his foes. There were twelve months more before the end of the first civil war, but the fighting was confined to skirmishing and raiding.

Notes to Chapter Six

1. *The Court and the Country,* P. Zagorin, Cambs. 1971; *Two Cultures/ Court and Country under Charles I,* P.W. Thomas, in *Origins of the English Civil War,* ed. Conrad Russell, 1973; also Prof. Trevor-Roper's *The English Gentry 1540-1640* in *Economic History Review,* suppl #1, and Laurence Stone's *The Causes of the English Revolution,* pps 78 9l.
2. When William Prynne was passing through Chester in 1637 on his way to imprisonment, King Charles had prosecuted John Hampden for failure to pay his allotment of the ship-money tax. Pym and Hampden both made their wills and settled their estates on closely interlocked groups of trustees. It appears that they, along with Sir Arthur Haselrig and Oliver Cromwell, were in the very act of emmigrating to New England when they were stayed by an order of the Privy Council, (May 1, 1637) *Historical Collections,* i 2, 409, Rushworth, 1659, London.
3. "It was easy to hang or imprison one man, or even ten men, for mutiny or tax refusal, but it was impossible without a disciplined standing army to hang or imprison whole villages and counties. The point was, as the Deputy Lieutenants of Shropshire reported, that they had a 'persuasive, but no compulsive power'. The King did not have the physical power to force the major part of his subjects to perform actions they did not want to perform." *Origins of the English Civil War, Problems in Focus Series,* ed. Conrad Russell, 1973
4. *William Davenport and the silent majority of Early Stuart England,* J. S. Morrill, *Journal, Chester Archealogical Soc.,* Vol 581975, pps 115 et seg.
5. *CR 63/2/19,* Chester R. O.
6. Sir Peter Daniel's son and namesake was at Grays Inn with John Bradshawe. Sir Peter Daniel was brother-in-law of Sir Richard Grosvenor of Eaton (1584-1619). Grosvenor had been married to the daughter of Peter Warburton, Judge of the Cornmon Pleas. John Bradshawe's wife was a neice of Peter Warburton. It seems a remote connection to be called cousin, but not untypical of Stuart times. One other remote connection exists; Sir Richard Grosvenor's grandmother, Anne (d: 1559) was a daughter of Roger Bradshaw of Haigh in Lancashire.
7. Sir Peter Legh of Lyme was party to a family settlement made in 1619, between Francis Bradshawe of Bradshaw Hall in Chapel-en-le-Frith, on the one part, and Sir Peter Leigh (sic) of Lyme in the county of Chester, knight, Peter Bradshawe of London merchant tailor and Henry Bradshawe

the younger of Marple in the said county of Chester gentleman (,) of the other part" in which Francis Bradshawe conveyed in trust to Sir Peter Legh, Peter Bradshawe, and Henry Bradshawe all his manors, houses, and lands in Abney, Hope, Eyam, Foolowe, Great Hucklowe, Longson, Moniash, Bowden, Bradshawedge, and Chapel-en—Ie-Frith, "in consideration of natural love and affection.". *Wooley Charters*, xii.93

8. Lyson's Magna *Britannia*, Vol 2, 1810, pg 490, says that Charles I granted the manor of Congleton, in fee-farm, to "Ditchfield and others" and that some years later it was in the possession of the family named Toxteth. See also *Pat Roll 2484*, M.I., and PRO.
9. *Cal of State Papers, Dom.*, Chas I, 1639, 302.
10. A *Bradshaw House* stands on the B 5081 road between Swan Green and Allostock, not far from Peover hall, but the significance of the name of the name is not known.
11. Unfortunately the Mayor's accounts for this year are amongst the few that are missing from the fine collection which still exist in the possession of the Corporation of Congleton; J. P. Earwaker.
12. One must recognise the existence of other John Bradshaw's who could have been the Steward of Congleton.
13. Sir William Brereton's troop of Parliamentarians was supposed to have stabled their horses in St. Mary's during the seige of Biddulph Hall. They were blamed for smashing mediaeval glass and carrying away prereformation furniture, including the organ, which they burned in the field below the village. This seems unusual given Brereton's stated toleration of diverse religious beliefs.
14. Davenport Hall was owned by John Davenport (1606-1643) whose uncle was Francis Bradshawe of Chapel-en-le-Frith. Somerfield Hall was owned by Somerfield Oldfield, Chief Sergeant-at-Law of Chester from 1638 until his death. Yeaton Hall seems to have been the property of Sir William Brereton. Little Moreton Hall was owned by William Moreton (1577-1654) whose son was King Charles's Ambassador to Genoa and Turkey. Rode Hall was owned by Randle Rode (1602-1663) who was married to the daughter of William Moreton of Little Moreton Hall. Great Moreton Hall was owned by John Bellot (d: 1659), Sheriff of Cheshire in 1640; his sister was wife of Peter Legh (1599-1641) fourth son of Sir Peter Legh of Lyme. John Bellot's mother was Amy, daughter of Anthony Grosvenor of Doddleston, a younger son of Grosvenor of Eaton.
15. W. B. Stephens, *History of Congleton*, (Manchester Univ. Press, for the Congleton History Society), picture facing pg 79.

16. The term *cousin* encompassed many distant relatives.
17. Thomas Parnell (1625-1685), son of Tobias Parnell, painter and gilder of Congleton. His uncle Richard Parnell was Mayor of Congleton in 1647. Thomas married, in 1674, Anna Grice of Kilosty, county Tipperary, Ireland.
18. Samuel Roe (Wroe, Rowe)
19. *Congleton, Past and Present*, Robert Head, 1887.
20. Another John Bradshaw *of Congleton* made his will, 22nd March 1654, (*Pell 224, PCC*) which was proved 1st April 1659, seven months before John Bradshawe the Regicide died. John Bradshaw (d; in April) was descended from the Bradshaws of Darcey-Lever and must have been born about 1620/21 because he entered Grays Inn 1638/9. In his will he named his father, Lawrence Bradshaw of Hope, Lanes, his son Thomas, and his daughters Penelope and Frances. To further compound our confusion he named "John Bradshawe, Sergeant-at-Law" as one of his Trustees. His other Trustees were Thomas Mawdesley citizen and grocer of London, and Roger Kent of Congleton. His brother Ralph Bradshaw of Pendleton married Rachel Penn the aunt of William Penn, founder of Pennsylvania.
21. J.O. Halliwell. Ed, *The Autobiography and Correspondence of Sir Simonds D'Ewes*, 2 vols., (1845).
22. Probably John Bradshawe, the future Regicide.
23. John Bradshaw of Bradshaw near Bolton.
24. John Bradshawe, the Regicide, was closely associated with Thomas Fell.
25. January 3rd, 1642, Sir Edward Herbert, Attorney-General, went to the House of Lords and, in the King's name, accused high treason against Lord Kimbolton and five members of the Commons (Pym, Hampden, Holles, Strode, and Haselrig) for having attempted—1st, to subvert the fundamental laws of the kingdom and to deprive the King of his lawful authority; 2nd, to alienate the people from the King by odious calamities; 3rd, to raise an army against the King; 4th, to engage a foreign power—Scotland—to invade the kingdom; 5th, to annihilate the rights and the very existence of parliaments; 6th, to excite against the King and the parliament seditious assemblages for the purpose of securing, by violence, success in their criminal designs; and 7th, to levy war against the King.
26. Issac Pennigton was Lord Mayor of London and Lieutenant of the Tower during the Commonwealth and conducted Archbishop Laud to his execution. Earlier he had reported to Laud over his proposal to establish a Puritan lectureship at Chalfont St. Peter, Bucks, where he had inherited The *Grange* as his country residence. His Vicar, James Bradshaw was an orthodox clergyman, and rebuffed Pennington's proposal. Bradshaw was

forced from his post during the Commonwealth. John Milton's friend Thomas Ellington came to Chalfont St. Peter to tutor Pennington's children. In 1654 Issac gave *The Grange* to his son and namesake who became stepfather of Gulielma Springett. Gulielma Springett married William Penn, the founder of Pennsylvania.

27. The titles of a few of these publications: *Mercurius Anlicus—Mercurius Britainnicus Rusticus Pragmaticus Politicus Publicus Dirunal Paper—Dirunal Occurrences—A Perfect Dirunal of Some Passages in Parliament—London Intelligencer.*

28. William Bradshaw of Haigh, Lancashire, was 8th son of Roger Bradshaw of Haigh, a staunch Roman Catholic family. William had five brothers who were priests and three sisters who were Nuns. This family variously spelled their surname, Bradshagh, Bradshaw, and Bradshaigh.

29. William Radcliffe, Richard Howarth, Rowland Hunt, William Dean, John Hartley, John Gaskell, Edward Holbrook, Roger Worthington, Richard Meare, Thomas Lancashire, Richard Lomax, Thomas Minshull, Edward Johnson, Lawrence Owen, Robert Lever, Nicholas Hawett, Thomas Ellinworth, Michael Buxton, Ralph Wallin, and Hugh H. Williams Edwd Baines, ed by John Harland, *History of Lancashire*, Vol II, 319. (1868).

30. John Bradshaw of Bradshaw (1614-1666/7), son and heir of John Bradshaw (1583-1665/6). The senior John Bradshaw was at Grays Inn in 1602 and served as Justice of the Peace and Commissioner for Recusancy.

CHAPTER SEVEN

The Committeeman

*Without question, when he first drew the sword,
he threw away the scabbard.*
The History of the Rebellion, Earl of Clarendon

✠

THROUGHOUT THE FIRST civil war, the English people were surrounded by enemies and allies, victories and defeats, devastation and death. The war was fought in the very heart of the realm—in their own homes, farm fields, and towns. In every country village and isolated manor the people had hidden their treasure and were prepared to flee to the woods at the first approach of any soldiers of either side. Vicious skirmishes between feuding family groups settled very large issues but only confused other local residents. War became an excuse for personal revenge, plunder, and arbitrary taxation.

Issue number 88 of the news pamphlet the *Scottish Dove*[1] printed a short poem that "was found in a church 25 June 1645";

*Why where are we now, sure all is not right,
They take our Courage, that send us to fight,
Alas the Poore Souldier that ventures his life,
Getts nothing to maintain himselfe and his wife
But asking for money is answered with no.*

The whole apparatus of the royal court was gone. The administrative business of national government was vested in parliamentary committees at London. Few men dared take upon themselves individual responsibility for action and took instead the anonymity of committee membership. John Bradshawe seems to have been one of the few exceptions.

Parliament decreed a Committee of Safety on July 4, 1642, to care for the public defense and see the orders of Parliament were executed. It was restructured into a Committee for Both Kingdoms in 1643. There followed the Committee for Advance Money, for Sequestration, for Compounding with Delinquents, for Taking Accounts of the Kingdom, for Plundered Pinisters, for Removing Obstructions in the Sale of Delinquent's Lands, for the Relief of Those Who Surrendered on Articles of War, for the sale of Crown Lands, and the Committee for Both Kingdoms (called the Derby House Committee), which superseded the Committee of Safety.

Parliament was desperate for money to suppress the Irish rebellion and punish the Catholics who had the signed the Oath of Kilkenny. A joint committee for both houses was set up to arrange with the city of London a loan of £50,000. It was the first body of this kind which we find mention. The Commissioners for the Affairs in Ireland succeeded the joint committee and met at the Guildhall commencing February 1642. John Pym, Denzil Holles, and Henry Vane were among the commissioners.

A group of London merchants calling themselves the Adventurers proposed to finance a private army to conquer the Irish rebels, seize Irish estates from the rebels, and promise to settle (adventure) the protestant religion upon those estates. The scheme, effectively a government lottery, was approved by the commissioners in March, inviting subscriptions of £200 upward. An ex-officio market sprang up, and shares of the *Adventurers for Land* were sold, traded, and assigned long before the drawing of lots for particular lands.

Members of Parliament and private speculators were quick to contribute £600 for the promise of 1,000 acres in Leinster, £450 for the same in Munster, and £200 in Ulster. Independents contributed nearly twice as much as Presbyterians. Royalists contributed less than 10 percent. Cromwell personally contributed more than £2,000 in three installments. At the end of July, the House of Commons asked the treasurers of the Adventurers for Land to hand over £100,000 from the sum already collected. It may be coincidental that on June 4, Parliament had passed an ordinance for securing the sum of £100,000 agreed to be lent to Parliament by several companies and citizens of London "for the use of the kingdom." In July 1643, Parliament brought in the "doubling Ordinance," whereby the land allocation was doubled for each Adventurer who made an additional payment equal to one fourth their original subscription. Ultimately Parliament owed £360,000 to 1,360 subscribers and others. They had to allocate the whole of Leinster, Ulster, and Munster to the Adventurers.[2]

The Commons and the Lords voted an ordinance for temporary weekly assessments from London, Westminster, and Southwark. In February it was extended to all of England and Wales. Central and local committees were assigned the task. Lancashire was assessed £500 weekly. The committee for Lancashire consisted of Sir Ralph Ashton, James Stanley, Baronets, Ralph Ashton, Richard Shuttleworth, Alexander Rigby, John Moor (Moore), John Atherton, Richard Holland, Edward Butterworth, John Bradshaw (of Bradshaw), Peter Egerton, George Dodding, Nicholas Cunliffe, and Thomas Fell, Esquires, Robert Cunliffe, Robert Curwen, and John Nowell, gents.

Instructions were sent to Sir William Brereton, Sir George Booth, and the other deputy lieutenants of Cheshire to assess £62 from the city of Chester and £175 from the county each week. The Cheshire committee consisted of Sir George Booth, Knight and Baronet; Sir William Brereton, Baronet; Henry Mainwaring, Henry Brook, Robert Dukenfield, Henry Vernon, John Crewe, John Bradshawe, and William Marbury, Esquires. Marbury, a moderate supporter of the conflict against the king, was Bradshawe's brother-in-law. Over time, Booth, Mainwaring, and Vernon would come into conflict with Brereton and Bradshawe.

At this time it appears John Bradshawe, serving on the Cheshire committee, was residing in Congleton. Another of his creditors writes a pleading letter:

> *Good Cousin, I received your letter by Mr Watson from whom att several tymes I have understoode with griefe the contents of this. I acknowledge your overfaithfulness to my brother & your love to mee, which aggravates my sorrow, and my shame, to see soe good a friend, soe great a sufferer; but soe it is with mee at present that I cannot satisfye you in your inst ant and reasonable demande, my own necessities are soe pressing, which ere long will be soe visible uppon mee, that you will believe that this is no feigned storie & soe far yet credit mee, that it shall*

be through want of means, not of honesty or affection, if it appeare otherwise unto you, then Your loving cousin JAMES DAVENPORT Sutton September 2 1642

Endorsed by Bradshawe,
James Davenpts l're
7ber ye 2d 1642

Addressed To my very loving Cousin
John Bradshawe Esquire att Congleton
these present Seal, a chevron between 3 cross crosslets

James Davenport, son of the Royalist lord chief baron of the Exchequer, left England soon thereafter. Perhaps Bradshawe assisted him in his flight, as could be inferred from Lady Mary Davenport's subsequent letter.[3] Gibson places Bradshawe in London as early as 1640 but retaining his house in Congleton. W. B. Stephens[4] thought Bradshawe had left Congleton in August 1642. It certainly appears that soon thereafter John Bradshawe had taken up residence in Basinghall Street, adjoining the Guildhall, London. Thomas Parnell (b: 1625), Bradshawe's young secretary from Congleton, resided with him. Samuel Roe was another of Bradshawe's secretaries and assistants.

Financial difficulties continued to plague Parliament. Having failed to raise enough money by persuasion, an ordinance "for assessing of all such as have not contributed on the Proposition of both Houses of Parliament . . . for raising of money, plate, horses and horsemen" was passed in November. A central committee was established. Officially it was known as the Committee for the Advance of Money or the Committee at Haberdasher's Hall. John Bradshawe's friend and patron, Sir William Brereton, was one of the original sixteen committee members.[5] The mayor and the council of London had made the Haberdashers Hall available for an agreed rental. Initially the committee's work was administrative, not judicial. Residents of London and others who had estates within a twenty-mile radius were assessed. Only those whose total property did not exceed £100 were to be exempt. All others were assessed one fifth of their personal estate and one twentieth the value of their real estate, payable in four installments. MPs and lords were assessed by their respective houses.

Public faith bills, issued and secured on faith of the government to repay, were to earn 8 percent interest per annum. The grant of a public faith bill was conditional upon payment within ten days of summons for payment of assessment.

Not everyone was happy to pay their assessment. In the decade commencing 1640, England was more heavily taxed than it ever had been or would be again until the twentieth century. By May, Parliament provided the committee with powers of enforcement. The Committee for Advance of Money spawned the Committee of Lords and Commons for Sequestration,[6] also known as the Goldsmith's Hall Committee, which was formed to seize and put in safe custody (sequestrate) the offices, income, goods, and estates of "Malignants or notorious delinquents" in every shire. Malignants were Papists, i.e., Roman Catholics or, occasionally, Anabaptists and other dissenters. Delinquents were those who had not paid their assessments, had been in actual war against Parliament, had assisted the king, or had resisted the National Covenant. Those who refused payment or attempted to hide assets were fined the full amount of their assessment without hope of repayment.

Goods and property were seized from those who did not pay their fines. Sir Inigo Jones, King Charles's surveyor, was assessed £1,000 but attempted to conceal his goods, plate, and wagons. Seized possessions were sold, after due advertisement, at the Guildhall. Auctions by the candle were held; the final bid determined when a small lighted candle expired. One notorious low bidder was accused of placing himself near the candle and by some surreptitious means blowing it out.

Robert Bostock, a contemporary London bookseller, reported the sale of hundreds of books seized from the rich libraries of Sir John Pennington, Sir William Parkhurst, and others. His reports remain in State Papers 20/7 at the Public Record Office in Kew. It is interesting to note there is no specific sale of any work by William Shakespeare, but copies were sold of Bacon's *Henry 7*, Ben Johnson's *Playes*, Pembroke's *Arcadia* (imperfect), *Orlando Furioso*, *Edimon*, *Edward ye 3rd*, *King Arthur*, *Plutarch's Lives*, *Euphues*, *Purchas Pilgrimage*, "old 1617," and *Bradshawe on ye Thessel*.[7] One book, simply called *Playes*, sold for sixpence.

The work of assessment, already undertaken, combined with the work of sequestration and seizure was a tremendous undertaking. Paid officers of the central committee, not all of whom were MPs, were appointed:

1) A treasurer at £150 per year, plus a percentage of receipts, Lawrence Newman (d: June 1644), followed by William Lane, Samuel Grosse.

2.) A clerk, or secretary, at £4 per week with benefit of collecting a fee for copying orders. These fees became considerable after a rule of the committee that all petitions or complaints to the committee should be accompanied by an official copy of the last order in the case, Mr. Piggott.
3.) A registrar at £150 per year, Martin Dallison.
4.) An examiner of witnesses at £100 per year, Edward Carey, followed by John Birchenshaw.
5.) Six attendants, or collectors, allowed 6s. 8d. per day when on duty and 6d. in the pound on all money brought in, plus traveling expenses.
6.) A legal counsel at £150 per year, John Bradshawe.

Good records of the Committee for Advance of Money still exist. Seven order books of the Committee for Sequestration are in existence but very few original papers. The post of legal counsel was filled by John Bradshawe, but at what date is uncertain. Hugh Bellot believed "it is permissible to presume that he took up his abode in the City with a view to this appointment." In the scattered records[8] of the committee, Bradshawe is variously called counsel-at-law, attorney general for sequestrations, and solicitor for the commonwealth.

A schedule of the delinquencies of each offender was drawn up, his estates were valued, and he was invited to appear and urge any arguments why the committee should not fine him a sum in proportion to his estate and the severity of his delinquency. One fifth of a sequestered estate was set aside for the support of the offender's family. That portion was increased to one third for Roman Catholics not directly involved in supporting the Royalists.

Not all cases came before the committee. County committees enforced most local sequestration, and many were never appealed. As early as December 1642, the county of Cornwall had begun sequestration, and Parliament only gave national legitimacy to the fearful process. Obviously the local machinery came into the hands of a set of Parliamentarian minor gentry, not the old Royalist county magnates. Some members of county committees protected their friends and falsely accused their enemies. Rewards of 5 percent were offered, and unscrupulous informers accused their neighbors in return for reward money.

Among the nineteen Lancashire sequestrators appointed to value and take possession of the delinquent's assets were Thomas Fell of Ulverston,

John Bradshaw (1583-1665/6) of Bradshaw, his brother-in-law Edward, his son-in-law John Hartley of Strangewayes, his nephew William Ashurst, and relatives of his late father-in-law Peter Ashton. William Ashurst is particularly interesting because he, along with John Bradshawe the regicide, was a financial agent for Sir William Brereton, member of Parliament for Cheshire.

Brereton returned to Cheshire in 1643 and immediately began to consolidate his personal power. As chief military commander for the county, he had the sole right to make military appointments and coordinate local strategy and tactics. Full administrative power in the county was exercised by "the said Sir Wm Brereton together with the deputy lieutenants," or any two of them. His signature was required on every important county governmental action. He effectively established and controlled local committees for the advance of money, for the examination of ministers and schoolmasters thought to be delinquent, and for the sequestration of delinquents. He selected committeemen who supported his objectives rather than those of the old and more neutralist group of leading gentry. He established local sequestration committees in the five eastern Cheshire hundreds, much to the bitter opposition of Sir George Booth, Henry Mainwaring, Wilbraham, Stanley, and their supporters. He was managed to place loyal friends on important committees of Lancashire, Staffordshire, Shropshire, Lancashire, Surrey, and Pembrokshire. His intrigues in Wales brought him into conflict with the titular major general for North Wales, Sir Thomas Myddleton of Chirk Castle. Brereton waged a war by correspondence through John Bradshawe, William Ashurst, and other agents in London. Middleton, an MP and head of the powerful family of London merchants, was certainly the focus of Brereton's secret campaign, but there was also a powerful group in London and Westminster acting on behalf of Middleton. Their hidden names are represented by numbers, as yet undecoded, in Brereton's letters.

Bradshawe succeeded in stirring up the entire city of London in February 1643/44. The sheriffs of London, the Court of Aldermen, and the Committee of the Miltia appeared at the door of the House of Commons, and when called in, Sheriff Foulke explained, "the Occasion of their coming, at this time, was upon the Occasion of the late Ordinance for the Weekly Meal; and some Misunderstandings growing between the Committee at Salter's Hall, and the Committee of the Militia, by the Carriage and Artifice of one Man, whom he was to name, Mr. Bradshawe. He then said, he was commanded, and by reason of some Aspersions cast upon the Committee of the Militia by the said Mr. Bradshaw(e), enforced to enumerate the good and faithful Services performed the Publick by the said Committee II. He then delivered the Act of the Common Council of London, dated 3rd February 1644."

From London, Bradshawe wrote to Brereton on March 12, 1644/45: *I have been unwilling of late to write, although you have favored me with your lines. Truth is our business is not so well managed here as we could wish. We hope well of amendment. The Lords have not yet perfected Sir Thos. Fairfax's list. Sir William Waller and Col. Cromwell are abroad toward the west, whence we expect good tidings. The Committee here have concluded upon the way to raise £80, 000 speedily for the advance of Sir Thos. Were we true to ourselves all would be well quickly.*

An anonymous author addressed a message, in rhyme, to Parliament, June 3, 1645:

> *Wise men labour*
> *Good men grieve*
> *Knaves plot*
> *Fools believe*
> *Good Lord from heaven*
> *Shew mercy to us*
> *For knaves and fools*
> *will else undo us.*

An intriguing entry appears in the proceedings of the Committee for Advance Money at this time. Thomas Tresham of the Strand in London was assessed £500 on March 19, 1644/45. A few months later came an order to bring in Mr. Bradshaw, who was to pay Mr. Tresham's fine, but Bradshaw told the committee's messenger that he "would not be ordered by no prating scrivener." It is not certain this Bradshaw and the John Bradshawe who was so actively involved as legal counsel for the Committee of Sequestrations were the same man. It could indicate minor conflicts between the two committees were continuing.

Appeals against local sequestrator's decisions were made to the central London Committee; and it was they, in theory, who made the final judgments for sequestration or granted relief to the appellants. There were hundreds of cases to be examined, framed, presented, and heard before the committee. Brereton must certainly have been influential in placing John Bradshawe into the workings of the London Committee.

Appeals were heard after Bradshawe examined the merits of the case. Case after case was assigned to Bradshawe for examination. His name appears so often in the records that his name begins to appear as simply Mr. B. As the workload increased, it seems the committee was often happy to leave the work and the judgments to Bradshawe.

A case in point: Edmund Shallcrosse, rector of Stockport near Marple Hall, was ejected from his living, and his goods were confiscated in August 1644. Some of the books[9] from his extensive library were placed in the keeping of George Newton, John Bradshawe's brother-in-law. After Shallcrosse's death in 1646, testimony was given: "Edward Hill, of Stopforth (sic), glazier, knew Mr. Shallcrosse, formerly minister of Stopforth, who about the year 1641 refused to let to farm the tithes of Marple to the townsmen of Marple at their own rates, but offered them the same at such rates as was conceived they might well gain at. And that about two years after Articles were exhibited against the said the said Mr. Shallcrosse for delinquency, who thereupon appealed to the Committee of Lords and Commons for Sequestrations, and went several times to London about the same business, and was once going to have the same heard and had a convoy of horse of the Parliaments party, and some of the King's party came forth of Dudley Castle and (he) then was by them slain. And this depondent further saith that he was servant to the said Mr. Shallcrosse for seven years before his death, who did acquaint this examine that he found much opposition by Sergeant Bradshawe, who then was Solicitor for the Commonwealth—He also saith that the tithes of Stopforth are reputed to be worth £400 by the year or thereabouts, and saith that he hath heard generally reported that Sir William Brereton had a power invested in him to place or displace such ministers as were scandalous or delinquents. And he further saith that he believed if the said Mr. Shallcrosse had complied with the desires of the said Mr. Bradshawe and his father and brother that the said Mr. Shallcrosse would not have been sequestered."[10] William Nicols, DD,[11] was nominated to the rectory; but he, being in the hands of Sir William Brereton and the Committee for Plundered Ministers, was never instituted. The committee appointed Thomas Case, MA.

In another case, Samuel Shipton, cleric, of Alderley in Cheshire, was judged a delinquent. He appealed his case to the Committee for Sequestration in May 1647 wherein he claimed he was sequestered for words only. He said he had taken the National Covenant, May 11, 1646, before his appeal to the committee. John Bradshawe, counsel-at-law to the committee, reported: "This is the truth of Mr. Shipton's case and in my opinion he deserves as much favour and haste as the Committee's rules will permit, his offense being only speaking of words.... I must say it hath been very rare that any sequestration hath been for words only, without actions. But such is his destiny to which he submits. Besides composition for his temporal ties, he irrecoverably loseth his living of more than double worth to the other, which he cannot compound for."

Nevertheless, as late as 1650, John Winnington of Rudheath, in Cheshire, was sequestered because he called the Parliament men "traitors and hoped to see Colonel Brooke and President Bradshawe hanged."

In the city of London, a vacancy existed among judges of the Sheriff's Court at the Guildhall. The right of election was claimed by both the Court of London Aldermen and the London Common Council. John Bradshawe was chosen by majority ballot of the councilors on September 21, 1644; Richard Proctor was chosen by the aldermen. William Steele was an unsuccessful candidate who was, or would become, a Brereton supporter. Disregarding the aldermen, the Common Council selected Bradshawe and administered his oath of office on the twenty-fourth. Proctor brought an action against the council in the King's Bench, but it did not come to final hearing until February 1655, by which time Bradshawe had held the post for more than twelve years. The King's Bench rejected Proctor's suite.

Lady Davenport addressed a letter, dated September 30, 1644: *to the right wor^{ll} (worshipful) my very worthy good cozen John Bradshawe, Esqr att his house in Bassinghall Streete London.*

Seventy-two-year-old Lady Mary Sutton Davenport and her husband, Sir Humphrey Davenport of Sutton, were sequestered Royalists and living in greatly reduced circumstances. Sir Humphrey, aged over eighty at this time, was Bradshawe's and Brereton's old friend and fellow at the Society of Gray's Inn. Davenport had been raised to the bench as a judge of the Common Pleas in 1630. It fell to him to deliver the court's judgment against John Hampden on the ship-money tax case. Although he agreed with the majority that the king had the power to impose the tax, he found in Hampton's favor on the technical point that the writ was bad law. King Charles named him Lord Chief Baron of the Exchequer in 1631. Impeachment proceedings to remove him as a judge were brought against him in the Lords, 1641, but were allowed to drop. When the king withdrew to Oxford, Davenport joined him there and remained as Royal Chief Baron of the Exchequer until January 1643/44 when overtaken by ill health. He died in Cheshire, March 1644/45.

Her ladyship begins by acknowledging the receipt of Bradshawe's letter of the seventeenth (of which no copy has been found). She thanked Bradshawe for his kind enquiries after her husband's health, which she said was reasonable: *but very weake both in body and mynde.*

She expressed her sorrow that Bradshawe should suffer for his good will to her son and excuses the latter insofar as he had for the last four or five years not received one penny profit from his estates in Oxfordshire. Her son, she says, is away; and she is not sure whether he is in Paris or at Blois, but a letter addressed to Mr. Bradley at the College du Turnay, Paris, might reach him. Finally, Lady Davenport concluded: *for myne own plticular, I shall never be wanting to yor assistance herein to the utmost of my ability w^{ch} (God knowes) is but weake: and had I power to my will neither you nor any other should suffer for any of my sonnes debts, and so I beseech you conceive of me, and I shall as truly take this business into my thought as if it were myne owne and I will use the best meanes I canne for yor indemnity and so wth myne & Mr Davenports harty well wishes unto yrselfe and my good cozen yor wife I take leave and shall ever remayne*

30 Sept 1644 yr truly loving cozen
Mary Davenport

Addressed To the right wor^{ll} my very Worthy good cosen John Bradshawe Esq att his house in Bassinghall Streete, London these present
Endorsed in the handwiting of John Bradshawe A lire from my Lady Davenpt dated 30 Dec (qy Sept) 1644.
son James & ye intention touch^g her to save me harmless concerning my Ingagemen^t for him

Octagon seal
a lion rampant

In October, Bradshawe was employed by Parliament to prosecute the Irish rebels, Connor Macguire, 2nd Baron Enniskillen, and his companion, MacMahon, for their part in the Irish rebellion of 1641. Bradshawe was joined by Richard Newdigate and William Prynne as joint prosecutors. The rebel lords were condemned and executed early the next year.

William Prynne was hammering Parliament for establishment of rigid ecclesiastical discipline, i.e., Presbyterianism and the suppression of Independency. In January, the House of Commons approved the establishment of the Presbyterian form of church government with no toleration of other beliefs. John Lilburne attacked his old friend of earlier years in an unlicensed publication, *Letter to Prynne*, "I am not against Parliaments setting up a State-Government for such a Church as they think fit . . . for my part leave them to themselves . . . so that they leave my Conscience free to the Law and Will of my Lord and King."

Enforcement of strict religious conformity demanded that the dissident press be muzzled, and this job was handled by Parliament's Committee for Examinations. John Milton's *Areopagitica*, published on November 24, 1644, advocated freedom of the press.

It is difficult to fathom Bradshawe's political convictions at this time. Political convictions then were defined in terms of religious convictions. Bradshawe had long been closely associated with Sir William Brereton's group of Cheshire Independents and dissidents—seldom with any of the Cheshire Presbyterians. Strangely, he was appointed junior counsel for the Presbyterian Parliament in 1645.

The king and his forces had slipped out of Oxford and were proceeding north toward Chester. Sir William Brereton wrote to John Bradshawe: *1645. May 14 The siege is drawne up close to Chester and the last evening I had intelligence that the people there was in great distresse, having little support them besides the expectation of speedy reliefe. Much disappointed that King is at liberty to interrupt all this. I had intended to come up to London in a few dayes, but the condicon of things stands soe hazardous that I thinke it not fitt to leave them yet till this storme be over though my forces here be soe weakened that I cannot act as I would and thinke if I come up I might doe that service for my country which will not otherwise be done.*

On the very day this letter was dated, John Lilburne was once again summoned before the Committee of Examinations on the charge of printing *Letter to Prynne*. He boldly denounced the intolerance of Parliament and shortly after published *Reasons of Lieu. Col. Lilburnes Sending his Letter to Mr. Prin*. The Independents had remained loyal to Parliament, said Lilburne, while Prynne was guilty of "bloody, unchristian and dividing practices." Prynne declared that Lilburne had private unlicensed presses "alwaies at his command."

A few days later, James Davenport wrote to Bradshawe:

Good Cousin, I thanke you ever for your kindness toward mee & that yet in my lasting miserie you are pleased to give mee your friendly advice & assistance in my endlesse business wherewith I shall acquaint my friends in the countrye: I am exceedingly sorry to heare you are still tormented for mee & will forthwith write that those to whom I entrusted the discharge of that debt to Mr Boys wch was Mr Wade, Mr Coker, & Mr Walthall that they may render theire account why interest is not paid as formerly & and that they assist you so farr as they are able; soe desiring my service to bee presented unto my Cousin your good wife & your selfe I remaine

Your affectionate Kinsman & Ser^t J.D.
Paris May 25 1645

> Addressed, *To my very Loving Cousin John Bradshaw Esquire these present.*
> (In another hand writing) *Endorsed in the handwriting of John Bradshawe*
> *ffrome James Davenport   neewe Blackwell Hall*
>
> *C***. 25th May 1645*

John Lilburne was arrested on June 18 on the charge of printing *Letter to Prynne* but released soon thereafter. He was arrested again on July on charge of uttering slander against the speaker of the house. Again, on August 9 he was arrested for an unlicensed publication and committed to Newgate prison. There he remained until October 14.

Two letters, the first dated September 11, 1645, and both addressed to John Bradshawe Esq. at his *howse in Bassinghall Street London* were sent by Mr. Phillip Osborne at Lady Mary Davenport's insistence. Lady Davenport craves Bradshawe's intercession with his brother, Col. Henry Bradshawe, on behalf of Mrs. Anne Warren who appears to be a kinswoman of Lady Davenport. While John Bradshawe was occupied in London, his brother Henry Bradshawe had taken a place on the local committee of sequestration in Macclesfield hundred. Mrs. Warren owned a £150 annuity secured upon her nephew's sequestered estate. She was not receiving the income from the annuity.

From the second letter it appears that Bradshawe made the requested application to his brother, Col. Henry Bradshawe, who had taken the matter in hand and recovered for Mrs. Warren £5 of the arrears with a prospect of the recovering the balance. "It comes at a good tyme to supply her want of clothing against this cold tyme," Osborne told Bradshawe.

Lady Davenport gave John Bradshawe some of her husband's books. Osborne assured Bradshawe that her Ladyship is *much troubled* that he should make any scruple about the books and assures him that he has them by her free consent,

and without any p'ticular opposicon to yor selfe by the trustees who are now verry well satisfyed that my La; may dispose of them at her pleasure.

If Bradshawe refused them, her Ladyship would imagine that it was out of *some displeasure conceived*. It was obvious from this bequest that Sir Humphrey Davenport was dead.

Sir William Brereton surrendered his military command in accordance with the Self-Denying Ordinance in June, and it appeared he would now assume a dominant role in the Commons. Brereton, however, like Cromwell, was restored to command before October. Between September and December, Parliament appropriated £15,000 for the military crisis in Cheshire. Brereton appointed John Bradshawe and William Steele as his agents to receive the money and see it delivered to Cheshire. Out of the money, Bradshawe paid some of the county's debts in London and paid part of his brother's arrears.

On November 24, 1645, John Bradshawe, Thomas Fell, Francis Bacon, and Nicholas Bacon were called to be members of the Grand Company of Ancients at Gray's Inn. Francis Bacon, son of John Bacon of Kings Lynn, had been presiding judge at the trial of Macquire and MacMahon, the Irish rebels.

The Ancients were a group of about thirty, selected from barristers with at least ten years experience, sons of judges, and persons of distinction chosen for membership in the inn—"not so much to make the laws their study, much less to live by the profession, having large patrimonies of their own, but to form their manners and preserve them from the contagion of vice." Sadly, the war had disrupted the whole administration of the Society of Gray's Inn. Some of the members had joined the king, some the forces of Parliament; some were Presbyterian and some were Independent. For Parliament's cause were the Earl of Warwick, Sir William Brereton, Sir Arthur Haselrig, Denzil Holles, Alexander Rigby, Ferdinand Lord Fairfax and his son Thomas, Christopher Fulwood, and others.

January 26, 1646, an upper chamber in Holbourne Court, later called Finch's Buildings, that had formerly been occupied by Sir George Ratcliffe was assigned on a twenty-one-year lease to Bradshawe, and he built two additional chambers. In 1650, Bradshawe surrendered these chambers to William Steele, recorder of London. Chambers on the ground floor of Goodricke's Buildings, number 14 South Square, are described in 1668 as "lately Bradshaw's."[12] Elections to Parliament were held in the autumn. As one of the MPs for the county of Cheshire, Brereton was the leading military and civilian leader for Parliament in the area, including the surrounding counties. He tried to get Sir Richard Skeffington (his brother-in-law) and John Swinfen elected MPs for Staffordshire. John Bradshaw[13] was his nominee for burgess of Newcastle-under-Lyme. Two of the elected burgesses would be MPs for the borough of Newcastle. Bradshaw came under attack from Christopher Tomkinson who, when asked how he stood, replied, "Not with Mr. Bradshaw by any means, for I hold Mr. Terrick the honester man . . . for when Sir Francis Wortley came to Congleton with prisoners (including a relative of Tomkinson's) Mr. Bradshaw counseled him not to part with them? without money for they were able men." Brereton rose to Bradshaw's defense by pointing out that Bradshaw was in London at the time of the said rumor, he had advised the Royalist Wortley. Brereton had miscalculated the mood of the county. Samuel Terrick was elected.

Calls for peace were sweeping the counties, and Sir George Booth gained the election in Cheshire County for his son, George Booth the younger, with the support of the antimilitaristic faction and the powerful prewar gentry. He took his seat alongside Brereton as the second MP for Cheshire.

After a long siege, the city of Chester surrendered to Brereton and his Parliament forces on February 3, 1645/46. The king fell back once again to Oxford. Other Royalist strongholds fell in quick succession.

The surrender of Chester was negotiated by the mayor and a group of aldermen, including Edward Bradshaw and his brother Richard Bradshaw. Edward had remained in the city during the Royalist occupation but exhibited Parliamentary loyalties.

By-elections were called to replace the two Chester MPs who had been disqualified from taking their seats in 1644. Brereton had groomed Capt. William Edwards and John Bradshaw,[14] a local lawyer, as his nominees for the seats. In the end it appears that Bradshaw was not put forward as a candidate.[15] The city chose Edwards and John Ratcliffe.

They had opposed the Royalist faction but were determined to keep the city from becoming subject to Brereton's county committee at Nantwich. Edwards was mayor of Chester in 1646.

As military conflict was coming to a close, political conflict was just beginning. Grievances were being expressed, reforms were named, actions were suggested, and always appeals for the commonweal of the English people. The party of Presbyterians and the party of Independents were the primary opponents.

Independents, sometimes termed Congregationalists, generally agreed with the Presbyterians on religion but differed as to the mode of church government and consequently with the mode of political government. The small gothic chapel at Duckenfield, Cheshire, is acknowledged the first Independent church that was set up in England. Col. Robert Dukenfield commenced it in 1644. Soon thereafter another was set up at Stockport.

Another group, afterward call the Levelers, was forming around John Lilburne. Lilburne had been released from the tower in October. The House of Commons acquiesced to one of his many petitions and discharged him from the old 1638 Star Chamber fine. The Lords concurred, assigned John Bradshawe and John Cook as Lilbourne's counsel, and agreed to hear his case anew. Bradshawe and Cook gathered and presented the facts admirably; and the Lords, on February 12, 1646, obliterated of the Star Chamber conviction "as illegal, and most unjust, against the liberty of the Subject, and the Law of the Land, and Magna Carta." Bradshawe and Cooke were so successful in their presentation that the Lords proposed to grant Lilburne £2,000 in reparations. Those reparations, however, would have to be granted by the Commons.

In April, King Charles cut short his hair, donned a false beard, and slipped away from Oxford with only two companions. Nine days later he surrendered to the Scottish army at their headquarters between Nottingham and Newark. He hoped to convince the dispirited Scots to join with him, their Scottish king, against the English.

Lilburne stepped up his attacks. The Lords issued a warrant for Lilburne's arrest on June 11 on the charge of publishing a pamphlet in which he called the king a traitor and accused the Earl of Manchester with complicity. He countered by accusing the Lords in Parliament of usurpation, perjury, injustice, and breach of the great trust in them imposed. On July 11, the Lords pronounced Lilburne guilty of contempt and sentenced him to be fined £2,000, suffer close imprisonment without writing instruments during the pleasure of the house, and be barred from holding any civil or military office.

Despite being so closely confined and observed, Lilburne was able to publish two comprehensive unlicensed pamphlets in October and November: *The Charters of London* and *Londons Liberty in Chains*. He must have had a collaborator outside prison. Lilburne had procured a Latin copy of the old franchises and liberties of London. Lilburne knew little Latin, so he sent it to a friend for translation. The translator remains unidentified, but he was also the author of the opening section of London's Liberty and author of its inspiration, Protestation, which had been read in protest outside the Guildhall in September. Lilburne's anonymous friend may have also helped with *England's Miserie and Remedie* published in October 1645. He described himself on the title page of *England's Miserie* as an Utter Barrister who knew the gossip and workings of London. Bradshawe cannot be discounted as Lilburne's collaborator.

Bradshawe, Sir Rowland Wandesford, and Sir Thomas Bedingfield were nominated as commissioners for the great seal on October 6, 1646. The House of Lords, however, overruled this Bradshawe's appointment.

Bradshawe continued his work with the Committee for Sequestration. On December 18, he addressed a letter to Henry Wrigley, John Ogden, John Smith, and the gentlemen of Oldham Parish in Lancashire: *I am a witness of the executing of a deed by and which you have the whole Rectory of Oldham settled in as good a way as you can wish upon yor church of Oldham and Shaw Chapell. I have sent you by this bearer an order I procured before for £ 40. to be allowed for mayntenance of a Minister at Shaw Chapell.*

This was a result of one of Bradshawe's examinations before the committee. Thomas Asheton of Chadderton[16] had been fined £1,414 as a delinquent. The fine was reduced to £514 provided that Asheton paid £50 annually to Oldham Chapell for a preaching minister and £40 annually for the same purpose to Shaw Chappell.

This year the traditional joyous winter season was dismal. All the old saint's days had been abandoned. London apprentice boys asked for substitutes. The House of Commons ignored Christmas as a papist frippery and remained in session the whole day. The ancient celebrations and masques of the Inns of Court were not observed.

Slowly some attempt to restore peacetime government and administration of justice began. The Scots kept their royal prisoner in respectful custody because possession of him gave them influence over

Parliament. The Scots wanted the money they had been promised as the price for handing over the king and returning home. The Independents feared the presence of a Scots army on English soil and wanted an end to the Solemn League and National Covenant. The general population wanted the end of high taxation and a return to peace even if it meant compromising with the king. The king wanted his royal prerogatives back, and he did not want to compromise. The army wanted possession of the king and money for their destitute troopers. The Presbyterian majority in Parliament, headed by Holles, wanted the New Model Army disbanded.

The majority of the army was for liberty of conscience, as they called it: "that . . . every Man might not only hold, but preach and do in Matters of Religion what he pleased," so said Richard Baxter, the Puritan minister. Even worse, Baxter felt the idea of independency in religion had fostered the idea of independency in politics, and that lead to talk of state democracy. "A few fiery, self-conceited men kindled the rest, and made all the noise and bustle and carried about the Army as they please." These men had been seduced by John Lilburne's pamphlets, even though he was imprisoned, Baxter said, and that afterward they were called Levelers. Lilburne himself confessed, "I made a vigorous and strong attempt upon the private Soldiery . . . with an abundance of study and paines, and the expence of some scores of pounds." Lilburne's primary agent and messenger was an army officer, Edward Sexby, a convinced Republican.

The hostilities which heretofore had been between Parliament and the king now became hostility between the Parliament and the army. Of primary importance was pay for the army. Foot soldiers were eighteen weeks in arrears, and dragoons were forty-two weeks in arrears. Next in importance to the arrears was the question of indemnity from prosecution or acts that the soldiers had committed during the war. Finally there was the question of freedom in religious choice.

In January, Parliament paid £200,000 to the Scots who, in return, went back across the border. Although not implicit in the agreement, the king was delivered into the hands of Parliament in February. It was reported that the king said, "Then I am bought and sold!" Nine parliamentary commissioners, three lords, and six commoners escorted the king and his modest court to Holdenby House in Northamptonshire. For the next six months he was pressurized to agree to the abolition of the Episcopacy and the establishment of the Presbyterian form of church government. For the Independent majority in the army, headed by Cromwell, and the Independent minority in Parliament, headed by Vane, the establishment of bishops or presbyters was equally abhorrent. Civil and military commanders were now openly antagonistic.

Holles's party carried another step through Parliament in February. All the army was to be dismissed except 5,400 horse, 1,000 dragoons, and enough infantry to garrison only forty-five castles and fortified places. Sir Thomas Fairfax was proposed as general-in-chief, and no officer under him would have rank higher than colonel. There was no mention of the arrears owed to the army, much less a bonus for their past services.

A general council of the army was held on March 1, after which they broke their camps and moved closer to London, encamping at Saffron Walden. The House of Commons was thrown into panic. They voted an assessment of £60,000 a month for one year to pay the soldiers. Petitions were voted requiring the army to stay at least twenty miles out of London. This was passed on March 17. A plan was proposed to reduce the army by sending part of it to Ireland. A deputation from the Derby House Committee was sent to Saffron Walden to ask Fairfax how the army would react to such a plan. Fairfax called a council of officers whose resolution was that they must first know who would be their commanders, what would be their pay, and when the Commons proposed to pay their arrears and bonuses before they even considered the plan. This was outright mutiny against the Commons and the Derby House Committee, but the government had no physical means to suppress it; there were few Presbyterian sympathizers in the army camps. They called five army officers—Lilburne (probably Robert, John's brother), Ireton, the two Hammonds, and Grimes—to appear at the bar of the house and be examined.

Notes to Chapter Seven

1. Written in a contemporaries' hand on the final page of the newsletter *The Scottish Dove,* No 88, in the *Thomason Tracts,* E 290, British Library.
2. Number 254 of the 1360 subscribers was Elizabeth Bradshaw of St. Katherine's, widow.
3. The dates of these letters are contested. Hugh Bellot's manuscript dates them 1642. A. Craig Gibson, in *Trans. of the Hist Soc of Lancs & Ches,* New Ser. Vol 11, dates them 1644/45. Although Bellot's date of 1642 is not impossible, I have accepted Gibson's dating on the assumption that Lady Davenport would have found it difficult to be in correspondence with Bradshawe in September 1642. Sir Humphrey Davenport served King Charles as Lord Chief Baron of the Exchequer until he was replaced, as a result of his ill-health, by Sir Richard Lane in January 1643/44. Davenport died in March 1644/45.
4. *History of Congleton,* Manchester Univ Press for the Congleton History Society, W.B. Stephens, ed., pg 73.
5. Other members were, Sir Thomas Middleton, Lord Brooke, Edmund Prideaux, Lord Howard, William Purefoy, Walter Long, John Pym, Earl of Manchester, Lord Say & Sele, Sir Thomas Soame, Mr. Spurstow, William Strode, Sir Henry Vane the younger, Sammuel Vassall, and Lord Wharton.
6. *Committee for Sequestration, April, 1643*—Lords; Earl of Pembroke Earl of Northumberland, Earl of Rutland, Earl of Manchester, Earl Bullingbroke, Earl of Salisbury, Earl of Kent, Earl of Warwick, Lord Howard, Lord Say & Sele, Lord Wharton, Lord North, Lord Grey de Wark, Lord Howard, and one other Lord Neconham ? : Commons; Sir Thomas Barrington, Sir Peter Wentworth, Mr. Holland, Mr. Pym, Mr. Bond, Mr. Browne, Mr. Prideaux, Mr. Lisle, Mr. Glyn, Mr. Ellis, Mr. Gordon, Mr. Ashurst, Mr. Chas Woodhouse, Mr. Barnadston, Mr. Trenchard, Sir Thomas Middleton, Sir Gilbert Gerrard, Mr. Sergeant Wild, Mr. "Solicitor," and two others.
7. Probably a booke called *An Exposition on the second Epistle of Paule to the Thessalonians* written by William Bradshawe and Master Thomas Gattiker, first printed 20 March 1620 and reprinted 1641.
8. In 1878 J.P. Earwaker, East *Cheshire, Past and Present,* "Amongst the State Papers at the Records Office are a series of interrogatories administered in the trial of some persons suspected of delinquency . . . In these many alien subjects are touched upon . . . These papers are at present very roughly

indexed and I had to read over many hundred sheets of MSS *State Papers, Domestic, Interregnum Letters,* Vol 308 . . . . Every page had to be cead thoroughly for fear any little entry might escape unnoticed."

9. *Harle Mss* 1999, 2130; "Bookes out of the Closet; or Studie 588 of all sorts, Bound Bookes, paper bookes, the Court Roulles, and out of the Parlour 2 Statute Bookes, 1 Red Rudge and 4 Blankets that the Bookes are packed up in . . ."
10. J. P. Earwaker, *East Cheshire, Past & Present*, (1878). Vol I, 386-87
11. Henry Heginbotham, *Stockport Ancient & Modern*, (1892). William Nichols, D.O., was Rector of Cheadle but had been removed by Brereton and the deputy lieutenants of Cheshice in 1644. Nicols was brother-in-law to the first wife of John Bradshaw of Bradshaw in Lancashire.
12. Hugh H. L. Bellot, Barrister-at-Law Inner Temple, *Gray's Inn and Lincoln's Inn*, (1925).
13. *Add'l Mss 11332.* ff 70 119-20; D. Underdown, *Recruiter Elections*, EHR lxxii,252-6. All historians have assumed this was John Bradshawe the regicide. This is by no means certain. There were other Bradshaws in Newcastle from an early date. T Pape, *History of Newcastle under-Lyme*, (1938); John Bradshaw was enrolled as a Burgess of Newcastle in 1579. John Bradshaw in mentioned in Newcastle's charter of 1590. "John Bradshawe of London, ffencer" paid an assessment of 6d. for a tenement in the iron market, "next adjoyninge the said yron Hall" in 1608. John Bradshaw was admitted as a burgess in 1629. "John Bradshawe, Assize broker" appears in 1637, and one of the same name appears as the "supervisor of highways" with Richard Bowker, in 1639. In August 1641, John Bradshaw (without the appended "e") of Congleton" was chosen Steward for the town of Newcastle-under-Lyme and served for the next eighteen years, until 17 Nov 1659, by which time he was dead, It has been generally accepted that this was the regicide, as previously noted there was at least one other "John Bradshaw of Congleton" who died early in 1659.
14. *Add'l Mss* 11333, f. 83, and *Victoria County History of Cheshire* call him "John Bradshaw a local lawyer working for the Committee of Compounding" which would therefore identify him as John Bradshawe the regicide. There is, however, the problem of the other John Bradshaw, Attorney-General of Cheshire, who was not the regicide. James Croston, F.S.A., *Nooks and Corners of Lancashire and Cheshire*, 40, makes the mistake of confusing the two, Bradshaw and Bradshawe, when he imagines that the regicide was named Attorney-General of Cheshire in 1637. This last Attorney-General John Bradshaw was more likely Brereton's nominee for Chester. He was

half-brother to Edward Bradshaw, alderman of Chester, and to Richard Bradshaw, Brereton's Quartermaster. Edward was Mayor of Chester in 1647 and in again in 1653; Richard in 1648. Richard was Ambassador to Hamburg during Cromwell's Protectorate. These Bradshaws, descended from the Bradshaws of Aspull, would have held greater influence in Chester city than John Bradshawe the regicide. Edward remained in the city during the royalist occupation and was prepared to surrender the city to Brereton when the siege ended. Richard served as one of Brereton's commissioners for negotiating the surrender. It is clear from Brereton's correspondence that he termed both Richard Bradshaw and John Bradshawe the regicide his *kinsmen*.

15. *The Letter Books of Sir William Brereton*, Vol II, Rec Soc of Lancs & Ches, Ed. by R.N. Dore, 1984; Brereton wrote to John Bradshaw on 30th December 1645 to mention the drawbacks Bradshaw would have as a candidate Letter # 1148.

16. *Cal. of Proceedings, Comm. for Compounding,*; 22 October 1646 Testimony from J. Bradshaw, sheriff John Bradshaw of Bradshaw, sheriff of Lancashire. and Ralph Assheton, that Edmund Assheton's son James of Chadderton may not be prejudiced as to the settlement made on him by his father on his marriage, because of adhering to Parliament, the old man having called him a rebel, and threatened not to leave him a foot of land if he could help it.

CHAPTER EIGHT

Time of Trial

> *Hellish Complotment! which a League renews*
> *Lesse with the men, than the actions of the Jews*
> *Such was their Bedlam Rabble, and the Cry*
> *Of Justice now, 'mongst them was Crucified*
> *Pilates Content is Bradshaws Sentence here;*
> *The Judgment Hall's removed to Westminster . . .*
>
> **Works of the Great Monarch &**
> **Glorious Martyr King Charles I, 1649;**
> **Thomason Tracts, E1220.**

✠

IT HAS BEEN often repeated that John Bradshawe was an obscure provincial lawyer chosen to preside at the king's trial because no greater judge could be found for the post. Lord Clarendon said that Bradshawe was little known in halls of Parliament but much in favor among contentious petitioners of the city. Presumably he had in mind the contentious John Lilburne, William Prynne, and others. A different picture could be drawn by reading the contemporary records.

Certainly Bradshawe's tireless activity as Attorney General for Sequestrations and Junior Counsel to Parliament would not have gone unnoticed. He had demonstrated his considerable legal skill before the House of Lords in the reversal of Lilburne's Star Chamber conviction. It was both houses that appointed and confirmed him chief justice of Cheshire. The Commons had attempted to appoint him one of the keepers of the Great Seal. At Parliament's order he had prosecuted the state trials of Macguire, MacMahon, and Jeffreys. As previously noted, it is difficult to understand his appointments from the Presbyterian-controlled House of Commons unless these were made on the perception of Bradshawe's alibities. Bradshawe did not agree with the Presbyterians, but he had taken the Solemn League and Covenant. All along the way he had made a few allies and many powerful enemies.

Some historians have been confused by a document that exists in the House of Lords manuscripts.[1] It is a petition, without heading, calling for the establishment of the Presbyterian church in England, signed with approximately ten thousand names. It seems to date from late 1647, or perhaps slightly later. The list of signatures is headed by that of "John Bradshaw." It has led some to think that John Bradshawe the regicide favored the Presbyterians. This signature is surely not the signature of John Bradshawe the regicide, who was firmly Independent, but that of John Bradshaw of Bradshaw who was a Presbyterian.

On February 23, 1647, the House of Lords ordered the hearing of charges brought against Cecil Calvert, Lord Baltimore. Dr. Walter Walker, a judge of the admiralty and prerogative courts, and John Bradshawe were assigned counsel for the state and the merchants against Baltimore.[2] Bradshawe and Walker won a judgment for the state and the merchants.

Throughout the first civil war, the university establishment at Oxford had grudgingly supported the king. They seemed to have little choice. The king had chosen Oxford as his headquarters. During the uneasy peace, Parliament thought it high time to deal with the Royalist influences in the universities. An ordinance of May 1, 1647, established a committee to visit and reform the University of Oxford. Sir William Brereton was one of the committee, and William Prynne was one of the visitors. Dr. Samuel Fell, dean of Christ church and vice chancellor of Oxford, resisted the visitors and maintained that the king was the only visitor established by ancient charters, and that these new visitors were come by an ordinance to which the king had not given his consent. Fell was imprisoned at London from October until May or June the following year for resisting. The university requested legal counsel to argue their case before the committee.

Prynne confidently supported the university's request. In private he asked the committee to approve the request and assured them that no counsel in England would agree that the king was the only visitor. In fact, he said, it could be shown that no king had ever claimed that privilege, and King Charles in particular had disclaimed it. This skirted the issue of whether the two houses of Parliament held the virtual power of ordinance without the king's assent. It was a key point to the university's case. The university had spoken with Matthew Hale and Chaloner Chute of the Middle Temple in preparation for their hearing.

Mr. Cheynill and Mr. Wilkinson, two of the visitors, suggested that Hale, Chute, and John Bradshawe be assigned as counsel for the committee. This effectively banned Hale and Chute from being counsel for the university. Bradshawe prepared the committee's case and ignored Hale and Chute, probably because of their prouniversity opinions.

Late in November, the university approached John Herne of Lincolns Inn, John Latch, Francis Phillips, and Mr. Leigh of the Inner Temple.

The committee under the chairman Francis Rous,[3] MP for Truro, began hearings at London in the Painted Chamber. Dr. Morley of the university apologized to the committee for any slur to Parliament and once again pleaded that the university had no counsel. He questioned whether John Bradshawe, or indeed any other, should be counsel to the committee, who were to be the judges of the matter. There was some applause followed by debate.

Bradshawe immediately launched into the principal point—the king's sole right to visit. John Selden, the great legal historian and one of the committee, interrupted, saying he thought it unfit that Bradshawe should "enter the main cause, or the heart and bowels of the business before the University had counsel."[4] The question of Counsel was carried in favor of the university by two votes. Dr. Morley asked for Hale, Chute, Hearne, Latch, Phillips, and Richard Newdigate. They were approved. Col. Herbert Morley, a committeeman, remarked that if the university had this many counselors, there would not be able lawyers enough left in town to plead for them.

A few days later, the university's counselors asked for a formal statement of the charge. The committee thought this a waste of time for *the doctors knew it, for they had given in their answer to it*. Bradshawe told them that disobedience and contempt to the authority of Parliament might be the charge. Chute seized upon this point and suggested that Sir Robert Harley bring in the university's charters for examination on that point. He insisted that the committee had exceeded Parliament's ordinance. Specifically that the Parliamentary oath of loyalty was to be given with five commissioners present, but the committee had said one was sufficient. Further, that it was against the law for any man to be both a judge and a party to the contest. Finally, the commission was written in English while all commissions under the Great Seal were usually issued in Latin. Prynne answered this last point by saying that the ordinances were in English and that most of the scholars had been soldiers. If the commission were not in English, they would not have understood it. The committee ruled against the university and removed Vice Chancellor Fell and others.

Phillip Herbert, the Puritan Earl of Pembroke and a member of the Committee for Sequestration, was appointed Parliament's chancellor of Oxford. He was probably one of Bradshawe's strongest allies. Pembroke died in 1649, and Oliver Cromwell was chosen chancellor of Oxford.

The point of this reform was not lost on the Oxford colleges. At the start of 1648, George Bradshaw,[5] the new master of Balliol, commanded that no reference to the king or queen was to be made in chapel prayers or in the ancient grace said before meals in the Great Hall. The text of the prayer had long been hung up in the hall pasted on an old wooden table. He demanded it be taken down. With a flourish he scratched out the very names of the king and queen.

How had it come to this? Ever since that fateful summer of 1642, opponents of the king had held to the belief that once they had gained military victory, the king must grant all their demands. The government of England would rest in the hands of the House of Commons, shored up by the influence of the Lords, under the respected figurehead of the king.

The king believed differently. Even in defeat and confinement he continued to risk his life and freedom on the principle of his divine right to personally rule the realm. He pretended to agree to concessions, played for time, and devised secret plots. He wrote to William Tyringham, "some designs for our present enlargement will speedily be put into execution . . . money is our only want you are at present provided to furnish us with five hundred pound . . . without delay . . . Deliver that sum to this bearer, and if possibly without noise, in gold, to whom you may give credit, though we must not give you his name, for he desires to be concealed . . . communicate this negotiation to no one living."[6] In the spring of 1648, one of these secret plots was revealed. A Scottish army invaded northern England, and Royalist uprisings broke out in South Wales, East Anglia, and Kent. From the Continent, King Charles's son wrote a secret commission to Sir Edward Hopton "to raise a regiment of horse and a regiment of foot, and kill, slay, or put to flight any who oppose." By the end of summer, however, it had all come to nothing, and the Royalists had been defeated everywhere.

The king played a dangerous game, and he knew he might be secretly assassinated as previous kings of England had been. In fact, the army officers guarding the king foiled some assassination plots.

Bradshawe, in his role of chief justice of Flintshire, appointed John Edisbury to the office of clerk of the court for the counties of Denbigh and Montgomery in 1647. John Edisbury was the steward of Chirk Castle for Sir Thomas Middleton, William Brereton's old adversary. Appointing Edisbury as clerk may have been Bradshawe's attempt to heal that rift between Middleton and Brereton. Bradshawe had presided over the Cheshire county assize in April 1648, despite the threat of Royalist plots and the Scots invasion. He was presented with a petition complaining of forestalling of corn and victuals (i.e., an attempt to corner the food market). It was pointed out that although there was enough corn in the county, there was a shortage in the markets because forestallers were buying up whole quantities of barley and other corn. The petitioners, one of whom was Edward Burghall, master of Bradshawe's old school at Bunbury, requested the laws against forestalling be strictly enforced. Bradshawe's holographic marginal note on the petition says, "I like it well that this good and wholesome Lawe be put in Execution and am for that purpose hither sent amongst you. But to take any order herein before the abuse be presented in an orderly way is against the Law." He then asked that the petitioners present the names of any offenders. It was reported[7] that Bradshawe delivered a three-hour speech to a jury at Cheshire in June, during which he declared, "This man, who calls himself King, is more cruel than Nero."

For some reason, Bradshawe's Cheshire judicial circuit had included Nantwich but omitted the city of Chester.[8] In response to complaints, Bradshawe wrote:

Sir, I have rec'd one from you and 3 other aldermen by this last Post which is the first Time I heard from you since I was by the Parliament appointed for that service at Chester. You well know the occasion for omitting Chester the last time and if the like other said sad impediment do not happen you may be assured I will no way alter from the usual place of holding the grand sessions, nor shall I be less affectionate to your city than any of my predecessors in office have been, wherein I may do you real good; and I shall hope also that yourself and the other Governors of the City and Assistants in office to you will be evermindful of the Cities true welfare which at present consists in nothing more than in a cheerful and constant compliance with the directions of Parliament and in them with the kingdoms true interest which is the Duty and Direction of every honest Englishman to do. And in so doing and not otherwise no man shall more willingly comply with you nor which himself more enabled to serve you than, Your old Acquaintance and well wishing friend, Jo: Bradshawe. Grayes Inn 1 August 1648. Endorsed on the back *for the Right Worshipful Mr. Ro: Wright, maior of Chester.*

On the nineteenth, the house ordered Bradshawe to go on his circuit.

The House of Commons, now exercising all the functions of the old officers of the Crown, responded to a new call for sergeants-at-law on October 11, Sir Thomas Widdrington, Sir Thomas Bedingfield, Mr. Keble, Mr. Thorp, and "Mr. Bradshaw, of Gray's Inn, to be of that number." On day one of the commissioners of the Great Seal, Bulstrode Whitlocke advised Bradshawe to be like his predecessor celebrated by Chaucer, "A Sergeant-at-Law, wary and wise." This creation was a necessary first step toward filling the many vacant positions among the judges of the Common Pleas, who were recruited from the ranks of the sergeants. It had been the custom for newly appointed sergeants to present gold rings to the king, queen, and high court judges. Inscribed on the rings were the sergeant's mottos. Whitlocke says that Bradshawe's motto was "Pacis justicia basis." Watson gives it as "Regi serviri libertas."

Bradshawe, Cromwell, their Independent allies, and the army councils believed that no sovereign immunity from prosecution could be exercised for the king, but to secretly assassinate him would be as unlawful as any other murder. The king, like any other Englishman charged with capital crimes, should be tried by the common law of England. John Canne wrote that those who determined to try the king "took no dark or doubtful way; no indirect by-course, but went in the open and plain path of Justice, Reason, Law, and Religion."[9] The authority of the English people was declared to be above that of the king. On November 20, 1648, the army presented to the Commons their remonstrance demanding that the king be brought to trial, that any future sovereign should be elected by the people, that Parliaments should be annual or biennial, and that the elective franchise should be extended.

Throughout the summer, the Presbyterians in Commons began to gain the ascendancy. Cromwell and many of his fellow soldier members were absent, engaged in suppressing Royalist uprisings. Presbyterians in Commons tried to negotiate a treaty with the king, but by November they saw no sign the king would concede, although they continued to promote the so-called Treaty of Newport. On the morning December 5, the Commons countered the army's remonstrance by carrying a motion—that the king's concessions to the propositions of Parliament were sufficient grounds for settling the peace of the kingdom. The following morning, as the unsuspecting Parliament began to assemble, Col. Thomas Pride and his regiment barred any member who was not of the Independent faction. The restrained Presbyterian and other non-Independent members were locked in Mr. Duke's alehouse, commonly known as Hell, under the old Exchequer Court.

Cromwell had arrived in London the night before, fresh from his victory over the Duke of Hamilton's Scots army, and sat in the Commons the following day. Several petitions were offered to the Parliament against the king. At the same time, Ireton's regiment petitioned Cromwell. It was moved to charge the king with capital crimes, and a committee was appointed to draw up the charges. Cromwell rose to announce that "if any man moved this upon design, then I should think him the greatest traitor in the world, but since Providence and Necessity had cast them upon it, he would pray to God to bless their counsels, tho' he was not prepared at present to give them advice."

Throughout his futile negotiations with the Presbyterians, the king had been at Hurst Castle in Hampshire, having been moved there from Carisbrooke Castle on the Isle of Wight. The king was now moved to Windsor Castle. Col. Thomas Harrison was commissioned to guard the king while the reduced House of Commons made preparations for his trial.

Commons sent up to the Lords an ordinance for impeaching Charles Stuart, King of England, of high treason, and trying him by commissioners to be nominated in the ordinance. It was rejected by the sixteen Lords who remained in London. Upon hearing of the rejection, Commons overwhelmingly voted an act that contained three watershed resolutions: first, that the people, under God, are the origin of all just power; second, that the Commons of England, being chosen by and representing the people, are the supreme power of the nation; and third, that whatsoever is enacted or declared the law by the House of Commons assembled in Parliament, it has the force of law through the consent of the king and the House of Peers be not had thereunto. Forty-six members were present in the house, and the act passed by a narrow majority of six votes. There was no going back now.

They then proceeded to establish a High Court of Justice to try the king and examine witnesses. One hundred thirty-five commissioners were named to the court, of which twenty or more were enough to constitute a quorum. The commissioners included a Scottish peer, an Irish peer, a knight of the Bath, four sons of English peers, eleven baronets, members of the Commons, army officers, lawyers, citizens, and country gentlemen. The precedent for this high court was based on the style of a court established by Queen Elizabeth for the condemnation of Mary Queen of Scots.

The high court, as originally nominated, represented "the most respectable and substantial elements in the country,"[10] but in the end the three Lord Chief Justices, Oliver St. John of the Common Pleas, Henry Rolle of the Chancery, and John Wilde of the Exchequer, refused to participate. On the whole these judges' refusal seems to have been on grounds of deviation from established legal procedure rather than on moral objections. If Charles Stuart have been indicted by a bill of the grand jury, arraigned and made to plead guilty or innocent before a petty jury, they most probably would have agreed to try him and pronounce sentence. Oliver St. John had been an outspoken opponent of the king for many years, and he had been cocounsel with Bradshawe in the prosecution of Judge Jenkins. As solicitor general in 1641, he had advocated circumventing the normal rule of law in arguing, before the Lords, the case for a Bill of Attainder against Strafford, saying, "it was never accounted either cruelty or foul play to knock foxes or wolves on the head . . . because they are beasts of prey." He was related to Cromwell by marriage. St. John was descended from the cadet branch of the St. John's of Bletsoe, whose ancestry descended from Sir John St. John and his wife Alice Bradshaw of Haigh in Lancashire. The arms St. John are quartered with the arms of Bradshaw at St. Mary's church in Bletsoe.

Many others, including General Fairfax, did not attend or attended only briefly. It must be said that some refused to participate simply out of a sense of personal danger. There were many absentees who asked to be excused because of incapacity, illness, or injuries.

Two of the commissioners of the Great Seal, Bulstrode Whitlocke and Sir Thomas Widdrington, absented themselves. Whitlocke's case was more complex. Nearly ten years earlier he had served as chairman of the committee charged with hearing the charges of high treason against Strafford. John Pym had chosen Whitlocke for the post of chairman for the very reasons that John Bradshawe was about to be chosen judge of King Charles. He was a promising newcomer of recognized legal experience; and he was supported by powerful friends, known for his moderation, and not regarded as a Commons man. After the Commons had succeeded in securing Strafford's execution with a Bill of Attainder, Whitlocke swore to never again take part in a capital case. After the king's execution, Whitlocke remained Bradshawe's friend and spoke of the nation's present alterations brought about by unavoidable necessity. He served on the board of governors of Charterhouse with Bradshawe and Cromwell. He received a pardon after the Restoration, busied himself writing, made the acquaintance of William Penn, and died 1675 in some degree of poverty.

Cromwell was the first president of the commission, and shortly thereafter, Ireton was the second. Bradshawe was named but as an assistant only. Later he was promoted to the rank of commissioner.

Sir William Brereton was strangely absent from most these proceedings. He may have been recovering from the injuries he had recently received. In a narrow London lane, he had come face-to-face with William Compton, the Royalist earl of Northampton, who immediately gave challenge. Brereton refused to fight and turned to leave. Northampton furiously inflicted several sword cuts on Brereton before being restrained by his companions. We have no way of knowing if Bradshawe was present at the scene.

Christmas came and went under the Puritan regime, although it was much less to the taste of the rigid Presbyterians than to the more liberal Independents. On Saturday, two days before Christmas, a compromise was attempted. The fierce party in the Commons pressed for the king's trial. Those of more moderate opinion urged that the king was already defeated, and no further action was required except to defend the realm against future tyrants. Nicholas Love expressed the opinion that even if the king were brought to trial, it would come to nothing because the "King could clearly acquit himself." Whitlocke and Widdrington made brief appearances, sided with the moderates, and went on to a secret meeting in Speaker Lenthall's chamber. Various compromises were advanced from the establishment of a regency in the name of King Charles's youngest son, seven-year-old Henry Duke of Gloucester, to the formation of an outright republic. No agreement was reached, and another meeting was scheduled for Monday, Christmas day.

Still there were joyous celebrations and feastings, but on a greatly reduced scale. The king celebrated Christmas at Windsor. On that day, while the Commons was meeting, William Fielding, Earl of Denbigh, attempted to secretly present Cromwell's last compromise offer to the king. Denbigh had gone to Windsor ostensibly to visit his brother-in-law, the Duke of Hamilton, who was also held captive there. In reality it was to offer these final terms to the king; Charles was to abandon his negative statements, he was to consent to the abolition of the episcopacy, and he was to abjure the Scots. Speaker Lenthall, who must have been privy to Denbigh's mission, said on Saturday night: *"if the King come not off roundly now in point of concession, he would be utterly lost."* The king either refused to see Denbigh or rejected the offer and continued his dinner.[11]

Whitlocke and Widdrington were called to attend the commission, but they silently left London on the morning coach for Reading where the spent the night. They reached Whitlocke's house near Wallingford on the following day. The country's two most eminent lawyers had now divorced themselves from the king's trial. On January 6, Whitlocke returned to London and received a communication: "It is this day ordered that the Commissioners . . . do meet on Monday (8th January) . . . in the Painted Chamber." The Painted Chamber was chosen in preference to the Exchequer Chamber, it was stated, because there had been a quarrel about drinking to Henry, Duke of Gloucester, as "Harry the Ninth" in the Exchequer Chamber. So at that late date, some commission members still may have held hope that a regency might be established and the king's trial averted. There were suggestions that the Duke of Hamilton be tried first, and by such example, the king might be brought to his senses. Denbigh's failure was not yet generally known. Only fifty-two of the one hundred thirty-five commissioners attended, and having conducted little business, they adjourned until Wednesday.

Bradshawe may have been at Marple Hall in Cheshire with his brother for the Christmas season because on January 10 the commissioners meet in the Painted Chamber to name a president of the high court. John Bradshawe, who was in the country, was selected.[12] William Say was ordered to take his place until his return. A special summons was sent for Bradshawe. Bradshawe appeared on the twelfth to attend the commission. According to the former order, he was called to take the place as president of the court.

He made an earnest apology for himself to be excused; but therein not prevailing, in obedience to the desires and commands of this court he submitted to their order, and took his place accordingly. There-upon the court ordered that he should have the title of Lord President, as well without as within the said court—against which title he pressed much to be heard to offer his exceptions, but was overruled.[13]

Clarendon saw it differently, "When Bradshawe was first nominated, he seemed much surprised, and very resolute to refuse it; which he did in such a manner, and so much enlarging upon his own want of abilities to undergo so important a charge, that it was very evident he expected to be put to that apology. And when he was pressed with more importunity than could have been used by chance with great humility he accepted the office, which he administered with all pride, impudence, and superciliousness imaginable."[14]

Counsel to prosecute the king were selected: William Steele,[15] Isaac Dorislaus, John Cook, and John Aske.[16] Steele later was excused because of illness. Edward Dendy was chosen sergeant-at-arms.

There were meetings on the fifteenth and seventeenth. Draft charges against the king were presented, debated, and amended. Administrative orders were approved. The college of heralds was consulted about the dress for the officers of the court. Railings were ordered to be made and set up at the south end of Westminster Hall where the court would set. Provisions and temporary lodgings were arranged for Bradshawe at Sir Abraham Williams's house in Palace Yard. The sword of state and the mace were to be carried before him on his official progresses.

Much has been made of Bradshawe's high-crowned hat as representing some statement of arrogance. In viewing it at the Ashmolean Museum at Oxford, it seems to be a particularly uncomfortable headgear. It must have been the choice of the Heralds of the College of Arms. The Speaker of the House and the Lord Chancellor wore round high-crowned beaver hats in the middle of the seventeenth century; judges wore the coif, a black cloth cap which they continued to don into the twentieth century whenever they passed the death sentence. Wigs and three-cornered hats only came into England after the Restoration. Bradshawe's hat, however, does have one innovation. It's lined with small plates of sheet iron. There had been rumors of death threats against Bradshawe.

Figure 12. Bradshawe's armored hat at the Ashmolean Museum, Oxford

Assuming that the authority of court was now legally constituted and all preparations were in place, the king's trial could begin. A last meeting on the nineteenth was tumultuous. Algernon Sydney attended for his second and last time. He wrote to his father, the Earl of Leicester: *I did positively oppose Cromwell and Bradshawe, and others who would have the trial to go on, and drew my reasons from these two points. First, the king could be tried by no court, secondly that no man could be tried by that court. This being alleged in vain, and Cromwell using these formal words, 'I tell you we will cut off his head with the crown on it', I replied 'You may take your own course, I cannot stop you, but I will keep myself clear from having any hand in this business', immediately went out of the room and never returned.*[17] The charge against the king was again considered and amended that day.

While these discussions progressed, the king was being brought from Windsor in a closed coach drawn by six horses. He spoke to no one, and the troop of horsemen accompanying him kept at bay the few curious people standing alongside the road. The king had received formal notice of his impeding trial but knew nothing more. He had not seen the act for setting up the court, nor did he know the names of his judges. It seems he was prepared to resist any effort to remove his divine right, and if necessary, die a royal martyr. What could the court do if he refused to plead or even cooperate with the whole affair? The king's refusal could be a dangerous snare. There had already been recognition of this difficulty, and the ordinance January 6 contained a special provision in case the king should refuse to plead to the charge against him.

There was an ancient concept in English law that jurisdiction was based on consent, and that it was objectionable to try a man without his consent. How that consent was obtained was not material. After the choice of trial by combat was abolished in the Middle Ages, for centuries thereafter the prisoner was asked, How will you be tried? The acceptable answer was, By my God and my country. He then had the ability to plead to the charge, and if he did not, an effort was made to persuade him.

In 1752, George Smith Green published *Oliver Cromwell an Historical Play* in which he imagined a conversation between Cromwell, Ireton, and Bradshaw on the morning of the king's trial:

> Cromwell—*"Mr. President, you are welcome, Be brief, I pray, and tell my son and me The issue of last Night's elaborate Toil; What new Discovery you've made in Law, To set a Gloss upon this gloomy Business, And satisfy the gaping, murmuring Multitude?"*
>
> Bradshaw—*"The king, himself, will furnish us with that. His evil Counsellors have bid him question by what Authority we hold our Court: And, till that Interrogative is answer'd—He's not to plead, but frustrate his Arraignment. By which Device he will be deem'd contemptuous; and may, by standing mute, be press'd to Death."*

Torture as a means of extorting a confession had long been officially outlawed by English common law, although King James violated the law in the case of Guy Fawkes who in 1605 was certainly threatened with torture and most probably actually racked in the effort to gain his confession.

A defendant who refused to plead when brought before a court threatened to balk every attempt of judgment. To deal with such cases, the punishment called "peine forte et dure" (the strong and hard pain), or pressing to death, was brought into use. According to common law, it did not legally constitute torture, and it survived until 1772. By standing mute in contempt of the court and dying without being convicted, the accused saved forfeitures and was able to pass on his estates and possessions to his heirs.

Stow, in his *Survey of London, 1720*, described the manner of pressing to death: "The criminal is sent back to the prison whence he came, and there laid in some low dark room, upon bare ground on his back, all naked, except his privy parts, his arms and legs drawn with cords fastened to several parts of the room; and then there is laid on his body, iron, stone, or lead, so much as he can bear; the next day he shall have three morsels of barley bread, without drink; the third day shall have to drink some of the kennel water (stagnet water from a puddle in the prison) with bread. And this method is in strictness to be observed until he is dead." Sometimes a sharp stone or piece of timber was placed under the back of the prisoner to hasten his death.

A strange case exists in London's County Court, April 16, 1656: "Record of arraignment of John Thompson for the death of John Bradshawe, with a record that the same John Thompson stood mute and was therefore[18] sentenced to peine forte et dure."

When Major Strangeways was condemned to this punishment in 1658, a heavy piece of iron was laid crosswise over his heart; and his friends, or the prison attendants, stood upon the iron—he died within eight or ten minutes.[19] In another recorded case, the accused, after experiencing a few minutes of the pain, agreed to plead and be tried. In 1726, a man accused of murder refused to plead and was pressed for one and three quarters of an hour, after which he pleaded not guilty and was then tried, convicted, and hanged. There was one recorded case of pressing to death in America: that of Giles Corey who refused to plead to the charge of witchcraft in 1692.

George Smith Green missed one crucial point in his imagined conversation. By law, *peine forte et dure* could not be applied in treason cases, and King Charles was to be charged with high treason. Refusal to plead to a charge of treason, as to that of a misdemeanor, was taken as a guilty plea. Bradshawe would never have even contemplated King Charles's death by pressing because he knew the law. Cromwell would have realized, or been counseled by Bradshawe, the subsequent effect that the Crown and all royal possessions would have been inherited by the king's eldest son; clearly not a happy conclusion for the regicides.

On the twentieth, the king was brought by barge from St. James palace to the house of Sir Robert Cotton adjoining Westminster Hall within the precinct. Meanwhile several members of the high court were meeting in the Painted Chamber to agree what was to be said to the king when he appeared before them. There is no official record of their debates; but Sir Purbeck Temple, a Royalist plotting the king's escape, said he heard them talking.[20] This is a very strange account. Tempe said that he bribed the custodian of the Painted Chamber to secrete him in a hole in the wall behind the wall hangings. "When they had finished their prayers," said Temple, "came the news that the king was landing at Sir Robert Cotton's house, at which Cromwell ran to the window, looking on the king as he came up the garden. He turned as white as the wall, he speaks to Bradshawe and Sir Henry Mildmay how they and Sir William Brereton had concluded on such a business, then turning to the board said thus My masters, he is come, he is come, and now we are doing that great work that the nation will be full of. Therefore I desire you to let us resolve here what answer we will give the king when he comes before us, for the first question he will ask us will be by what authority and commission we do try him. To which none answered presently. Then, after a little space, Hen. Marten . . . rose up and said 'In the name of the Commons in Parliament assembled and all the good people of England'. Which none contradicted . . ." A message from the Commons was brought in asking that members of the Commons presently in the Painted Chamber come to the House. At a second gathering in the Painted Chamber after midday, it was decided that "in case the prisoner shall in language or carriage toward the court be insolent, outrageous or contemptuous, that it shall be left to the lord president to reprehend him therefore and admonish him of his duty or to command the taking away of the prisoner and, if he see cause, to withdraw or adjourn the court. But as to the prisoner's putting off his hat, the court will not insist upon it for the day, and that if the king desire time to answer, the lord president is to give him time." The members of the court then marched to Westminster Hall.

Figure 13. Plaque set in Westminster Hall marking the site of King Charles' trial

Colonel Fox and twenty pikemen lead the procession followed by the crier, the ushers, and the court messengers. Colonel Humphreys bearing the sword of state, and Sergeant Dendy carrying the mace, preceded Lord President Bradshawe. The hem of Bradshawe's long black tufted gown was borne by a train bearer. Upon entering the hall, Bradshawe proceeded to the south end and took his seat in the prepared crimson velvet chair behind a desk. A crimson velvet foot cushion was placed before him. All the other members of the court followed in file and took their seats on each side and behind Bradshawe. The sword and mace were laid on a table in front of the clerks. Opposite the table and behind the bar, facing Bradshawe, another crimson velvet chair was prepared for the king.

The crier called—Ho Yes! Ho Yes Ho Yes! All manner of persons that have anything to do in this Court, come and give your attendance. Ho Yes! Every man keep silence upon pain of imprisonment and hear the commission of this Court read, which is authorised by an Act of the Commons of England in Parliament assembled.[21]

The act was read, and the roll call was made, each commissioner standing up when his name was called. Sixty-eight[22] of the original 135 commissioners were present. There was a reported disturbance when Fairfax's name was called, although none of the licensed accounts of the trial note this incident. He was not present, but his wife was, seated high up in the galleries reserved for dignitaries. Clarendon said she cried, "He has too much wit to be here!" Rushworth remembered it differently—"the Lady Fairfax . . . interrupted the reading of the following names of the Commissioners, etc, by speaking aloud to the Court . . . that her husband . . . was not there in person, nor would ever set among them, and therefore they did wrong to name him as a sitting commissioner." It was variously unofficially reported that the court suffered her rebuke in silence or that troops leveled their guns at her.

Twelve men were sent to fetch the king.

Notes to Chapter Eight

1. *House of Lords Mss, 1514-1711*, New Ser, Vol II, 471
2. Lord Baltimore was the Catholic proprietor of the Maryland colony. There was a protestant faction in the colony. They had driven out the proprietary Governor and Parliament was unable to exercise the control that they claimed. The conflict taking place in England was reproduced on a smaller scale in the American colonies. Parliament threatened to revoke Baltimore's charter. Bradshawe dealt with a case before the Committee of Sequestration in which Richard Austin, an informer on behalf of the state, was examined. Lord Baltimore had contested with Thomas, late Lord Arundel of Wardour, about the right to the manor of Sembley and Hooke farm in Wiltshire. On the basis of Bradshawe's examination of Austin and his report to the Committee the case was decided against Baltimore. Lord Arundel had been lord of the manor of Glossop, Derbyshire, and it was he who appointed John Bradshawe the Steward of Glossop manor in 1630. Arundel had also been brother-in-law to Pembroke, they both having married daughters of the Earl of Shrewsbury.
3. *Burke's Extinct Baronetages, Burkes Commoners* Francis Rous of Lanrake, Cornwall was M.P. for Tregony 1625/6, for Truro 1640/1. He was Speaker of the Short Parliament. His brother Robert was married to John Pym's sister. His nephew, Major Anthony Rous, was married to Mary daughter of William Bradshaw, Esq., of Lancashire. Anthony was M.P. for Cornwall, 1653 and 1656 and Navy and Admiralty Commissioner in 1653.
4. Antony Wood, *History & Antiquities of the University of Oxford*, (1767).
5. George Bradshaw was tutor to John Evelyn, the diarist. Evelyn wrote of his dislike of George Bradshaw and of John Bradshawe, the regicide. George was eldest son of Nicholas Bradshaw Rector of St. Mildred Breadstreet London (1604) and Rector of Ockham in Surrey (1635). George's brothers Richard Bradshaw and Robert (of Balliol College in 1635, aged 16) were required to compound for their estates and their cases were reviewed by John Bradshawe. A funeral brass commemorating Nicholas Bradshaw and his eighteen children remains in Ockham church. Nicholas, matriculated Balliol College 6th November 1590 aged 15, B.A. 1594, M.A. 1599, was the author of *Canticum Evangelicum Summan Sacri Evanglli Contenens* published in London 1635.
6. Letter dated 10th April 1648—Geo. Lipscomb, *History and Antiquities of the County of Buckinghamshire*, vol IV, (1847), 377

7. *Mercurius Electicus*, 21st-28th June 1648, and 6th-13th February 1649, *Thomason Tracts* E. 450 and E. 542, British Library.
8. J. Hall, *History of the Town and Parish of Nantwich, Cheshire*, (1883)
9. *The Golden Rule of Justice Advanced*, (London, 1649), 96-97
10. C.V. Wedgewood, *Trial of Charles I*, (Collins, London, 1964),
11. *Mercurius Melancholicus*, 25 Dec 1648, 1 Jan 1648/49, C.V. Wedgewood in *Trial of Charles I*, 77, expresses doubts about Denbigh's mission. David Underdown in *Pride's Purge* acknowledges Wedgewood's doubts, "But it accords too well with the rest of the known facts about the compromise scheme to be disregarded."
12 *Minutes of the Commission.*
13. Foss, *Biographical Dictionary of the Judges of England*, 232
14. Clarendon, *The History of the Great Rebellion*, vol III, 373
15. William Steele had contested with Bradshawe the election for Judge of the Sheriff's court in 1644.
16. John Ashe was Bradshawe's fellow member on the Committee for Sequestrations.
17. R. W. Blencowe, *Sydney Papers*,
18. *Middlesex County Session Rolls*, Vol III, 1625-1667, (Greater London Council, 1947).
19. George Ryley Scott, London, *The History of Torture Throughout the Ages*, (1940)
20. *Exact and most impartial accompt of the trial of 29 regicides* (Marten's trial), 248
21 Horace Walker, *Collection of Notes at the King's Tryall*, Walker rendered the traditional "Oyez" as "Oh Yes."
22. Commissioners present, 20th January 1648/49, at Westmister Hall

John Bradshawe, Seriant at Lawe, Lo. President

Oliver Cromwell	Henry Ireton	Sir Hardres Waller
Will Goff	Cornelius Holland	John Carey
Valentine Wauton	Thomas Harrison	Edward Whaley
Thomas Pride	Issake Ewer	Francis Allen
Tho. Lord Gray of Grooby	Will. Lord Monson	John Moore
Sir John Davers	Sir John Boucher, Knt.	John Alldred
Isack Pennington, Aldrmn of London	Henry Marten	Henry Smith
Sir Thomas Maleverer, Bt.	Will Purefoy	John Barkstead

John Blackston	Gilbert Millington	Sr Will Constable, Bt.
Edmund Ludlow	John Hutchinson	Sir Michael Livesley, Bt.
Robt Tichborne	Owen Roe	Robert Lillborne
Adrian Scroope	Richard Deane	John Okey
John Hughes	Daniel Blagrave	John Dixwell
Simon Mayne	James Temple	Peter Temple
John Browne	John Jones	Thomas Lister
Peregrine Pelham	Thomas Wogan	Francis Allen
Thomas Chaloner	Will Saye	Francis Lessells
James Chaloner	Houmphrie Edwards	Gregory Clement
John Fry	Sir Gregory Norton, Bt.*	Edmund Harvie
John Venne	Thomas Scott	Will Cawley
Anthony Stapley	John Downes	Thomas Horton
Thomas Hammond	John Lisle	Nicholas Love
Vincent Potter	Augustine Garland	

* Sir Gregory Norton of Broadbridge in Bosham, Sussex, married Martha Drewe, daughter of Bradshawe Drewe and great-granddaughter of Ellis Bradshawe (d;1545) of Broadbridge. Martha survived Sir Gregory Norton (d; 1652) and remarried Robert, 4th Viscount Kenmure *Victoria County History, Sussex*, Bosham.

CHAPTER NINE

Judgment Day

> *Peruse over all our books, records, and histories,*
> *and you will finde a principle in law,*
> *a rule in reason and a trial in experience,*
> *that treason doth ever produce*
> *fatal and final destruction to the offender.*
> **Third Part of the Institutes of the Laws of England,**
> **Concerning High Treason, etc.**
> **Sir Edward Coke, 1st publ 1644**

✠

COLONEL HACKER AND twenty-two officers escorted the king and his retinue of servants into Westminster Hall within a quarter of an hour after the call. The king wore a black satin suit trimmed with lace. Fastened on the blue ribbon across his chest was the bejeweled Star of the George Order of the Garter. He carried a small white stick with a silver handle. Methodically he seated himself as he sternly surveyed the members of the court and the people in the galleries at either side. He rose and turned around to look at the guards on the left side and the great multitude of spectators on the right of the hall. That is the official account. Unofficially it was reported that the spectators were not admitted to the hall until after the charge was read. Whichever account is correct, it is mutually agreed that the Lord President Bradshawe began with an address to the king.

"*Charles Stuart, King of England, the Commons of England assembled in Parliament, being sensible of the evils and calamities that have been brought upon this nation and of the innocent blood that hath been shed in it, which is fixed upon you as the principal author of it, have resolved to make inquisition for this blood, and according to the debt they owe to God, to Justice, the kingdom and themselves, and according to that fundamental power that is vested, and trust reposed in them by the People have resolved to bring you to trial and judgment, and have therefore constituted this high court of justice, before which you are now brought. Where you are to hear your charge, upon which the court will proceed according to Justice."*

Solicitor General John Cook, standing at the right hand of the king, began to read the charge. The king reached out with his stick and tapped Cook on the shoulder two or three times saying, "*Hold!*" As he withdrew his stick, the silver handle fell away. This was conceived an ill omen, and the king was distracted when forced to retrieve the handle and place it in his pocket. Bradshawe ordered Cook to continue. After a few minutes the king once again interrupted,

The king; "*By your favour,* **Hold**"!

Bradshawe: "*The Court commands the charge shall be read; if you have anything to say, after, the court will hear you*".

The general thrust of the charge was "*that he the said Charles Stuart being admitted King of England, and therein trusted with a limited power to govern by and according to the laws of the land and not otherwise nevertheless, out of a wicked design to erect and uphold himself an unlimited and tyrannical power . . . He . . . for the accomplishment of such his designe and for the protecting of himself and his adherents . . . hath traitorously and maliciously levied war against the present Parliament and the people therein represented.*"

It was unofficially reported that Anna Lady de Lille (or Lisle), widow of a French Royalist who had served the king, raised a tumult during the reading, and members of the guard branded her shoulder and face with a smoldering musket fuse to chastise her. The king was said to be much distressed at the spectacle.

Figure 14. The King's Trial in Westminster Hall

The reading of the charge continued, "*And the said John Cook by protestation saving . . . the liberty of exhibiting . . . any other charge against the said Charles Stuart and also of replying to the answers which he shall make, . . . doth for the said treasons and crimes . . . impeach the said Charles Stuart as a tyrant, traitor, murtherer (sic) and public and implacable enemy of the commonwealth of England . . .*" As these last words were read out the king laughed aloud.

Bradshawe: "*Sir, you have heard your charge read containing such matters as appear in it. You find that in the close of it, it is prayed to the court, in behalf of the Commons of England, that you be put to answer to your charge. The court expects your answer and are willing to hear it.*"

It was then, according to an unofficial account, that the gate to the hall was thrown open and the multitude of spectators rushed in, unaware of Lady De Lille's outburst and unaware of the exact statement of the charge. The crowd's noisy entrance supposedly drowned out the king's reply. Remember that the official account says the multitude had already been surveyed in the hall by the king. The propaganda battle over the accounts of the king's trial had begun. The king and began by citing the abandoned Treaty of Newport.

The king: "*First I must know by what power I am called hither, before I give answer . . . I was not long ago in the Isle of Wight . . . there I entered into a treaty with the two Houses of Parliament . . . we were upon a conclusion of the treaty. Now I would know by what authority (I mean lawful, for there are many unlawful authorities in the world, robbers by the highway, taking men's purses by illegal ways) but I would know by what authority (lawful) I was carried thence till I came hither. That I would fain know. When I know a lawful authority then I will answer. Remember I am your King, your lawful King and what sin you bring upon your heads; beside those other judgments you bring upon the land. Think well upon it, I say, think well upon it before you go from one sin to greater. I know no authority you have . . ."*

Even though he knew that he had been militarily defeated, the king may not have been aware that he was also politically defeated by the Act of Commons proclaiming themselves the supreme power in the nation without the consent of the Lords or the king.

Figure 15. John Bradshawe, seated right center, faces King Charles standing left

After a brief exchange with Bradshawe about the authority of the Commons, the king concluded, *"show me by what lawful authority I am seated here and I will answer it. Otherwise I will not betray the liberties of my people."*

Bradshawe: *If you acknowledge not the authority of this Court, they must proceed.*

The king: *"I do tell you Sir, England was never yet an elective kingdom, it was a hereditary kingdom for near this thousand years*[1] *... Your authority raised by a usurped power I will never—I will never betray my trust. I am entrusted with the liberties of my people. I do stand more for the liberties of my people than anyone that is seated here as a judge ... I will not betray the liberties of my people."*

Bradshawe, *"Whether you have not betrayed your trust in good time when you have given your answer, will appear. You, instead of answering, interrogate the court, which doth not become you in this condition. If this be all, you have already been told your answer."*

The king asked that a witness be called to testify that he had been brought from the Isle of Wight by force. He further insisted that he did not come as submitting to the court. Bradshawe countered that the *"interpretation doth not belong to you . . . The court will consider what to do with you."* Once again the king insisted that he was more for liberty than any of his judges. Seeing that he would get no answer, Bradshawe commanded the guard to remove *"the prisoner."*

"The King! shouted the indignant Charles. The court was adjourned until the Monday following."

The commissioners of the court had intended that the king would be confined to Sir Robert Cotton's house until the trial was completed, but the king had a desire *"to lye in one of his own house and be with his children."* This was allowed despite the fear of another attempted escape, and the king was conducted back to St. James Palace. Two soldiers were ordered to keep watch within the royal bedchamber. The king refused to go to bed on Saturday night.

The commissioners attended a solemn fast at Westminster on Sunday where they heard lengthy sermons from two moderate preachers, Mr. Sprigge and Mr. Foxley, and one firebrand, Mr. Hugh Peter. The crowds that gathered outside expected to see the king, but he didn't appear.

Seventy commissioners entered the great hall on Monday afternoon. After the opening formalities and the entrance of the king, the prosecutor addressed Bradshawe

John Cook: "*My lord, my humble motion to this high court in the behalfe of the people of England, is that the prisoner may be directed to make his positive answer, either by way of confession or negation. Which if he shall refuse to do so, that the matter of charge may be taken pro confesso,* (i.e., a plea of guilty) *and the court may proceed according to justice.*"

Bradshawe: "*Sir, you may remember at the last court you were told the occasion of your being brought hither and you heard your charge read against you, containing a charge of High Treason, and other crimes against this realm of England. You have heard likewise that it was prayed in the behalf of the Commonwealth that you should give an answer to the said charge that thereupon such proceedings might be had as should be agreeable to justice. You were pleased to make some scruple against the authority of this court You did divers times propound your question and you were often answered Sir, the court has since that time taken into their serious consideration what you then said and they are satisfied fully with their authority and they hold it fit you should stand satisfied therewith too. And they do require that you should give a positive and particular answer to this charge that is exhibited against you. They do expect you should either confess or deny it. If you deny, it is offered in behalf of the Commonwealth to be made good against you . . . Sir, the court expects that you apply yourself to the charge not to lose any more time, but to give a positive answer thereunto.*"

the king: "*When I was here last, it is very true I made that question, And if it were only my particular case I would have satisfied myself with the protestation . . . against the legality of this court. And that a King cannot be tried by any superior jurisdiction on earth. But it is not my case alone, it is the freedom and liberty of the people of England . . . I did expect particular reasons, to know by what law, what authority, you did proceed against me here. And, therefore, I am a little to seek what to say to you in this particular, because the affirmative is to be proved, the negative is often very hard to be done . . . But since I cannot persuade you to do it, I shall tell you my reasons as short as I can . . . I conceive I cannot answer at this time till I be satisfied of the legality of it. All proceedings against any man whatsoever . . .*".

Bradshawe: "*Sir I must interrupt you which I would not willingly do but that which you do is not agreeable to the proceeding of any court of justice, as all who know what belongs to justice know . . . it seems you are about the entering into arguments and disputes concerning the authority of this court . . . You must not do it. If you take upon you to dispute the authority of this court, we may not do it, nor will any court give way unto it. You are to give your punctual and direct answer either affirmative or negative whether you will answer your charge or no and what your answer is."*

The king: "*I do not know the forms of law. I do know law and reason though I am no lawyer professed. I know as much law as any gen. in England . . . I cannot yield unto it.*"

Bradshawe: "*I must again interrupt you; you may not go on that course. You speak of Law and Reason. It is fit there should be law and reason and they are both against you in the proceedings. The vote of the Commons of England in Parliament, that is the reason of the kingdom. It is the Law of the kingdom, and they are these that have given you that law according to which you should have ruled and reigned. Sir you are not to dispute our authority . . . it will be taken notice of that you stand in contempt of court.*"

The king: "*I do not know how a King can be a delinquent, but by all law that I ever heard of all men, delinquents . . . may put in demurrer, and to demur against any proceedings is legal. I do demand that and to be heard with my reasons.*"

Bradshawe: "*Sir you have offered something to the court. I shall speak something unto you, the sense of the whole court. They overrule your demurrer . . . We sit here by authority of the Commons of England, and that authority hath called your ancestors (the greatest of them) to account.*"

The king: "*I deny that. Show me one precedent.*" [2]

Bradshawe: "*This point is not to be debated by you; neither will the court permit you to do it.*"

The king: "*I say, sir, by your favour, that the Commons of England was never a court of judicature. I know not how they came so*".

Here the king offered a fine point of law. Parliament had been established, centuries before, as the *curia regis*—a court of law. Its official title was still the High Court of Parliament. The current problem was that Commons had dissolved the Lords and stood as the single chamber of Parliament. Sir Edward Coke had described the workings of the High Court of Parliament: "*This Court is aptly resembled to a clock which hath within it many wheels and many motions . . . if the motion of the lesser be hindered, it will hinder the motion of the greater.*"

Bradshawe was not prepared to debate the point: "*You are not to be permitted to go on in that speech and these discourses*".

Bradshawe ordered the clerk to read a prepared statement: "*Charles Stuart, King of England, you have been accused on behalf of the people of England of high treason and other high crimes and treasons which hath been read unto* you. The court requires you to give a positive answer, whether you confess or deny the charges, having determined that you ought to answer the same."

The king continued to dispute, "*I do require that I may give in my reasons why I do not . . . .*"

Bradshawe: "*Sir, 'tis not for prisoners to require.*"

The king: "*Sir, I am not an **ordinary** prisoner.*"

The wrangling continued until finally Bradshawe ordered the king removed. A default of plea and contempt of the court was recorded against the king. It constituted a plea of guilty. In point of law, the trial phase was now over . . . the court could now enter the sentencing phase.

Seventy-one commissioners were seated in the court on Monday afternoon. After the opening formalities and the entrance of the king, John Cook addressed Bradshawe and the Court : "*this is the third time . . . the prisoner hath been brought to the bar, before any issue joined in the case. I did at the first court exhibit a charge against him: containing the highest treason that ever was brought upon the theatre of England. That a King of England, trusted to keep the law, that had taken an oath so to do, that had tribute paid to him to that end, should notwithstanding out of a wicked design to subvert and destroy the said law and introduce an arbitrary and tyrannical government . . . I did humbly pray . . . that he might speedily be required to make an answer to that charge. But, my lord, instead of making any answer, he did then dispute the authority of this high court. Your lordship was pleased to give him a further day to consider and put in his answer . . . But: my lord, he was then pleased to demur to the jurisdiction of the court. My lord, this hath been a great delay of Justice. Therefore I shall now humbly move your lordship for speedy judgment against him. My lord, I might press your lordship that (according to the known rules of law of the land) if a prisoner should stand mute or contumacious and shall not put in an issuable plea to the charge given against him, whereby he may come to a fair trial, that (,) by an implicit confession (,) it may be taken pro confesso, as it hath been done to those who have deserved more favour than the prisoner at the bar hath done . . . if your lordship and the court be not satisfied hereupon, I have on behalf of the people of England several witnesses to produce . . .*"

Still Bradshawe held out one more opportunity and addressed the king: "*Sir you have heard what is moved by the counsel . . . the court cannot forget what dilatory dealing they have found at your hands. They might in justice if they pleased, according to the rules of justice, take advantage of these defaults and proceed to pronounce judgment against you. Sir, in plain terms (for justice knows no respect of persons) . . . you are to give your answer, your final and positive answer (in plain English) whether you be guilty or not guilty of these treasons laid to your charge."*

The king paused for a while and then spoke.

The king: *"When I was here yesterday, I did desire to speak and began to speak for the liberties of the people of England. I was interrupted. I desire to know yet, whether I may speak freely or not."*

Bradshawe: *"Sir, if you answer your charge, which the court gives you leave now to do, though they might have taken advantage of your contempt, yet if you be able to answer to your charge, when you have answered, you shall be heard at large to make the best defense you can . . . But Sir, I must let you know from the court, as their commands, that you are not to be permitted to issue out into other discourses till such time as you have given a positive answer to the charge . . . And this is their final command."*

The king: *"For the charge I value it not a rush . . ."*. He then again launched into his reasons for failing to acknowledge, the court. Bradshawe interrupted the king, the king interrupted Bradshawe. Bradshawe ordered, *"Clerk, do your duty."*

"Duty?" cried the king. The clerk once more read the charge and demanded a positive response.

The king: *"Sir, I say again to you . . . so that I might give satisfaction to the People of England . . . that I have done nothing against that trust that hath been committed to me, I will do it. But to acknowledge a new court, to alter the fundamental laws of this kingdom . . . Sir, you must excuse* me."

Bradshawe: *"Sir, this is the third time you have publicly disowned his court and put an affront upon it. How far you have preserved the fundamental Law and freedom of the subject, your actions have spoke it, For truly, Sir, men's intentions are used to be shown by their actions, You have written your meaning in bloody characters throughout the whole kingdom. But, Sir, the court understands your meaning. Clerk, record the default. And, gentlemen you that brought the prisoner, take him back again".*

The king: *I have one word to you. If it were only my own particular indeed I would not . . .*

Bradshawe: *"Sir, you have heard the pleasure of the court; and you are (notwithstanding you will not understand it) to find that you are before a court of justice."*

The king, in a lower voice, as he was taken away: *"Well, Sir, I find I am before a power."* No man had ever publicly spoken to the king in the manner that Bradshawe had spoken; no body of men had ever publicly regarded the king in the manner he had just been regarded by the high court.

The court adjourned to the Painted Chamber and gave notice that it would reconvene to Westminster Hall at 10:00 AM the following morning, Wednesday the twenty-fourth. In actual fact, they did not return to the hall until Saturday the twenty-seventh.

Evidence from twenty-nine sworn witnesses[3] was and heard by a committee in the Painted Chamber throughout the twenty-fourth and twenty-fifth. On the morning of the twenty-fifth, the commissioners made orders to prepare the dean's house at Westminster Abbey for Bradshawe's residence and to command the keeper of Ludgate Prison to bring Colonel Fox, who was in charge of Bradshawe's personal guard, from his confinement in prison to the commission. It appears Colonel Fox had been committed for debt. Bradshawe was being moved to a more secure residence. Some Royalists were outraged at Bradshawe's challenges to the king. Bate's *Elenchus*, published after 1660, tells that a Mr. Burghill armed himself with a sword and pistol intending to assassinate Bradshawe. He lay in wait outside Gray's Inn but missed his target because Bradshawe did not return to Gray's Inn that night. No date for this event was mentioned.

Evidence submitted by the witnesses was heard at length by the commissioners to prove the charge. The business of the day was concluded.

The court, taking into consideration the whole matter in charge against the king, passed these votes following as preparatory to the sentence against the king but ordered that they should not be binding finally to conclude the court.

Resolved upon the whole matter that this court will proceed to sentence of condemnation against Charles Stuart, King of England.

Resolved that the condemnation of the king shall be for a tyrant, traitor, and murderer.

That the condemnation of the king shall be likewise for being a public enemy of the Commonwealth of England. That the condemnation shall extend to death.

Memorandum that the last aforenamed forty-seven commissioners were present at these votes.

Mr. Scott, Mr. Marten, Colonel Harrison, Mr. Lisle, Mr. Say, Colonel Ireton, and Mr. Love . . . or any three of them . . . were ordered to draft the king's sentence, but to leave blank the manner of his death. An order was issued summoning all members of the court, then present in and about London to attend the following day.

In spite of the summons, only sixty-three, including Bradshawe, attended in private. The draft sentence was debated, amended, and ordered to be lettered. An order was issued that the king was to be brought to Westminster on the next day to receive his sentence. Two ladies, Mistress Massey and Lady Aubigny, tried to gain admittance to plead for the king. They were refused.

Mary Pope had published several treatises dedicated to the king and the Lords calling for divine retribution against the breakers of the Solemn League and Covenant. Allegedly she had made various wagers, totaling £15, that the king would be restored to all his dignity within six weeks. Lady Aubigny and her recent husband, Lord Newburgh, had laid plans for the king's escape.

On Saturday morning, according to Sir Roger Manley,[4] Mary Bradshawe rushed into her husband's chamber, fell upon her knees, and began to weep. She asked Bradshawe to have nothing to do with the king's sentence for fear of the anger of God. "*You have no child,*" she said, "*and why should you do so monstrous an act to favour others.*" Bradshawe sent her away with, "*I confess he hath done me no harm, nor will I do him any, but what the Law commands.*" Four years later, when Cromwell dissolved the Parliament and the Council of State, Bradshawe mused, "*If this is no Parliament, then I am the King's murderer.*"

Figure 16. Lord President John Bradshawe

Sixty-eight commissioners gathered for the preliminary meeting in the Painted Chamber where they read the completed sentence. Instructions were prepared for the reading and publication of the sentence in the court. Three resolutions were agreed. The tenor of these shows that the commissioners still held a slim hope that the king would recognize the court.

That in case the king shall submit to the jurisdiction of the court and pray a copy of the charge, that then the court do withdraw and advise.

That in case the king shall move anything else worth the court's consideration, that the Lord President upon advice of the said assistants do give order for the courts withdrawing to advise.

That in case the king shall not submit to answer and there happen no such cause of withdrawing, that then the lord president do command the sentence to be read, but that the lord president should hear the king say what he would before the sentence and not after.

This last point was good English law. Any prisoner sentenced to capital punishment was considered already dead in the court's eye and therefore incapable of being heard. King Charles was gambling to the bitter end that he could continue to disavow the court's authority and still openly address the court after the cruel sentence, thereby gaining public sympathy. It was a gamble he would lose.

Bradshawe, in a scarlet robe, lead the rest of the commissioners to their seats in Westminster. After the usual preliminaries, the king was brought to the bar. Bradshawe rose to address the Court:

Bradshawe: *"Gentlemen . . .".*

The king: *"I shall desire a word to be heard a little; and I hope I shall give no occasion of interruption."*

Bradshawe: *"You may answer in your time. Hear the court first."*

The king: *"If it please you, Sir, I desire to be heard; and I shall not give any occasion for interruption; and it is only a word. A sudden judgment . . ."*

Bradshawe: *"Sir, you shall be heard in due time; you are to hear the court first."*

The king: *"Sir, I desire; it will be in order to what I believe the say; and therefore, Sir, A hasty judgment is not so soon recalled."*

Bradshawe: *"Sir, you shall be heard before the judgment be given; and in the meantime you may forbear."*

The king: *"Well Sir, I shall be heard before judgment be given?"*

Bradshawe: "*You shall. Gentlemen, it is well known to all or mosyt of you here present that the prisoner at the bar hath been several times convented and brought before the court, to make answer to a charge of treason and other high crimes exhibited against him in the name of the people of England.*"

Two ladies, disguised in masks, cried out from the galleries, "*It is a lie, where are the people or their consents . . .*" *Oliver Cromwell is a traitor*. Axtell ordered his troop of guards to force the ladies to unmask, saying: "*Shoot them if they say one word more.*" But the ladies had retired from the hall. It was presumed they were Lady Fairfax and Mrs. Nelson.

Bradshawe resumed. After summarizing the past proceeding, he concluded: "*(the court) are resolved and are agreed upon a sentence to be pronounced against this prisoner . . . But in respect he doth desire to be heard before the sentence be read and . . . the court hath resolved that they will hear him.*" Turning to address the king, he cautioned that the court would hear no dispute concerning their authority: "*but, sir, if you have anything to say in defense of yourself concerning the matter charged, the court hath given me in command to let you know they will hear it*".

The king acknowledged Bradshawe's instructions and then sprung a new ploy: "*I desire before sentence be given that I may be heard in the Painted Chamber before the Lords and the Commons . . . but if I cannot get this liberty, I do protest that these fair shows of liberty and peace are rather specious shows than otherwise and that you will not hear your king.*"

Bradshawe: "*Sir, you have now spoken?*"

The king: "*Yes, sir.*"

Bradshawe: "a*nd this . . . is a further declining of the jurisdiction of this court, which was the thing wherein you were limited before.*"

One commissioner of the court, however, was moved by the king's appeal and raised an interruption. John Downes was sitting behind Bradshawe. "*Have we hearts of stone? Are we men?*" he said aloud. Others tried to quiet him. Perhaps because the interruption was becoming heated, the king continued to speak.

The official account is at variance with other accounts on what happened next. In 1660, John Downes printed his own version[5] as a way of mitigating a charge of high treason threatening him. He said Cromwell told him to sit still and be quiet. Downes replied: "*No I cannot be quiet*" and rose to his feet and audibly addressed the whole court: "*I am not satisfied to give my consent to this sentence, but I have reasons to offer against it. And I desire the court may adjourn to hear me. Nay,* replied Bradshawe;

if any of the court is unsatisfied, the court must adjourn . . ." which sounds more like a rebuke to Cromwell's *"sit still and be quiet"* than it does to Downes's request. Bradshawe consulted his assistants, John Lisle[6] and William Saye, who were seated on either side of him. Downes's outburst was in direct violation of the court's specific instructions, formulated on January 12, which stipulated that "none of the Court doe speak but the Lord President and the Counsell. And in case of any difficulty arising to anyone, that he speak not to the matter openly, but desire the Lord President that the Court may please advise."

The official account, from Bradshawe's journal,[7] relates that Bradshawe asked the king, *"You say you do not decline the jurisdiction of the court?"*

The king; *"Not in this that I have said."*

Bradshawe then adjourned the court for one-half hour to consider the king's request. No mention is made of Downes's outburst.

The court withdrew to the Court of Wards chamber for an acrimonious debate. Downes told Bradshawe that the king was making some condescension, offering peace, and desiring to speak it to Parliament. Cromwell told Bradshawe that Downes: *"doth not know that he hath to deal with the hardest hearted man upon earth . . . whatever he pretends of dissatisfaction, that he would only save his old Master"*. Bradshawe made the decision that the king's offer was just another way of denying the court's authority. In the end Downes left the chamber and took no further part in the trial. He did, however, sign the death warrant for the king's execution sometime later.

The court reassembled, and a short exchange between Bradshawe and the king concluded:

The king: *"I doubt not but I shall give some satisfaction to all here and my people after that. And therefore I do require you, and you will answer it at the dreadful Day of Judgment, that you consider it once again."*

Bradshawe: *"Sir, I receive direction from the court."*

The king: *"Well, Sir."*

Bradshawe: *"Sir, this I have in charge from the court that if this must be reinforced, or any such thing of this nature, your answer must be the same. And they will proceed to sentence, if you have nothing more to say."*

The king: *"I have nothing more to say. But I shall desire that this may be entered what I have said."*

Bradshawe began his address to the king, which would last about forty minutes. Much of it would be in accordance with the views of any modern representative democratic government, although it must have sounded very revolutionary to King Charles:

Bradshawe: *"I speak these things the rather to you because you were pleased to let fall the other day, you thought you had as much knowledge in the law as most gentlemen in England. It is very well, Sir. And truly, Sir, it is very fit for gentlemen of England to understand that law under which they must live and by which they must be governed, But you know, Sir, what the Scripture says, "They that know their master's will and do it not." What follows? The law is your master. Sir, as the law is your superior, so truly, there is something that is superior to the law, and which is indeed the parent or author of the law, and that is the people of England . . . This we learn, the end of having kings or any other governors is for the enjoying of justice, that's the end*[8] *. . . NOW, Sir, if so be the King will go contrary to that end, or any other governor will go contrary to the end of his government, Sir, he must understand that he is but an officer in trust and he ought to discharge that trust for the people, and if he do not they are to take order for the animadversion and punishment of such an offending governor. For the great bulwark of the liberties of the people is the Parliament of England. And by subverting and rooting that, which your aim hath been to do, certainly at one blow you had confounded the liberties and the property of England."*

He rounded on the king's claims of hereditary sovereignty stretching back over a thousand years: *"you know well you are the 109th King of Scotland, for not to mention so many kings as that kingdom according to their power and privilege have made bold to deal withal, some to banishment, some to imprisonment, and some out to death, it would be too long . . . we will be bold to say that no kingdom hath yielded more plentiful experience than your native kingdom of Scotland hath done concerning the disposition and punishment of their offending and transgressing Kings, etc. Sir, it is not far to go for an example very near you, your grandmother*[9] *set aside and your father*[10] *an infant crowned. And the state did it. Here in England hath not been a want of some examples. They have sometimes been bold (the Parliament and the people of England) to call their Kings to account, as may appear if we look into the Saxon's time, the time before the Conquest. Since the Conquest there want not some precedents neither; King Edward the Second, King Richard the Second, were dealt with so by the Parliament as they were deposed and deprived.*[11] *And truly, Sir, whoever shall look into their stories, they shall not find the articles that are charged upon them to come near to that height and fatal catalogue of heinous crimes that are laid to your charge. Sir, you were pleased to say the other day where you are in descent and I did not contradict it. But take it altogether, Sir, you were as the charge speaks and no otherwise admitted King of England, but for that you were pleased then to allege, how that almost for a thousand years these things have been. Stories will tell you otherwise if you go higher than the time of the Conquest. If you come down since the Conquest you are the twenty-fourth King from William called the Conqueror, you shall find more than one half of them come in by the state and not merely upon point of descent . . . And truly, Sir, what a grave and learned judge[12] in his time and well known to you once said . . . that although there was such a thing as a descent many times, yet the Kings of England ever held the greatest assurance of their titles when they were declared and approved by Parliament . . . although its true by law the next person in blood is by the law of descent usually designated, yet if there were just cause to refuse him, the people might do it. For there is a contract and bargain made between the King and his people, and the oath is taken for the performance, and certainly, Sir, the bond is reciprocal, for you are their liege lord so they are your liege subjects . . . Thus we know now, the one tie, the one bond, is the bond of protection that is due from the sovereign, the other is the bond of subjection that is due from the subject. Sir if this bond be once broken, farewell Sovereignty. For whether you have been (as by your office you ought to be) a protector of England, or the destroyer of England, let all England judge, or all the world that hath looked upon it yet it must not be denied that your office was an office of trust, and indeed an office of the highest trust lodged in any single person . . . If instead of being a conservator of the peace you will be the grand disturber of the peace, surely this is contrary to your office, contrary to your trust let all men know that great offices are sizable and forfeitable as if you had it but for one year or for your life.*

Sir, the charge hath called you a Tyrant, a Traitor, a Murderer, and a public enemy to the Commonwealth of England. Sir, it had been well if that any of these terms might rightly and justly have been spared, if any one of them at all." The king interjected: *Hagh!*.

Bradshawe was near concluding now: *"As I said at first, I know it cannot be pleasing to you to hear any such things as these are mentioned to you from this court, for so we do call ourselves and justify ourselves to be a court, and a high court of justice, authorized by the highest and sublimest court of the kingdom, as we have often said, And though you do yet endeavour what you may to discount us, yet we do take knowledge of ourselves to be such a court as can administer justice to you and we are bound, sir, in duty so to do. Sir, all I shall say before the reading of your sentence it is but this . . ."*

He admonished to king to repent of his sins, and concluded: "*I shall not trouble you further, I shall—*"

The king: "*I would desire only one word before you give sentence. And that is that you would hear me concerning those great imputations that you have laid to my charge.*"

Bradshawe: "*Sir, you must give me now leave to go on, for I am not far from your sentence and your time is now past.*"

The king: "*But I shall desire you hear me a few words to you, for truly whatever sentence you will put upon me in respect of those heavy imputations that I see by your speech you have put upon me. Sir, it is very true that—*"

Bradshawe: "*Sir, I must put you in mind . . . you have disowned us as a court and you look upon us as a sort of people met together . . . You disavow us as a court, and therefore for you to address yourself to us, not acknowledging us as a court to judge of what you say, it is not permitted. And the truth is, all along from the first time you were pleased to disavow and disown us the court needed not to have heard you one word more. For unless they be acknowledged a court, it is not proper for you to speak. Sir, we have given you too much liberty already and admitted too much delay, and we may not admit of any farther. Were it proper for us to do, we should hear you freely, and we should not have declined to have heard you at large, what you could have said or proved on your behalf, whether for totally excusing, of for in part excusing, those great and most hainous (sic) charges that are laid upon you. But, Sir, I shall trouble you no longer . . . What sentence the law affirms to a traitor, tyrant, a murderer and a public enemy to the country, that sentence you are now to hear read unto you, and that is the sentence of the court.*"

The lengthy sentence detailed the charges and the king's refusal to plead, taking note that this refusal constituted a confession, and ended: "*For all which treasons and crimes this Court doth adjudge that the said Charles Stuart, as a tyrant, traitor, murderer and public enemy to the good people of this nation, shall be put to death by the severing of his head from his body.*"

Bradshawe: "*This sentence now read and published, it is the act, sentence, judgment and resolution of the whole court.*" The court stood to consent the judgment.

The king: "*Will you hear me a word, Sir?*"

Bradshawe: "*Sir, you are not to be heard after the sentence.*"

The king: "*No, Sir?*"

Bradshawe: "*No, Sir, by your favour, Sir. Guard, withdraw your prisoner.*"

As the king was being taken away, he cried out, "*I am not suffered to speak. Expect what Justice other people will have!*" This must have surprised Bradshawe because the king, having claimed to know as much law as any gentleman in England, would surely have known that prisoners were not permitted to speak after sentence. They were considered, in the eyes of the law, to be already dead. The king had waited too long to play his trump card. He had lost the gamble, and he would soon lose his head.

Notes to Chapter Nine

1. King Charles was extending his contention back beyond the Norman Conquest, the removal of Edward II, the murder of the Princes in the Tower, and the "election" of Henry Tudor. Hereditary Kings had been deposed and sometimes murdered in England before, but never before in public.
2. The greater Barons of England, a Parliament of sorts, had forced King John, Edward II, Richard II, and other Kings to be called to account, but the House of Commons had never presumed to interfere.
3. Witnesses produced and sworn in Court to give evidence to the charge against the King:

   Henry Hartford of Stratford upon Avon
   Edward Roberts of Bishop Castle, county Salop, ironmonger
   Will Bayne of Wixall, county Salop, Gent.
   Robert Lacey of the town of Nottingham, painter
   Robert Loade of Cotham, county Notts, tyler
   Samuel Morgan of Wellington, county Salop, feltmaker
   James Williams of Rosse, county Hertfordshire, shoemaker
   Michael Potts of Sharpreton, county Northumberland, vintner
   Giles Grice of Wellington, county Shropshire, Gent.
   John Vincent of Damorham, county Wilts., Gent,
   George Seely of London, cordwainer
   John Moore of city of Cork, Ireland, Gent.
   Thomas Ives of Boysett, county Northampton, husbandman
   James Crosby of Dublin, Ireland, barber
   Thomas Rawlins of Hanslopp, county Bucks, Gent.
   Richard Blomfield, citizen and weaver of London, 35
   John Thomas of Llangollen, county Denbigh, husbandman, 25
   Samuel Lawson of Nottingham, maltster
   John Pyneger of Heanor, county Derby, yeoman
   George Cornewall of Aston, co Hereford, ferryman, 50
   Thomas Whittington of town of Nottingham, 22
   Will Jones of Uske, county of Monmouth, husbandman, 22
   Houmfrey Browne of Whitsondine, co Rutland, husbandman, 22
   Arthur Yonge, citizen and barber surgeon of London, 29
   David Evans of Abergenny, county Monmouth, smith, 23

Diogines Edwards of Carston, county Salop, butcher, 21
Robert Williams of psh of St Martins, co Cornwall, husbandman, 23
John Bennett of Horwood, county York, Glover
Samuel Burden of Lyneham, county Wilts, Gent.
Thomas Reed of Maidstone, county Kent, Gent.
Henry Gooch of Grays Inn, co Mddlsx, Gent.
will Cuthbert of Portington in Holderness, Gent., 42
Richard Price of London, scrivener
James Morgan
Will. Arnop

In addition, Mr. Houlder was brought from prison but was forgiven from giving testimony because of self-incrimination.
4. *De Rebellione* appeared, in French, in 1686. Sir Roger Manley died in 1688, and an English translation of his book appeared in 1691.
5. "A true and humble representation of John Downes Esg" (1660). He escaped death at his trial and obtained permission to leave England. He probably died in America.
6. John Lisle escaped to Vevay in Switzerland after the Restoration. He was murdered there by an Irish Royalist in 1664. In England his widow, Alice, was tried and convicted in 1685 for sheltering a preacher, John Hickes, and sentenced to be burned alive, she then being aged over 70 years. Her sentence was commuted to beheading, a fate she suffered, at Winchester. She was the first victim of Judge Jeffrey's infamous "Bloody Assizes."
7. J. G. Muddiman *The Trial of King Charles the First*, (1928).
8. Compare Bradshawe's statements with the Declaration of Independence written by the British colonists of North America in 1776: "We hold these truths to be self evident that all men are created equal. That they are endowed by their Creator with certain inalienable rights. Those among these are the right to Life, Liberty, and the pursuit of Happiness. That to secure these rights, Governments are instituted among men, deriving their just powers from the consent of the governed. That whenever any Form of Government becomes destructive to these ends, it is the Right of the People to alter or abolish it, and to institute new Government . . . . The history of the present King of Great Britain is a history of repeated injuries and usurpations, all having in direct object the establishment of an absolute Tyranny over these States . . . He has abdicated Government here by declaring us out of his Protection and waging War against us. He has plundered our seas, ravaged our Coasts, burnt our towns, and destroyed

the lives of our people. He is at this time transporting large numbers of foreign Mercenaries to complete the works of death, desolation and tyranny already begun with circumstances of cruelty and perfidy scarcely paralled in the most barbarous ages, and totally unworthy the Head of a civilized nation . . . ."

The opposing view was stated in a pamphlet *Reason Against Treason or A Bone for Bradshaw to Pick*, published in 1649. "The People upon their choice of a King do irrevocably alienate their liberty; neither let any man be so brain sick as to believe . . . that regal Authority is derived from man . . . and therefore it is a muddy and cloudy search, to trace into the first root of Jurisdiction, since it is not grounded in man. Proof of this we have had brought to us from the remotest parts of the World . . . the discoveries that have been made . . . . do sufficiently demonstrate that men . . . do by the light of nature subject themselves to one as their King; and shall we that have for almost a thousand years upward in our generations flourished under the government of Kings in all variety of blessings, against the commandment of God, murder them, dishonour them, and banish them?"

9. Mary, Queen of Scots.
10. King James VI of Scotland and, later, King James I of England.
11. The treatment of Edward II and, later, Richard II at the hands of their captors was inhumane but conducted in secret. Edward II, after being deposed and confined in 1327, was secretly murdered in a particularly brutal way. A hollow, open-ended cow's horn was forced up his anus and through it a red-hot iron was pushed into his bowels, leaving no external tell-tale mark of physical injury on the King's body. Richard II was quietly starved to death in confinement. Ironically it was Richard II who had commissioned the rebuilding of Westminster Hall where Charles now stood in trial.
12. Bradshawe was probably referring to Lord Chief Justice Sir Edward Coke (1552-1634). King Charles had suppressed the printing of Coke's "Second Institute." "The King fears it may be to the prejudice of his prerogative, for Sir Edward is held too great an oracle amongst the people, and they may be misled by anything that carries such authority as all things do that he either speaks or writes . . .", Lord Holland to Secretary Dorchester

CHAPTER TEN

Execution

*Our thoughts are lofty, proud, and full of ire
We can be good, or bad, as times require.*

✠

AFTER PASSING SENTENCE on the king, Lord President Bradshawe reassembled the members of the high court in the Painted Chamber to consider the time and place of the king's execution. Waller, Ireton, Harrison, Deane, and Okey were appointed a committee to provide recommendations. John Downes seems to have returned from his self-imposed exile and joined the other sixty-three commissioners. The court was adjourned until eight o'clock on the following Monday.

The king was conducted to Sir Robert Cotton's house and then to St. James Palace. That evening he requested to see his children and Dr. Juxon, bishop of London. After a short consultation, the request was granted. On Sunday the king attended church, under guard, at St. James Palace where the bishop preached before him.

Only fifty commissioners presented themselves early Monday morning. The committee report, recommending that the king be executed the following day in the open street before the Banqueting Hall, was received and approved. A death warrant had already been drawn on parchment. It was signed and sealed.

At the high Co(urt) of Justice for the tryinge and judginge of Charles Steuart Kinge of England January xxixth Anno D(omini) 1648 (1649 new style)

Whereas Charles Steuart, King of England, is and standeth convicted and attaynted and condemned of High Treason and other high Crymes. And sentence upon Saturday last was pronounced against him by this co(ur)t, to be putt to death by the severinge of his head from his body, Of w(hi)ch sentence execuc(i)on yet remayneth to be done. These are therefore to will and require you to see the said sentence executed in the open Streete before Whitehall uppon the morrowe, being the Thirtieth day of this instant moneth of January between the houres of Tenn in the morninge and Five in the afternoone of the same day w(i)th full effect. And for soe doing this shall be yo(u)r sufficient warrant. And these are to require All Officers and Souldiers and other the good people of this Nation of England to be assisting unto you in this service. Given under o(ur) handes and Seales.

To Col. Francis Hacker, Col. Huncks and Leivetent Col Phayre and to everyone of them

In 1981, Professor A. W. McIntosh examined the facts of the death warrant and wrote a very interesting analysis for the House of Lords Record Office. McIntosh speculated that the warrant was engrossed on Saturday, January 27, and at least the first twenty-nine signatures were appended. Either late that evening or over the weekend, it emerged that many more members of the high court were to sign the warrant. Space at the bottom of the warrant was barely sufficient for so many, and not all signatures could be obtained on Saturday. On Monday some changes were made to the warrant and additional signatures obtained.

Fourteen members—Allured, Carew, Corbet, Chaloner, Clement, Danvers, Downes, Fleetwood, Lilburne, Mauleverer, Moore, Norton, Wogan, and Wayte—are not listed as in attendance at the Painted Chamber on Monday, yet their signatures appear on the death warrant. Four are listed as attending—Francis Allen, John Alnaby, John Lisle, and Nicholas Love—but their signatures do not appear on the warrant.

The "bright axe for executing malefactors" was known to be somewhere in the Tower of London, but no one of the committee could say exactly where, so an order was sent out to Col. John White or any other officer in the tower to deliver the axe, when found, to Edward Dendy, Esqr., Sergeant at Armes, or his deputy.

Meanwhile others acted with more privacy and behind the curtain, among whom Saint-John and Vane. Indeed this whole day's work was acted with all the deepest secrecy and darkness, and yet most of the actors still seemed to have had some inclination to save the king's life if they could get terms of security with him.

Some fifty years after the king's execution, Mrs. Thornton of Yorkshire, daughter of Christopher Wandesford, told the historian Echard[1] that Mr. Rushworth, Lord Baltimore, William Lilly, and others "suspected to be papists" met in the London house of William Wandesford on January 29 as a close committee to consult on the king's death. They instructed Rushworth and another to met with the king and "use all their art and arguements, to persuade him to recede something from his former resolute stifness in insisting so much on his own innocency . . . and to own himself, at least in some measure, to have been the cause thereof, and so justifying their proceedings; which if he would do, all of them . . . promised to serve him to their utmost and set him upon his throne again." The king, according to the account, rejected their offer as breaching his honor, cause, and conscience. Accordingly they advised him that he would be sentenced to death the next day, to which the King replied: "God's will be done . . . Such is the account given by a person of unquestioned reputation, who died in the year 1705, of which the reader is left to make his own judgment." There is a slight confusion here: those who reputedly called upon the king on the night of the twenty-ninth would not have advised him that he would be sentenced to death the next day but that he would be *executed* the next day.

At nine o'clock in the morning of Tuesday, the thirtieth, Bradshawe met other members of the court in the Painted Chamber. An order was prepared directing Mr. Marshall, Mr. Nye, Mr. Caryl, Mr Salway, and Mr. Dell to attend the king at St. James Palace and "administer to him those spiritual helps as should be suitable to his present condition." In all likelihood their purpose was to present the king with his death warrant. Lieutenant Colonel Goffe was ordered to conduct them to the king. The king refused to confer with them, having previously conferred with Dr. Juxon.

The court ordered that the scaffold be draped in black almost as an afterthought. The king was brought on foot through St. James Park to the cabinet chamber in Whitehall at about ten o'clock. The scaffold was not ready, so the king was forced to wait his death. At noon the king took a bit of bread and a glass of claret. About an hour later, Colonel Hacker, Colonel Tomlinson, Doctor Juxon, and other officers and soldiers conducted the king through the Banqueting House and out an opened window onto the scaffold. The king was disappointed to find that the gathered crowd was being held back at some distance. Fearing that his final words would not be heard, the king addressed Colonel

Tomilson: "*I shall be very little heard by anybody here; I shall therefore speak a word unto you.*

Indeed I could hold my peace very well, if I did not think holding my peace would make some men think that I did submit to the guilt as well as to the punishment; but I think it is my duty, to God first, and to my country, for to clear myself as an honest man, a good King, and a good Christian. I shall begin first with my innocence . . ." He then declared that he did not first make war on Parliament or encroach upon their privileges. He professed that *ill instruments* between Parliament and himself *have been the chief cause of all this bloodshed.* He confessed, referring it seems, to his acquiescence in the execution of the Earl of Strafford, "*I will only say this, That an unjust sentence that I suffered to take effect is punished now by an unjust sentence upon me.*"

He then said that he would prove himself a good Christian by forgiving "*all the world, and even those in particular that have been the chief causers of my death: who they are God knows, I do not desire to know; I pray God forgive them.*" He asks that they "*endeavour the peace of the kingdom.*"

He interrupted his speech to briefly rebuke a gentleman who was examining the axe: "*Hurt not the axe, that may hurt me.*"

Summing up, he revealed his vision of the people and government: "*For the People . . . their liberty and freedom consists in having government, those laws by which their life and their goods may be most their own. It is not in having share in government, sirs; that is nothing pertaining to them; a subject and a sovereign are clear different things . . . I am the martyr of the People.*" Finally he asks to be excused for not putting his thoughts "*in little more order, and a little better digeste*d."

Once again he cautioned: "*Take heed of the axe, pray, take heed of the axe.*" He put his long hair under a cap and asked the masked executioner: "*Does my hair trouble you?*" The executioner requested that all the king's hair be put under the cap. The king told the executioner that he would say a short prayer and then thrust out his hands as a sign to strike. He removed his cloak and doublet, then put his cloak over his waist coat. After some discussion about the height and fastening of the block, he laid his head upon it. Some of his hair protruded from under the cap, and the executioner pushed it back. Alarmed by this unexpected touch, the king spoke out: "*Stay for the sign.*" The executioner assured that he would.

After a short pause the king gave the sign, and the executioner neatly severed his head from his body with one practiced blow. As dictated by tradition, the second executioner held up the severed head and showed it to the assembled crowd. There is disagreement whether the usual cry of "*behold, the head of a traitor*" was proclaimed. The king's body and head were placed into a coffin, covered with velvet, and taken back into the Banqueting House. It was all over by two o'clock, three hours before the expiry of the death warrant.

Figure 17. The execution of King Charles, at the Banqueting Hall

The crowd then pressed forward to edge the gory scaffold where many paid the soldiers to dip their cloths into the damp blood. The object of this display must have varied; some took symbols of the king's punishment for crimes, some took reliques of a martyr, and some took magical tokens of God's blessing and healing just as they had sought the king's touch when he was living. Handfuls of bloody straw were hawked by the soldiers to ready purchasers.

Some persons, allegedly Parliamentarians, demanded that the king's body be opened to make a search for such symptoms as might disgrace his person or his posterity. An unidentified intruder prevented the autopsy, probably on the basis that no such order had been given by Bradshawe and the court.

Later in the afternoon, the court met again and appointed a committee to make an account of the money that had been disbursed and would be disbursed for the services to the court in trying, judging, and executing the king. The accounts of the committee were to be presented to the House of Commons. Lord President Bradshawe asked that sufficient remuneration be disbursed to the guards that "have so freely and cheerfully attended the Lord President and the Court." Captain Blackwell was in charge of the Parliamentary purse.

Lord Southampton sat with King Charles's body in the Banqueting Hall overnight; and he later told of observing a visitor, whom he took to be Oliver Cromwell, approach the body about 2:00 AM. After staring at the body for some time, the visitor sighed, *"cruel necessity."*

Thomas Tropham, Lord Fairfax's surgeon, was appointed to embalm the king and sew the head to the body. He performed the procedure in the presence of many spectators, explaining to them afterward that he had been sewing on the head of a goose.[2] Some witnesses reported that this took place in the kitchen of the dean's house at Westminster Abbey, the house that had become John Bradshawe's home during the trial.

Meanwhile the court issued orders to apprehend and examine all those who had spoken or done anything against the actions of the court, specifically William Evans. Subsequent to this order, William Evans, John Hall, and a Mr. Nelson were accused on testimony of witnesses and committed to the marshall of the army.

Lord Grey was paid £100 out of the Haberdasher's Hall on January 31, "to be disposed of for the service of the Commonwealth as he shall think fit." Perhaps this was secret payment for the executioner.

A plain lead coffin, reputedly costing six shillings, was procured to receive the king's body. On November 17, the coffin was driven to Windsor Castle and delivered to the king's servants—Thomas Herbert, Anthony Mildmay, Mr. Preston, and John Joyner—who placed it in the former king's bedchamber overnight. The next day it was moved to the Dean Hall. Parliament ordered the king's burial be entrusted to the Duke of Richmond and that expenses not exceed £500. A request was made to Colonel Whichcot, governor of Windsor Castle, that internment might be made in St. George's Chapel, according to the form of the Common Prayer. Whichcot refused on the basis that Parliament would hardly permit the form that they had abolished. Whichcot ordered an ordinary grave to be dug in the body of the church at Windsor, but the duke and other lords persuaded an old knight to tap the floor until he secretly discovered a vault in the middle of the quire and then claim that it had been accidentally found. The ordinary grave was dug in such a way that it came up against the side of the discovered vault. When this was done, the side of the vault was broken open. Looking in through the small opening, the gravediggers determined it to be the tomb of Henry VIII. There just happened to be a convenient spot for a coffin inside. King

Charles's coffin was placed there in silence on Friday, February 9, 1649, covered with its black velvet pall and forgotten. After the Restoration, a search was made for the king's burial place, but due to alterations in the church, it could not be found, so Lord Clarendon said. Mr. Herbert wrote down the story of the burial, but his papers were not published until after his death in the eighteenth century.

How strange to consider that the construction of King Henry's tomb, the tomb in which King Charles now lay, would have been overseen by Laurence Bradshaw, the surveyor of the king's works at Windsor (and other royal palaces) when Henry VIII died. Laurence Bradshaw was known to have carried out other works at Windsor, and there is a reference to *Bradshaws Rails* in Windsor Great Park. It is equally strange to think that Henry Bradshaw, attorney general to Henry VIII, must have solemnly stood by the vault when King Henry was interned there in 1547.

Aubrey, the antiquarian, said that he had heard a rumor to the effect that the body of King Charles had been secretly buried in sand at Whitehall, and the actual coffin was filled with *rubbish and brick-bats* and delivered to Windsor.

In 1696, King Henry's vault was reopened to receive the small royal coffin of a stillborn child—a child of the future queen Anne. It was lowered down on top of a strange coffin covered in black velvet. If anyone suspected it to be the coffin of Charles the First, they raised no question at the time.

One hundred and sixty-four years after the king's burial, workmen carrying out excavations under the choir of St. George's chapel accidently breeched Henry VIII's tomb. Peering in, they could see three coffins, two of which were those of King Henry and Queen Jane Seymour. The third, still covered with a black velvet pall, excited their curiosity. It was presumed to contain the remains of Charles I. The Prince Regent determined to clear up the question by opening the third coffin.

On April 1, 1813, in the presence of the prince, Sir Henry Halford, and other dignitaries, the tomb was opened. The velvet pall was removed revealing a plain lead coffin bearing the inscription King Charles 1648.

The official record reads: "A square opening was then made in the upper part of the lid, of such dimensions as to admit a clear insight into its contents. These were, an internal wooden coffin, very much decayed, and the body carefully wrapped up in cere-cloth, into the folds of which a quantity of an unctuous or greasy matter, mixed with resin, as it seems, had been melted so as to exclude, as effectually as possible, the external air. The coffin was completely full; and from the stickiness of the cere-cloth, it was difficult to detach it from the parts which it enveloped. Wherever the unctuous matter had insinuated itself, the separation of the cere-cloth was easy; and when it came off a correct impression of the features to which it had been applied was observed in the unctuous substance. At length the whole face was disengaged from its covering. The complexion of the skin was dark and discolored. The forehead and temples had lost little or nothing of their muscular substance; the cartilage of the nose was gone; but the left eye, in the first moment of exposure, was open and full, though it vanished almost immediately; and the pointed beard, so characteristic of the period of the reign of King Charles, was perfect. The shape of the face was a long oval; many of the teeth remained; and the left ear, in consequence of the imposition of the unctuous matter, between it and the cere-cloth, was found entire—It was difficult, at this moment, to withhold a declaration that, notwithstanding its disfigurement, the countenance did bear a strong resemblance to the coins, the busts, and especially to the pictures of King Charles the First, by Van Dyke by which it had been made familiar to us. It is true, that the minds of the spectators of this interesting sight were well prepared to receive this impression; but it is also certain, that such a facility of belief had been occasioned by the simplicity and truth of Mr. Herbert's narrative, every part of which had been confirmed by the investigation . . . When the head had been entirely disengaged from the attachments which confined it, it was found to be loose, and without difficulty, was taken up and held to view. It was quite wet, and gave a greenish red tinge to paper and linen which touched it. The back part of the scalp was entirely perfect, and had a remarkably fresh appearance; the pores of the skin being more distinct, as they usually are when soaked in moisture; and the tendons and ligaments of the neck were of considerable substance and firmness. The hair was thick at the back of the head, and, in appearance, nearly black. A portion of it, which has since been cleaned and dried, is of a beautiful dark brown color. That of the beard was a redder brown. On the back of the head it was more than an inch in length, and had been probably cut so short for the convenience of the executioner, or perhaps by the piety of friends soon after death, in order to furnish memorials of the unhappy King—On holding up the head, to examine the place of separation from the body, the muscles of the neck had evidently retracted themselves considerably; and the fourth cervical vertebra was found to be cut through its substance transversely, leaving the surfaces of the divided portions perfectly smooth and even; an appearance which could have been produced only by a heavy blow, inflicted with a very sharp instrument, and which furnished the last proof wanting to identify King Charles the First."[3] Halford reported that he could see into the burst coffin of Henry VIII but saw only a skeleton that carried the remains of a beard. Queen Jane's coffin was undisturbed.

Figure 18. Halford's drawing of King Charles's severed head

Halford made a drawing of Charles's head before returning it to the coffin. He quite openly, and with the tacit approval of all present, took a few relics: part of the hair and beard with a bit of cerecloth attached, the severed part of the neck vertebra, and a tooth. These relics were lodged at Helford's country seat, Wistow Hall, a few miles from the city of Leicester, where they remained for seventy-five years and were occasionally viewed by Halford's friends.

In 1888, Sir Henry St. John Halford, grandson of Sir Henry Halford, presented a small ebony box containing the royal relics to Edward Prince of Wales (the future King Edward VII). Edward gave Sir Henry St. John a less-than-cordial reception but accepted the box nevertheless. Edward then obtained Queen Victoria's permission to return the royal relics to

King Charles's tomb. On Thursday, December 11, 1888, Mr. A. Y. Nutt and three workmen carefully opened the floor and then the tomb. The workmen discreetly withdrew from the chapel. The question then arose as to how the small box was to be deposited into the four-foot depth of the tomb; it couldn't just be dropped. Mr. Nutt made a sling of his own handkerchief, which he offered to the prince. The prince then lay on the floor and lowered the box in its temporary sling down onto the lid of King Charles's coffin.

After the Restoration, the search for the king's executioner had been pursued with vigor. Despite these efforts, the executioner was not satisfactorily identified. Many were suspected, and at least one was executed for the act.

The trial of a certain William Hulett Hewlett was held on October 15, 1660. Richard Gittens testified that he and Hewlett were sergeants in Colonel Hewson's regiment in 1649. According to testimony, Hewson called Gittens, Hewlett, and thirty-six others together a day or two before the king's execution, made them swear an oath of secrecy, and then asked if any would undertake to execute the king. He promised a hundred pounds ready payment and preferment in the army. All refused but Gittens testified, later at the hour of execution, he saw Hewlett "as near as I can guess . . . He had a pair of frieze trunk-breeches, and a vizor, with a grey beard, and after that Col Hewson called him Father Grey-Beard, and most of the army besides; he cannot deny it." Hewlett was later promoted to captain lieutenant, according to Gittens. Captain Toogood testified that Colonel Hewson had told him, about 1650 in Dublin Castle, that Hewlett either cut off the king's head or held it up and said, "Behold the head of a traitor." Toogood also testified that Hewlett himself had confessed to act. Many other witnesses were examined, in proof that Hewlett was the person who beheaded King Charles . . . assisted William Walker the other executioner. Rev. Mark Noble acknowledged that Hewlett was executioner but maintained that it was William Walker who beheaded the king and Hewlett who held up the severed head.

Over the years, other persons—Hugh Peter, Col Pride, Coronet Joyce, even Lord Fairfax and Oliver Cromwell—were suspected. John Dixwell supposedly confessed. Lord Stair, a Scottish judge, was named as the man who executed Charles the First, because he had sworn to "be revenged on Charles for the seduction of his sister, which Charles had accomplished when Prince of Wales. Lord Stair confessed this many years after on his death-bed. He died in a garret in Saint Martin's Lane"[4]

Another account, supposedly related by Archbishop Jennyson, the former vicar of Saint Martin's, has been quoted. According to this account, Jennyson said that an unknown young woman asked him to visit her dying father in a yard in King Street, Westminister. The woman said her father was under a great distress because he had cut off the king's head. Jennyson arrived too late, and the man was dead, so no deathbed confession was obtained. It was determined that the man had been a cattledrover or butcher at St. Ives in Huntingdonshire. He was brought up to London by Oliver Cromwell about the end of 1648 and ever after lived on a yearly pension, in obscurity and under an assumed name. The young woman disappeared, and Jennyson could find nothing further.[5]

Richard Brandon, known as *young Gregory*, the experienced common executor who beheaded Lord Strafford and Archbishop Laud, was the obvious suspect, but he died in 1649 and was buried in Whitechapel churchyard. Wedgewood and other historians concur on their belief of Brandon's guilt and that the second executioner was Brandon's usual assistant, Ralph Jones, a ragman.[6] In 1826, Henry Ellis, keeper of the manuscripts at the British Museum, announced that he had discovered the proof of Brandon's guilt and provided excerpts from three quarto tracts given the museum by King George III in 1762: "(1) The confession of Richard Brandon the hangman (upon his death-bed) concerning his beheading of his late majesty. Printed in the year of the hang-man's downfall, 1649;[7] (2) The Last will and Testament of Richard Brandon printed in the same year; and (3) A Dialogue or Dispute between the late hangman and Death, in verse, without date."

Whether Brandon's confession is an authentic account, as Ellis believed, or the invention of a contemporary pamphleteer, remains unproven. It is certainly inventive. In it Brandon is said to confess that he had thirty pounds for his work, all paid in half crowns, within an hour after the fatal blow was struck. He also had an orange stuck full of cloves and a *handkicher* out of the king's pocket. A gentleman in Whitehall offered twenty shillings for the orange, which Brandon said he refused, and he afterward sold it for ten shillings in Rosemary Lane.

Notes to Chapter Ten

1. Echard, *History of England*, vol II, 641
2. Seward's *Biographiana*, Vol II, p.442
3. W.D. Fellowes, *Historical Sketches of Charles the First*, (London 1828)
4. *Dryasdust's Literary Curiosities*
5. W. D. Fellowes, *Hist Sketches of Chas First*,
6. London, 1964, C.V. Wedgewood, *The Trial of Charles I,*
7. *Thomason Tracts, E.561.14,* British Library.

CHAPTER ELEVEN

Keeping the Lid on Chaos

*These are the repairers of the breach,
the restorers of paths to dwell in.*

Isaiah 58:12

✠

THE LAST DAY of January 1649 dawned on a kingdom of England without a king—at peace but devoid of effective civil or ecclesiastical government. Seven years of intermittent war had divided the shires and exhausted the people. Nearly every great aristocratic house was missing the family head or a son. Whole families of common people had been wiped out. Farming was abandoned in many places, and animal herds were depleted. Floods had devastated much of the countryside. Surviving soldiers depended upon "free-quarter" for food and lodging, much to the anger of the common householder who was forced to provide these necessities with only Parliament's promise of compensation at some time in the future. Imports were uncertain, and trade with the American colonies was suspended. Merchants of the city of London had contributed huge loans to the war and now sought repayment in cash or concessions. Many people doubted Parliament could rule, or even survive.

Sovereign authority rested with the purged House of Commons and the truncated House of Lords. It mattered not whether they ruled by the will of the the people or at the point of the sword—they were the only authority in existence, a government of necessity, more conservative than radical. Gerald Winstanley said: *"you are like men in a mist, seeking freedom, and know not where or what it is: and those of the richer sort of you that see it, are ashamed to owne it."* Sir Arthur Haselrig observed, in retrospect, force "was very much upon us. What should we do? We turned ourselves into a Commonwealth." Authority had been established by an uneasy alliance between commanders of the army and committed Independents in the Rump Parliament. The voice of the civilian Parliament gave a velvet glove to cover the army's iron fist. The army grandees were professing their submission to the authority of a civilian Parliament, but a good many of them, not the least of whom was Lt. General Oliver Cromwell, had seats within the Commons despite the Self-Denying Ordinance.

The rank and file of the army was unrewarded and unpaid. They saw themselves poor and unrepresented while their commanders became rich and more powerful. They needed reassurance that just and equal government could be dispensed by Parliament. A few units mutinied and seized what they wanted, but much of the destruction attributed to Cromwell's embittered and war-weary soldiers was, in fact, the act of criminals posing as soldiers. Cromwell ordered arrest of the perpetrators, be they soldier or civilian. Fairfax, commander of the army, recovering from old wounds and the gout at home, took no part in government. King Charles had warned that the lower orders could never be successfully manipulated by Parliament but would "call for parity and independence liberty . . . destroy all rights and properties, all distinctions of families and merit, and by this means this splendid and excellently distinguished form of government end in a dark, equal chaos of confusion".[1]

The Rump Parliament needed speedy and pragmatic solutions to what were perceived as temporary political problems. Counter-revolutionary forces had to be suppressed and government firmly settled. Only then could they tackle the fundamental and permanent changes promised by the revolution. "Having negotiated the rocks of revolution and let the storm spend itself around them, the Rumpers had brought the ship of state back into safe waters, somewhere calm to drop anchor,"[2] but within its own ranks the Rump was plagued by malcontents. It was becoming evermore difficult to distinguish Royalist sympathizers from disillusioned anti-Rump agitators. Calls for a new Parliament were rejected for fear that Royalist or Presbyterians MPs would once again be returned. The problem for the Rump Parliament was that, out of the four hundred ninety members who had been sitting in Commons, November 1640, only ninety remained in January 1649. The dissident's members had been ejected by Pride's Purge. The House of Lords had less than fifteen members. No one had previously envisioned a Parliament that could oppress the very people whom it was supposed to represent. That accusation had been hurled at the king who never claimed to be a representative of his subjects or subservient to the common law. In fact it was said Parliamentarian tyranny would be contrary to the interests of its very members, peers, and Commons alike. "Slavery would be our own condition if we should go about to overthrow the laws of the land, and the property of every man' estate, and the liberty of his person. For therein we must needs be as much patients as agents, and must everyone in his turn suffer ourselves, whatever we should impose upon others," they declared. Unlike the king who claimed his power by divine right of inheritance or conquest, peers and MPs maintained that "they have . . . their own power, being parts and special members of the people, and, also, they have their high places in Parliament, either from the people's express or tacit consent".

Among the impatient voices raised within Parliament and its army were those of John Lilburne, William Prynne, Richard Overton, the Levelers, and the Presbyterians. Lilburne and the Levelers called for an expansion of, but not universal, male suffrage. Very few, other than Gerrard Winstanley and the Diggers, asked for a new constitution based upon political liberty accompanied by social equality and suffrage without property qualifications. Thomas Rainsborough had stated the case for political liberty in straightforward terms at the Putney Debates of 1647, "For I really think that the poorest he that is in England hath a life to live . . . and therefore, truly, Sir, I think it's clear that every man that is to live under a government ought first . . . consent to put himself under that government . . . I do not find anything in the law of God that a lord shall choose twenty burgesses and a gentleman but two, or a poor man shall choose none."

John Milton called for an oligarchy of rich Puritans. Richard Overton, a vigorous Republican, was sceptical of God's supreme laws and urged a Moralist theology and government. Royalist propagandists made the most of these divisions and pointed to the distinct possibility, now that Parliament had destroyed the king and the court, that the vulgar multitude would intrude and dictate to their betters.

Yet England's revolution had been no secret murder of a king by power-hungry peers. This bad king had been done away with in the glare of public view. General Harrison, at his execution in 1660, continued to proclaim, "Throughout the war the things that have been done have been done upon the Stage, in sight of the Sun." Parliamentarians had drawn a clear distinction between their resistance, to preserve the fundamental laws of England, and the resistance of mere private men to legally constituted authority.

No one was quite sure just how far resistance to magistrates and the established courts could be justified, particularly when a private man took individual initiative to maintain his liberty. William Bridge wrote in 1643, "we take not up arms not as private men. But as subjects united and joined in the representative body of the kingdom." Parliamentarians consoled themselves with the belief that individual discontent could be channeled upward through just lesser magistrates to a just and benevolent Parliament. Concerted action by dissident groups would have to be crushed.

On February 3, the Parliament appointed a new High Court of Justice to try five captured Royalist peers who had aided the Scottish invasion: the Duke of Hamilton, Earls Holland and Norwich, Baron Capel, and Sir John Owen. Only John Bradshawe, the new court's president, and Vincent Potter had been members of the earlier high court which sat in judgment of King Charles. John Cook and Attorney General Anthony Steele were appointed prosecutors. Bradshawe was permitted to name a deputy judge to take his place on the Guildhall court bench where he still sat.

James Hamilton, 3rd Marquis, 1st Duke of Hamilton, and Earl of Cambridge, insisted he could not be properly tried in an English court because he was a Scottish peer. Bradshawe curtly informed him he was tried not as Duke of Hamilton in Scotland but by his other dignity as Earl Cambridge in England. Hamilton countered that he was an alien, born in Scotland before his father became a naturalized Englishman, therefore not subject to trial in England. Bradshawe knew, however, that Scottish children born after the union of Scotland and England in 1603 were granted citizenship of England just as by the same union English children became citizens of Scotland. Within a week after the death of Charles I, Scotland had declared for King Charles II and was thereby in revolt against Parliament. Finally Hamilton insisted that he was a prisoner of war whose life and personal safety had been guaranteed by the army in the articles negotiated for his surrender at Uttoxeter. He asked for more time to prepare his defense and call witnesses from Scotland. Bradshawe reminded him that he had been in custody for the past six months—more than enough time to have prepared a defense. It was known that Hamilton had contrived to bribe his guard and escape confinement at Windsor Castle after the king's execution. He was recaptured in London after a thorough search of Sir John Owen's house. No immediate answer was given Hamilton's request, and the court adjourned.

In the Tower of London the prisoners sought out John Lilburne, who advised them to claim the court lacked jurisdiction and delay the trial until a new Parliament could be called. Lilburne professed that he was: *"much concerned in that fatal president of that abominable and wicked court."*

At the next sitting of the court, Hamilton's request for more time was denied. Counsel was appointed for Hamilton: Mr. Heron, Mr. Parsons, Mr. Chute, and Mr. Hale. Some of these same lawyers had argued the case of Oxford University against Bradshawe in 1645. Hamilton's lawyers argued that army's Articles of Capitulation at Uttoxeter, August 25, 1648, had indemnified the duke from prosecution as a prisoner of war. Prosecutor Steele held that Hamilton's escape from Windsor had ended the army's obligation to protect him as a prisoner. Col. Robert Lilburne, John Liburne's brother, who had negotiated the articles with Hamilton, testified that in preserving the duke's life, he only did so "to preserve him from the violence of the soldiers and not from the justice of Parliament." Hugh Peter, who also had been at Uttoxeter, rose to his feet and shouted to the court that if this was true it should have been made abundantly clear in the articles. Bradshawe looked coldly at his old compatriot and said: *"you say well for the future, but it is now too late."*

These trials, particularly that of Hamilton, were putting a severe strain on the relations between Parliament and the army. Hugh Peter felt the honour of the army was being impuned. Cromwell, who had been a friend of Capel, vaccillated, feeling that Capel was now too dangerous to live.

Capel chose to act for himself and did a gallant job, according to Lilburne. Using Lilburne's words, Capel stoutly said: *"I am an Englishman . . . the Law is my inheritance."* He demanded of Bradshawe: "Where is my Jury? I hope you will not deny me the benefit of the Law, which you pretend you have fought this seven years to maintain." Capel claimed, as an English peer, the right to be tried by his peers—the House of Lords. Bradshawe told him: *"My Lord Capel, let me tell you you are tried before such Judges as the Parliament think right to assign you and these Judges have already condemned a better man than yourself. As to the defense of merits, the Parliament has become the supreme power in the state and to levy war against the Parliament was treason. The supposed promise of General Fairfax was never ratified by the Parliament; and, at most, it could only exempt the prisoners from being tried before a council of war, without precluding any proceeding which might be necessary for the peace and safety of the kingdom."* The army commander, Lord General Fairfax, avoided involvement.

On March 6, all five prisoners were condemned to death. The army council met to debate whether it should mediate with Parliament for the lives of any of the condemned men. For two days their sentences were appealed to the House of Commons. George Goring, Earl of Norwich, was reprieved by the tiebreaking vote of the speaker. Sir John Owen was reprieved. Baron Arthur Capel's appeal was unsuccessful, as was that of Henry Rich, Earl of Holland. The Puritan Parliamentarian Robert Rich, Earl of Warwick, brought his influence to bear in an unsuccessful attempt to save his brother Henry. Hamilton's appeal was not considered. The three condemned men were beheaded in the presence of Lord President John Bradshawe and other members of the high court on March 9. The iron will of Parliament prevailed over the conscience of the army.

While these trials were occupying Bradshawe, the House of Commons was voting acts to establish unicameral power in the ravaged country: "February 6th—the House of Lords is a useless and dangerous thing and by a vote of 44 to 29 it is abolished; February 7th—voted that the office of a king in this nation, and to have the power thereof in any single person, is unneccessary, burdensome, and dangerous to the Liberty, Safety and public Interest of the People of this Nation; and therefore ought to be abolished"; February 7, a committee composed of Edmund Ludlow, John Lisle, Cornelius Holland, Luke Robinson, and Thomas Scott was appointed to draw up a list of nominees for the Parliament's new executive body—an exalted Council of State.[3] February 8, Bulstrode Whitelocke and Sir Thomas Widdrington, commissioners of the Great Seal, took the old seal to the house, where it was ceremoniously broken in pieces; a new seal is prepared bearing the legend, "In the first year of Freedom, by God's blessing restored." February 13, members of the Council of State are elected, each member taking the engagement, thereby binding himself to concur in the "settling of the government of this nation for the future in the way of a republic without King or House of Lords." The council was given executive powers for one year despite the army's demand that its powers cease after April.

John Bradshawe was nominated one of the members of the Council of State. Other nominees included the earls of Denbigh,[4] Mulgrave, Pembroke,[5] and Salisbury; lords Grey, Munson, and Fairfax; General Lord Grey and Viscount Lisle; and the heirs apparent to the earls of Stamford and Pembroke; Bulstrode Whitelocke, Henry Marten, Sir Henry Vane Jr., Oliver St. John, Chief Justice Henry Rolle, Sir Arthur Hasilreg, Sir Gilbert Pickring, Sir James Harrington, Alexander Popham, Denis Bond, Rowland Wilson, Phillip Skippon, and Lieutenant General Oliver Cromwell. Thomas Harrison and Henry Ireton were rejected by the Commons because of their perceived radical support of the military coup. It was, on the whole, a council of moderation and determined to keep the revolution from spinning out of control into anarchy. The only nominees who were not members of the House of Commons were Alderman Rowland Wilson, Lord Chief Baron Wilde, Maj Gen Skippon, and John Bradshawe.

The council became an established institution. Nineteen members approved the king's execution and the removal of the House of Lords. Twenty-one did not so approve but were willing to accept the situation. They held their first meeting on Saturday night, February 19, with Cromwell in the chair. Subsequent meetings elected a new chairman at each sitting until March 10. On that day, the day following the execution of Hamilton, Holland, and Capel, the council made four momentous decisions: (1) A president to be chosen from among the members of the council; (2) Mr. Sergeant Bradshawe to be president; (3) if Mr. Bradshawe be absent at any meeting, the council to act as though he were there; (4) Mr. Bradshawe to be desired to attend this afternoon.

On the twelfth of the month, Bradshawe was made chief justice of Wales and Flintshire, adjoining Chester where he already occupied the post of chief justice. Also on that day Bradshawe signed the first of a flood of orders he would sign as president of the Council of State:

> *The Parliament hath resolved for the more effectual carrying on the Warre in Ireland to send thither twelve thousand men whereof 8 thousand foote 3 thousand Horse & one thousand Dragoons, for the transportation of soe great a number all the ports from the mouth of the Severne to the North of England, afford not sufficient shipping. Wee hope those men will be speedily ready, and if shippping be not prepared to transport them, they will continue here to the burthen of the Country, and that place want their service. If they can be early there*

will be a great advantage to our affairs by taking the field before the Enemy can be able to doo it. Wee therefore recommend it to yor care to consider how shipping sufficient & convenient for such a purpose may be taken up and sent to Chester & Leverpoole waters for this service, and that you presently certifie us how many ships and of what burthen, will be sufficient for this affaire, and at what rates they will be had, and in what manner, whether by the month, or for the service.

Signed in ye name & by order of ye Councell of State appointed by authority of Parliamᵗ Jo: Bradshawe prsidt

Derby House
12 Marty 1648/9
Exʳ G Frost, Sectry Commʳˢ of Navy [6]

On March 15, the council appointed Oliver Cromwell commander-in-chief of the troops for Ireland. The same day, Bradshawe called a forty-one-year-old London poet and pamphleteer, John Milton, to take the post of secretary for foreign tongues in return for an annual payment of £300. Milton's *The Tenure of Kings and Magistrates* identified him as an avid supporter and propagandist of the new government. Milton's early biographer said that he procured the post "by means of a private acquaintance." John Bradshawe knew Milton and had acted as his solicitor in litigation. There was a later incorrect assumption that Milton's mother was from the Bradshaw family. Luke Robinson could vouch for Milton's proficiency in Latin, the language chosen by the Commonwealth for international correspondence after dispensing with the French tongue.[7] Robinson had been Milton's fellow student at Christ's College, Cambridge. Some historians suspect that Bradshawe had also been at Christ's.

Bradshawe also employed his own two long-serving private secretaries, Thomas Parnell and Samuel Rowe, whom he had brought from Congleton and seemingly paid from his own purse. The council employed and paid Gualter Frost Sr. (40s. daily) and his son, Gualter Jr. (20s. daily), as their official secretaries. In addition there were four clerks (28s. 8d. among them) and twelve messengers (5s. daily and 6s. a mile riding charges). Bartholomew Hall (£100 annually) was responsible for answering antigovernment pamphlets, and Ambroise Randolph (£80 annually) was responsible for the State Paper Office. Thomas Scott received £800 per year for carrying on intelligence, and Denby received 20s. daily for being sergeant-at-arms. Messrs. Goodwin and Sterry received £200 annually as chaplains to the council. Richard Scutt was keeper of Whitehall Palace with a staff of five servants and three porters. Richard Nutt was master of the Commonwealth barge, assisted by Thomas Washborne and other watermen.

Bradshawe was seen to be a prolific and tireless worker and must have kept his learned secretariat busy. The sheer volume of documents he produced while attorney to the Committee of Sequestrations has been noted. We know that he attended 319 of the total 321 Council of State sittings in the first year and was late only twice. Thomas Scott the spymaster, next best, attended 224 times and was late thirty-one times. By contrast, Whitelocke attended just seventy-one times and was late twenty-six of those; Cromwell attended eighty-one times coming late thirteen times. The council usually assembled at 7:00 or 8:00 AM and sometimes met twice a day. The average attendance was thirteen, and nine members constituted a quorum. By contrast, Parliament met only 232 times that year. Doubtless Lord President Bradshawe was dedicated to his responsibilities, but while most of the order books of the council still exist, the remaining letter books, warrants, recognizes, and passes of the period 1649-1660 are so few as to hinder any serious attempt to prove Bradshawe's executive abilities and political reasonings.

Bradshawe's correspondence has turned up in scattered private collections,[8] like that of March 29, 1649, Derby House, addressed to Lord Fairfax. It directed him to take measures for the security of Montgomery and Harwarden Castles in Flintshire and also Chirk castle, the dwelling house of Sir Thomas Middleton, and was signed John Bradshawe and impressed with the seal of the council.

Bradshawe made another order to Fairfax in April. Gerrard Winstanley and his colony of *Diggers* had begun to farm the commons of St. George's Hill, about eight miles southwest of Kingston, Surrey. They planned to plow up the ground of Oatlands and Windsor Great Park to create a commune of five thousand people. Complaints were lodged with the council, and Bradshawe requested Fairfax to send troops to disperse the Diggers.

The Rump originally specified that the Council of State should operate without a head, fearing the power of an individual *grandee*. Members of the council were changed each year as the Rump removed their opponents and ineffectual members. So rapidly did Bradshawe rise to power, and so tenaciously did he hold on to it, few dared challenge him. On March 16, the Council of State took the unprecedented move of electing Bradshawe the permanent president of the Council of State, an office he would retain off and on throughout the coming years. He took, at least ceremoniously, preeminence over the other councilors who were sometimes called lord commissioners. Considering that Bradshawe was not a member of Parliament and that his fellow lord commissioners—St. John, Rolle, Haselrig, Vane, Whitelocke, Cromwell, and five peers—were, then Bradshawe must have been highly esteemed. He was now the chief executive of the English republic. The *president*, which title Parliament allowed to Bradshawe, was an office roughly styled on the chairmanship of the late king's Privy Council. Even after Parliament adopted a motion that the chairmanship of all committees should be rotated on a monthly basis, Bradshawe managed to retain his permanent chairmanship until December 31, 1651.

In the early meetings of the council, there was jealousy, and perhaps some envy. Whitlocke felt Bradshawe's only intended role was "to have gathered the sense of the Council, and to state the question, not to deliver his own opinion, yet he spent much of their time urging his own long arguments, which are inconvenient in state matters." These statements must be tempered in the knowledge that Whitelocke had avoided taking a direct part in the king's trial and had been a close friend of the executed Earl of Holland whom Bradshawe had condemned to the block. Whitelocke's annoyance with Bradshawe's long arguments may have been caused by other factors.[9] Despite these reservations, which Whitelocke probably never uttered aloud, there seemed to no ill will between the two men, and they worked together. It is known that Whitelocke accepted at least one of Bradshawe's invitations to dinner.

In the spring of 1649, the council nominated Whitelocke as ambassador to Holland. He protested his lack of qualifications and his wife's poor heal in refusing the post. Dr. Issac Dorislaus, the former Cambridge lecturer who had helped frame charges against the king, was appointed. At the Hague in May, a gang of English Royalists brutally murdered him. A year later Anthony Ascham, English ambassador to Spain, was murdered in Madrid by Royalists agents. The Continent was not a safe place for representatives of the English Republic.

Many early edicts signed by Bradshawe dealt with the Navy,

> *March 26: We are informed that within the manor of Downton parcell of the Lands of the late Bishop of Winchester there is a very great*

common called the Franchise upon part whereof containing about five hundred acres are growing great store of very good and young Timber Trees of Oak Ash and others which is considered may be very useful for the service of the Navy of the Commonwealth, the place being within 16 or 18 miles of several Sea Towns. We desire you forthwith to dispatch thither some fit and faithful man well experienced in those affairs to survey and view the said Timber, and to make a report to this Council of the present, or future fitness of the Timber for the use of the Navy, and withall his judgment of the present value, and this we desire you to do with all expedition. We having written to the Contractors to forebear the sale thereof till the Council can be informed of the usefulness and fitness for the public service.

Signed in the Name & by the Order
Order of the Council of State appointed by the Authority of Parliament

Jo: Bradshawe Pres'dnt
to E.G Frost Sec'ty Commissioners of the Navy [10]

Another, signed and dated the following day,

To the Commissioners of the Navy: E. G. Frost, Secretary; At the Council of State at Derby House. Whereas the place of Cook in the Ship Swiftshore is become void by the death of Thomas Holtshipp, late Cook thereof; And whereas Thomas Faithfull hath been recommended by yourselves to be a person fit to execute that place; You are therefore required to enter the said Thomas Faithfull, Cook accordingly in the said Ship, with such allowance of diet and wages for himself and 5 servant as is usual in a Ship of that rate; And for your so doing, this shall be your Warrant.

Signed in the Name and by Order of the
Council of State appointed by authority of Parliament.
John Bradshawe President.

In April, Colonels Blake and Popham reported that men aboard their ships were about to mutiny. The council sent Hugh Peter to Gravesend with instructions to lecture the mutinous crews. At Sandwich, Peter fell seriously ill. The council voted £20 for Col. John Humphrey to take a physician to aid Peter. An unsigned letter, probably from Bradshaw, was sent with Humphreys.[11]

> *To Hugh Peter, Sr. Wee have received information that at present you are sicke in Sandwich for which wee are very sorry and doubting much whether in that place you can have such Physitians as are acquainted with your Condition and for want thereof be prejudiced or endangered, Wee desired Colonell Humphreys to visit you and bring with him such a physitian as upon Consultation with Dr. Gourdon shall be fit to take Care of your health. Wee being very sensible of your good affections & faithfull service to the Commonweal that would not be wanting to doe any thing in our power that might tend to your accomodation or recovery and recommend the success of all to the blessing of God.*
>
> *Derby House 9 May 1649*

On July 6, Parliament considered an act for revising the duchy and county palatine seals of Lancashire and entrusting them to the care of John Bradshawe who was to be the chancellor for the duchy. The act failed to pass but was brought forward again on the twenty-eighth and passed. Speaker Lenthall delivered the seals to Bradshawe on the thirtieth, and on August 1, Bradshawe took the oath of the distinguished and formerly lucrative post of chancellor. Thomas Fell was appointed vice chancellor and Bartholomew Hall was appointed attorney general. Bradshawe's office was to end August 10, 1650. It seems inconceivable that Bradshawe could add this extra burden onto his already heavy schedule, but he did exactly that.

He immediately undertook the work of the chancelor's office, which was overwhelming. On the eighth he adopted new forms for the duchy process, follwed with further instructions for the new style of orders to be issued in the duchy and Commonwealth's name. On the twenty-first he summoned the attorney general and deputy auditors to his house to discuss arrears. County court sessions had not been held, and Bradshawe said, "there hath been little looking after (of late) the fines and forfeitures of recognizances in Lancashire." On the twenty-third Bradshawe asked for particulars of outstanding amounts. He appointed November 6 for the Michaelmas Court sitting at Lancaster and ordered Thomas Fell to be present there. On the fifteenth he issued directions to all officers, ministers, and clerks belonging to the duchy, then in London, to appear at the duchy chamber the following morning at eight o'clock. On December 4, Bradshawe asked the attorney general to consider the act for selling the late king's lands and to determine what lands the Commonwealth possessed in the duchy.

Bradshawe and Fell were continued in office for twelve months from July 18, 1650, and again by successive acts until September 16, 1653. Six days later Bradshawe told William Jessop, clerk of the duchy council: "*I cannot but think that Parliament now sitting will take care for continuance of the Duchy Court and distributing of right unto the Duchy tenants by somewhat of the old way until they have provided a new model for them and all the rest under government.*" There had been no slackening of the workload; between February and July, Bradshawe had applied the duchy seal to 161 documents. Parliament had determined to sell duchy forests and lands. Crown and duchy fee farms and honors were gradually sold off so that eventually the duchy, as a landed estate, ceased to exist, but its legal jurisdiction and that of the county palatine of Lancaster were kept alive. The forests of Needwood, Enfield, and Ashdown were surveyed, valued, and sold to meet the arrears of army pay.

One of the pressing difficulties facing the fledgling government was how to silence the Royalist press. A tome, *Eikon Basilike,* supposedly authored by King Charles in defense of his personal credo and heroism, was being circulated in London. It was immediately accepted by the masses, making the martyred king the most prominent icon of the age. It was printed on the press of William DuGard, headmaster of the Merchant Taylor's school. DuGard, an intimate friend of John Milton, was apprehended in the act but not immediately confined. His printing press was destroyed, and Bradshawe told the Merchant Taylor's Company to dismiss him. Another tract appeared on London's streets entitled "Reason against Treason or A Bone for Bradshaw to Pick.—Now if you will demand of him who shall be Judge of the Kings misdemeanors or delinquency . . . that is, the Representatives of the People, that is the Parliament, that is the House of Commons, that is the Army, that is the Council of State, that is a company of men in whom neither Faith, Oath, nor Altar take place," it said. "Fairfax, also with Cromwell, Ireton, Steele, Bradshaw, and many others . . . over all of them there is spread a heavy night, blackness and darkness, and an image of that which shall receive them . . . Now every Englishmans choice lyeth thus; whether he will yield his subjection on to Charles, the second the indubitable Sonne and heir of Charles the first, of bleeding memory . . . or whether he will give up his obedience to I know not, nor he knows not what Laws, nor when enacted, nor by what Authority ratified and confirmed? . . . And if this Council of State must be our Law givers, I will hold my—to Cromwell's nose."

The council moved against the Royalist Dr. John Barwick, one-time fellow of St. John's College, Cambridge. Barwick and his brother, Edward, had been privy to the murder of Thomas Rainsborough, the escape of Sir Marmaduke Langdale from Pomfret Castle, and private communication with Prince Charles. Through a man named Bostock, who belonged to the post office the council, obtained incriminating letters written to and from the Barwick brothers. They were imprisoned in Westminster Gate-House on a warrant signed by Bradshawe on April 9. Barwick was brought before Bradshawe and Sir Henry Mildmay for examination. Barwick said that he was threatened with torture by Mildmay, "who in Wickedness, Abusiveness, and cruel Threatening was almost superior to that most impudent Brawler Bradshawe himself." Barwick was near death from consumption when he was confined in the tower on Bradshawe's warrant of the twelfth. Barwick was sure that Bradshawe ordered the lieutenant of the tower to let him die in "some Dungeon of that Prison, secluded from the Company of all mankind, but of a stern morose Jailor." Despite all his privations, Dr. John Barwick survived more than fifteen months in prison. Edward Barwick was released but died soon after.

The Council of State attempted to remove from public view all symbols of the Stuart Kings, but it would become a long-term task. Among the council's first resolutions was an order to emblazon the sterns of Republican ships with the twin arms of England and Ireland. An ensign bearing a red cross on a white background, the Cross of St. George, was ordered for each ship. As late as 1650, Bradshawe was still writing the commissioners of the militia in County Hereford:

We are informed that there are several churches and other public places, in your counties, there remain standing the arms and picture of the late king, which have been ordered to be taken away . . . appoint some fit persons to make due and strict searches in all churches, halls, and other public places . . . give your express order for the taking away and destroying all the same arms and pictures . . .

In 1651, instructions were issued to Edward Carter, surveyor general, to stringently remove all royal arms and insignia, whether they be in chambers or windows of chambers or any other public or private place.

In April 1649, the Council of State recommended a new design for the Commonwealth's coins. The dead king's face peering out from the old coinage was a constant reminder of his fate.[12] Sir Robert Harley was turned out from being master of the mint for refusing to coin money after the king was beheaded. Some years later, when Bradshawe as chief justice of Chester came to visit Harley at Ludlow, Harley shut his doors against him. After the Restoration, John son of Thomas Woodward petitioned King Charles II "to be put in possession of the house and office of Assay Master of the Mint, held by his father till the late troubles, when John Bradshawe, so called President of the Council of State, on Oct 23, 1649, dismissed him for refusing obedience to the usurped powers and put in Samuel Bartlett, on this Woodward's father went to Virginia publicly declaring that he would not see England again until his Majesty's return."

Figure 19. Coin of King Charles (left) and coin of the Commonwealth (right)

The Royalist newsletter *Mercurius Pragmaticus,* for June 12,[13] printed a supposed letter from John Bradshawe's mother, introducing it thus, "Sir, it's a sign how you mind her business when you lose her letter and let it corne into my hands, but I be so honest as to return it in her own language," then printing it in full, "To the worshipful John Bradshaw in his chambers in Grays Inne, these, etc . . . Son John. When you have dispatched the business I last wrote about I pray you to bring my petticoat downe, for I think I can sell my best here for as much as it cost me. Send my linens and my prints and pewter pot and wheele. Pray you buy me a black bag for a girl of 10 years old, of taffity. the taffity is cut in three and then it will not be above half a crown or 7 groats. When it is cut it must be a yard long. Pray you be sure to buy them, for they are for one who has given me money for them, and you shall have it when you corne down. Remember my love to your wife and children. So I rest your loving mother, Sara Bradshaw." This attack, indicative of the petty nature of some contemporary propaganda, was apparently intended to prove Bradshawe's humble background. It failed to recognise that subject letter was intended for a different John Bradshaw, not the Lord President John Bradshawe. Lord President Bradshawe had no children, and his mother, Catherine, had long been dead. It is little wonder the many John Bradshaws continue to confuse us today given that his own contemporaries could not distinguish between them.

Not only the Royalist press but other dissident voices were speaking out in print. As early as February 23, the Council of State had issued an order for the apprehension of one Thompson, the printer of a protest from the ejected and secluded members of the Long Parliament. John Lilburne published a pamphlet called *England's New Chains Discovered*. His break with England's new rulers was now nearly complete. It mattered not that Bradshawe and John Cook had eloquently obtained for Lilburne a reversal of his Star Chamber sentence and reparations of £2,000 some three years earlier. Forgotten too was was his family association with the Bradshaws.[14] Just eight days after Bradshawe had taken his seat as lord president, he was entrusted with the singular power to sign council warrants for the apprehension of all those who spoke or acted against the safety of the Commonwealth. He quickly issued a warrant for Lilburne, Overton, Walwyn, and Prince to appear before the council at Derby House. When Lilburne appeared, Bradshawe informed him of the charge and gave him leave to speak. *"Well, Mr. Bradshawe with your favour—I am an Englishman born and bred and brought up, and England is a nation governed bounded and limited by law and liberties,"* answered Lilburne. He adopted his usual tack of denying the authority of the council. Bradshawe countered, *"Lieutenant Colonel Lilburne you need not be so earnest and have spent so much time; This Council doth not go about to try you."* Still Lilburne refused to admit any knowledge of his tract, *England's New Chains*. All four of the men were interrogated and then ushered out of the chamber. Lilburne told how he put his ear to the door and heard Cromwell thump the table and say, apparently addressing Bradshawe, *"I tell you sir, you have no other way to deal with these men but to break them to pieces."* After deliberating until midnight, the council committed the prisoners to the Tower awaiting trial.

While Lilburne was prisoner he continued to send forth pamphlets for publication. The most telling of these was *The Impeachment of*

Cromwell and Ireton published on August 10. After insulting Cromwell and Ireton, Lilburne wrote that Bradshawe was the hired mercenary of the other two, a theme that would be echoed by Clarendon, other Royalists, and some historians to this day. Lilburne received a long letter of empathy from Thomas Verney.[15] In Lilburne's *Hue and Cry after Sir Arthur Haselrig*, dated August 18, 1649, he refers to Verney's letter, saying that Haselrig and Bradshawe were employing *one Thomas Verney . . . a quondam Cavalier to plot and obtain the taking away of his life* by getting him to commit to writing something that could be used against him. Refusing to be drawn, the ever-cautious Lilburne sent copies of Verney's letter to be presented at the council. *"And yet,"* Lilburne says in a bitter summing up, *"the said Verney continues as great with Bradshawe and other of the thing called the Council of State to this very day as if he were their Alpha and Omega."*

The Rump House of Commons intended the Council of State to perform the role of executive body with power to charge the revenue, settle the militia, settle tumults and give commissions to raise arm forces on any emergency, advance trade and plantations, control the stores and magazines, and provide such a navy as it should think fit. The council had the authority to send for any person, any records or writings, and administer oaths for discovery of truth with the power to imprison and take bonds from any who refuse obedience to them. They had the authority to send ambassadors and settle amity with foreign nations. Lilburne said the council was the supreme power in England. "Bradshaw, by his office, was in some measure the first man in the nation. He was to receive foreign ambassadors, and to represent, in his own person, upon occasions of public solemnity, the executive government of the Commonwealth of England," says Godwin.[16]

One other officer of the civil establishment was viewed by some as possessing supreme power: the Speaker of the House William Lenthall. Lenthall had been seen to subject himself to the will of the house when the king demanded to know the whereabouts of the five members in 1642: *"May it please your Majesty, I have neither eyes to see nor tongue to speak in this place but as this House is pleased to direct me, whose servant I am here."* No doubt this reassuring expression was remembered by the Rumpers in 1649. However, as a figurehead of civil government, Lenthall took ceremonial roles formerly reserved for the king. A solemn thanksgiving was held in Christ Church, Newgate Street, followed by a sumptious banquet given by the lord mayor and corporation in the

Grocer's Hall. The order of precedence was determined by the Council of State: the speaker, members of Parliament, and the Council of State were to dine by themselves. At their table, Speaker Lenthall sat at the upper end with the army commander Fairfax and Lord President Bradshawe on either side, then came Whitelocke, Lisle, Pembroke, and Cromwell. A satirical tract published soon thereafter imagined speeches delivered at the banquet: "Oh, this is a blessed day, Mr. Speaker and mervilous in our eyes, to see you become our Supreme Head and Governour, now that we have cut off the king's head . . . you, my Lord President, who deserve so much in the settling of this republick . . . I should have placed you uppermost, for I know none so fit to have represented the supreme authority as you that commanded the cutting off of it . . . It was a dangerous piece of work, indeed: and I was afraid, as you are . . . I think my brethren carried it off a little better than myself; for my guts began to crow after their old tune, and wrought like bottle-beer, inasmuch that I wished for Colonel Pride to stop the bung-hole, till the troopers relieved us."

Just a year before the Restoration, the reinstalled Parliament swore loyalty to Lenthall as the father of the nation. A Commonwealth warship had been named *Speaker* and a frigate named *President* in honor of Lentahall and Bradshawe.

Parliament determined to remove the busy Council of State from the overcrowded Derby House in Cannon Row and arranged a more prestigious place for them in Whitehall.

About this time, John, Lord Belasyse, son of the Royalist Duke of Ormonde, arrived in London. A German count named Altoine, confined in the tower, said Belasyse had met him on the Continent and offered command in a Royalist army being raised to conquer England. Belasyse was arrested and brought before the Council of State sitting in the Queen's Presence Chamber in Whitehall palace. Belasyse vehemently denied Altoine's charge and demanded trial by combat. Bradshawe told him that was an old athiestical law and sent him to the tower. Belasyse was sure that Bradshawe had coopted Count Altoine to falsely accuse him. Belasyse became one of the six members of Charles II's secret supreme council, the Sealed Knot. Other members were Lord Loughborough, Sir William Compton, Col. John Russell, Col. Edward Villers, and Sir Richard Willys. Belasyse was the only Roman Catholic member.

In spite of their earlier amicable association, Bradshawe and his old acquaintance, William Prynne, were now at odds. Bradshawe's respect for Prynne's rebelliousness had evaporated. They engaged in a bitter battle at the council. Prynne had been imprisoned on June 30 for his pamphlets attacking the Parliament. He blamed Bradshawe and continued to publish pamphlets challenging the legality of his imprisonment. Bradshawe wrote to Prynne's jail keeper:

Sir: We have been informed, that Taunton is an unfit place for the imprisonment of Mr. Prynne, where he is now; we therefore desire you to give order for the removal of the said Mr. Prynne to Pendennis Castle; and he be there kept upon the same Warrant upon which he hath been prisoner at Dunstar Castle and now at Taunton, till further Order. And that while he is there in restraint, he may have liberty to go to publick Ordinances of Gods worship, if he shall desire the same. Signed in the name and by order of the Council of State, by authority of Parliament. John Bradshawe, President.[17]

Two years later he was offered freedom if he promised no further pamphlets against the government; he refused. After another year and one half, he was released without conditions. In December 1654, the two men met face-to-face at Gray's Inn. We have only Prynne's account of the encounter, which is not flattering to Bradshawe. He says Bradshawe conceded the illegality of Prynne's imprisonment but defended it on the grounds of self-preservation, just as Prynne had defended the historical self-defense of Parliament's sovereignty as valid. Prynne rejoined that the comparison did not suit the question. He thought Bradshawe and Cromwell were self-serving tyrants and their protestations of liberty hypocritical. He was sure the *strange corrupting tranforming venom . . . in Sovereign powers and dignities* seduced men from their legal foundations and led them to violate their oaths and Christian obligations. Prynne was instrumental in the Restoration and was awarded the post of keeper of the records in the Tower of London by King Charles II in 1660. He found the records in decay and described how he was almost choked by the dust of crumbling parchment which left him at the end of each day as black as a chimney sweep. Presumably, if he had found Bradshawe's papers, he would have happily delivered them to his royal masters.

Prynne's vision of a godly Christian government—compassionate, pious, humble, honest, and plain—was supported by other radical voices urging that "all costly pomp and state hereafter be suspended until the desolations and spoils of the poor people be repaired." The magnificent royal library at Whitehall was rifled by Hugh Peter before the Council of State could appoint Bulstrode Whitelocke as its keeper. Still many of the Rump were no Philistines, and they feared embezzlement of the king's valuable treasures. Orders were issued to inventory, value, and sell some of the booty, "except such parcels therof as shall be found necessary for the uses of the state." The Council of State was given power to determine what should be retained to the limit of £10,000. This was later enlarged to £20,000, but the council simply ignored this upper limit and reserved for the state great quantities of the royal family's personal possessions, well above the value of that limit, drawn from London's royal houses and palaces as well as provincial ones. They reserved more than £10,000 worth of the king's furniture, tapestry, etc. for the use of the council alone. This was not the *Liberte, Fraternite, Equalite* of the 1789 French Revolution which dispelled the treasures of France. This new civil regime was moving toward preserving the kingdom's heritage and the restoration of some of the traditional patterns of ceremony and grand spectacle, acknowledging Henry Savile's observation that the mass of people is guided more by ceremonies or show than matter in substance.

Richly furnished apartments were placed at the disposal of Lisle, Grey, Holland, and other members of the Council of State. Hugh Peter, now chaplain to the Council of State, was quartered at Whitehall palace in three or four decent and well-furnished rooms at the front of the house. John Milton also had furnished chambers. No doubt these apartments were furnished with rich carpets, hangings, and furniture drawn from the royal inventory.

In April, Parliament ordered a new mace to replace the old royal one. In May the Council of State ordered Edward Denby, its sergeant-at-arms, to confer about providing the council with their own mace. Parliment's new gilded mace was delivered in June at a cost of £137 1s.; the council ordered their own in July at a cost of £151 10 s. 4 d. Denby was assigned the job of bearing the mace before Lord President John Bradshawe. He also had the job of protecting Bradshawe and the council with his team of security men, armed guards, Whitehall police, ushers, and doorkeepers. Cooks provided meals for the council's table and the commissioners ordered St. James Park to be stocked with deer so that a regular supply of fresh venison was available. On one ocassion three fishermen supplied the council's table with a huge sturgeon—a fish formerly reserved only for ruling kings.

In addition to his official lodgings in Whitehall, Bradshawe had his own house provided by Parliament: the dean's house in Westminster Abbey. In a paper bearing his signature dated January 10, 1652, he says: *"I was settled there by the Parliament at the tryall of the King and Lords, and was in possession when the Governors were appointed."*[18] The governors of the school and alms houses of Westminister came there in early 1650, and they quickly arranged a forty-year lease of the dean's house to Bradshawe. Dr. John Williams, the Royalist lord keeper, had been the last dean of Westminster, but he left about 1646.[19]

On November 20, 1650, Bradshawe surrendered to the Society of Gray's Inn the three upper chambers in Holbourne Court, two of which he had built.

Five thousand pounds had been provided to furnish Bradshawe's needs before the king's trial. Subsequently, a grant of £1,000 was ordered to be paid forthwith to Bradshawe for his services to Parliament. Then a committee composed of Sir William Brereton, Lord Lisle, Whitelocke, Cromwell, and others was appointed to consider what lands were available, out of which a grant to the full value of £2,000 annually could be settled on Bradshawe and his heirs. The lands chosen were Summerhill (a.k.a. Somer Hill),[20] the seat of the Royalist Earl of St. Albans in Kent (valued at £1,000 a year), and Fonthill Gifford,[21] the seat of Lord Cottingham in Wiltshire (valued the same). The act settling these estates was passed by the house. The Earl of St. Albans's estate, however, was encumbered with previous debts, and Bradshawe's grant would be challenged in a 1654 petition to Parliament from Thomas Brewer, William Pawlin, Elizabeth Quested, and Ann Bewick, creditors of the earl.

Royalists made much of Bradshawe's ambition and and alledged he was greedy for personal reward. During the eighteenth century, John Adams, the American president, was similarly castigated, but he was defended by his biographer: "That he was ambitious of public honors must be admitted; for, in a Republican government, public honors are the evidence of public approbation. Ambition is criminal only when it seeks the honors without deserving them." Bradshawe received a new commission as chief justice of Chester in July[22] with Thomas Fell as his deputy.

Not everyone was so liberally rewarded as Bradshawe. Colonel Rosworme, the hero of the seige of Manchester, was treated with "gross ingratitude (by) the perpidious townsmen of Manchester." He submitted a petition to Fairfax, Bradshawe, and Cromwell asking their help in the collection of his back pay. Only Bradshawe took action and addressed a letter:

> *For the town of Manchester and particularly for those who contracted with Lieut. Col. Rosworme, these: Gentlemen The condition of the bearer being fully made known and his former merit attested to us by honourable testimony and very well known to yourselves, himself also*

being by birth a stranger and unable to present his compliments in ordinary legal form give us just occasion to recommend him to you for a thorough performance of what by your contract and promise is become due unto him for his special service done to your town and country, whereto we conceive there is good cause for you to make and addition and that there can be no cause at all for your backwardness to pay him what is due. As touching that which is otherwise due to him from the state after some greater business are over, he may expect to be put in a way to receive all just satisfaction. In the meantime we commit him and the promises to your consideration for his speedy relief and we require you to give us notice of your resolutions and doings therein, within one month after the receipt hereof. Signed in the name and by the order of the Council of State appointed by authority of Parliament.

John Bradshawe
Whitehall 7 July 1649
President

Two years later Rosworme, still awaiting payment, presented a further petition to Parliament complaining that his wife and children were living on the charity of strangers.[23] In the following month Rosworme was, perhaps at Bradshawe's recommendation, appointed engineer general of all the garrisons and forts in England at a salary of 10s. per day, later doubled. After 1659, nothing is heard of this accomplished German soldier who fought for the England Parliament.

Bradshawe was not averse to recommending the cases of his loyal friends and acqaintances. Lord President Bradshawe wrote to the Committee for Compounding:

Gentlemen; The Bearer, my old friend (Mr. Hugh Middleton) and Schoolfellow seeks (as he tells me) a Messengers place amongst you. He hath done and suffered for the parliament so much as I could wish to meet with an opportunity to help him in a larger measure to a substenance than by troubling you with this Recommendation. But his present desires being for this place of a Messenger I willingly for him make it my request to you he may find your favor herein which I should not do if I had not Confidence of his diligence & fidelity in performance of the trust you shall commit to him in the advancement of the service you have in hand. So with my heartiest salutations I rest and will be Your Friend ready to serve you.[24]

To prove this was written by Bradshawe himself and not by one of his secretaries, the note is in Bradshawe's characteristic "court hand."

Although it is technically "secretary hand," few, if any secretaries in public or private service, were writing like that by the 1640/50s.

Bradshawe also wrote in favor of Lord Mohun, Baron of Okehampton, John Pennington, George Warburton of Arley[25] and Tim Turner, bencher of Gray's Inn. Bradshawe's support of petitioners even reached to the American colonies. Bradshawe addressed the governor of Virginia, October 11, 1649:

Sir—we are informed by the petition of some of the people of the congregation of Nansamund in Virginia, that they had long enjoyed the benefit of the ministry of Mr. Harrison, who is an able man, and of unblameable conversation, who hath been banished by you for no other cause but that he would not conform himself to the use of the Common prayer book. We know you cannot be ignorant that the use of the common prayer book is prohibited by the Parliament of England, and therefore you are hereby required to permit the same Mr. Harrison to return to his said congregation to the execise of his ministry there unless there be sufficient cause as shall be approved by the Parliament or this Council, when the same shall be represented unto us of your compliance herein. We expect to receive an account from yourself by the first opportunity.[26]

On the evening of July 10, Oliver Cromwell departed London in a coach of state drawn by six huge Flanders mares. His bodyguard was eighty men, "the meanest whereof a Commander or Esquire, in stately habit with trumpets sounding, almost to the shaking of Charing Cross had it now been standing," He traveled by way of Windsor and Bristol to Ireland, a scene of distracted plunderings, excommunications, treacherous conflagrations, and universal misery and blood and blunder, such as the world before or since has never seen.[27] Innumerable parties contended for control: Anglo-Irish Catholics of the Pale, old Irish Catholics, the English and Scottish Ulster Presbyterians for King and Covenant, the Duke of Ormonde's Royalist confederation of mixed creeds for king and no covenant. The Duke of Ormande's son was Lord John Belasyse, who was imprisoned in London on Bradshawe's warrant. Against all these forces stood Gen. Michael Jones[28] and the forces of the Republic of England who wanted neither king or covenant.

John Bradshawe wrote to Col. John Raymond, July 26:

These are to will & require you forthwith to cause those Company's of foot which you have raised to march with all expedition to Chester or Liverpool in order to (your ?) present transportation to Dublyn. And you are to be careful to keep good Discipline among your soldiers and pay your quarters as you march to prevent the oppression of the County & alienation of the hearts of the people thereby from the present Government.

Whether Bradshawe meant that caution to apply to the hearts of the people in Ireland, as well as the people of Lancashire and Cheshire, can only be guessed.

Cromwell departed for Ireland with thirty-two ships in early August. Reverend Hugh Peter was still dealing with the mutinous condition of the navy. Peter was sufficiently recovered from his springtime illness to write to Bradshawe and explain that "we had to pay dear enough for ships, and meet with a very hard people to doe themselves good" in order to transport Cromwell and his troops to Ireland. The crossing was rough, and Peter said that Cromwell "was as sick as ever I saw a man in my life, we have heard nothing from him."[29]

Cromwell arrived in Dublin to find that Michael Jones had inflicted a defeat upon the odd alliance of Protestants and Catholics. Still, Cromwell favored a swift and bloody final campaign to save the dwindling treasury of Parliament. A month was spent in remodeling Jones's Army, "And now have at you, my Lord Ormond! You will have men of gallantry to encounter; whom to overcome will be honour sufficient and to be beaten by them will be no great blemish to your reputation. If you say, Caesar or nothing: They say a Republic or Nothing."

In a letter dated September 16, 1649, Cromwell addressed the Honourable John Bradshawe Esquire President of the Council of State and described the storming and capture of Tredah.

Back in London, Bradshawe addressed orders on behalf of Council of State to Wm Lenthall, Speaker, Anthony Edwards, Mayor, and other persons appointed in city and county of Gloucester, for preserving the peace of the Commonwealth.

Bradshaw was still finding time to deal with minute navy details:

> *Whereas we are informed that the Ship Leopards Whelp is a fit Vessel for this Winters service. We have therefore thought fit and do hereby require you to fit her with such a quantity of Victuals and otherwise necessaries as you conceive she will bear not hindering her sailing, and for your so doing this shall be your Warrant*
>
> *Given at the Council of State at Whitehall the Sixth of October 1649, Jo: Bradshawe, president* [30]

Bradshawe's Press Act had been passed chiefly in response to John Lilburne's flood of antigovernment pamphlets. Lilburne was indicted for high treason and brought to the Guildhall on October 25 and 26 for trial. Peter Warburton, judge of the Common Pleas, was appointed one of the trial commissioners but took no active part. Justices Keble, Heath, Thorpe, Jermin, and four other common-law judges presided over the court. Edmund Prideaux, attorney general, was the prosecutor. A jury was empaneled. The Council of State detemined this was to be no high court, which Lilburne could challenge. Lilburne in fact did not challenge the legality of the court but instead chose to refute each point of law. He wrangled on the indictment and assignment of counsel. *"Mr. Bradshawe,"* said Lilburne, *"was my Counsel before the House of Lords in 1645,"* but *"when brought before the Council of State, I saw no accuser, no prosecutor, no charge or indictment but all the crime that there was laid to my charge was Mr. Bradshawe's very seriously examining me questions against myself and committed me to prison for treason upon the same general grounds that as Counsel he had formerly controverted and declared illegal."* Mr. Justice Jermin reminded him that Mr. Bradshawe was now styled "The Lord President of the Council of State." Lilburne took no notice and claimed the same privileges which Bradshawe had extended to the Duke of Hamilton. Amidst cheers of his supporters, he was acquitted by the jury but recommitted to the tower while Bradshawe and the council hesitated for a fortnight. Bradshawe then issued a warrant for his release:

> *Whereas Lieut. Col. John Lilburne hath been committed to the Tower, upon the suspicion of High Treason, in order to his Trial at law: which Trial he hath received and is by them acquitted: These are to will and require you upon sight hereof to discharge and set at liberty the said Lieut. Col. John Lilburne from his imprisonment; for which this shall be your sufficient warrant. Given at the Council of State at Whitehall this 8th Day of November 1649.*
>
> *Signed in the Name and by the Order of the Council of State, appointed by authority of Parliament.*
> *John Bradshawe, President*
> *To the Lieutenant of the Tower of London or his Deputy*

Figure 20. Free Born John Lilburne

Lilburne's immediate reply was his pamphlet *Truth's Victory Over Tyrants*, but the Leveler's appeal was gradually diminishing. "He was a brave soldier and an exceedingly able man but with no sense of proportion, he became a more unwilling fanatic." For the next eighteen months, Lilburne published no contentious pamphlets and devoted himself to his family and the business of soap boiling. Exiled to the Continent, he returned to England, again was exiled to Jersey, imprisoned at Dover, and became a Quaker in 1655. In the last year of his life he wrote Margaret Fell[31] to confess his conversion. He died at Etham in 1657. As a Quaker and a Leveler, Lilburne could not be interred just two miles northwest in the old church of St. Alphege at Greenwich, where John himself claimed to have been born and where other members of his family were buried.[32] Instead his body was taken to London and buried without pomp at the new churchyard of Bethlehem by Bishopsgate.

While dealing with the Leveler's press, Bradshawe was also countering the vicious attacks of Royalist propagandists. The *Royall Diurnall* for March 26 to April 3 says, "but no laws shall be of force but what proceeds out of the mouths of Regicides, Jack Cade (Bradshawe I should say) and his fellow Rebels . . . As the head of this monstrous government is, so must the body be; A chaos of Tyranny Injustice, &c., where the lust of every Tyrannt becomes a Law themselves being both Judges, Parties, and Jury.—for 14 April to 23 April; The Functo are now in so stinking a fear of the King and Scots agreement, that Lt. Col. John Lilburne thinks soap will be a very good comodity at Westminster these few days. Another order was to remove all Persons whose abode shall seem prejudicial or dangerous to the Functo 20 miles from them, this is the property of a Fratricide or Regicide, that he thinks (like Cain) that everyone that but dwells near him hath a mind to kill him; this is the disease Rebels sometimes in seeking to prevent, turn their own executioners, as Hoyle, Judas, Achetophel &c. who knows but Mr. Bradshaw make of this approved remedy; I hear the Disease is predominate in his conscience already."

Milton was commissioned to examine copies of *Mercurius Pragmaticus*, edited by Marchmont Needham. Needham wrote:

No favour is durable from those 'Hobnayle Functo Birds.' Who is secure in what they bestow? Have they not bestowed largely on divers, and recalled their grants (?) . . . a Fairfax, Cromwell, a Bradshawe, a Steele, Cooke, Aske, &c. or any Regicide may have part of their inheritance, and none other.

Bradshawe signed a warrant for Needham's arrest, dated June 18. After six months in Newgate gaol, Needham changed sides and became editor of *Mercurius Politicus* at £100 per year paid by the Council of State. Milton supervised Needham's work. A Royalist described the first edition, "Now appeared in print as the weekly champion of the New Commonwealth and to patter the King with the basest of scurrilous raillery Mr. Marchmont Needham, under the name of Politicus a Jack-of-all-sides, transcendentally gifted in appropious and treasonable droll and hired therefore by Bradshawe to act the second part to his starched and more solemn treason; who began his first diurnal with an investive against Monarchy and the presbyterian Scotch Kirk and ended it with an Hosanna to Oliver Cromwell who in the beginning of June returned by way of Bristol from Ireland to London."

Figure 21. Eikon Basilke

One other Royalist publication remained. Throughout 1649, editions of *Eikon Basilke* had been printed and circulated. In later editions, one of the king's prayers, known as Pamela's prayer, was interpolated. Milton, who had been given the job of replying to this popular Royalist icon, recognized Pamela's prayer as a direct plagiarism from Sir Philip Syndey's *Arcadia* and pointed that out in his new book, *Eikonoklastes*. The Royalists were shocked at the charge their martyred king stole from another man's work, claiming it as his own. To explain how this could have happened, they charged that Bradshawe and Milton had coerced William DuGard's cooperation in a plot to insert Pamela's prayer in his later editions. A certain Dr. Bernard was said to have stated that he often heard Bradshawe and Milton laugh at inserting this prayer out of Sir Philip Sydney's *Arcadia*. This charge doesn't seen to stand, however, since Milton's first edition of *Eilkonoklates* appeared in October 1649 and DuGard wasn't imprisoned until February 1650. At Milton's intercession, Bradshawe released DuGard in April. Dugard was reinstated as headmaster of Merchant Taylor's School in September. DuGard would become printer for the council. One of DuGard's famous pupils was Elihu Yale, whose name is remembered in Yale University.

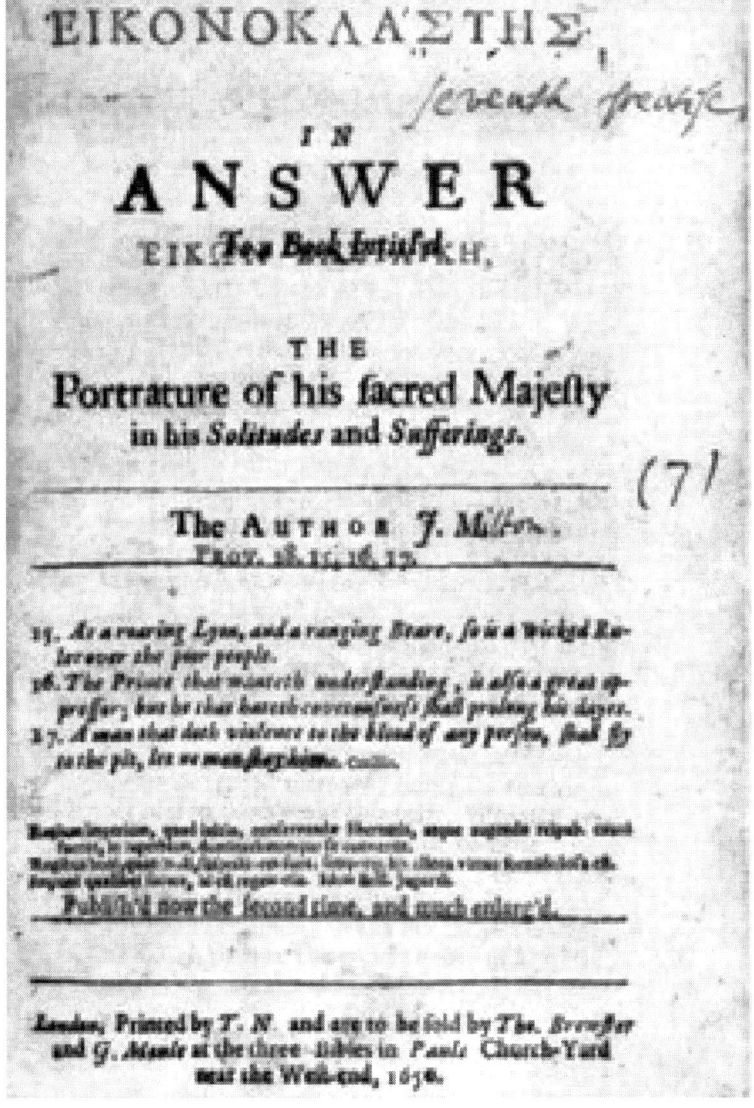

Figure 22. Eilkonoklates, Milton's answer to Eikon Basilke

At the first meeting of the second Council of State, Bradshawe was again elected lord president. Milton was put in charge of the State Paper Office in Whitehall and the following letter was dispatched to Baker, Weckherlin, and Willingham:

> *Sir—we are informed that there are several letters and other papers of public concernment that are in your hands which we have thought fit should be brought into the paper office at Whitehall, both for safe keeping of them and that they might be ready for public use upon all occasions. We therefore desire you to deliver all the said papers to Mr. Milton, whom we have appointed to receive the same and see them safely and orderly disposed in the said office.*
>
> *Signed in the name and by the order of the Council of State.*
> *Jo: Bradshawe, President.*

Some years later, after Bradshawe had left the presidency, an order for delivery of documents specifically identifies a bundle of "all the papers that Ambroise Randolph[33] had from Lord Bradshawe when he was President delivered out of the Library of Lord Bradshawe." After the Restoration, a king's warrant dated October 2, 1660, ordered John Thurloe[34] to deliver to the keeper "all those papers, books, and records of state . . . heretofore delivered unto you by Ambroise Randolph Esq, late clerk of the said papers, and likewise all those papers, books, and records of state delivered by the said Ambroise Randolph to Bradshawe and by him left with you." The Bradshawe bundle of papers do not appear to have been received from Thurloe and are not accounted for today.[35] Not all men respected public records. Bradshawe did, so did William Prynne, but Hugh Peter wanted to send "all our old Records to a firey Martyrdom in Smithfield."

Anxious to know who their friends were, the council devoted considerable effort to enforcing the Engagement (an oath of allegiance to the Commonwealth) on all Englishmen eighteen years and older, at home or abroad. Formerly, the Engagement had been required only of government officers and ministers. Presbyterian ministers of Lancashire and Cheshire objected on the grounds that it was inconsistent with the covenant and it was imposed by usurpers. The Royalist city of Chester presented difficulties, and Mayor Richard Bradshaw[36] reported to the lord president:

I had hoped to give you numerous account of subscribers to the engagement within this city but there being none here specially commanded to take subscriptions since the passing of the Act and to give you the whole truth there is not one justice of the peace, mayor, recorder, or other except Mr. Aldersey and myself that have either taken the engagement or given countenance to they that have.

If there was difficulty administering the Engagement at home, there was even greater difficulty abroad. The Commonwealth was faced by hostility from almost every government in Europe and a campaign of sabotage by exiled Royalists there. Hamburg had traditionally been a close trading partner of England. The Company of Merchant Adventurers had a permanent colony there, and the president of the Adventurers often served as the English government's representative to the city. The senate of the city of Hamburg issued a decree forbidding English residents from taking the Engagement, and the council wrote to ask why. Hamburg blamed the problem on Royalists who intimidated some of the city magistrates. By May the matter was solved, and the Commonwealth's resident at Hamburg, Richard Bradshaw,[37] reported the English merchants had all taken the Engagement. Royalist attacks continued, however, and Richard Bradshaw received insults and death threats.

Cromwell wrote Lord President Bradshawe from Cashel on March 5 describing the surrender of Cahir and Kilhnan Castles and the capture of Lord Dunboyne's stronghold.

The University of Oxford was preparing to elect a chancellor in the spring of 1650. Bradshawe and Fairfax were candidates. Bulstrode Whitelocke, deeply depressed after his wife's death, was encouraged to stand for nomination but he refused. Cromwell was elected.

Friends encouraged Whitelocke to marry again and even suggested a suitable widow, Mary Wilson. Whitelocke would, ultimately, marry her. Rowland Wilson, a member of the Council of State and former alderman of London, died in February, leaving his widow Mary and ten children. Wilson's elaborate funeral took place in March. The Lord Mayor and Lord General Fairfax led the procession with Bradshawe and Whitelocke directly behind them. Many of the London Trained Bands that Wilson had commanded marched in the procession. As they made their way through the narrow streets, a crowd of noisy onlookers raised a cry against Bradshawe, "Here is the rogue that judged the King!, Kill him! Kill him! Let us tear him to pieces!" Bradshawe, who had been threatened with death before, appealed to Whitelocke to stay by his side, and the two escaped down a side street before the cortege reached the church. Whitelocke's "Diary" relates a more alarming narrative of the event and suggests that Royalist agitators had planned the attack, knowing that after they murdered Bradshaw they could safely escape through the assembled throng.

These were, without doubt, genuine Royalist threats. Eusebuis Andrews, former secretary to the late Lord Capel, was preparing to leave England when he was persuaded to subscribe to a new Royalist plot. John Barnard, a former major under his command, introduced Andrews to two Royalist cavaliers, Captain Holmes and John Benson, who proposed to enlist dismissed Parliamentarian officers. Barnard was a secret spy of the Council of State, probably recruited by Thomas Scott, the Council's spymaster. Scott delayed Andrews's arrest until other cavaliers were drawn into the trap. Andrews became convinced that the whole plot was a delusion but while preparing to leave the country was arrested at Gravesend on March 24. In London, Andrews was interrogated by Bradshawe, Mildmay, and Scott, and committed him to the tower on the charge of treason on the evidence set forth in a "narrative" provided by Andrews himself. Andrews charged that Bradshawe had set spies to entrap him. Bradshawe acknowledged and defended the practice. After sixteen weeks in the tower, Andrews was brought before the High Court of Justice and condemned on his own "narrative." The usual sentence for treason—to be hanged, drawn, and quartered—was commuted to beheading which was carried out on August 22. Benson was hanged. Ashley was condemned and later pardoned. Barnard was rewarded, but four years later he was hanged at Tyburn for robbery.

While this was taking place, Bradshawe was made one of the governors of Charterhouse in place of Lord Roberts of Truro. The patent for his appointment bears the signatures of Speaker Lenthall, Lord Lisle, Lord Chief Justice St. John, the Earl of Salisbury, Lord Lefforway, Sir William Armyne, and John Selden.

Cromwell arrived back in England during the Eusebuis Andrews affair. On the way to London he paused at Windsor where he held court and listened to "any man that hath business, to speak to him." On June 27, Bradshawe wrote to Colonel Reade notifying him of the resolution of Parliament appointing Cromwell captain general of the army. Fairfax was retired on a pension of £5,000 per year.

A few months later Captain General Cromwell took his army northward to confront Prince Charles and the Scottish Covenanteers. The Commonwealth was now under great threat.

Notes to Chapter Eleven

1. In his Answer to the Nineteen Propositions in 1642 the late King had propounded a view that the English constitution was a balance between monarchy, aristocratic and popular forces, and that the power of the two Parliamentary houses was more than sufficient to restrain to power of tyranny. This view was shattered by the events of the first Civil War when the Parliament accused the King of instituting a lawless form of personal rule which destroyed property rights of peers and MPs and turned them into fellow-servants with "the meaner sort of people"; the King accused the Parliament of a tyranny which caught and enslaved the affection of the credulous common people.
2. Sean Kelsey, *Inventing a Republic*, (Manchester Univ. Press, 1997)
3. The powers of the Council were broadly drawn:—1. To oppose the pretensions of Charles Stuart, 2. to direct the Militia, 3. to use means to subdue Ireland, Guernsey, Jersey, the Isles of Scilly and Man. Forty-one names were proposed of which only about a half had shown themselves to be wholly committed, either by having signed the King's death warrant or by making a declaration of dissent before the execution. Several were well-known moderates.
4. Basil Fielding, 2nd Earl of Denbigh, was brother-in-law of James, Earl of Hamilton, who had been condemned by Bradshawe's High Court.
5, Phillip Herbert (1584-1650), 4th Earl of Pembroke, Lord Chamberlain to King Charles the First, had broken with the King and sided with Parliament pragmatically accepting the idea of Civil War and its consequences saying "war be what it will, you know might overcomes right . . . if they deny me my honour, they cannot deny me my age, and that it is that makes me honourable." He had been patron of both Bulstrode Whitlocke and John Bradshawe. Bradshawe was Chief Steward of Pembroke's manor of Glossop in 1637; Whitlocke became Pembroke's deputy Keeper of the Forest and Great Park at Windsor after Pembroke was made Constable of Windsor Castle and Keeper of the Forest in 1649. John Bradshawe, while Chancellor of the Duchy of Lancashire, appointed Pembroke to the post of Monmouth Steward.
6. Pierpont Morgan Library, New York
7. *Scobel p 155*; Parliament unanimously agreed a bill "that all books of law be translated into English; and all proceedings in any court, except the Admirality Court, after Easter 1651, shall be in English only . . . and

all writs & etc shall be in a legible hand and not in court hand." French had always been the language of the English court system and Bradshawe, as a Sergeant-at-Law, would have been skilled in that tongue. Bradshawe would have had, almost certainly, considerable skill in legal Latin.

8. *Rpt on the Mss of F.W. Leyborne-Popham,* (HMSO 1899), 11, 55; Other letters in the collection include—January 17, 1649/50 ¬ Council of State to Col. Robert Blake ; Instructions for the General appointed to command the fleet for the Southern expedition; page 56; February 12, 1649/50—Council of State to Cols. Popham, Blake, and Deane: Whitehall, Commission appointing them Commanders of the Fleet for the ensuing years—signed by Bradshawe, seal, parchment.
9. Whitelocke's beloved wife, Frances, had been ill since April and he was shattered by her untimely death in May. She was sister to Francis, Lord Willoughby of Parham. Whitelocke's grief was so all-consuming that he lost interest in his work. His friends, perhaps including Bradshawe, feared for his life. Only the welfare of his ten children kept him committed to life.
10. *Add'l Mss 63,788*, folio 59, British Library.
11. *State Papers* 25, vol 94, 152, (P.R.O.)
12. It is apparent that both types of coin continued in circulation. At the Middlesex Sessions of 1 September 1657, a True Bill was returned that Anthony Bradshaw, labourer, late of the parish of St. Leonards Shoreditch, county Middlesex, made "of copper brasse tinne and other mixed metals certain false and counterfeit moneys;" King Charles half-crowns, and "The Commonwealth of England half-crowns."
13. *Thomason Tracts E 560*—19.
14. Lilburne's aunt was Mary, daughter of John Bradshaw of Bradshaw, Lancashire.
15. M.M. Verney, *Memoirs of the Verney Family,* Vol III, 142
16. *History of the Commonwealth of England*, Vol iii, 185.
17. *British Library,* Shlf Mk 1129.h.7 (3).
18. J. Armitage Robinson, *The Abbot's House at Westminster*, (Cambridge. Univ. Press, 1911)
19. Again, how strange to find an earlier Bradshaw connection with this house. In 1575 Lady Elizabeth Russell had sheltered there because of the plague. The birth of her child in the house of Westminster Abbey was announced to Queen Elizabeth and a grand christening was held in the Abbey church—a certain Mrs. Bradshaw was Midwife of the child and took a prominent part in the ceremony bearing the baby Elizabeth on

a "mantel of crimson velvet garled with gold, having also over the face a lawne striped . . . lace of gold overthwart and powdered with gold flowers white wrought thereon." Mrs. Bradshaw received a gift of 3 lie from the Queen. Lady Elizabeth Russell was the learned Elizabeth Cooke, sister of Lord Burghley's wife Mildred, and sister of Francis Bacon's wife, married firstly Sir Thomas Hoby. He died at Paris in 1566 and eight years later she married secondly to Lord John Russell son of the Earl of Bedford. Russell died in 1584 and his widow composed his epitaph in the Abbey.

20. Summerhill (Somer Hill) was a splendid Tudor mansion near Tunbridge. It was the seat of Richard Burgh, Vsc. Tunbridge and Earl of St. Albans, who married Francis the widow of Robert Devereux, Earl of Essex, the ill-fated favourite of Queen Elizabeth I. Richard's son Ulrick Burgh succeeded in 1636. He fought for the King in 1645 and was created Marquis of Clanricarde. His estate at Summerhill was sequestered and given to his step-brother Robert, Earl of Essex, the Parliamentary General. Upon the death of Essex in 1646 the estate again came to the hands of Parliament. Bradshawe died in possession of Summerhill. Hasted, the historian of Kent, repeated an inaccurate legend; "Several people now alive (in 1782) remember an old man in the neighborhood who was reputed to be a natural son of John Bradshawe and reported to have been once possessed of Summerhill," *History of Kent*, vol II, pg 340. John Bradshawe's will disproves any question of such a succession, and there is no mention of an illegitimate son fathered by Bradshawe. Of such gossip history is often made.

21. The estate, dating from the 12th century, encompassed nearly all the parish and much of the land in nearby parishes. It was centered on Fonthill Gifford manor house. It is sometimes described as lying in Wiltshire and sometimes in Somerset. In 1621 it was the possession of the infamous Meryvyn Touchet, Earl of Castlehaven, who was attainded and executed for felony sex crimes. King Charles I granted it to Francis Cottington, Baron of the Exchequer, who died in exile 1652. A vellum survey commissioned in 1658 by Bradshawe described the Fonthill estate as containing 2668 acres and 39 perches, and the demesnes of the honor of Summerville (Summerhill?), being parcel of the land belonging to "the right honourable and faithful patriot of his country, John Bradshawe, Lord President of the Council of State anno libertities Angliae restitutae secundo annoque Dom: 1650." Rev. John Watson said the survey existed at Marple Hall in the 18th century. John Watson said that Mr. T. D. Lingard possessed original papers from the Bradshawes of Marple among which was a blank document for the appointment of a Bailiff of the Fonthill estate. He describes it as

retaining an oval seal of red wax bearing the arms, two bends, between two martlets, crest a lion. In 1651 Bradshawe purchased the entire Hundred of Dunworth which greatly expanded his estate.

22. Eight days earlier a John Bradshaw had been nominated Attorney-General for Cheshire and Northern Wales 20 July, 1649. He was not John Bradshawe the Regicide. Peter Bradshaw, a Merchant Tailor of London and distant cousin of John Bradshawe, was Savoy Manor Steward in the Duchy of Lancaster.
23. *The Case of Lieut. Col. Rosworme*, (Chetham Society, 1844-45), 215-247.
24. State Papers 28/258. 30 Oct 1649
25. George Warbuton of Arley was a distant relation of Lord President Bradshaw's wife.
26. *Virginia Historical Magazine*, Vol 5, 229. Rev. Harrison would return to England and marry the daughter of Edward Bradshaw, brother of Richard Bradshaw of Chester.
27. Carlyle, *Cromwell Letters and Speeches*,
28. Gen. Michael Jones drew a bill, dated 11 July 1649, to pay Alderman Richard Bradshaw of Chester 442 £. Richard Bradshaw assigned Jones's bill to his agent, James Wainwright. Richard Bradshaw, who would become the Commonwealth's Resident in Hamburg, was a sizeable merchant of Cheshire. *Cal of State Papers 1647-1660* and Addenda 1625-1660, HMSO.
29. *Perfect Occurences of every daies journall*, No. 139, (Aug 24 1649), 1253.
30. Private collection, Mr. Christopher Godber, Northamptonshire, 2001.
31. *Thirbeck Papers, Library of the Society of Friends*. Margaret Fell, wife of Judge Thomas Fell of Ulverstone. Judge Fell sat on the bench with John Bradshawe in the County of Cheshire, Denbigh, and Flintshire. Margaret Fell, *The Mother of Quakerism*, was converted by George Fox, whom she would marry after the death of Judge Fell.
32. *Memorials in Greenwich Old Church,* Lansdowne Mss Vol 938, folio 112 "On a stone in the wall of the north side of the north aisle of the church—In the never dying memory of Thomas Hixon of Greenwich Esq. Wardrobe keeper to Queen Elizabeth and King. James; married Margaret daughter to Thomas Manley and had issue 5 sons and 3 daughters viz. Robert dyed young Humphrey Hixon of Greenwich Esq Keeper of the standing wardrobe there now, who married the daughter of John Bradshaw of Bradshaw in com. Lanc and hath issue Robert, John, Tho, Franc, Elizabeth, Beatrix, Jane, Susanna, Care, and Mary Hixon . . . . Margaret married to Richard Lilburne of Durham Esq. who died An. Dom. 1619 . . ."

33. Ambroise Randolph (or Randall) and William Boswell were Keepers of the State Papers from 1629 into the Commonwealth period.
34. Thurloe was Cromwell's Secretary of State during the Protectorate and head of Cromwell's network of spies. He replaced Thomas Scott who had held a similar position under Bradshawe and the Council. Bulstrode Whitelocke became a close friend of Thurloe. Thurloe's life was spared after the Restoration in return for providing a detailed statement of the current diplomatic situation.
35. Robert Thomas Fallon, *Milton in Government*, (Pennsylvania Univ. Press, 1993), 12
36. Richard Bradshaw, son of Roger Bradshaw of Aspull and Pennington in Lancashire, was only distantly (if at all) related to Lord President John Bradshawe. Both Richard and his brother Edward had been Aldermen and Mayors of Chester. They were supported by Sir William Brereton who also supported the Lord President.
37. Richard Bradshaw was appointed English Resident for Hamburg on 15th March 1649/50 by the Council of State. He sailed for Hamburg on 30th of the same month. John Milton's letter, 2nd April, 1650, to the government of Hamburg announces the appointment of Richard Bradshaw a England's permanent envoy to Hamburg. It seems this appointment was intended to impress the Hamburgers with the seriousness of England's concern by "naming to the post the nephew of of John Bradshawe," *Milton in Government*. Richard, although supported by John Bradshawe and often called his *nephew* by contemporary as well as modern historians, was not his nephew. *Resident Bradshaw* has also been confused as *President Bradshawe*. It is also said that Richard was *Cromwell's envoy to Hamburg* but it is apparent that John Bradshawe brought both Richard Bradshaw and John Milton into government service while Cromwell was otherwise engaged in Ireland.

CHAPTER TWELVE

King Charles II Invades England

> *He either fears his fate too much,*
> *Or his deserts are small,*
> *Who dares not put it to the touch,*
> *And win or lose it all.*
>
> **The Marquis of Montrose**

✠

CHARLES STUART, THE eldest son of King Charles the First, celebrated his twentieth birthday on May 29, 1650, in exile at Breda in the Netherlands. His hopes of establishing a Royalist base in Ireland had been scuppered by Cromwell. In the previous year he had begun secret negotiations with Scottish commissioners, but behind their back he was pressing his courtier, James Graham Marquis of Montrose, to gather German recruits and conquer Scotland so that he need not bend to the demands of those Scottish commissioners.

The commissioners were not deceived, and they prepared a belated birthday gift. They hanged, drew, and quartered Montrose at Edinburgh. With no other option available, Charles concluded the Treaty of Breda with the commissioners and took the Presbyterian Solemn League and Covenant before entering Scotland.

The English Parliament was aware of what was transpiring and resolved to invade Scotland rather than allow the Scots to set up a hostile kingdom. An unidentified correspondent wrote from Breda: *"the royall party here seems to be exceedingly crestfallen, and much cast down, by the reason of the falling off of many in place and authority, who formerly promised them aid and assistance, and that which doth at present so much distaste them is the receipt of an extract from Hamburgh; wherein is intimidated the arrival of Mr. Richard Bradshaw, Resident for the Parliament of England, who was very joyfully received, and entertained with a gallant volley of great shot, and a noise of trumpets. Upon his going to audience, he was accompanied with several coaches, and divers English merchants, and others of good quality; where having delivered his embassie with excellent grace and singular oratory, the States seemed to be exceedingly pleased thereat, showing good affection to the present Government of England . . ."* From the west of England, however, the Royalist Colonel Keane reported his meeting with a secret supporter in England: "He assures me that if Parliament be well busied in Scotland the City will also raise them a new trouble. Upon some conference he had lately with Bradshaw (the Regicide), he was told by him he wondered much that all the fair and foul means they could use yet not anyone cavalier was heartily converted to them."

Parliament received reports that the colonists in Barbados and Virginia were supporting the king.[1] Shortly after the establishment of the Commonwealth, Parliament had revoked the powers granted in 1643 to the Warwick Commission headed by Robert Rich, Earl of Warwick, and entrusted the entire care of the colonies to Bradshawe's Council of State. The council, already staggered by the volume of their work, was accustomed to perform its work through standing committees under the close oversight of Lord President Bradshawe. The council's Admiralty Committee was primarily responsible for the colonies. John Bradshawe signed a Parliamentary commission appointing Col. Edward Popham, Col. Richard Deane, and Col. Robert Blake commissioners of the admiralty for the year 1650.[2] In addition to this committee, there was another appointed especially for colonial affairs. Then on March 2, 1650, the council issued an order that the entire Council of State, or any five of its members, should constitute the Committee for Trade and Plantations. Prince Charles ignored any claim of the council's control. From Breda on June 3, a royal commission was issued for Governor Sir William Berkeley and sixteen other men to constitute the Council for Virginia. They were ordered to immediately build forts and bulwarks "for the better suppressing of such of our subjects as shall at any time rebel against Us or our Royal Governor there, and for the better resisting of foreign force which shall at any time invade those territories." In July the Council of State issued a warrant for Daniel Goodkin to export thirty barrels of powder, ten tons of shot, and fifty arms to New England. The actual contest for control of the colonies, however, would have to await the outcome of the Scottish war.

In preparation for war with Scotland, the Council of State had locked up many Lancashire Presbyterians and Royalists on suspicion of raising Royalist plots. At their order, Col. Robert Dukinfield imprisoned Sir Roger Bradshaigh of Haigh[3] and several other Lancashire gentlemen at Chester Castle. Sir Thomas Middleton of Chirk Castle was confined.[4]

Captain General Cromwell and his nineteen-thousand-man army moved into Scotland shortly after the Treaty of Breda was concluded. He was short of provisions, and seven thousand of his army had fallen sick. He planned to ship his suffering soldiers back to England from Musselborough. He wrote Bradshawe a letter dated July 30 addressed, in full, to the Right Honourable the Lord President of the Council of State. Frustrated from disembarking at Musselborough, Cromwell was driven eastward and encamped his army near Dunbar. They were without tents. At their back was the cold North Sea; facing them was the Scots army of twenty-three thousand men. There were no ships to evacuate them. The English were in perilous circumstances.

At the darkest moments of Cromwell's troubles, Bradshawe devised a secret plan to split the Scots army. Bradshawe wrote to Henry Ireton in Ireland to inquire what troops and horse could be spared from there for a landing on the west coast of Scotland. Bradshawe's letter, apparently of August 2, is not found today, but Ireton's reply is worth quoting in full for it reveals Bradshawe's hand in the detailed planning:

> *My Lord, Since my dispatch to your Lordship by Sir Robert King and Col. Herbert, I received letters from the Lord President of Connaught, and Col. Venables, wherein they signify me, that upon letters they received from your Lordship (to know what forces they could spare out of Ulster to be sent to Scotland, if occasion were) they had returned answer that, for foot, they conceived it very hazardous to send any, til that Province were wholly reduced, and also the Province of Connaught; but for horse (if I should not require them to any service in Connaught) they conceived four or five hundred might be spared, when it should please God to give Charlemont into their hands; upon which letters of theirs, having (at the same time with them) received your Lordship's letter to myself of the 2nd instant. I have sent them a copy of it, and (in answer to their own) have let them know, that (as to their sparing four or five hundred horse after Charlemont reduced) I conceive they may make that offer absolute (without expecting for it to be excused from the service into*

Connaught) because when they shall be otherwise free to prosecute the business of Connaught, I shall take order for the addition of so many horse from the army (to meet and join with them about Athlone, or where they shall appoint for that service) as they shall spare into Scotland: and (for the business contained in your Lordship's letter of the 2nd instant) conceiving the second part of your Lordship's offer (viz. that concerning Ayre and Arran and the parts between Longs Ryan and the River Clyde) to be more advisable and hopeful for us to do anything from hence, then that proceeding concerning Kirkcudbright, I have desired them to be preparing their horses and all things in a readiness for that design, against such time as your Lordship shall send them those lately levied foote (of Col. Lidcote's regiment, Sir William Coles, &c. which I suppose were intended for such purpose) with shipping provisions and money competent for such an undertaking; and that in this or what other design they (at their nearer distance) shall find more sensible and hopeful to the ends proposed by your Lordship, they would do the utmost they can (as God shall direct and enable them) when by your Lordship as aforesaid, or otherwise, they shall be fitted and furnished for it; and in the meantime, that in the third kind (which your Lordship's letter to me propounds) they will do something presently, even the utmost they can, and that with the more show of great preparations and forces intended the better; so as nothing be spoken tending to any design upon the coast of Ayre and Arran and, accordingly, that when they shall send out any vessels with soldiers in them to alarm them in Scotland, they be directed to go either to those parts of the coast, more northerly, beyond the river Clyde or (where they can without evident loss) really to land men, to get prey, take prisoners, destroy and make spoil as much as they can, until they find opposition; and then (going off to other places) to do attempt the like there also til like opposition; that so they make the enemy conceive, either that we have a design of invading them thereabouts, or else that our design is no more but to annoy them and make spoil, which may occasion them to keep forces and guards against us upon those coasts, and so answer, in some sort, your Lordship I send (of diverting part of their forces, or increasing their charge) and yet (by their employing of those forces where we intend not a real invasion, or by their keeping of them then and scattered all along their coast, as being only to resist robbers) to leave us the more facility of landing, and fastening with a stronger force *(where we do intend it) when we are ready for it; and in general, to those ends of diverting their forces, increasing their charge, and real annoying of them, I have earnestly pressed that nothing may be omitted or delayed; and, to this effect, as I have written to them one letter, and sent it (with a copy of your Lordship's to me) by sea to Wexford, so I have since sent a duplicate of the same by the way of Dublin. Now for the enabling and furnishing of them for a real attempt to fasten on some such place as Ayre or Arran (which indeed seem the most hopeful and advantageous for your Lordship's purpose) I humbly offer, that your Lordship would hasten over to them those foot aforementioned (whom when they come, I have advised them to put into their garrisons, and draw out as many old foot for this other service) that you would send them provisions and money sufficient for such a number of foot (with the horse intended) for three or four months, and that you would appoint the same vessels that bring these over, to stay in your service, and attend the further orders of Sir Charles Coote, or Col. Venables; by which, with the help of such other vessels, as (I presume by what your Lordship formerly appointed by way of preparation, in that particular) they may have already in the parts of Ulster, they may (probably) be able to transport both the horse and foot, according to your Lordship's intention. As for frigates, or ships of the force, to guard and assist them herein, or in sending out vessels manned with foot, to alarm the enemy, there is at present upon that coast the Hinde frigate, but (I believe) quite out of victual by this time (if for want of it she be not gone already) the President frigate (so soon as she comes with our money for which, or for her own victual she is yet stayed at Bristol, for ought I can hear) shall be halted away to the north, or else the Peter frigate instead of her: As for those that were heretofore appointed for Waterford river; the Hector is (for the present) sent with our ordnance, ammunition, &c. and to convey our provisions into the river of Limerick; the TrueLove frigate is already gone (according to her orders) into the north part of the channel (where I suppose she is or may be ordered to serve them in this degree) and the Peter frigate (being gone to convey over Sir Robert King and Col. Herbert, and to hast away our money and get victual for herself) shall at her return, be sent thither also, or else the President frigate (one of which I conceive necessary to be kept on the coast of Munster, and to serve for conveying over to us further supplies) the Mary flyboat being (as I formerly acquainted your*

Lordship) *gone in for Deptford; now (my Lord) for our present posture and condition (as to your further service here) I can but let your Lordship know that (the opportunity of conveying over our money by the TrueLove frigate, when the wind served, being neglected by the treasurer's deputy at Bristol (as I formerly acquainted your Lordship) I cannot since then hear a word of the money, nor know when I shall; but we have ever since, in expectation of it, been kept hovering in these parts, and not advanced westward for any further service, having nothing to do hereabouts but to hunt Torys and endeavour to get preys from them toward the maintenance of our men, and to spoil and waste those parts of the country that afford them shelter and subsistenance, which is the work we are now upon; but it is such, as I think, an army was never upon before, and though it may toil out and roast an army, it cannot deserve it in such a season as this is; and therefore I must needs say again, that the prejudice and retardment of your service, by neglect of that opportunity and delay of sending over money, is greater than can be valued. Hereafter I trust we shall have more frequent intercourse between us and our friends in Ulster, I having for that purpose wrote to them, and taken further orders otherwise, for the settling of two packet boats, one at Carlingford, the other at Wexford, to pass weekly between those two places; from which, to and from the remoter parts of our quarters in the north and south respectively, the conveyance of our letters by land will be much more safe, and with smaller convoys than the sending altogether by land from north to south. I cannot omit to acquaint your Lordship (to the praise and glory of the grace of our God) that it hath pleased him, since our poor and weak addresses to him by prayer and fasting, to stay his heavy hand in diverse places, beyond any rational expectation, as first at Clonmell (to cease it wholly in a manner) at Youghal and (since it carne to be ours) at Waterford, to abate it to a very small proportion; and the like change we hear from Dublin, in one weeks space; and this in a season most apt for increase. Thus he is pleased with his mercy and pity to overrun our repentance, and much more our reformation, and to show himself more quick and ready to pardon, than we break of our fines, but I hope (of his own grace, and by his own power and working, above and against the evil of our hearts and natures) he will, upon our continued seeking of him for it, be pleased to evidence further, and crown his merciful acceptance thereof, in discovering to* us, and taking away or abating as we; as well the occasions of this judgement, as the plague itself.

> Your Lordship's most humble servant,
> From the camp near Bartinglas,
>
> H. Ireton
> on the confines of Wicklow, Carlagh
> Kildare, Aug 28, 1650.

This duplicate I send by way of Dublin and Chester, having sent the original hereof by way of Waterford and Milford.
To the right honourable
Lord President of the council of state.
Haste, Haste.

Figure 23. Sir Henry Ireton

From this reply it must have been apparent to Bradshawe that the plan couldn't be organized in time to relieve Cromwell's army. With nothing more to do, he wrote words of encouragement:

Whitehall 30 August 1650—For his Excellency Lord General Cromwell these. My Lord, By the hands of this trusty bearer, accept I pray you of this paper remembrance and salutation from him who both upon the public and his own private account is very much your debtor, and with other your poor friends here prays for and adores the manifestations of Gods gracious presence with you in all your weighty affairs; My Lord, I forbear particularizing things here; only this, God is gracious to us in discovery of many of our enemies designs (which thereby have proved abortive) and delivering their Counsels in good measure into our hands; and in watching over the common safety, there is much acknowledgement due to the indefatigable industry of M. General Harrison, your faithful servant and substitute in that work here. Your Lordship will shortly hear of some numbers of godly persons in a regimental form here in London whose example will be followed by others of like good mind in Norwich, Kent, and other places, who have sent for Commissions of us for that purpose, and our resolution is they shall not want Encouragement. My Lord, I will trespass no further upon your time. The Lord of Hosts be with you: the God of Jacob be your refuge. The humblest of your wellwillers, friends and servants Jo: Bradshawe.[5]

In the midst of all this turmoil John Bradshawe took time to write an intimate letter to his neice, Sarah Fallowes, on the ocassion of her betrothal;

For my Loving Neece . . . I hear so well of your young man (Millington Coulthurst) *who seeks to you as I know nothing that can put me out of conceit with him but his insisting upon a larger portion than can at present be provided for you; yet I suppose he and his friends may consider so well of the matter as that Reason may take place at last, if they value you and your Friends more than ready money as I think they will: / I have written to you mother"* (Bradshawe's sister Anne Bradshawe Fallowes) *"& will give order that what is Reasonable / shall be done on your behalf. / wait upon God duly and dayly in your prayers & trust in him who alone can bring things to pass for your good, and so will do If you rightly depend on him . . . for if good for you, this your desire shall be accomplished, or otherwise he will provide better for you. / To his Grace and goodness I commend you & rest Your assured Loving uncle Jo: Bradshawe.*[6]

In the end the Bradshaw's plan to land an army in western Scotland was unnecessary. Cromwell engineered an impetuous breakout from Dunbar and shattered the Scots army on September 3. It was reported that three thousand Scots were killed and ten thousand captured. Others were *driven like turkeys by the English soldiers,* according to Whitelocke. The following day, Cromwell wrote Bradshawe the details, explaining that *some of the honestest in the army among the Scots did profess before the fight that they did not believe this king in his declaration.* London was ecstatic.

Parliament resolved to strike a special Dunbar medal for both officers and common soldiers. The Scottish prisoners were brought to Durham

Cathedral for imprisonment, where for lack of warmth they tore down some of the ancient woodwork and burned it.

Cromwell wrote again on the twenty-fifth and described to Bradshawe details of his march to Edinburgh, driving the Scots before him. "*I thought*, he says, *I should have found in Scotland a conscientious people and a barren country about Edinburgh on the contrary it is fertile for corn as any part of England but the people are so given to the most impudent lying and frequent swearing as is incredible to be believed.*" Cromwell had captured the city of Edinburgh and was besieging Edinburgh Castle.

Figure 24. The Dunbar Medal

The threat of a Royalist revival in England concerned Bradshawe and the council. In the heart of Sussex, Prince Charles's younger brother and sister were confined at Penshurst with a generous annual allowance of £3,000 provided by Parliament. Princess Elizabeth was just fourteen years old; her brother Henry, Duke of Gloucester, was eleven. With the arrival of their brother in Scotland, Parliament feared Penshurst could become a Royalist magnet. At the time Cromwell was beseiged at Dunbar, Bradshawe wrote to Colonel Sydenham, governor of the Isle of Wight, August 27:

The parliament hath appointed the two children of the late King who are now at the Earl of Leicester's at Penshurst shall be sent out of the limits of the Commonwealth; and have referred the same to this Council to see done accordingly; and until that can be done, we have thought it fit and necessary they be sent to Carrisbrooke castle; and have sent you this notice hereof before, that you might be ready for them. And for that we are informed, there are designs of mischief carrying-on in several places, we recommend that island to your especial care. And if there be any persons therein whom you shall judge may bring danger thereunto you are hereby desired and authorized to put them out of the isle and to seize upon and secure the horses arms and ammunition of any whom you shall suspect will make ill use of them to interrupt the public peace.

The young pair were removed to Carisbrook where Princess Elizabeth died the following year.

Edinburgh Castle fell to Cromwell in December. King Charles II was crowned at Scone Palace on January 1, 1651. The defeat of the Scot army at Dunbar had taken Charles out from under the thumb of the more strict Scottish Presbyterians. He laid plans to gather his continental friends and recover his English throne. Once his followers had affected a landing on the Kent coast and his army marched into Lancashire, he was sure the English would flock to his banner. Charles began to think of moving toward Lancashire where he envisioned a Royalist powerbase.

But Charles's plans were betrayed. Bradshawe's Council of State was working smoothly; and its intelligence network, headed by Bradshawe's chief spy Thomas Scott and his assistant, Capt. George Bishop, was the scourge of the Royalists. Bradshawe was the first to see their reports. He had been given the power to open any packets addressed to the council that arrived at night and summon the council if he saw fit. Sir Edward Nicholas wrote a warning to Sir Edward Hyde in May:

The King's business and friends in England are totally revealed by the many discoveries lately made there by the intercepting of Berkhead but especially by what Mr. Thomas Cooke hath (it is said) voluntarily discovered. He being a perfect and prudent Presbyterian, was (it seems) held fittest to be intrusted with the secrets of all his majesty's designs and friends in England, which he hath so fully and clearly made known to his old friend Bradshawe as it is said there are not less than 2000 noblemen and gentlemen of quality imprisoned and under restraint there at present.

So effective was the espionage conducted by Scott and Bishop that Bradshawe even heard rumors that Cromwell was becoming displeased with him. Thomas Scott was at Cromwell's headquarters in Scotland. From Whitehall, Bishop wrote to Scott on Christmas eve:

I have, in three or four letters since your departure, endeavoured to give you an account of some proceedings here, though happily you have more from nearer hands. The last told you the state of the present designs of your enemies; these two letters enclosed will give you a further account, when you have perused, you will find the enemy what and how they are . . . . The last night Mrs. Hamlim[7] *is gone for Holland, for the old crew of the designers in Hartfordshire, London, Kent &c. and from thence she is to go to Scotland for their commissions, which they only want. I have ordered her to come by land (if possible) and wait upon my Lord and you with what account she can learn from the enemy. Newcastle's man was with her: She is gone to the Earl of Newcastle; She shall have their names there. I have a copy of their letter and the figure. They write that all things are ready (except their Commissions.) It seems Dover is designed, and upon that surprise 4000 Dutch and English are to land in Kent, under command (as we think) of Newcastle (for we have a letter under his hand to the King wherein he begs it) and Lieutenant General Carpe, then the country is to rise. The High Court of Justice have condemned and executed, on Monday last, six of the rebels, the rest as soon as they can try them. One of the chief is very ingenious and begs his life upon discovery.*

This last was apparently the Thomas Cooke who would be mentioned in Edward Nichols letter to Hyde.

In contrast to Bradshawe's successes in London, Cromwell's reputation was waning, albeit ever so slightly. Since the enthusiastic reception of his Dunbar victory, the news from Edinburgh was worrying. Cromwell blamed Parliament's failure to supply money and supplies. There were several interesting letters to Cromwell immediately after Christmas. Elizabeth Cromwell wrote her husband a bit of advice:

think to write sometimes to your dear friend the Lord Chief Justice . . . if you would think of what I put you in mind . . . it might be to as much purpose as to others, writing sometimes a letter to the President, and sometimes to the Speaker. Indeed, my dear, you cannot think (of) *the wrong you do yourself in the want of a letter, though it were but seldom.*

Sir Henry Vane wrote:

I perceive that you can see light at the little crevice, since you can know the meaning of men whilst it is unciphered. They were the only reports amongst us here, which I make account you will laugh at sufficiently when you read them, but your good success will set it right again, and cause your temporising friends to hold fair with you; and your real friends will participate with you in all your changes, whatever the thoughts and jealousies of men be.

Bradshawe wrote to an unidentified person near to Cromwell, most probably Thomas Scott, December 24:

The little time allotted to me for particular transmission to any . . . whose letter of the 16th was glady received. Here the news being good and acceptable, (as regarded the Scottish campaign), *We are busy here with preparing reception for the Embassadors; one from Portugal . . . and Don Alonzo . . . the returning of Mr. Strickland as resident into Holland, is at present forborn.*

Bradshawe confided: "*The new High Court of Justice sitting at Norwich, began upon Friday; tried and condemned six upon Saturday, who were executed in the market-place yesterday; and are proceeding vigourously to the trial of the rest that had a hand in that mistimed insurrection of Norfolk. the terror of the example may happily do good and help prevent numerous mischiefs still plotting . . . Capt. Bishop intends to give you some account thereof.*" He then spoke of what he expected to hear from the Portuguese and Spanish ambassadors, concluding, "*Very hot many are for ownings and applications from Foreign States . . . God grant . . . that we may be independent enough . . . and that we only do all persons and nations justice, and casually provoke none; which would be the best way for subsistenance and establishment, and teach other nations . . . to value us aright, and to do as they would be done to. I fear our impotent haste to ingratiate with neighbouring nations hath done us neither honour or profit, and it seems to me by the murder and disgrace of our Ministers sent abroad, that God thought fit to give our forwardness that way a check, and teach us where our strength was, and our applications should be. But in these things I have many dissenting brethern, and I write to one much abler to judge, and therefore forbear.*"

He then confessed his own suspicion that he would be forced from the presidency of the council:

Our second year is drawing on apace to a conclusion: God give us a good exit, and much good may it do them that covet to be our successors; modo sal va sit republica. Some of us shall entertain our dismissions with much contendness. Much talk there is of things and persons, relating to the succeeding choice, wherein I may not be particular. Hugh Peter hath arbitrated between me and Lord ? General? Hammond making me pay soundly for my coming into Hanworth at annunciation next . . . if I live so long I hope . . . to attain to some fresh air to recover health somewhat impaired, and prevent more waste and spoils . . . present my humblest service to my Lord General, and my respects to our other good friends . . .

The reference to Hanworth may relate to the purchase of a house that Bradshawe later—it was said—owned at nearby Walton-on-Thames or Feltham.[8]

A month before the first meeting of the third council, Captain Bishop plucked up his courage and wrote directly to Cromwell in support of Bradshawe:

It is very much whispered that there shall be another president and some forbeare not to say that your lordship does not favour him that is now in that place. pardon me my lord if I presume to acquaint you with what is muttered by some; what representations may be made, I know not (I trust the Lord doth give you wisdom to discern such things) but this I presume I may say safely, that he hath a plaine and upright heart full of courage and nobleness for justice and the commonwealth, and is so elaborate that whosoever succeeds him, the commonwealth will find a great miss of him.

Since the middle of the year, the inland post had been handled by Edward Prideaux, the postmaster as well as attorney general. Identifying the handwriting and seals of suspected correspondents and opening their letters was a tactic employed by both Royalist and Commonwealth spys. The council had ordered Sergeant-at-arms Denby to guard their own letters, but they were obviously suspicious of interceptions. Within the year there would be an enquiry into the opening of packets between England and Scotland sent on the business of Capt. George Bishop.

The third Council of State met on February 19, 1651, when Bradshawe was for the third time elected lord president. This council was to cease at the end of the year. Just eight days before the first meeting, Bradshawe wrote to Col. Richard Deane and the committee for Trinity House asking them to hire fifty captains and two hundred fifty seamen for the fifty boats prepared by order of the committee for transportation of soldiers to Scotland. Captains were to be paid thirty shillings a month, mariners twenty-one shillings. Trinity House replied that very few could be found at those low wages. Bradshawe authorized an increase of ten shillings for the captains and a shilling or two more for the mariners.[9]

It is apparent that several conciliatory letters, unfound today, were exchanged between Bradshawe in London and Cromwell in Scotland as evidenced by this one written the day before the opening of the third council:

For his Excellency the Lord General Cromwell, These . . . My Lord I return you my humble and hearty thanks for your late noble and friendly letter, whereby I have the comfort and assurance of your lordship's fair interpretation of my past and (so I dare call them) well meant actions, which I shall not deny to account for or justify to any man living so soon as to yourself; of whom I shall ever have that esteem as becomes me to have of one who daily approves himself religion's and his country's best friend and who may justly challenge a tribute of observance from all that sincerely wish them well, in which number I shall hope ever to be found.

My lord I have ('tis true) taken the boldness to write some few letters to you since your late departure hence and I have the satisfaction enough that they were received and are not displeasing to you. Your application to the Gentlemen, named in youri, who is of so known fitness and ability to procure your effectual returns was an act in my apprehension endeavouring of your usual prudence and tending to the advantage of the public affairs committed to your trust and care; neither can any wise man justify any charge of summing neglect of others in that respect. I am sorry your lordship hath been put to any expense of your so precious time, for removing any such doubts; but there my ever careful friends, who have created your Lordship this trouble, have I must confess occasionally contributed to my desired contentment, which is and ever hath been, since I had the honour to be known unto you, to understand myself to be retained and preserved in your good opinion. And if my faithful endeavours for the public and respects unto your lordship in everything wherein I may serve you may deserve a countenance thereof I may not doubt still to find that happiness and this is all the trouble I shall give your lordship as to that matter.

We are now beginning with a new councell another year. I might have hoped either for love or something else, to have been spared from the charge but I could not obtain that favour; and I dare not but submit, when it is clear to me that God gives the call. He also will, I hope, give this poore creature some power to act according to his mind and to serve him in all uprightness and sincerity in the way wherein He hath placed me to walk.

My Lord I have no more, but to recommend you and all your great affairs to the guidance mercy and goodness of our Good God and to subscribe myself in all truth and affection.

Your lordships ever to be disposed of Jo: Bradshawe

Whitehall 18 Feb 1650 (1651 new style)

The Customer who wronged Sir James Lidd is ordered to restore and satisfy and come up to answer his charge which probably will fall heavy upon him.

Ten days before Bradshawe's letter was written, Cromwell fell dangerously ill. Ever audacious, he had attacked Charles's headquarters at Stirling Castle in the midst of a raging blizzard. His army was driven back, and he caught a persistent fever that hung about him into the summer. The men of London were alarmed at the reports of Cromwell's illness.

Bradshawe was amongst them and wrote his concerns. Cromwell humbly replied:

To The Right Honourable the Lord President of the Council of State; These, Edinburgh 24th March 1650 (1651 new style)

My Lord I do, with humble thankfulness acknowledge your tender respect for me expressed in your letter and therewith to inquire after one so unworthy as myself.

Indeed, my Lord your service needs not me: I am a poor creature: and I have been a dry bone; I am still an unprofitable servant to my master and you. I thought I should have died of this fit of sickness; but the Lord seemeth to dispose otherwise. But truly my Lord I desire not to live, unless I may obtain mercy from the Lord to approve my heart and life to him in more faithfullnes and thankfulness and to those I serve in more prof i tableness and diligence. And I pray God your Lordship and all in public trust may improve all those unparalled experience of the Lord's wonderful workings in your sight with singleness of heart to his glory and the refreshment of His People; who are the apple of His eye; and upon whom high favour the express and sent your enemies; both former and latter who have fallen before you did split themselves

This shall be the unfeigned prayer of My Lord your most obedient servant Oliver Cromwell.

Sir Henry Hyde, a cousin of Sir Edward Hyde (later Lord Clarendon), was beheaded March 4, 1651. He had assumed the quality of an ambassador from the king to the Grand Seignor with a design to seize the English estates there and affront Sir Thomas Bendish, the old resident. Hyde asked that his trial be conducted in the Italian language, having been long out of England. This was taken as an example of his vanity and pride. No doubt this execution added to Clarendon's eternal hatred of Bradshawe.

A sizeable responsibility of the Council of State was the approval of warrants for money. On April 29, Bradshawe sent order to Sir Thomas Wollaston and the Treasurers of War:

> *These are to will and require you out of such Moneys as now are; or next shall be to be sent to the Lord Deputy Ireton for the pay of the forces in Munster to transmit to Mr. Charles Walley at Chester, or elsewhere upon Bills of Exchange from him so much Money as shall beby him taken up for six hundred and forty barrels of wheat and three hundred weight of Cheese, to be provided by the said Mr. Walley and Captain Edward Pierce for the use of the forces in Ireland; the sums not exceeding four thousand six hundred Pounds; Of which you are not to fail; and for which this shall be your warrant. Given at the Council of State, at Whitehall the 25 Martii 1651.*
>   *Signed in the name and by the Order of the Council of state,*
>   *Appointed by the Authority of Parliament.*
>   *John Bradshawe, Lord President* [10]

Other eyes were watching the money for Ireland. The Middlesex court session of July 26 heard testimony against John Rose and John Page for endeavoring to rob the state's wagons on the highway being laden with money for the use of the army that is in Ireland.

Cromwell's relapses in illness were now so serious that Parliament, through Bradshawe and the council, requested Cromwell to return to the milder climate of England. Bradshawe dispatched two London doctors, Dr. George Bate and Dr. Laurence Wright, to attend him home.

I have received yours of the 27th of May, Cromwell writes, *with an Order from the Parliament for my liberty to return unto England for change of air that thereby I might the better recover my health. All which came unto me whilst Dr. Wright and Dr. Bates whom your Lordship sent down were with me.*

Within three weeks Cromwell was in the field again, but Needham's *Mercurius Politicus* observed in June, "The beauty of the summer is passing away very fast and yet we are not upon any action." Two more letters to Bradshawe dated in July contained news of Cromwell's actions. Part of his army, under command of Lambert, was dispatched by sea into county Fife, behind the king's headquarters.

James Wainwright wrote Richard Bradshaw at Hamburg with the news that Sterling was taken. He also informed him that Lord President Bradshawe had ordered a ship to bring him home from Hamburg.

By August, Cromwell's army was as far advanced as Perth. Charles had little hope of recruiting any more Scots. He aimed for the only way still open, southward toward England. Bradshawe wrote to the governor of the Mount and Dennis Fort in Cornwall:

"By Letters this day received from Scotland, we have notice that while our Army is in Fife (where it is in good condition) the Scots Army is Marched Southward with intention for England and we doubt not but this March of theirs will tend much to the shortening of the work. That there is a party on this side them will be able to give impediment to their March, and if need be to fight them, and that the Lord General will send a sufficient force seasonably upon their Rear, yet for that we conceive their party here will not fail to do their utmost in this conjuncture; to execute any designs they may have laid against any Garrison in this Commonwealth, the better to countenance and give advantage to their cause . . . we therefore commend it to your care to have a more especial watchful eye . . . that you may discourage and prevent any attempts on the execution of any designs the Enemies have upon it." [11]

Lambert's cavalry harried Charles's flanks, and Cromwell persistently trailed him at a discreet distance. It seems Cromwell had not anticipated Charles's entrance into England, and he said as much in a letter to Speaker Lenthall. Charles had been foolishly assured, and inaccurately as it turned out, that the Presbyterian ministers of Lancashire would join the Royalist cause.

The alarm in London was great. Lucy Hutchinson says, "city and country were all amazed, doubtful of their own and the Commonwealth's safety." Even Bradshawe, stouthearted as he was, feared for his neck.

The old matter of Dr. John Barwick, still confined in the Tower of London, resurfaced. John Otway of Grey's Inn despaired of Barwick's life and took upon himself the task of preparing a decent burial for his old friend. He coopted some other gentlemen of Grey's Inn to go directly to Bradshawe, still a bencher at the inn. These gentlemen realized Bradshawe was their most powerful member. Bradshawe, according to later narration,[12] broke "into a violent passion against Mr. Barwick . . . not only as a traitor to his Country, but as one that was guilty of the highest Contumacy, and had most ungratefully refused the Favours offered him by the Commonwealth, against which he had committed such heinous Crimes, and which might have long since most justly taken away his Life, as a capital Enemy to the Government; adding, that he wondered what evil Genius had induced so many Gentlemen of that Inn, his dear Collegues of whom he had conceived better Hopes, to desire any Acquaintance with so great an Enemy and Pest of the Commonwealth". Bradshawe warned them to be very cautious with whom they cultivated friendship and avoid all contact with Barwick. In the end Bradshawe gave leave for them to choose one from their group to visit Barwick and carry him what friendly message or other relief as they thought fit. Bradshawe signed a warrant to permit Mr. Otway to the prison cell of Barwick. Barwick would remain confined for another year.

There was a further danger of Royalist Irish coming across the sea to join the king at the seaport of Bristol. Throughout Cromwell's illness Bradshawe had put the western militia in readiness to block any of Charles's supporters. In April the council ordered that Bradshawe notify the commissioners of the militia to raise ten thousand men for regiments in Ireland. An act of Parliament, July 1, ordered the sheriff of Cheshire and certain others to hold enquires weekly, if not more often, respecting strangers resorting to the county, conspiracies, secret meetings, and correspondence with Charles Stuart. In July, Bradshawe ordered the mayor of Gloucester to intercept the post and call a public meeting to apprise himself of conspiracy threats.

A passport was issued by John Bradshawe to Henry Eccleston of Eccleston, esq., and his two servants:

> *These are to will and require you to permit and suffer the bearers hereof Henry Eccleston of Eccleston, Esq., with John Clayton and Thomas Lee his servants to transport themselves and necessaryes beyond the Seas they carrying nothing with them prejudiciall to the State. Of wch you are not to faile and for wch this shall be your warrant. Given at the Councell of State at Whitehall this 22th of July 1651.*
>
> *Signed in ye Name & by Order of ye Councell of State Appointed by Authority of Par.*
> *Jo: Bradshawe, Prsd^{t}.*

To all Customers Comptroullers and Searchers
And all other officers
of the Ports and Customs.[13]

Henry Eccleston, eldest son of Royalist Thomas Eccleston who was killed at Warrington 1646, was about fourteen years old in 1651. He was probably Roman Catholic.

Reverend Christopher Love, zealous Presbyterian chaplain of Col. Venn's Parliamentary regiment, had opposed the execution of King Charles I. In 1651, he joined a plot against the Commonwealth. A certain Colonel Titus was commissioned by Dr. Drax, Mr. Jenkins, and other Presbyterian ministers to carry letters to and from France. The replies were secretly read at Love's house. On October 18, 1650, a pass was obtained from Bradshawe, perhaps by design, for Love's wife, Mary Stone Love, to proceed to Amsterdam, doubtless in connection with the plot. Bradshawe's intelligencers exposed the plot. At the order of Lord President John Bradshawe, Rev. Love was arrested on May 14, 1651, on charges of corresponding with Prince Charles and the former Queen Henrietta-Maria. Love was tried before the High Court of Justice on July 20, 21, 25, and 27 and condemned to death by beheading on Tower Hill. Love made a last plea for mercy to Parliament in which he acknowledged nearly all the accusations. His sentence was carried out on August 22. On that day, Wainwright wrote to Richard Bradshaw:

This was a sad day . . . Mr Love's head was cut off upon Tower Hill.

The historians Echard and Kennett both mention the story of a reprieve from Cromwell, supposedly intercepted and destroyed by Royalists. This seems unlikely, however, since any supposed reprieve would have come from Bradshawe, not from Cromwell who was otherwise occupied. Three days after Love's execution, Lord President Bradshawe wrote to the Lord mayor of London,

There is an intention to make a solemn funeral for Christopher Love, lately executed for High Treason; James Winstanley, his brother-in-law, is a principal person in it; he is to be carried from Merchant Tailor's hall, one of the most public places in the city. We do not judge it fit that he who was such a notorious traitor while he lived and died such an ignominious death for the same should have a solemn burial.

The mayor was commanded to keep the Merchant Tailor's Hall closed and send for Winstanley. Love's body was privately buried. Shortly after Love's death his widow married Edward Bradshaw of Chester, the brother of Richard Bradshaw the Commonmwealth Resident in Hamburg.[14]

Rumors still circulated in London. James Afflack was called before the court to answer for dispersing of false news saying that Major General Massey "did with a party of horse, take at Edinburgh six-and-twenty of the Parliament's Commissioners, and said that none of the news was to be seen in the books."

On August 10, the Council of State stayed all ships bound for Virginia.

Bradshawe wrote to the mayor of Gloucester restating the prohibition against correspondence with Charles Stuart. On the fifteenth he wrote the commissioners in the Isle of Wight:

We formerly gave you directions for drawing forth some Horse out of the Militia Horse of your County in pursuant of an Order of Parliament of Eight of April last, for raising of three thousand Horse and one thousand Dragoons . . . we having at present an occasion for making use of Train Horses sooner than they can be conveniently had from the several Cities and Counties where any of them remain any of them yet undisposed of have taken care for the speedy buying of them here . . . we therefore desire you to raise for each of fifteen Horse and Arms that are remaining in your Island, the sum of Nine Pounds of such person or persons as were to have found them and pay it unto the Receiver-General of Assessments or your County to be by him paid over to such as this Council shall appoint.

As the threat to the north of England became ever more dangerous, Bradshawe and George Bishop took on additional burdens. Bishop was agent for intelligence communicating directly with the Committee for Examinations, and Bradshawe held the "power of the Committee of Examinations in himself, at such time as other members of the Council shall be at Parliament." The council had power to imprison or take bonds from anyone who refused obedience to them. This power had been handed to Bradshawe as indicated by an order issued August 13:

"The Lord President to send for Col. Fortescue, and examine him concerning the reports which he has made in the North of the greatness of the Scot's Army and give order for his close restraint: also to send for Mr. Dixon, the surgeon, and Mr. Inglish, the merchant, both Scotchmen, examine them, and if he see cause, committ them."

Col. John Okey wrote to Lord President Bradshawe from Sterling Castle on the nineteenth, reporting the capture of Sterling town and the pacification of the country so that: *we may now march with 100 horse from this place allover the West and South.* He continued *The Lord hath done great things for us in these parts, whereof we have great cause to be glad, and we are confident also he is doing great things for you in England.*

Wainwright wrote to Richard Bradshaw: *The enemy is got into the heart of England almost . . . The General (Cromwell) is not yet corne up; we are making a force out hence to meet him; I cannot tell what else to write, but it was a foul temptation for our General to let them corne in.*

Whitelocke said that no affair could have been managed with more diligence, courage, and prudence, and that peradventure there was never so great a body of men so well armed and provided that got together in so short a time as were those sent to reinforce Cromwell.

Harrison took charge of the reinforcements and traveled northward. By August, Charles's army had crossed the English border, pausing briefly at Carlisle. At Shrewsbury, Charles turned from the London road and headed to Worcester where he awaited the Earl of Derby who was coming from the Isle of Man with three hundred gentlemen. Bradshawe, Scott, and Bishop had prevented the risings in Kent and Norfolk. Satisfied that some Lancashire Catholics posed no further threat, the council released Sir Roger Bradshaigh from Chester Castle on his own recognicence. Having failed to enlist strength in Lancashire, it now appeared that Charles was making for Gloucester city. Bradshawe has anticipated that. The trap was set.

On the sea, Parliament's ships were seizing prizes. The newspaper *Mercurius Scoticus*, August 20, reported that Capt. Peter Escot's ship, the *Convet Frigate*, had brought two prizes into Leith harbour: a Dutch Pinke of 120 tons and another of 160 tons. In addition, after a three-hour fight, they had sunk another loaded with wine and ammunition. Only ten hogsheads of wine were saved. In the encounter the captain was wounded, one Manley was slain, who with Mr. Wells the surgeon and *Lieutenant Bradshaw* behaved themselves stoutly, the enemy being about five hundred highlanders with muskets, bows and arrows. Lieutenant Bradshaw is not further identified.

On the twenty-third, Cromwell asked the council to send vast quantities of ammunition to Gloucester city. On the twenty-fifth Bradshawe sent the mayor of Gloucester ten acts of Parliament and proclamations concerning Charles Stuart.

The very same day, Col. Robert Lilburne's dragoons and foot soldiers caught Lord Derby's force in Wigan Lane and cut them to pieces. Before the battle, Derby had learned the Presbyterians and their ministers were refusing to cooperate in the Royalist uprising. With a degree of fatalism, he castigated them:

If I perish I perish; but if my Master perish, the Blood of another Prince, & all ensuing Miseries of this Nation, will lie at your Doors.

He commanded only six hundred horses against Lilburne's dragoons and three thousand foot, but he sustained the bruising battle for two hours. Seven shots hit his breastplate; he received five or six sword cuts on his arms and thirteen cuts in the beaver hat which covered his steel cap. Two horses were killed under him but still he escaped and fled to join the king in Worcester. From Haigh Hall above Wigan Lane, Roger Bradshaigh and a few of his servants descended to the silent battlefield. Among the dead he found Lord Withington, Colonel Bointon, Colonel Trollop, Colonel Gerald, Major Anderton, and his kinsman Sir Thomas Tyldesly, Derby's second in command. Sir William Throgmorten was found among the wounded and carried back to Haigh Hall where he eventually recovered.

John Bradshawe signed a warrant of the council appointing Charles Austin master gunner of the *Mermaid* frigate, Whitehall, August 29.[15]

From his camp near Wrexham, August 31, Charles promised royal pardons to all who would join him now, with the exception of Cooke, Cromwell, and Bradshawe. Four prominent Cheshire men who apparently were thinking of abandoning their Parliamentarian views were specifically pardoned: John Crewe of Crewe, Edward Hyde of Norbury, Henry Brooke of Norton, and Thomas Marbury of Marbury. Thomas Marbury of Marbury was a half brother of Bradshawe's wife! The others had ties by marriage or close friendship to the Marburys and the Bradshawes of Marple. John Bradshaw of Bradshaw near Bolton, though a strong Presbyterian, refused to join Charles. The Parliamentarian army of more than twenty-eight thousand men converged on Worcester.

Charles had less than that number, and he was pinned inside the city. Cromwell's old soldiers were weary, and the new recruits sent from the south were untested. The mayor and aldermen of the city of Gloucester sent Cromwell forty barrels of strong "beere," praying favorable acceptance thereof as a sign of the "good affection of this corporation." On the morning of September 3, Cromwell went into a nearby wood and made a pact with the devil, so said Colonel Lindsay, one of Cromwell's men who supposedly witnessed the event. Royalists later made much propaganda out of Colonel Lindsay's story.

London awaited news with bated breath. Major General Philip Skippon had mustered the London regiments against a possible breakout of the royal forces from Worcester. Hermann Mylius, a newly arrived diplomat, wrote in his diary: *The Parliamentarians now handle no matters of state unless public. They are all busy with arms, camps, musters, defense works, taxes, collections, supplying reserves, fortifying ports and garrisoning fortifications, nearby, overseas and abroad, while their own civil and domestic affairs in these boiling whirlwinds are not at all attended to, one and all postponed.*

Cromwell's forces fell on Worcester like the hammer of God. The Royalists were crushed. Col. Henry Bradshawe, John Bradshawe's elder brother commanding Parliament's Macclesfield militia, was wounded in battle. King Charles II escaped, and after hiding in the Boscobel Oak and then wandering about the English countryside for ten weeks, ultimately reached Paris. Wainwright wrote to Richard Bradshaw that Buckingham, Poyntz, and Captain Hinde, the great robber and Charles's scout master general, had escaped. Hinde would later attempt highway robbery on Cromwell and Lord President Bradshawe.

The city of Gloucester elected Cromwell their high steward. Colonel Lambert laid waste to Royalist's estates around Worcester. Chirk Castle, the home of Sir Thomas Middleton, was bombarded and nearly destroyed. Cromwell returned to a hero's welcome in London on the twelfth. His baton was hung up in Westminster Hall. He never took the field of battle again.

Seven thousand Scottish and Royalist prisoners of war were paraded through London. Mylius noted in his diary that among the captives were two regiments of Spaniards and some companies of Venetians. The Tower of London was full of captured earls and generals, and some common soldiers were soon shipped off to work in the West Indies canefields.

The contest for supreme authority in the Commonwealth now began in earnest. Mylius notes that the holding of new Parliamentary elections: *is not merely a question of constitutionality and legitimacy. That is the field of maneuver which will decide whether power will be in the hands of one group of contenders or another group of contenders . . . Cromwell understands what is at stake, Vane understands, Scot and Haselrig understand . . . (Cromwell) alone holds the direction of political and military affairs in his hands. His ONE equivalent to all, and, in effect, King.*[16]

Cromwell attended the Council of State eight times in September, sixteen times in October, and eleven times in November. James Wainwright wrote to his master, Richard Bradshaw:[17]

Great matters have been moved in Parliament but all differed . . . This quarter will tell how you shall be governed, and what great man we shall have either as King or Protector; we must have some such thing; I do not see how it will be avoided; tho' modesty and other circumstances may keep us from it.

James Stanley, Earl of Derby, was captured near Nantwich in Cheshire some days after the battle. Although he believed he was entitled to the immunities of a prisoner of war, he was imprisoned in Chester Castle. A court martial was convened to try him on the charge of treason. Col. Henry Bradshawe was sufficiently recovered to sit as a member of the court. Derby was condemned and sentenced to beheading at Bolton on October 15. Several appeals were lodged on Derby's behalf but all failed. Rumors circulated that John Bradshawe actually issued a pardon, but it was intercepted on the way to Lancashire. Other rumors held that Derby's execution was due to the inveterate malice of John Bradshawe originating—it was said—because Derby had refused to name Bradshawe vice chamberlain of Chester in 1638. Once again the confusion of the various Bradshaws named John fueled this rumor. The John Bradshaw who was refused the office is identified as the "Attorney General of Chester," an office that Lord President John Bradshawe never held; another John Bradshaw did.

At the end of October, John Bradshawe signed a warrant instructing Mr. Edward Annesley, storekeeper of the armory at the tower, to deliver to Lord General Cromwell a fair suit of arms to be removed from the armory at Greenwich and presented as a gift from the Council of State.[18]

With the northern counties cleared of the Royalist threat, the civil courts resumed sitting. The act of May 10, 1650, made adultery a capital crime without benefit of clergy; several executions took place. At Chester assizes held on Nov 7, 1651, a man was sentenced to death by Chief Justice John Bradshawe for misconduct with a married woman.[19]

Just three days before, Bradshawe had been in London attending to matters of state as evidenced by this order addressed to the commissioners of the navy:

These are to authorize and require you to cause the Shipps and Vessels appointed for the winter guard, A list whereof is hereunto annexed, to be rigged, victualled, and fitted forth to sea with all necessarys wi thin your off ice from time to time as shall be occasioned. And for so doing this shall be your warrant given at the Council of State at Whitehall, on the 4th day of November 1651. Signed in the name and by order of the Council of State appointed by the authority of Parliament. John Bradshawe, Ld President[20]

When the fourth Council of State was appointed, Parliament voted that perhaps at Cromwell's instigation the permanent presidency enjoyed by Bradshawe should cease. Accordingly, chairmen were to be chosen to preside for periods of four weeks or less. On the last day of November, James Wainwright wrote to Richard Bradshaw, who was then in Chester:

Your hint of a head makes me a little fearful, excuse it I do write in the dark . . . I perceive there is something in the Parliament's last vote either against men's honour or profit, that none should continue chairman of any Committee of Parliament above one month, and it shall extend to the President of the Council. (Therein I am confident they are deceived, for there is neither profit nor honour, as the parties suggest that were the cause, but a favour and a great ease: I need not tell you it will be his profit).

Nevertheless, Bradshawe was the first elected on December 1, followed by Bulstrode Whitelocke on the twenty-ninth and Sir Arthur Haselrig on January 26.

On December 12, Bradshaw wrote to Colonel Duckenfield, who had subdued the Isle of Man:

Sir—Wee have received your letter of the third of December wth the papers enclosed on the goods in the Isle of Man like to be prize, as we have done other letters from you since the takeinge of that of that place. All wch letters are referred to consideration, and though you have yet had no returnes yet it hath been under consultation to settle such establishment and prepare all things necessary for that place, of w you will speedily have the particulars, this being only to lett you know that your service in reducing that Island is acceptable to the Councell, and for wch wee returne our hearty thanks. You shall wth what expedition we can, receive more full directions touching the matters offered to consideration in yor Letters.[21]

Notes to Chapter Twelve

1. Two days after the King's Birthday, a Charter was issued for the establishment of Harvard College in Cambridge, Middlesex, Colony of Massachusetts Bay, "for the education of English and Indian youth." Signed by Thomas Dudley, Governor.
2. *Landsdowne Mss,* 115, 98, British Library.
(3) Roger Bradshaigh of Haigh,
4. James Wainwright, steward to Richard Bradshaw, the Commonwealth Resident in Hamburg, wrote to his master on 28th March, "we have many of your acquaintance in Lanc., Chester, Salop, and Wales, of the gentry secured under suspicion of holding correspondence with the Scots, and some receiving commissions fro-that Scots King: I believe many are clear; Mr. Wm Ashurst, Shuttleworth, Holland, Egerton, Hoult, Bradshaw, Booth, Standish, Lo: Milnes, Chumley, Kilmurye, Hen. Leigh, Lo: Harbart, Sir Thomas Middleton and son, and many more in these counties and in North Wales." Wainwright was wrong about Middleton.
5. Henry Ellis, *Original Letters & c.,* 2nd ser 4 vols, (1827).
6. Original letter, dated from Westminster 29 August 1650, sold recently by Maggs Brothers of London. Sarah did marry Millington Coulthurst, but not until 5th October 1653. Sarah's sister married Ralph Furnivall in 1650 and was "bewitched to death" in 1654. Sarah's sister Hannah married Thomas Acton a lawyer of Chester who was preferred by Lord Bradshawe, and Sarah's brother Lt. Col. William Fallowes (1625-1677) married Alice (Alicia) daughter of Hugh Hollinshead. Lt. Col. William Fallowes served in Col. Henry Bradshawe's regiment at Worcester. After his death his widow married John Bradshawe of the Inner Temple, London, in 1678. John Bradshawe (d; 1706) of the Inner Temple was the son of Col. Henry Bradshawe.
7. Perhaps an alias of one of Bishop's spies.
8. John Bradshawe wrote to the parishioners of Feltham, Middlesex, 4th November 1650; "Neighbour and Friends. the Parliament of England having been pleased to confer an Interest upon me amongst other things of the Tithes of your parish and my desire being that you that you of that place should fare you better for it in what concerns you touching spirituals I have thought fit hereby to signify unto you my purpose of providing you every Lord's day and other fitting time an able and faithful minister to dispense unto you the mysteries of the Gospel you being as I hear very much in want of such a person. My purpose also is through

God's acceptance to settle a competent maintenance for such a minister for all time to come to come out of what is the eight of you of the parish to pay without putting you to any other charge. In the mean time my Request to you is that you would bless God for these opportunities and means of grace and make the best use of them for God's glory and your own Souls good which that you may do Is my hearty prayer and desire and so far as shall be in my power shall be my sincere Endeavour who through God's providence am related to your neighborhood and shall be ready and willing to assist and further you in any way." *Trans of Hist Soc of Lancs and Ches*, vol II, NS 41, *Bradshaw Papers in the Possession of Rowson Lingard*, ed. by Craig Gibson.

9. *Appendix to the 8th Report of the Historical Mss Commission*, page 247. From a large collection of letters in what was formerly the Sunderland Library in the Batchelor's Gallery at Blenheim Palace.
10. Private collection of Mr. Christopher Godber, Northamptonshire, 2001
11. Original letter, dated 9 August 1651, sold to private collector by Maggs Brothers of London in 1935. Recently resold by Maggs Brothers.
12. Peter Barwick, *The Life of the Reverend John Barwick, D.O.*, (London 1744).
13. *Report of the Lancs Rec Office for 1960*, Scarisbrick Muniments.
14. John Milton had written to the Burghers of Hamburg, at the time of Richard Bradshaw's appointment; "More than once we have written concerning the Contrversies of the Merchants, and some other things which more nearly concern the Dignity of our Republic, yet no answer has been returned. But understanding that Affairs of that nature can hardly be determined by Letters only, and that in the meantime certain seditious Persons have been sent to your city by *** (presumably "Charles" Stuart) authorized with no Commission than that of Malice and Audaciousness, who made it their business utterly to expatriate the ancient trade of our People in your City, especially those whose fidelity to their Country is most conspicuous; therefore we have commanded the worthy and most eminent Richard Bradshaw to reside as our Agent among you, to the end that he may be able more at large to treat and negotiate with your Lordships such matters and Affairs, as are interwoven with the Benefit and Advantages of both Republics. Him therefore we request you, with the soonest to admit to a favourable Audience: and that in all things that Credit may be given him, that Honour be paid him, as is usual in all Countries, and among all Nations paid to those that bear his Character . . . Westminster, April 2, 1650." *Works of Milton*, 1738, 2 vols.

15. *Stowe Mss. 427* f.3., British Library
16. Leo Miller, *John Milton and The Oldenburg Safeguard*, (New York, 1985).
17. Richard Bradshaw, Resident at Hamburg, had returned to England and was at the time of this letter (29 Sept, 1651) in Chester. Wainwright had written to Richard Bradshaw on 24th June "My Lord President tells me you are sent for . . . and if a ship is not gone yet (it) is with all expedition; and this was in answer to my pressing of him for answer to your letter."
18. *Rawlinson Manuscript*, Bod. Lib., f.85, 395.44 (19) F.A. Inderwick, K.C., *The Interregnum,*
20. *Add'l Mss 22,546*, fol 41, Brit Lib.
21. *Manx Society,* Vol IV, VII & IX.

CHAPTER THIRTEEN

Subduing the Colonies, Breaking Bradshawe

The disorders of the Mother Country were the safeguard of the infant liberties of New England
Gov. Winthrop of Massachusetts

✠

THROUGHOUT BRADSHAWE'S PERMANENT presidency, the Council of State exhibited a great interest in colonial matters. The Crown's monoply of the new world colonies had died with King Charles I, and a new structure of colonial administration was needed. In the years of civil war, the colonies had gone, out of necessity, from closely controlled enterprises to nearly self-governing powers. From 1649 and into early 1650, the Admiralty committee of the Council of State was particularly active in reporting matters directly affecting the Bermudas, Virginia, and Maryland. Commissioners had the power to appoint and remove all colonial governors and other officials and also general authority to do everything they might consider advantageous to the colonies.

The American colonies, with the exception of New England, sided with the Royalists and refused to acknowledge the jurisdiction of Parliament. In effect they recognized the authority of Charles II, but at the same time they realized he had no power to exercise it, particularly after his defeat at Worcester. Puritan New England demonstrated an inclination to accept Parliament but not their complete authority. Massachusetts went even further in asserting that their royal charter exempted them from acts of the English Parliament.

Parliament aimed their administrative control primarily at the West Indies. The proprietor there had been sequestered, and thus his properties came under control of Parliament. They appointed governors for St. Christopher, Nevis, Montserrat, and Antigua. In 1645, the Earl of Carlisle submitted to Parliament and recovered his proprietorship of Barbados, which he leased for twenty-one years to Lord Willoughby of Parham. At the same time he appointed Willoughby[1] as governor general. Barbados had become known as *Little England,* a rallying point for the Royalist cause largely due to the influence of Col. Humphrey Walrond and his brother Edward. Opposing the Walronds was Col. James Drax (or Drake?) and some supporters of Parliament. Willoughby was forced to accept the power of the Walronds who attempted to clear the supporters of Parliament from the island. Twenty of the leading inhabitants were labeled disturbers of the peace, arrested, and their properties were confiscated. Many of these wisely left Barbados before their trials, but some who remained were treated cruelly. Captain Tienman and Lieutenant Brandon were disenfranchised, their estates seized, their tongues cut, their checks branded with the letter *T,* and both were banished. In addition to the so-called disturbers of the peace, another one hundred Independents had left the island. They included plantation owners, merchants, and shipowners. One by one these deportees arrived in London and lodged their complaints before Bradshawe and the Committee of the Admiralty.

On June 29, 1650, the council issued an order that Lord President Bradshawe and Col. Phillip Jones were to speak with the Commissioners for Sequestration concerning "John Webb's business, whose tongue was bored through with a hot iron at Barbados, that something may be done for his relief and in compensation for his suffering."

London was not nearly so concerned for suffering. On Christmas Eve day, a true bill was returned at Middlesex sessions, indicting Peter Wright, alias Beale, for being an English-born Roman Catholic priest. He had returned to St. Martin in the Fields parish "traitorously and as a false traitor of this Commonwealth did stay was and remained." Since the days of Queen Elizabeth, this had been a capital offense. Accordingly the court gave judgment:

He shall be led back again to the place from whence he came, and from thence be drawn upon a hurdle to the place of execution, and there be hanged by the neck and then be cut down alive, and his entrails and privy members to be cut off and be burned in his sight, his head to be cut off and his body to be divided into four parts, and then to be disposed at the pleasure of the Parliament.

Bradshawe, however, took interest on some suffering persons. The children of the Earl of Derby petitioned the committee for compounding one fifth of the late father's estate for their maintenance. Testimony had been taken from William Stelfox of county Chester to the effect that the Countess of Derby with her husband (James, 7th Earl of Derby) on the Isle of Man had taken goods from a ship, the *Mary of Liverpool*, and traded with the King of Scotland, adding that the goods were woolen goods belonging to Robert Massey of Warrington and the countess had twenty-three tailors at work to make garments (presumably for the king's troops). Also the countess regretted that Capt. George Bradshaw, a Royalist privateer who took the ship, had not thrown the crew and passengers into the sea as rebels and traitors. As a result, the countess lost her portion of the earl's estate, but Bradshawe made a motion on behalf of the children, and they were awarded one fifth on February 26, 1651. On May 19, Bradshawe wrote in the name of the council to Col. Thomas Birch, saying that Captain Sherwin had taken Captain Bradshaw and brought him back to Liverpool. Included was an order for the trial of Captain Bradshaw. On the same day a similar order was sent to Major General Mytton. Four years later, the protector's Council of State ordered Captain George Bradshaw, of the *Betty* privateer, to report to the council to answer for plundering a Dutch ship, the *Hope of Delfhaven*. After the Restoration, Francis Mason of Shropshire filed a declaration that he had been a Lieutenant to Capt. George Bradshaw on a frigate called *The Michael*. Capt. George Bradshaw is otherwise untraced.

John Bradshawe prepared a rough draft act declaring that Barbados, Antigua, the Bermudas, and Virginia were rebels. It was reported by Parliament on September 19, read a first and second time on the twenty-seventh, and passed with Bradshawe's amendments on the October 3. Those guilty of rebellious proceedings were labeled "notorious Robbers and Traitors, and such as by the Law of nations are not to be permitted any manner of Commerce or Traffic with any people whatsoever." In anticipation of this, Governor Willoughby of Barbados, the richest and most prosperous English colony, had called for his island to be armed against Parliament. Barbados had a commanding position in the international market for sugar. London merchants and the deportees living in London were most hurt by this embargo.

The governor and Council of Barbados heard that "those persons lately gone from Barbados have made it their business to begat a broil betwixt this island and the persons that now govern England." Willoughby showed some intent to restore order in Barbados and prevent a total break with Parliament. Slowly he courted support from the island's moderate party, ousted the Walronds, repealed the Act of Sequestration, and showed favor to the dependents of banished persons. He dispatched Capt. George Marten, a person of standing in Barbados, "to satisfy the whole nation . . . and to prevent all misunderstanding and to settle a perfect and free trade with them." Doubtless Willoughby thought George Marten could enlist support from his brother, Col. Henry Marten, who was a member of the Council of State. Willoughby was anxious to obtain a commission from Parliament. A number of persons banished from Barbados travelled to England in the same ship as Captain Marten, and they swelled the ranks of those already in London who opposed any moderate treatment of Willoughby's administration.

Merchants of London and planters with interests in Barbados petitioned the Council of State for permission to conduct a limited trade there with five or six ships if the islanders would submit to Parliament. If the islanders refused to submit, the petitioners asked for letters of marque to exercise acts of hostility against them. Capt. George Marten was among the petitioners. Two days later the exiled Barbadian planters submitted a petition asking that Edward Winslow, a New England Puritan, replace Willoughby as their governor. In this document, George Marten is described as an agent from Barbados come to London only to invite those who had fled or been banished from the island to return home. Bradshawe jotted two pertinent questions on the reverse of the document, and they can be read today:[2]

whether Mr. Marten have any instructions in writing or declaration? . . . if Lord Willoughby have power there, how came more banished persons over?

Willoughby was informed by letter of Marten's efforts on his behalf but warned "that Marten was like to be hanged for speaking for him." The efforts toward conciliation had come too late.

Trade in and out of Virginia and the West Indies came to be dominated by the Dutch as Cromwell's Scottish war dragged on. Dutch merchants assisted the struggling colonists with capital, technology, credit lines, markets, and slaves. As a result of this foreign trade, the colonies were supplied with non-English manufactures, and their produce was shipped directly to continental markets. Parliament was receiving very little income or produce from their own colonies, but until Charles II's invasion was quelled, nothing could be done. After Cromwell's defeat of the Scot's army at Dunbar, the threat looked less dangerous.

Despite Cromwell's demands on Parliament's dwindling resources, Bradshawe assembled a sea-borne Barbados assault force of seven ships and mustered 820 men under command of Sir George Ayscue. Capt. Michael Pack was second in command. Daniel Searle and Michael Pack were appointed commissioners for reducing Barbados. Searle was to succeed Willoughby as governor general. On January 22, the fleet was ready to depart. John Bayes, one of the displaced Barbadians living in London, wrote to the council to ask that he be allowed to join the Barbados fleet. Then Cromwell fell ill in Scotland. The Council of State took over from the Committee of the Admiralty and decreed that the whole council, or any five of them, to be a committee to consider the business of plantations. The Barbados fleet was diverted to the Scilly Islands where they helped Blake defeat some assembled Royalists.

The new world colonies began to submit, without hostility, to Parliament's authority. Affairs with Maryland were concluded. Bradshawe's Committee of Examinations was ordered to report of the advisability of commissioning William Coddington governor of Rhode Island. David Kirke of Newfoundland submitted to the orders of the Council of State.

John Bayes wrote to Bradshawe:

My Lord, I humbly sent to your honour the reasons why I have not subscribed some expositions with or appended to this honourable Council by many, the Inhabitants belonging to the Island of Barbados and fellow suffers with myself." Bayes makes it clear that Captain George Marten was departing in Ayscue's fleet and had asked Bayes if he thought *"that those ships which Parliament did send to Barbados were sufficient to reduce the island, if the inhabitants were unanimous.*

Bayes said he feared the government of Barbados would eject Willoughby, who then could come home to his wife in England and enjoy his estates here:

All that I desire is that Barbados may be brought back under the power of England, says Bayes, *and may be governed by Commission from your honour to whom by order of Parliament it is now committed; and then I shall be sure to enjoy liberty both spiritual and temporal . . .*

In July 1651, rich hangings and other furnishings were taken from the inventory of the late king's goods to adorn the room where Bradshawe's Committee of Examinations sat.

On the nineteenth of that month, Ayscue's fleet[3] was victualled at Plymouth for a nine-month voyage and ordered to set sail at the first opportunity without waiting for further orders. On August 27, Ayscue was in the Canary Islands from where he addressed a letter to Bradshawe. He reveals that he had sailed with sealed council orders which, when opened at sea, commanded him to divert to Lisbon and there seek Prince Rupert's Royalist fleet. He reported meeting two Flemish men-of-war about thirteen or fourteen leagues out of the Port of Lisbon who told him that Rupert was not on that coast and was last seen in July. The Portuguese refused to fight, although provoked, and Ayscue steered to the Cape Verde Islands for water, from thence to Barbados "where I shall endeavour to show myself."

Sixteen hundred and ten Scottish prisoners were earmaked for transportation to Virginia on condition that Virginia guaranteed them Christian usage. A few days later the council drew appointments for Capt. Robert Dennis, Richard Bennett, Thomas Stagg, and Capt. William Claiborne to be commissioners for reducing Virginia. Several ships were put at their disposal, and Dennis was made commander-in-chief. They were ordered to join Ayscue in Barbados before proceeding to Virginia. The Council of State wrote the news of Cromwell's victory at Worcester to Ayscue: *to make use of in promoting the work he has in charge.* This letter was given to the Virginia fleet for delivery to Ayscue; one hundred narratives of Cromwell's victory at Worcester were printed and delivered to Edward Winslow with order that he send them to New England.

The Virginia fleet was dispatched in late September carrying the news of the Worcester victory to Ayscue. Storms in the Atlantic scattered the little fleet, and Captain Dennis's ship, *The John*, foundered. Dennis, Stagg, and Robert Watts were castaway. About two hundred men were lost.

The Barbados fleet arrived in Carlisle Bay October 1651 and established a blockade, creating consternation on the island. Asycue wrote to Lord President Bradshawe, enclosing a duplicate of his previous letter. One man had been lost to sickness on the voyage. He had surprised fifteen ships, mostly Dutch, and overpowered them. This created some difficulty in finding enough seamen to man the prizes. He sailed under the guns of the island's fort and engaged in a gun battle. One of his seamen was killed. Ayscue said he would make *"this stubborn little island know their duty to the Commonwealth of England."*

Back in England it was time for Cromwell to settle scores after his triumph at Worcester. John Bradshawe signed and dispatched an ornate document to Alban Cox, governor of Guernsey:

There is a Commission for a Marshall Court, issued by the Lord General in pursuance of an Act of Parliament for the trial of certain prisoners(,) in which you are named a Commissioner of (,) therewith you are hereby to take note, and be at the Starr Chamber on Thursday the three and twentieth of this instant October at nine of the Clock in the forenoon to put the same Commission in Execution, We desire you not to fail to appear at the time and place aforesaid, that the business may not be delayed, but effectually presented dated from Whitehall, 16 October 1651.[4]

At the end of the year, Henry Ireton, Cromwell's son-in-law, died in Ireland. Cromwell insisted there be a magnificent state funeral. The Council of State agreed and dispatched a chariot with six horses and other equipage to Bristol. Ireton's coffin arrived in Bristol on December 17. On Christmas Eve the coffin, on one of two black draped chariots, began a six-day procession toward London. The Lord General's Regiment of Horse accompanied the procession. The council determined the internment would be in Henry VI's chapel at Westminster Abbey and Parliament approved. The coffin lay in state at Somerset House throughout January while funeral arrangements were finalized. On February 6, a solemn procession followed the coffin down the Strand to Westminster Abbey. No doubt Bradshawe and all the members of the council accompanied the procession. Cromwell commissioned William Wright to prepare an elaborate marble monument, which the council paid for out of its contingency funds. Dr. George Bate wrote that Cromwell had given Ireton:

that vain glory which himself had often declared against.

The revolutionary English republic became a force of international standing after Worcester. All the European powers rushed to recognize the republic and dispatched diplomats to London. The council was overwhelmed with ambassadors. Parliament resolved to press its advantage by passing the Navigation Act, which required that all goods imported into England be carried on English vessels or on vessels of the county where the cargo originated. This was a direct challenge to the Dutch trade with the English colonies and with mainland England. Richard Bradshaw wrote from Hamburg to Lord President Bradshawe:

It having pleased God to give us safe arrival here . . . in the ship Lion accompanied by all the merchant ships &c . . . the Senate gave order to salute us at our landing with some ordinance: the like respect we received from two of the King of Portugal's ships lying in the river ready bound for Lisboa, (which I was told) was done by order of his ambassador 'here lately come from Sweden.

Ayscue wrote to Bradshawe that he had taken a Dutch galleote hoy which had unloaded in Barbados before they came. Another Dutch ship of sixteen guns was taken, bound for Barbados, with horses, beer, and some general provisions. In all he had taken fourteen vessels, but few are worth much. Anything worthwhile Ayscue promises to send back by the best ship. He reports that declarations have been sent to the island without reply. He had no physical way to reduce the island except by cutting off their trade and creating alarm. However, the Barbadians were bouyed up upon receiving news that Charles II was near to London and Cromwell was slain. That rumour was prevalent in Holland. The arrival of a vessel from Barnstaple in November with printed copies of Cromwell's victory at Worcester soon scotched all rumors. A small force under command of Captain Morris landed at a place called the *Hole* and dispatched the news among the Barbadians.

Capt. Michael Pack reported to Bradshawe in February that he had joined with the Virginia fleet early in December. Pack organized a landing party five hundred strong that included 130 of the Scottish prisoners from the Virginia fleet. He attacked the island while Governor Willoughby and his chief men were feasting some twelve miles away. In the attack his force killed forty of the islanders, captured fifty or sixty, and routed another one thousand: *which run away and we took of their great guns from the shore, which were at that place . . . the Lord Willoughby who is as unworthy a person as any among them and sought nothing more that the ruin of the place.*

An influential Barbadian, Thomas Modyford, sent Pack a private letter requesting a private meeting in some remote place. At the arranged meeting place no boat could land, so Captain Pack swam ashore. After several meetings arranged with Seale, Modyford agreed to declare for Parliament on January 3. Modyford's secret agreement was betrayed to Willoughby by a sailor who swam ashore from Captain Heath's ship. Modyford's faction drew up men, and with Pack's men they faced Willoughby's forces, at a distance of little more than a mile, for eight days. Luckily it rained so hard that the soldiers could hardly keep their matchlocks lit. Articles were signed, and the island surrendered on January 12. Willoughby went to Guiana and then came home to England in 1655. He was imprisoned in the tower for about two years. After the Restoration he returned as governor of Barbados and was drowned in a hurricane that swept the island in 1661.

The Virginia fleet had departed Barbados December 14. Virginia submitted to Parliament without resistance three months later. Richard Bennett[5] replaced Sir William Berkely[6] as governor. This was temporary appointment, pending the decision of the English government. The Commonwealth oath of "Engagement" was required of Virginia's residents in April.[7]

In London the fourth Council of State had met and once again elected John Bradshawe as lord president, but Bradshawe's stranglehold on the office was loosening. He only held the presidency for one month. In February a dispute arose at Committee for Examinations, which was normally Bradshawe's personal baliwick with assistance from George Bishop. Henry Marten had managed to assume the chair. Bradshawe retaliated by coming into the committee *in state with a great guard before him.* It was even claimed that after he had secured reelection to the council in the same month "it was spoken by one of the Council of State that they kept him in for fear he should have hanged himself."[8] Major changes were in the offing: John Milton was nearly blind, and the council's general secretary, Gaulter Frost, died. Old Georg Weckherlin, Milton's predecessor as Latin secretary, was recalled from retirement and appointed assistant secretary to the Committee for Foreign Affairs. In a short time Weckherlin was near death.

Milton addressed a letter:

the Honourable the Lord Bradshawe, 21st February; My Lord, Be that it would be an interruption to the public wherein your studies are perpetually employed I should now venture to supply this my enforced absence with a line or two though it were my only business (and that would be no slight one) to make my due acknowledgement of your many favors. Which I both do at this time and ever shall; . . . I thought my part to let your know . . . that there will be with you tomorrow . . . a gentleman whose name is Mr. (Andrew) Marvell; a man whom both by report and the converse I have had with him (I can recommend as) of singular desert for the state to make use of; who also offers himself if there be any employment for him.

Bradshawe brought this suggestion before the council without success. Marvell attracted the attention of Cromwell, who appointed him tutor to William Dutton, Cromwell's ward. Marvell and Dutton went to live at the house of John Oxenbridge at Eton College.

John Thurloe, a protegee of Judge Oliver St. John, was presented to and accepted by Parliament as clerk of the council replacing the deceased Gualter Frost. Thurloe went into the county for two weeks, perhaps to consult about his future important role. Cromwell was beginning to install his own men into the council's secretariat. Thurloe had recovered money and rents for Cromwell in the Court of Admiralty and the Committee for Compounding. He had sponsored Cromwell's son, Richard, at Lincoln's Inn. On April 22, a blow was struck at the power of the council's president when it was ordered:

All warrants, or papers which are to be signed by the Lord President or any five of the Council, to be examined and countersigned by the Clerk of the Council (Thurloe) or his assistant, before being brought in.

Cromwell had installed his own spy within the heart of the council.

All this time the council had received none of the Barbados letters from Ayscue and Pack, with the exception of the news that Ayscue had arrived in Barbados. The council had written to Ayscue on February 13 to report their lack of news and note that the Virginia fleet will have "informed him of the signal victory at Worcester . . . the (Scottish) prisoners on board that fleet will sufficiently inform him of their condition." Finally on April 23 the council received a packet of letters. Among the packet were Michael Pack's letter to the "Right Honourable the Lord President of the right honourable Council of State" and a letter from Col. Thomas Modyford to the right honourable John Bradshaw, Esq., a member of the honourable Council of State.

Modyford says he will endeavor to deserve the unexpected civilities he has received from John Bayes and tells Bradshawe: [*you*] *have sweetly captivated my mind, and clearly fixed it in true affection to your service.* He offers Bradshawe advice on enlarging the English dominions in the West Indies by acquiring Guiana. Included was a statement of considerations for the settlement of Guiana and the places controlled by the Dutch. Willoughby had already settled 150 men there, and as *Barbados cannot last in an height of trade three years longer,* it is considered that there should be a place where this great people may find maintenance and employment, for which the Commonwealth should disburse £20,000. Bradshawe jotted notes on the reverse of the document.[9]

The English realized that the Dutch had acquired de facto supremacy in foreign trade. England's economic growth was threatened on nearly every front the East Indies, the West Indies, and Africa by Dutch competition. Nearer to home, Dutch herring buses brought great wealth to the United Provinces and maintained supremacy over the herring fishery in the Narrow Sea (the English Channel) and northward, where English kings had long claimed sovereignty. John Selden's *Mare Clausum*, claiming supremacy of the narrow sea, printed by royal decree in 1635, was translated from Latin by Marchmont Needham and reprinted by DuGard, the Council of State's printer, in 1652.

The Republic of England declared war on the United Provinces of Holland in July 1652. As early as June 25, the day before Admiral Robert Blake sailed away to the north in quest of the Dutch herring buses, Parliament acted to claim maritime sovereignity. A resolution passed, "That it be referred to the Council of State to prepare a Declaration to assert the right of this Commonwealth to the Sovereignty of the Seas, and to the fishery: to be made use of when Parliament see cause." The council referred it to Bradshawe's Committee for Law and Examinations "to prepare a declaration—according to order of Parliament referring it to the Council to do so—for asserting the right of this nation to the sovereignty of the sea, and the fisheries, and to bring it to the Council with all speed; Lord Bradshawe to take care of it."

Bradshawe ordered William Ryley, senior keeper of the records in the tower, to make transcripts of several records in his charge referring to the sovereignty of the sea.[10] Among the State Papers[11] is a copy of the ordinance of King John, in Latin, French, and English, endorsed by Bradshawe:

A transcript of a record in the time of King John touching the striking of sail; brought in by Mr. Ryley, Keeper of the Records in the Tower, by order of the Council of State.

On August 23, one Paul Bradshaw, a distant cousin of John Bradshawe, petitioned the Council of State for the place of clerk at Woolwich rope yard, with what result is unknown. He was the fourth son of Peter Bradshawe (d: 1630), citizen and merchant of London, fourth son of Godfrey Bradshawe of Bradshaw and Abney Manor in Derbyshire. Two of his brothers, Edward and Francis, had been Royalist soldiers.

The Council of State ordered a warrant, dated September 27, to protect thirty-four men and a boy on the ship *Two Brothers of London* and eighteen men and a boy on another, *The Sarah Bonadventure*, both bound for Virginia, from being impressed into the service of the Commonwealth fleet. In October the council granted a pass to ten ships bound for Virginia: the *William & John*, the *John & Catherine*, the *Honour*, the *Planter*, the *Hopewell Adventure*, the *Golden Lyon*, the *Charles*, the *Anthony*, the *Margaret*, and the *John & Thomas*.

The fifth Council of State was elected by ballot as usual on November 24 and 25, 1652, and met first on December 1. Sir William Constable was president from November 22. He was succeeded by Bulstode Whitelocke on December 1 and Chief Justice Henry Rolle on December 29, who in turn gave place to Bradshawe on January 26, 1653, the Earl of Salisbury on February 23, and Denis Bond on March 23.

A potential recruit to Cromwell's cadre within the council, John Pell, had written to Bradshawe, December 15 (undated but probably 1652):

My Lord I have today spoken both with my Lord General and my Lord Chief Justice. The Councell's order in my behalfe was written a full month ago, viz. November 16. I hope your Lordship may today find an opportunity to add to the obligations Laid upon Your Lordships most humble servant . . . Pell.

The council did not appoint him. His brother, Thomas Pell, had been gentleman of bedchamber to Charles I but went to America about 1635. Thomas was a surgeon in the Pequot war, settled in Fairfield, Connecticut, and secured a large part of Westchester county New York which became the lordship and manor of Pelham. Perhaps his association with the royal family and Breda was enough to make Bradshawe and George Bishop suspicious. Nevertheless he was appointed by Cromwell, then chancellor of Oxford, to lecture on mathematics. Pell had been a brilliant lecturer on mathematics at Breda where one of his pupils had been William, 3rd Lord Brereton.[12] He invented the ÷ sign for division. Pell became Cromwell's agent in Switzerland after Cromwell dissolved the Rump.

On December 1, the council appointed a standing committee "for the businesse of Trade & Plantations & also for Forreigne Affaires," consisting of twenty-one members, among whom were Bradshawe, Haselrig, Whitelocke, Vane, and Cromwell.

Bradshawe was handling diplomatic relations in February with the aid of translations by John Milton. Bradshawe wrote to the Duke of Venice and the Senate, about 100 barrels of Russian Caviar:[13]

Most Serene Prince, most Illustrious Senate, our dearest friends; Certain of our Merchants, by name John Dickens, and Job Throkmorton with others, have made their complaints to us, That upon the 28th of November 1651, having seized upon a hundred Butts of Caviar in the Vessel called the Swallow, riding in the Downs, Issac Taylor Master, which were their own proper Goods, and laden aboard the same ship in the Moscowvite Bay of Archangel, and this by the Authority of our Court of Admiralty; in which Court, the Suit being there depending, they Obtained a decree for the delivery of said Butts of Caviar into their Possession, they having first given Security to abide by the Sentence of that Court: And the said Court, to the end the said Suit might be brought to a Conclusion, having written letters, according to Custom, to the Magistrates and Judges of Venice; wherein they requested liberty to cite John Patti to appear by his Proctor in the English Court of Admiralty, where the Suit depended, and prove his Right: Nevertheless the said Patti and one David Rutts, a Hollander, while this case depends here in our Court, put the said John Dickens, and those other Merchants, to a vast deal of trouble about the said Caviar, and solict the Seizure of their Goods and Estates as forfeited for Debt. All which things, and whatever else has hitherto been done in our foresaid Court, is more at large set forth in those Letters of request aforementioned; which after we had viewed, we thought proper to be transmitted to the most Serene Republic of Venice, to the end they might be assistant to our merchants in this Cause. Upon the whole therefore, it is our earnest Request to your Highness, and the most Illustrious Senate, That not only those Letters may obtain their due Force and Weight; but also that the Goods and Estates of the Merchants, which the foresaid Patti and David Rutts have endeavoured to make liable for Forfeiture, may be discharged; and that the said Defendants may be referred hither to our Court, to try what Right they have in their claim to this Caviar. Wherein your Highness, and the most Serene Republic will do as well what is most just in itself, as what is truly becoming the spotless Amity between both Republics: And lastly, what will gratefully be recompenced by the Good-will and kind Offices of this Republic, whenever Occasions offers. Sealed with the Seal of the Council, and Subscribed, President of the Council. Whitehall February—1652 (old style).

Admiral Robert Blake was the hero of the moment. He was known as a strong Republican, in sympathy with Bradshawe, Haselrig, and Vane. In the civil war he had emerged as the most competent Parliamentary commander in the west. Bradshawe's Council of State commissioned Blake general at sea. He was aged fifty and had never held a naval command before, and yet in the eight years of his life remaining, he made himself a peer of naval fame to Drake and Nelson, a feat even more extraordinary than that of Cromwell as a soldier. He recovered the Scilly Isles and Jersey for Parliament in 1650 and drove Prince Rupert's royal fleet from the sea off Portugal and the Mediterranean. John Milton drafted a letter for John Bradshawe:

To the most Excellent Lord Anthony John Lewis de la Cerda, Duke of Medina Celi, Governor of Andalusia: The Council of State constituted by Authority of Parliament, Greeting. We have received advice from those most accomplished Persons (Blake's fleet) *whom we have lately sent with our Fleet into Portugal, and pursuit of Traitors and for the recovery of our Vessels, that they were most civilly received by your Excellency, as often as they happened to touch upon the coast of Gallaecia, which is under your Government, and assisted with all things necessary to those that perform long Voyages . . . . Sealed with the Seal of the Council, John Bradshawe, President, Westminister, 7 November 1650.*

When the Dutch war broke out, Blake defeated the Dutch Admiral Tromp off Dover in May and DeWitt off the Kentish coast in September. He rashly attacked a Dutch fleet twice the size of his own off Dungeness in November and was defeated. This led to a complete reorganization of English naval administration. As Cromwell had reorganized the old ideas of ground warfare in the creation of the New Model Army, so Blake became the father of the modern navy. Blake's tactics would govern the pattern of naval warfare down to the days of Nelson. In March 1653, Blake destroyed seventeen Dutch warships and fifty merchantmen in a three-day battle between Portland and Calais.

It was also in March that Bradshawe began to recognize his own mortality. He made his last will and testament, dated March 22, in which he appointed his wife sole executrix and Thomas Parnell as one of the trustees.

Final victory in the Dutch war would not come during Bradshawe's administration. Cromwell wearied of Parliament. On the morning of April 20, Cromwell, accompanied by thirty musketeers, forcibly dissolved Parliament and locked the chamber doors. In the afternoon, Bradshawe and a few other council members attempted to hold a meeting. Cromwell, Harrison, and Lambert appeared at the door. Cromwell announced, "Gentlemen if you are met here as private persons you shall not be disturbed but if as a council of state, this is no place for you since you cannot know what was done in the house in the morning, so take notice that parliament is dissolved."

Figure 25. Cromwell dissolves Parliament

Bradshawe replied, *"Sir we have heard what you did at the House in the morning and before many hours all England will hear it. But Sir you are mistaken to think that Parliament is dissolved, for no power under heaven can dissolve them but themselves, therefore take notice of that."*

What answer Cromwell made to Bradshawe's bold statement we are left to guess. Sir Edward Nicholas says, *"when Bradshawe began to dispute that they sat by Authority of Parliament, he was told that if he and his company*[14] *would not depart by fair means, they should be forced."* Cromwell was quoted as saying to Desborough, *"my work was not completed till I dissolved in the afternoon the Council of State, which I did in spite of the objections of honest Bradshawe the President."*

Bradshawe had only assumed the presidency on that day, in the place of Denis Bond who had served the role for the twenty-eight days proceeding. Ludlow's *Memoirs* do not say that Bradshawe was presiding but clearly implies it. The latest day on which there is any record in the council's order book is April 15.

Godwin says, "Perhaps no man was ever placed in so illustrious a situation as that which Bradshawe occupied at this moment . . .

Cromwell was backed by all his guards, and by an army of the highest discipline, and the most undaunted and prosperous character. Bradshawe appeared before him in the simple robe of integrity[15] Thus ended the Commonwealth of England, after it had continued four years, two months, and twenty days."[16] The next day a paper was found posted at the House of Commons door: "This house to be let, now unfurnished."

James Wainwright wrote to Richard Bradshaw of April 30:

The Lady Bradshaw sent me yesterday two kittlings,[17] *the messenger told me they were to be sent beyond sea.*

Notes to Chapter Thirteen

1. Francis 5th Baron Willoughby of Parham was the brother of Bulstrode Whitelocke's first wife. He had supported Parliament against the King but became a royalist after being ejected from the House of Lords 8th September 1647 and imprisoned for four months. He agreed with the Earl of Carlisle, proprietor of Barbados, and was appointed Governor. He arrived in Barbados 29th April 1650 and was proclaimed Governor by the exiled King Charles II on 7th May.
2. *P.R.O.,* Kew, CO 1/11, folio 66.
3. Fleet for Barbados;

The Rainbow, Sir Geo Ayscue, Capt.	52 guns	280 men
The Amity Frigate, Michael Pack, Capt.	36"	150"
The Success, Edward Witheridge, Capt.	30"	90"
The Ruth, Edward Thompson, Capt.	30"	80"
The Brazil Frigate, Thos Heath, Capt.	24"	70"
The Malaga Frigate, Henry Collin, Capt.	30"	90"
The Increase of London, Thos Varvell, Capt.	36"	100"

4. *Add'l Mss 11,315*, fol 21, British Library
5. Richard Bennett was brother-in-law of Bulstrode Whitelocke.
6. Governor Berkeley belonged to a circle of playwrights, artists, and intellectuals—Ben Jonson, John Donne, Sir John Suckling, and Thomas Killigrew the impresario, playwright, and diplomat—who looked to Queen Henrietta Maria for patronage. Berkeley had written *The Lost Lady* in 1637, which was acted at Court and the Blackfriars Theatre. He purchased the Governorship of Virginia from Sir Francis Wyatt about 1641. In 1652 he retired to his estate in Green Springs. After the Restoration King Charles II said about Berkeley;—the old fool had hung more men in Virginia that my father did in the whole of England.
7. On 13th April 1652, a John Bradshaw and a Robert Bradshaw signed the Engagement in Virginia. *Virginia Colonial Abstracts*, (Balt. Gen Publ), vol 20.
8. T. Carte ed., *A Collection of Original Letters and Papers Concerning Affairs of England, 1641-1660*, 2 vols, 1739, vol I, pgs 443-445. State's Servants, G.E. Aylmer" 1973 pg 15. *Inventing a Republic,* Sean Kelsey, p 129.
9. *P.R.O.,* CO 1/11, folio 117.

10) *Harle Mss 4314.*
11. *Cal State Papers Dom, XXXV* 35.
12. William, third Lord Brereton, of Low Leighton in Ireland and Brereton in Cheshire, was son-in-law of Francis, Lord Willoughby of Parham. He was also a distant relative of Sir William Brereton of Hanforth, Bradshawe's early supporter.
13. *Works of Milton, 1738*, Vol II, 164.
14. Nicholas Papers, Camden Soc.
15. William Godwin, *History of the Commonwealth of England & c.*, 4 vols, (1824-1828).
16. Daniel Neal, *The History of the Puritans*, 1822.
17. In the 17th century *kitlings* were young cats, or young children.

CHAPTER FOURTEEN

The Wilderness Years

> *for freedom is the man
> that will turn the world upside downe,
> therefore no wonder he hath enemies*
>
> **Gerrard Winstanley**

✠

WHEN LORD GENERAL Oliver Cromwell dissolved the Parliament and seized executive power of government from Lord President John Bradshawe's Council of State, the fragile vision of an English Republic was destroyed by the power of a military coup—a coup backed by the most radical Puritan sectaries in the army. The religious malcontents within military ranks were breathing down the Lord General's neck demanding he choose between loyalty to his army and loyalty to his Parliament. Rumors, probably untrue, were being circulated to the effect that Parliament was planning to remodel the whole command of the army and remove Cromwell. He knew Parliament did not have the power to disband the army, but with the army's assistance, he had the power to dissolve Parliament. He chose to act on the day Parliament began the third reading of the bill for elections. That April morning in Parliament, Cromwell made his choice; he called his fellow MPs whoremasters, drunkards, unjust and corrupt, and a scandal to the gospel they professed, concluding, *"you are no Parliament; I say you are no Parliament; I will put an end to your sitting; call them in, call them in!"* About thirty musketeers ran into the chamber. He spied Parliament's new mace and said, *"What shall we do with this bauble? There take it away."* He turned on Speaker Lenthall and told Gen. Harrison to *"fetch him down."* Lenthall refused to come down except by force, to which

Harrison replied, *"Sir, I will lend you my hand."* Lenthall discreetly stepped down and vanished. Despite all that, Cromwell met no violent resistance. Some members stood up to shout their protests, but none drew their swords. Sir Henry Vane cried out, *"This is not honest, yea it is against morality and common honesty,"* to which Cromwell shouted back, *"O, Sir Henry Vane, the Lord deliver me from Sir Henry Vane!"* Tucking the hated bill for elections under his cloak, Cromwell turned his back and departed the house. Bulstrode Whitelocke wrote: *Thus was this great Parliament, which had done so great things . . . routed by those whom they had set up and that took commissions and authority from them; nor could they in the least justify any action they had done, or one drop of blood they had spilt, but by this authority. Yet now the servants rose against their masters,*

It is true that the army generals had received their commissions from the Long Parliament, but Parliament failed to see that they owed their very existence to an army they could no longer control. They had failed to consolidate civilian control over the army. The army was weary of legal and constitutional disputations. Cromwell was painfully aware to whom he owed his existence, but it was necessary to prove he controlled the army and the army be seen to control the county. That was his powerbase.

The bill for elections may have been a flawed instrument promoted by Sir Henry Vane, Haselrig, Bradshawe, and their Republican supporters. We cannot examine the wording of the bill. Cromwell took it away from Commons on the morning of April 20, and it is not to be found today, but Professor Blair Worden has aptly demonstrated[1] it provided for the Rump's final dissolution in the following November, with the seats to be redistributed on lines similar to 1649 agreement of the army officers. There was a danger that some powerful Royalists and Presbyterian malcontents would certainly have been elected, along with many of the contentious sitting Republicans. The night before he dissolved Parliament, Cromwell revealed to his supporters an alternative proposal recommending that Parliament hand over power to an interim Council of Forty composed of "men fearing God, and of approved integrity" nominated by itself and then dissolve itself until a totally new Parliament could be elected. Bulstrode Whitelocke and the speaker supported the proposal, and Cromwell believed that they would, with support of his other loyal supporters, forestall any further discussion of the bill for elections. When Parliament met on the morning of April

20 and began again to discuss the bill, not his own proposal, Cromwell was infuriated. He protested the Rump's haste in the bill for elections demonstrated a spirit "not according to God" or the whole weight of the cause which must be very dear unto us who had so often adventured our lives for it.

Sean Kelsey maintains that the bill for elections showed just how committed to a parliamentary republic the Rump had become. They saw the greatest threat to the survival of the parliamentary republic was the army's failure to believe in a "consistency of the civil authority by successive parliaments and the just and equal dispensation of justice throughout the Nation." Parliament chose to put their own seats to the choice of the electorate, and the possible return of a few elected Royalists to Parliament was not their worry. The bill was pressed not as a retaliatory measure but out of the desperate realization that the army's radicals were about to strike; therefore, the army's leadership must subdue them.

The army radicals had threatened to dissolve Parliament by force, and it was Cromwell who had rebuked them for such a suggestion and ultimately framed his own proposal for peaceful self-dissolution. As it turned out, he couldn't accomplish it. Vane and the Republicans thought the best that might be expected was to pass an electoral bill of the utmost integrity so that the army might be seen to have succeeded in their own obvious self interest. The bill was a testament to the conviction that a civil settlement by successive Parliaments was not only possible but, in the circumstances, positively desirable. Had not Cromwell rashly interfered, the bill for elections might have served as the keystone to John Cook's ideal of elective aristocracy: "An active minority, presumably many of them present in the House on the morning of 20 April 1653, spent four and a half years imaginatively molding a new state (albeit within quite inimaginative constitutional parameters) and were now prepared to send the ship of the Commonwealth sailing off on a course to be set by its electors. This was not 'throwing away the cause.' The wheel would have been firmly tied, not only by the likely return of those very Republicans who had plucked up the courage to seek popular mandate, but also by the simple, inescapable and politically defining fact that the Army would still be around to 'poyse the affairs of the whole Nation . . ."[2]

Bradshawe's position was unique in this conflict. Americans will recognize, more readily than Britons, the concept of a government chief executive who has no seat in the elected legislative branch of government. He remained a member of one of the Council of State's committees even though his strong republican feelings made him abhor Cromwell's dissolution of Parliament. After his initial condemnation of Cromwell's action, Bradshawe was silent and continued to demonstrate support for the army by serving as a commissioner for relief on the articles of war. In this Clarendon thought Bradshawe "rejoyceth . . . in the hope it may give him admission again into publique business." Cromwell, however, began to handpick his own assembly and bridge the dissolution with the outward appearance of peaceful continuity. He made no public utterances against Bradshawe and seemed to court his good will and retain his service well into 1654. In a conversation with Desborough, Cromwell had referred to honest Bradshawe, the president. After the dissolution, Cromwell could have easily arranged the deaths of Bradshawe, Haselrig, and Vane, but there was no need. Their teeth had been pulled. They had no powerbase and no military units at their command. Other opponents would be killed, converted, suppressed, intimidated, bought, or ignored.

It was said Bradshawe departed with great displeasure when ordered out of his Whitehall lodging, but there seems to have been no urgency to remove him. Bradshawe's niece, Elizabeth Furnivall,[3] died on June 16, so he may have been in Cheshire for the funeral. A polite hint was given on July 30, in an order from the new Council of State, that the lodgings "now Lord Bradshawe's" be appointed when he leaves to Colonel Montague, and it was not until September that they were assigned to Mr. Lawrence and Colonel Montague jointly.

Cromwell was now in a dilemma. He had closed the option of calling a new Parliament until the constitutional question could be resolved. There was no legal right to summon one since the Rump had not dissolved itself by consent. Even if new elections were called, the most likely members to be returned were his enemies: Presbyterians, Republican sympathizers, or crypto-Royalists. He threw the burden of constitutional decision upon the Council of Army Officers. Within the council of officers there were two factions. Major General Lambert favored a small governing council of ten or twelve men who would presumably settle the country and then bring Parliament back into the legislative role. The religious zealot Major General Harrison favored a Sanhedrin of seventy godly men who would follow the saintly example of biblical Israel. Cromwell mediated between the two, favoring the idea of saintly rule but preferring a larger, nominated rather than elected, assembly of one hundred forty. Temporarily, however, civil affairs were put in the care of small Council of State under Lambert's presidency in late April while nominations for a new assembly were submitted.

On July 4, the nominated assembly met and was addressed by Cromwell, who spoke with visionary Christian enthusiasm. He asked the assembly to sit no longer than November 4 and then give way to another body, nominated by themselves, who would take care of the succession of government for another year. He spoke of the time when the cleansed people of England would be fit to exercise their voting rights once again. The implication was that once a constitutional settlement was achieved, by about the end of 1655 Cromwell would consent to the return of a regular elected Parliament

The assembly decided to met in the House of Commons and call itself a parliament. A fanatical baptist and London leather seller, Praise-God Barebone,[4] was elected speaker, and the mace which Cromwell had taken away in April was returned to the chamber. It became known as the Little Parliament, or Barebone's Parliament. One of its first acts was to enlarge the Council of State to thirty-one members. Bradshawe was not included. Lambert had withdrawn from government, probably in disgust, and at his Yorkshire home he drafted a written constitution casting Cromwell in the role of a constitutional monarch.

George Bishop, Bradshawe's trusted spymaster, was discharged "from intermeddling in the foreign intelligence" in July.

In September, the Council of State took a petition from David Selleck of Boston New England requesting a license for his ships, *The Good Fellow of Boston* and *The Providence of London*, to pass to Virginia and Boston carrying four hundred Irish children to those plantations. A committee was appointed to examine the request, and on October 28 the license was granted.

All of Cromwell's talk of godly rule and the return of the saints emboldened provincial prosecutors to overzealously pursue evil doers. Bradshawe continued as chief justice of Chester and Flint. Because of the political upheavals, Bradshawe did not attend the September 1653 court at Chester but delegated responsibility to his deputy, Humphrey Mackworth, and to his fellow chief justice Thomas Fell.

At those sessions where Chief Justice John Bradshawe was not present, John Bradshaw, attorney general of Chester,[5] presented indictments against Ellen Stubbs, wife of William Stubbs of Warford, labourer; Elizabeth her daughter; and Anne Stanley, wife of John Stanley of Withington, laborer, for practicing witchcraft. Ellen Stubbs, Elizabeth

Stubbs, and Anne Stanley were accused of bewitching Anne, wife off John Lowe, at the earlier date of March 7, 1646. Ellen and Elizabeth Stubbs were accused of entertaining evil spirits and bewitching Thomas Grastie's black cow at Warford on October 9, 1652. Finally Ellen Stubbs and Anne Stanley were accused by fourteen witnesses of entertaining evil spirits and bewitching Elizabeth, wife of Ralph Furnival, Gent., on June 4, 1653, and other days at nether Aldersley, Cheshire. It was reported that Elizabeth languished until June 16 when she died. Elizabeth Furnivall was the neice of Chief Justice John Bradshawe!

Members of Barebone's Parliament must have approved of Bradshawe's legal judgment. Upon the creation of a new high court of justice, Bradshawe was appointed one of the thirty-two commissioners, November 22, 1653. The high court was constituted until August 1 following. This was among the last acts of this Parliament.

Barebone's Parliament foundered in November, and on December 12 they voluntarily dissolved themselves. The full powers of government returned to Cromwell's hands. On the sixteenth, Lambert and his council of officers promulgated the Instrument of Government, whereby the title of lord protector of the Commonwealth of England, Scotland, and Ireland was to be bestowed upon Cromwell, with whom a Council of State numbering fifteen men, elected for life, was to be associated. It was specified that a new four-hundred strong Parliament was to be elected, and it was to be called at least every three years. Once called, Parliament was to be kept sitting for at least five months. The date set for election was July 1654 with the first sitting scheduled for the anniversary of the Battles of Dunbar and Worcester. When everything was in place, executive authority would belong to the protector and his council; legislative authority would be vested in the protector and the Parliament. Arching over all was the Instrument of Government which the Parliament could not violate. In the interim, Cromwell and his council could make ordinances, subject to Parliament's subsequent approval upon their first sitting.

Cromwell said he longed for government by consent, but he was never able to be reconciled to Republicans like Bradshawe, Vane, Ludlow, Haselrig, and Marten. In February, Cromwell was advised by his Council of State to issue a new commission to Bradshawe as chief justice of Chester.

Cromwell concluded a peace with the Dutch, and on April 28 Wainwright wrote to Richard Bradshaw:

Yesterday was the Embassadors feasted at Whitehall in great state by the Protector; in a short time I believe his Highness will be Emperor of Great Britain and King of Ireland; something must be answerable to his power.

The April sessions for 1654 were held in Flint, so the women found guilty of bewitching Bradshawe's niece awaited their sentencing at Chester goal. On May 5, Wainwright wrote to Richard Bradshaw in Hamburg: "*I was this day a long time with my Lord Bradshaw, who wished me to remember him to you; he is come back from his circuit; he is still the honest man, I mean a true Englishman from bottom to top.*"

Figure 26. John Milton

Milton's *Second Defense of the English People* appeared in print at the end of May. Although overtly Cromwellian, it contained superlative praise of Bradshawe the pronounced Republican, Fairfax the darling of the Presbyterians, and Robert Overton whose sympathies were on the side of the Levelers. On the one hand it advised Cromwell to conciliate rather than alienate such friends of Liberty, whilst on the other hand admonished the others to cooperate with Cromwell in supporting the Commonwealth of the Protectorate. Milton appears to have sent presentation copies of his work to all those mentioned therein: Fleetwood, Lambert, Desborough, Pickering, Strickland, Sydenham, Montague, Fairfax, Whitelocke, Sidney, Whalley, Overton, Cromwell, and Bradshawe. Three copies were dispatched to Andrew Marvell at Eton with a letter explaining one copy was for Marvell himself, another for Oxenbridge, and the third for a person who must surely be Lord President Bradshawe. Marvell was instructed to very particularly see to the delivery of the third copy with its accompanying letter.[6] Milton would naturally have been anxious to know Bradshawe's reaction. Marvell wrote two letters back to Milton. The first is lost, but the second gives an incomplete, although interesting, report of Marvell's encounter with Bradshawe:

For my most Honoured Friend John Milton Esquire, Secretary for the Foreign Affairs, at his House in Petty France, these Honoured Sir I did not satisfy myself in the account I gave you of presenting your book to my Lord although it seemed to me that I writ you all which the messenger's speedy return from Eton would permit me; and I perceive that by reason of that haste, I did not give you satisfaction (either ?) *concerning the delivery of your letter at the same time. Be pleased therefore to pardon me and know that I tendered them both together. But my Lord read not the letter while I was with him; which I attributed to your dispatch of some other business tending thereto—which I therefore wished ill to, so far as it it hindered an affair much better and of far greater importance—I mean that of reading your letter. And to tell you truly mine own imagination, I thought he would not open it while I was there, because he might suspect that I delivering it just upon my departure might have brought in it some second proposition, like to that which you had before made to him to my advantage.*

The letter continues with praise for Milton and concludes:

I have an affectionate curiousity to know what becomes of Colonel Overton's business.

Figure 27. Andrew Marvell

It is dated from Eton, June 2, 1654. At that date, Col. Robert Overton was under suspicion in London of associating with Sexby, Wildman, and John Lilburne to foment Leveler plots among the northern army.

Cromwell attempted to purge the pulpits of unworthy churchmen. Committees of expurgators were constituted in each county to inquire into the conduct of ministers. In Cheshire, the committee consisted of fifteen laymen assisted by two noted ministers: James Marbury and Samuel Eaton. Among the laymen were Edward Bradshaw, the mayor of Chester; Humphrey Mackworth, deputy chief justice of Cheshire; and Sir William Brereton.

Upon his return from Cheshire, John Bradshawe presented to the Committee for Compounding the petition of the Dowager Countess of Derby for the restoration of her estates. He told the committee that it was specifically recommended by the protector.[7]

When the July elections came, Cromwell endeavored to exclude those extreme men of the old Parliament who, by their strong republican views, had given him so much trouble. The leading gentry of Cheshire met to agree a slate of four candidates as allocated by the Instrument of Government. All candidates were leading civilians, and they were to be returned unopposed. Ludlow says that even though the sheriffs and local returning officers were prepared to return, only such members as Cromwell's party "pointed out, yet many persons of known virtue and integrity were chosen to sit in that assembly and particularly the Lord President Bradshawe." This was Bradshawe's first election to Parliament. It is certain he was chosen for one of the seats for the county of Chester, the other the members being Sir George Booth, Henry Brooke of Norton, and John Crewe of Utkinton. It is claimed Bradshawe was also chosen in both Staffordshire and Lancashire.[8] Certainly Wainwright reported to Richard Bradshaw:

One of my Lord Bradshaw(e)'s gentlemen told me to-day, he is chosen in Staffordshire; if not there, in Cheshire or Lancashire; without doubt next post will tell you.

It is not impossible that Bradshawe's popularity in those counties could have resulted in his multiple election, but as I have already so often noted, John Bradshawe has been and continues to be confused with his identically named contemporaries.

John Bradshawe's father, Henry Bradshawe, the elder of Marple Hall, died in July and was buried at Stockport on August 4. John's elder brother, Henry, inherited Marple Hall as was the custom. No doubt

John would have been at Stockport for the burial. Wainwright said on October 13 that Mr. Samuel Rowe, one of Bradshawe's long-serving secretaries, was "abrod with Lord Bradshaw(e)."

About 125 MP's who had sat in the Long Parliament were selected for the 1654 Parliament. It was they, led by Arthur Haselrig, Thomas Scott, John Birch, along with John Bradshawe as a new Member, who would lead the first Protectorate Parliament. They assembled on September 3, although it fell upon a Sunday. Religious services were held at St. Margaret's church, and the members then repaired to the house. After about an hour they received a summons to attend the protector in the Painted Chamber, but Bradshawe and ten or twelve others shouted out, "Sit still," and remained seated. It was now obvious Bradshawe intended to take a stand on challenging the Instrument of Government. The first official act was the selection of a speaker, contested between Lenthall and Lord Bradshawe. The selection fell on Lenthall, Cromwell's choice. It was the first setback for the Republicans.

Cromwell's problem, says Professor Gardiner, lay in his difficulty of reconcilling Parliament and the army. This involved a deeper controversy. Were the people to be ruled for their own good by a godly Protectorate, or was the government to conform its action to the will of the people? The former view was maintained by the most prominent leaders of the army, the latter by Bradshawe and his Republican colleagues. Ludlow wrote:

and when it was debated whether the supreme legislative power of the nation should reside in a single person and the Parliament, Sir Arthur Haselrig and many others, especially the Lord President Bradshawe were very instrumental in opening the eyes of many young members, who had never before heard their interest so clearly stated asserted; so that the Commonwealth Party increased daily and that of the sword lost ground.

The next nine days were crucial.

By a vote of 136 to 140, a proposal backed by Bradshawe and Birch carried, and the house referred the constitution question to a grand committee. The Republicans were not so much attempting to deprive Cromwell of his power as asserting the permanent authority of the house. A paper of proposals, drafted by a member of the house, is attributed to Bradshawe. This attribution is confirmed by a letter from Joseph Jane to Sir Edward Nichols:

there came a report to the towne that they were in much disorder in England and that their Pa.r L, and Cromwell were not of a peece Bradshawe having moved to know whether they were a free parliament.[9]

In Bradshawe's draft, the absolute supremacy of Parliament was maintained but the Republicans were too weak to carry the whole program. Matthew Hale's adopted compromise that the government should reside "in a Parliament and a single person, limited and restrained as the Parliament should see fit" satisfied neither party.

In the American colonies, Roger Williams wrote to John Winthrop, Jr.:

I have this last week many letters from England: but all dated the first week of the Parliaments sitting: This house consisted most of Presbyterian factors . . . upon the grand question of the Supreme Legislative, the Lord Bradshaw(e) spake openly that if a Parliament were not supreme, then he a murderer of K. Cha. Sir Arthur Haselrig spake high; but the report is double; some say a vote past that would not dispute the point, some say they did dispute, & therefore a breach followed, & the imprisonment of Bradshaw(e) & Haselrig, & c. & it is said here (by Dutch news) 2 beheaded . . .

On the twelfth, Cromwell demanded the signatures of all members be affixed to a recognition that the fundamentals of the Instrument of Government would be preserved. Without their signatures, members were barred from the house. Before the night was out, one hundred members had signed. By the twenty-first, the number reached one hundred ninety, subsequently rising to three hundred. Bradshawe refused. In vain Bradshawe declared, as Lilburne had done before him, that if he must have a master, he preferred King Charles to Oliver.

Professor Gardiner said, "In protesting against the bonds of a written constitution on which the nation, Bradshawe, and the Haselrigs were doing, the business of posterity, Oliver was no less in insisting on conditions without which Parliamentary government is a vain show."[10]

Bradshawe attended the celebration of a fast at St. Margaret's Westminster and sat in the seat assigned him as an MP. He made no attempt to enter the house afterward. Bradshawe, Sir Arthur Haselrig, and others departed the Parliament less than two weeks after they had entered. They heard rumors of a plot against Cromwell.

In October, Bradshawe went on his northern circuit. At the autumn court sessions held in Chester, Ellen Stubbs, Elizabeth Stubbs, and Anne Stanley, who had been found guilty of death of Elizabeth Furnivall and not guilty of death of Anne Lowe, were sentenced to death by chief justices John Bradshawe and Thomas Fell. The three women were hanged at Boughton[11] October 17, 1654. At those same October Chester sessions, two days after the execution of the two Stubbs women and Anne Stanley, Elizabeth Johnson was suspected of witchcraft, but chief justices Bradshawe and Fell judged her an ignoramus.

Wainwright wrote to Richard Bradshaw on November 3:

I am returned out of the North, where I met with many of your friends, in particular at Wrexham, as I came with my Lord Bradshawe, where we did remember you, and commanded me to do it to you, and finding him remote from home we were singular merry.

On the first of January, Bradshawe surrendered his post as chancellor of the duchy of Lancaster to his friend Thomas Fell.

The seclusion from Parliament of those who refused to support the Instrument of Government was giving rise to considerable dissatisfaction. A curious combination of Anabaptists, Levelers, Royalists, and extreme Republicans became involved in a plot known as Wildman's plot. Milton's friend, Col. Robert Overton, had held conferences with Maj. John Wildman, but beyond expressing their mutual disgust about the exclusion of the MPs, there seems to have been no specific plan of action. Overton went back to his post in Gen. Monck's army in Scotland where he sounded out other disgruntled officers. Slowly a tentative plan developed: Monck was to be seized, Overton would take troops and horsemen to march on England where they would joined by Bradshawe and Haselrig. Vice Admiral Lewson would persuade a squadron of the fleet to join the plot, and it was supposed that Harrison, Alured, Sexby, Adjutant General Allen, Lord Grey of Groby, and Henry Marten would join. Wildman, however, was arrested in Wiltshire in the beginning of 1655 while in the act of dictating a *Declaration of the Free and Well-Affected People of England now in arms against the tyrant Oliver Cromwell, Esq.* Wildman was imprisoned at Chepstow Castle. Overton was committed to the tower and remained prisoner for more than five years. Sexby escaped the country, and the others suffered nothing more than isolation or dismissal from service.

Whether Bradshawe was actually engaged in the plot remains an open question. Certainly Thurloe thought so. From Thurloe's notes, never intended for publication, it is apparent that the conspiracy began in September 1654 when the MPs had been secluded. Thurloe may have known about it all along and had all the alleged conspirators under surveillance. Bradshawe is mentioned in the notes several times:

Petition drawn by Wildman and after (George) *Bishop had it and showed it to Bradshawe. The men they built upon was Sir George Booth, Bradshawe, Haselrig, G. Fenwick, Birch, Her(bert), Morley, Wilmers, Pyne,*

Scot, Allen, Pearson went like Hasel(rig) etc. Bishop like Bradshawe and their advices given by them. At the same time a petition from the City where Bradshawe advised in, and several met at his house, especially one (Col) Eyre, Sir Arthur H (aselrig), Scot, Col. Sankey, Weaver, directed both the bringing on and the manner of p(romoting) it. Sankey at Bradshawe's often, where Bishop met him—Col Eyre had been visited at his lodgings in Swan Alley in the Blackfriars by Dallington one of the conspirators to whom he admitted that he had fought for his liberty but had none.

From Dallington's later evidence given under examination, it is clear that Haselrig had given no pledges or even assurances. It can be assumed that the evidence against Bradshawe was no more reliable than that against Haselrig. Whatever Cromwell thought, no Republicans suffered punishment beyond that they already felt in their seclusion. Cromwell summarily dismissed Parliament on January 22, and it would be a year and nine months before he called another.

Katherine Bradshaw, wife of Richard Bradshaw, was back from Hamburg and Thurloe presented her to Cromwell at court in March. She was a friend of both Thurloe's wife and his mother-in-law.

Also in March, a Royalist plot to assassinate Cromwell, lead by Col. John Penruddock, was discovered. Cromwell was induced to divide the country in eleven districts, each commanded by an army major general assisted by a body of local commissioners. These major generals began to levy taxes and duties to support their administrations. They quickly came into conflict with the lawyers and the judiciary. One of the major generals proposed to clear the goals by mass transportation of the prisoners. Chief Justice Rolle ruled against a customs ordinance and was forced to resign. On the morning of May 30, Bradshawe was called before the council. He was at that moment sitting as judge in the Sheriff's Court at the Guildhall. The court was suspended until the afternoon as Bradshawe was led away. It was not initally clear whether he was summoned to give assurance of his submission to the Protector's taxation authority or to answer for his alledged involvement in the recent conspiracies. The question is not answered in the official records, but a newsletter dated June 9 states "the Lord Bradshawe hath been twice sent for by the Council for not paying his assize; Paise-God Barebones and some others also refuse it."[12]

The judiciary soon again clashed with the government, and on July 13 all the judges were summoned to Whitehall when Cromwell "gave them a very learned charge before they return to their several Councils."

He also ordered "that the Commissioners for giving relief on the articles of War should cease to sitt or act further upon the powers given to them. A newswriter of the day says; the Lord Bradshawe is out of his last public employment."[13] The writer forgot that Bradshawe was still Judge of the Sheriff's Court in the Guildhall and Chief Justice of Chester and Wales, but other reasons may have temporarily removed Bradshawe from public employment.

The court records for 1655 in Cheshire and Wales are sketchy, but by 1656 Bradshawe had acknowledged Cromwell's Protectorate. At the session of Chester held in the Common Hall of Pleas in Chester, on Monday (the last day of March 1656), before John Bradshawe, serjeant-at-law, Justice of Oliver, Lord Protector of the Commonwealth of England, Scotland and Ireland, and the dominions thereunto belonging, of Chester; and Thomas Fell, Esq., the other ustice of the said Lord Protector of the said county, several charges were laid. Ellen, the wife of John Beech (collier) late of Ranowe, in Cheshire, did execise and practice the "Invocation and conjuracon of evil and wicked spirits on 12th of September 1651 and did exercise certain witchcrafts upon Elizabeth Cowper, late of Ranowe, spinster, whereby she, from the 12th till the 20th of September, did languish and died 20th September. Also, Anne, wife of James Osboston, late of Ranowe, husbandman, practised certain wicked and divelish acts upon John Stevenson who died 20th September. Also, Anne Osboston," on November 20, 1653, "exercised certayn arts and Incantations" on Barbara Pott, late wife of John Pott. She died January 20 following. Anne Osboston practiced sorceries on John Pott. He died August 5, 1651. Anne Osboston used enchantments upon Anthony Booth, late of Macclesfield, thereby causing his death on April 1, 1652.

Indictments were returned, and Ellen Beech and Anne Osboston were imprisoned at Chester Castle to await trial at the next session. Seven days later, Bradshawe and Fell moved on to Wales.

Prisoners were brought forward at the great sessions of Flint, at Flint, on April 7, 1656, before John Bradshawe, serjeant-at-law, justice of Flint; and Thomas Fell, Esq., another justice of Flint.[14] Dorothy Gruff (Grydd) committed for felony. Discharged on her own bail. An entry, dated October 13, 1656, shows that Dorothy Griffith was again committed, this time upon suspicion of witchcraft and bound over to this assize, made a default. She bailed by herself, £ 40.

While Bradshawe was away, a case was heard at the Old Bailey in London, April 16, "Record of the Arraignment and trial of John

Thompson *pro morte Joh'is Bradshawe* (for the death of John Bradshawe)," with record that the same John Thompson stood mute and therefore sentenced to *peine forte et durer* (pressing to death.)[15] It is another confusing example of the many John Bradshawes.

Back in London after his circuit, Bradshawe was again summoned before the council, along with Lt. Gen. Edmund Ludlow and Col. Rich, on August 1. Rumor had it that the gentlemen were accused of "tampering with those people that would involve the nation in blood again and that they have endeavored where they have interest to dissuade the people from electing swordsmen Major Generals and Decimators."[16] The council demanded that Bradshawe take out a new commission from them for his office of Chief Justice of Chester and Wales. There were probably strings attached. Bradshawe flatly refused.

In a fiery confrontation with Cromwell, Bradshawe said: *"Sir, I require no new commission and I will have none. I hold the office by a grant from the parliament of England in the terms 'quamdui si bene gimirit.' And whether I have carried myself with that integrity which my commission extracts from me, I am ready to submit to a trial by twelve Englishmen to be chosen by yourself."*[17]

Two weeks after this encounter, Colonel Barkstead, lieutenant of the Tower, sent Thurloe secret information about a meeting which had been held the night of August 14 in the city of London. It was reported that Mr. Moyer, Major Salway, Colonel Webb, Colonel Rowe, Mr. Brandriffe, Alderman Tichborne, Lord Bradshawe, and one or two others had been nominated to act as a committee for the purpose of some uprising.[18] There is no suggestion in the report that Bradshawe was a party to the conspiracy but just that his name was being used. This was the Fifth Monarchist uprising led by Okey and Goodman. The only direct evidence against Bradshawe is his letter to those men in which he contends that the Long Parliament, though under a force, was the supreme authority of England.

Thurloe wrote to Henry Cromwell, Oliver's younger son and lord deputy of Ireland, informing him that Sir Henry Vane had been summoned to attend council and answer for his book *A Healing Question*. He adds that others have been endeavoring to create a disturbance, that Okey, Lawson, Rich, and Ludlow are being proceeded against while "Serjeant Bradshawe's commission as Chief Justice of Chester has been cancelled."[19] Vane was required to give keep the peace and post a security of £5,000. He refused and was imprisoned without trial at Carisbrook Castle.

By now Cromwell and Thurloe were becoming frustrated. Having tried every means to break Bradshawe's influence and link him to some conspiracy, they determined to block him from the new Parliamentary elections in Cheshire scheduled for the end of August. The Protectorate was desperately short of cash and looked to a cooperative new Parliament for supply.

Before each Protectorate Parliament, a county caucus of gentlemen was formed to settle on an agreed slate of candidates. In 1654, the caucus that had chosen John Bradshawe was composed of Thomas Mainwaring, Sir William Brereton, Thomas Stanley, Thomas Marbury,[20] Peter Brooke, and Jonathan Bruen of Stapelton. The caucus, which met on July 25, 1656, had a slightly different component; Stanley, Bruen, and Brooke were again members. They were joined by Philip Egerton the sheriff, Thomas Brereton of Ashley, Roger Wilbraham of Derfold, and John Arderne. The last four were disillusioned Parliamentarians, although Egerton was the son of a Royalist. The slate of candidates they chose was Thomas Marbury, Peter Brooke, Richard Legh of Lyme, and John Bradshawe.

Commanding the district, which included Cheshire, was Maj. Gen. Charles Worsley, who had a reputation as one of the most oppressive of all the major generals. He jailed couples who married contrary to the act of Parliament, closed ale houses and suppressed brewers,[21] and publicly punished idlers and loose persons, common tipplers, and Sabbath breakers. He scrupulously enforced the Decimation Tax by taking 10 percent from the income of Royalist sypathizers. When he died in June or July, his passing was unlamented.

Maj. Gen. Tobias Bridge[22] was appointed to replace Worsley, August 13, only a week before election day. From Middlewich on August 15, he reported to Cromwell:

yet notwithstanding my Lord Bradshawe hath a great party here in this county even amongst the commissioners some of whom have had divers meetings with the sheriff for the proposing of him. Mr. Marbury, Major Peter Brookes and Mr. Lee Legh of Lyme who chose for the next Parliament but after much debate and arguing with them concerning the Lord Bradshawe. I believe they are now satisfied to leave him out.

Other sources confirm that Thomas Croxton, governor of Chester, was to be the fourth candidate. Further discussion led to a compromise in which Bridge agreed to the gentlemen's slate so long as they undertook to prevent the election of John Bradshawe. Fully satisfied that the slate was now set, Bridge moved on to Lancashire the next day.

More interesting is Bridge's report that:

Notwithstanding the reports here of the Lord Bradshawe's restraints (at which I do not find the gentlemen any whit startled) . . . warrants are gone forth for the assizes to be held on the 6th of October in the same manner as formerly.

Dr. Denton wrote to Sir Roger Verney, from Alport:

Here hath been a strange rumour of the securing of Vane, Bradshawe, Ludlow, and other, but no certainty a little news doth well here.[23]

The Gentlemen Confederates (as the caucus had become known) soon began to have doubts about the possibility of preventing Bradshawe's selection. In the run-up to the election, they met several times at Lyme. Henry Bradshawe of Marple attended at least one meeting and firmly told the confederates that his brother, John Bradshawe, intended to stand and to serve if elected. Henry showed them a letter from his brother. The confederates were clearly rattled. Some of the confederates had been spreading rumours that Bradshawe would refuse to serve if elected or that Cromwell would arrest him before he could take his seat. More meetings were held, right up to the morning of the election when a final decision was reached to support their agreement with Bridge. George Booth accepted the nomination to stand in Bradshawe's place.

Bradshawe and his old patron and friend, Sir William Brereton, were now forced to take a stand against the confederates, hoping to be selected by acclamation. Henry Bradshawe thought that Brereton's popularity in the county was not sufficient to match John Bradshawe's, thereby embarrassing Brereton. Ludlow reported that a letter from Cromwell calling for the rejection of Bradshawe was read aloud by the sheriff in the election hall. That seems unlikely. Neither Brereton or Henry Bradshawe, who were present, make any mention of it. Cromwell's letter, however, was certainly circulating among the gentry.

According to Henry Bradshawe's account of the election, written in a letter to his brother dated September 5:

I do perceive you have a Hint of our late intended Election, the manageing whereof did not a little trouble me, yet I did not hold it safe further solely to discover myself then to testify my dissenting from both Sheriff and his favourites in his most apparent illegal proceedings; which was to his and their faces both in the Hall and upon the common excepted against and generally complained of . . . a great number of whose voters (,) if not the greater half (,) were also for you . . . both in the Shire Hall and upon the Common, you being in both places Nominated by the people of their free accord . . . the majority of people continued crying up your name and requiring the poll.

Despite this, the sheriff refused to allow a poll, and on a show of hands declared the four nominess of the confederates elected for the county of Chester. Bradshawe and Brereton were excluded. The city of Chester had its own MP; Edward Bradshaw, brother of Richard Bradshaw of Hamburg, was elected for the city of Chester in the 1656 election.

Later Brereton prepared a petition claiming the sheriff's declaration was false. "Sir William Brereton was duly elected one of the knights to serve in Parliament of the said County by the greater number of freeholders and such as had voices at the election. Nevertheless the said sheriff in pursuance of his design wilfully refused and would not grant the poll, but hath made return of knights to serve for the same county, omitting the said Sir William Brereton, although he was duly elected."

Brereton left Bradshawe out of the petition at Bradshawe's insistence, as a later letter will show.

Brereton presented his petition to a grand jury, backed by his own eyewitness testimony. The grand jury presented this in open court before Chief Justice John Bradshawe, but the panel from which this jury was chosen had been nominated by Philip Egerton, who was still sheriff. It came to nothing, and in any case, Cromwell excluded three of the four new Cheshire county MPs when they arrived in London. Wainwright wrote to Richard Bradshaw in Hamburg:

you need not be sorry for our friend (Lord Bradshawe) *he is far more safe as he is to be doing those public and private duties he is called unto . . . for if he had received the respects the country would have showed him, he had not obtained that they had chose him for.*

Bradshawe confirmed his own caution and concern to an unknown correspondent[24] on the September 16:

Your letter of the 12th instant is received and your former narrative touching the Cheshire Election carne likewise to hand for both which and your care, pains, and faithfulness therein expressed and by your actings manifested this return thanks and prayers . . . tend this same to those honest friends who have showed their good will in the late and troublesome business at Chester. I am much trouble(d) and startled at the Petition[25] your last letter speaks of and if any such thing be looke (d) upon as a Design in the countryverse of it, yet further to lessen me in your parts. I have a good title in my place as Parliament or Patent can make one, not impeached but confirmed rather by the Instrument of the present government which the Protector is sworn not to violate but to observe and cause to be observed. If either then the old law or the new stands or yet the Protector keep his oath I am safe enough and none needs to beg favour for me; But if force be determined and in any particular the law and property be trod under foot the case being every man's in the consequence of it I shall be content to suffer and tarry God's time for righting of one, Nor would have the time anticipated or my condition bettered by any unworthy application in my behalf. If the hand of violence prevent me from meeting the public Sessions (which by this time I suppose are warned and published) the county who will also therein suffer(,) may then consider what on your part is fit to be done and to whom to complain (if a Parliament be sitting). In the interim such courses as are now in agitation may be better forborne than proceeded in, neither can I look upon your Designers of them as wise or real friends. Thus much see you impart as any mind and Resolution as you shall see occasion. Concerning your Manchester Mistress my advice is you be assured in the 1st place that she be free to place her affection and unengaged to any other not preceding(,) If there be any strong suspicion of such a matter. Only if she do not be cleared Then Cooke will to it, that you can love her and in case you close that you can hope to live a contended and comfortable life with her in regard of what you can see and hopefully judge of her or else in the name of God meddle not but withdraw betimes and in the fairest manner you can that no Reflections be either upon her or yourself (write what happens hereupon). I would have you immediately upon receipt hereof repair to Marple and show these lines to our friend[26] there whose letters I have received and will answer you (God permits) by G.N[27] of Stockport. In the meantime I acknowledge his very great and affectionate care to me wards and think myself much in his Debt for it. Speak with W.W. also of these things and with whom else you will that they be not cojoined with the Devices and fair Glosses of those who carryon the Petition, If there be any further doings in it . . . (there follows a discussion of money that Bradshawe hopes to lend to his correspondent) . . . *be very careful how and with whom you converse never forgetting the honest heathens's advice honeste vivere nimini nocere suum eingue tribuere and always having in mind Paul's 3 Adverbs Pie Juste Sobrie.*

Bradshawe dispatched a second letter, dated September 27, to Henry Cromwell, the protector's younger son and at that time lord deputy of Ireland:

> *My Lord—I know It is not out of your Lordship's memory what passed at my last appearance before His Highness and the Council at which time I was occasioned to declare my purpose to procede in the execution of my judical office in the 4 counties to which I relate and the obligations upon me which neccessitated me to such Resolution. In pursuance thereof the assizes and great session are appointed to be held in those places respectively and those at Chester are to begin on Monday indecipherable word next this time of the year being the usual season for those occasions which in regard to myself and Duty I could no longer neglect. The conscientious consideration of what herein is incumbent upon me to do at least to endeavour (wherein the discharge of my Lord Protector's own oath as to doing Justice in those parts is also clearly involved) I hath been and with me the cogent argument to continue in the intention by me formerly Declared wherein for approbation I dare presume (any case and all circumstances duly weighed) your Lordship's own Judgement will concur as being satisfied that thereby I neither offend old Law nor new but should do both if I did otherwise and indeed besides wrongly my conscience with the hazard and Brand of perjury incur the penalty of forfeiting my office with such other penal blemishes as any honest man (in his right wits) would willingly avoid.*
>
> *My Lord: I have according to opportunities as the Lord hath been pleased to vouchsafe unto me and to the best of my abilities endeavoured in the course of that part of the magistracy entrusted to my charge to answer the ends of Government in being a terror to evil works and workers and a prayer for them that do well and I trust through your assistance of Divine Grace to hold on in so doing and when my call to further actings of this public nature through whatsoever providence shall cast it and I shall yet have the comfort of my Integrity and plain-heartedness in these things.*
>
> *My Lord: Your Ingenuity and candor to all and particular Respect often manifested to myself (ever by one to be great fully acknowledged and remembered) give me the boldness to transmit and Leave these lines with you. And if thereby and by your good means misconstruction may be prevented or any evil consequences thereof (whereof I am not conscious to myself of giving any real cause) I shall happily attain my designs and hope be engaged for all your noble favours to express myself at all times.*[28]

He entrusted delivery of the letter to the hands of Colonel Sankey, who Thurloe implicated along with George Bishop and Thomas Scott in the Wildman plot.

This was the closest Bradshawe would come to an apology for his quarrel with Cromwell.

Cromwell and Thurloe had been engaged in a running battle with the judiciary. Without their support he could not legalize his government. His dismissal of Chief Justice Rolle had angered many judges, and whatever their own personal opinions of Bradshawe, they would have stood by a colleague. It is obvious that his Cheshire friends strongly supported him. The council passed an order September 29, 1656, that Serjeant Bradshawe be permitted to go on his circuit. Whether this had anything to do with the intercession of Henry Cromwell is open to speculation.

Chester Sessions were held Monday, October 6, before John Bradshawe and Thomas Fell. Richard Golborne, constable of Chester Castle, brought Ellen Beech and Anne Osboston before the court. "They say that they are not guilty of the trepass or murders . . . and hereupon for good or evil do put themselves upon the country. John Bradshaw, Esq.,[29] who for the Lord Protector (i.e. the prosecutor) doth here on that behalf follow for the said Lord Protector doth the like." The jurors say they are guilty, sentenced to be hanged. They were hanged October 15 at Boughton about three o'clock in the afternoon. Anne Thornton was hanged at the same time. Sheriff Philip Egerton would have seen to the three executions.

Anne Thornton, late of Eyton in Cheshire, widow, of Febrary 9, 1655/56, and on other days and times at Eccleston, "not having God before her eyes, but by the instigation of the Devil being moved and seduced (did) with force and arms wickedly, devilishly, and feloniously (devise) exercise and practice certain devilish and wicked acts and Incantations called Witchcrafts, Inchauntments, Charmes, and Sorceries in and upon one Daniel Finchett, son of Ralph Finchett of Eccleston, yeoman, being an infant of the age of three days . . . whereby he, the said Daniel for the 9th February . . . until the 11th day of same month did languish, and die. And so the Jurors . . . upon their oath . . . Do say Anne Thornton . . . Upon the 11th day of February, at Eccleston, did kill and murder contrary to the form of the statute in that case made and provided, and againsts public peace."

It was during this time, according to Clarendon, that Cromwell endeavored to soften Bradshawe's opposition to the Protectorate policies. Bradshawe was offered a patent of nobility and a place in the proposed new Other House. Bradshawe steadfastly refused Cromwell's overtures. Whitelocke wrote, late in 1657: *the dislike between them was perceived to increase.* Godwin thought that Cromwell thrust first-rate men out of his government to make way for persons of inferior qualitites. He specifically named Vane, Bradshawe, and Harrison among the first-rate men; Thurloe, Lambert, and Lockhart among the latter.

A strange case was presented in a true bill at Middlesex court sessions, September 1, 1657[30]. "Anthony Bradshaw, late of the said parish, labourer, made of copper brass tin and other mixed metals certain false and counterfeit moneys—King Charles half-crowns and The Commonwealth of England half-crowns." Anthony put himself on the court and "did not fly."

It seems John Bradshawe's friends witnessed in him a sense of cynical humour that most historians haven't credited to this stern regicide. Sir William Pershall was a great friend of John Bradshawe and fellow member of the Society of Gray's Inn. During the Protectorate, Pershall found himself obliged to apply to Bradshawe for assistance. "I have heard Sir William affirm to the gentlemen, his friends," says Dr. Oliver, "at the club or meeting held at the Hen and Chicken Court, near St. Dunstan's Church in Fleet Street, where Sir William constantly resorted, that he had experienced (Bradshawe's) favours to himself and others." Anthony Windsor adds that on one occasion of Sir William calling on Bradshaw, the latter told him he was studying politics, to wit, a paper of Cecil's, "and pray you, see how you papists are to be dealt with." The sum of the paper was that the penal laws must never be taken off, but that "when Papists begin to be too popular and agreeable to their neighbours, and even to be thought to deserve the priviledges and freedom of other subjects . . . then to obviate and allay this good opinion, the ministry must be sure to fix some odious design upon them, which could never fail to be believed by the generality of the common people, and then they might put the penal laws into execution, to what degree they should think necessary against them."[31]

Lucy Walter, mistress of the future King Charles II, came into contact with Bradshawe. After the Restoration, William Disney stated that he had heard Bradshawe learned something about a pension or dowry paid to Lucy, alias Mrs. Barlow, from his Majesty. It seems Bradshawe had access to her papers and may have retained some evidences. A son, the future Duke of Monmouth, had been born to Lucy just ten weeks after the execution of King Charles I. It may have appeared to Clarendon, for reasons of royal succession, the story of a marriage between Lucy and Prince Charles should be suppressed at all costs.[32]

Bradshawe's wife must have died about his time, although one source reports that she died in late 1655. That seems inaccurate. In a codicil to his will, Bradshawe had made his wife the executor in September 1655. Wainwright had reported to Richard Bradshaw September 4, 1657:

I did your respects to the Lord Bradshaw and his Lady to their own hands this day at Yeld (Guild) Hall.

One thing is certain, she predeceased Bradshawe and was buried in Henry VII's chapel at Westminister Abbey.

Notes to Chapter 14

1. The Bill for a new representative: the dissolution of the Long parliament, April 1653, *English Historical Review*, lxxxvi, (1971), A. B. Worden. *The Rump Parliament*, (Cambridge Univ Press, 1974).
2. Sean Kelsey, *Inventing a Republic,* (Manchester, 1977).
3. J.P. Earwaker, *East Cheshire*, London, (1880), John Bradshawe's sister, Anne, married Ralph Fallowes of Fallowes Hall in Alderley. Their daughter, Elizabeth, married Ralph Furnivall of Milne House in Chelford in 1650. This was the Elizabeth who was "bewitched to death" in 1654. Ralph Furnivall died about 1661. Ralph and Elizabeth Furnivall had two daughters; Elizabeth, and Anne who married Philip Leycester.
4. Praise-God Barebone was one of three brothers, each of whom had a sentence for a given name; Christ Came Into The World to Save Barebone, and If Christ Had Not Died Thou Hadst Been Damned Barebone.
5. J. P. Earwaker, *The History of the Church and parish of St. Mary-on-the-Hill*, *Chester*, (1898). 28, 29—"This was John Bradshaw, of Congleton, Esq., the Attorney-General for the County Palatine of Chester, who although bearing the same names as the celebrated John Bradshawe, (Regicide) the Chief Justice of Chester, before whom the trial were held, was no relation to him. Much confusion has arisen between these two persons." See also C. L'Strange Ewen, *Witchcraft and Demonism,* (London, 1933),
6. *Bellot Mss*, John Rylands Library; According to Brayley, the antiquary, Bradshawe had a residence at Walton-on-Thames, a short distance from the back of Church Street in a small close. It would have been an easy twelve mile ride from Marvell's residence in Eton to Walton-on-Thames. In Brayley's time Bradshawe's house was let out in tenements to labourers and was still in that condition when Mrs. Anna Maria Hull visited in 1853. In her *Pilgrimages to English Shrines* Mrs. Hull gives a woodcut of the interior of a large room on the ground floor, showing a heavily-carved overmantle, paneled wainscoting and carved beams supported on massive fluted columns. Tradition reports two subterrean passages, one leading to the palace of Oatlands, and the other to the neighbouring demense of Ashley Park, said to have been the residence for a while of Cromwell.
7. *Cal Comm for Compounding,*1105.
8. *John Watson's Mss*, Bodlien Library.
9. *Nicholas Papers*, Camden Soc., vol II, 83
10. *Commonwealth and Protectorate*, vol III, 31

11. Spital-Boughton, an ancient Leper hospital and chapel, had become the execution place for Chester. George Marsh had been burned at the stake there in the time of Queen Mary. Registers of burials in Spital-Boughton, 1656—"Three witches hanged at Michaelmass Assizes, buried in the corner by the castle ditch, in the churchyard, October 8. Daniel Lyson, *Magna Britainnia*, Vol II, Pt II, Cheshire. (1810), 627. This date does not correspond with the court record for some reason.
12. Camden Soc. *Clarke Papers*, vol III, 42,
13. Ibid, vol III, 45. This, however, does not seem to be the case. The Commissioners for Relief upon the Articles of War reached a decision on Lord Montgomery's case, dated August 5th, 1655—signed by Bradshawe, Whalley, Hayes, Samuell, Warcupp, Oxenbridge, Rowe, and Bosvile. Cal of State Papers, Ireland, 1647-60.
14. *Flint Goal (jail) Book*, vol 3, 163
15. J. C. Jeaffreson, ed., *Middlsx County Records*,
16. Camden Soc. *Clarke Papers*, vol III, 68,
17. Ludlow, *Memoirs*,
18. Thurloe, State Papers, vol V, 304.
19. Ibid, vol V, 317.
20. Thomas Marbury of Marbury was half-brother of John Bradshawe's wife. Peter Brooke was Thomas Marbury's brother-in-law.
21. J. S. Morrill, *Cheshire 1630-1660: County Government and Society &c.*,(Oxford Univ Press, 1974), Bradshawe, as well as Cromwell, had been concerned that large quantities of malt from barley was being diverted into beer-brewing with consequent effect on food prices. Of concern also was the fear that ale-house keepers would take in wanderers and so increase the burden on the parish poor law. Cromwell, during the Protectorate, had written to Bradshawe "I desire that a more than ordinary care may be had in the suppressing the multitude of alehouses, and a severe punishment of the abuses thereof, for I fear that the dealing of Justices and grand juries have been too overly & superficial in that matter." The Justices of the Peace put into effect a plan devised by Bradshawe. According to the plan each township would be allowed two ale-houses, with extra allowance made in townships where there was a parish church, market towns, and on some major highways. Those which stood "forth on the common road," which could not "give lodging or entertainment to wayfairing men," or which could not give adequate sureties, were to be automatically suppressed. Col. Worsley was taking Bradshawe's plan to the limit.

22. L. J. Ashford, *The History of The Borough of High Wycombe*, (London, 1976). Nicholas Bradshawe was Mayor of High Wycombe in 1649/50 and had been summoned before the Council of State in London where several restrictions were placed upon his borough. He secured the Mayoralty for one of his collaborators in 1650/51. Once again the Council of State intervened, feeling that Nicholas and his friends were not well-affected toward Parliament. Stephen Bates was sent to High Wycombe to be Mayor at the Council's order. Nicholas Bradshaw rebuffed him. Maj. Gen. Tobias Bridge, a Col. at the time, was sent to High Wycombe in January 1656 to quell a dispute over misappropriation of charity funds. Blame was laid upon Nicholas Bradshaw who had been Mayor of High Wycombe in 1653/54, even though the alleged offense had occurred in many years before. Nicholas was not a royalist and even Col. Bridge did not accuse him of that. He had taken the Commonwealth Oath and had assented to the election of Thomas Scott, Lord President John Bradshawe's spymaster, as High Steward of Wycombe. In Cromwell's Protectorate parliaments Tobias Bridge and Thomas Scott represented High Wycombe. Nicholas Bradshaw resented the Commonwealth's central government interference in High Wycombe's local privilege. In 1663 he was once again Mayor. His son George Bradshaw was, briefly, Mayor in 1688.
23. Margaret M. Verney, *Memoirs of the Verney Family*, vol III, 283-4,.
24. The address is torn off. Hugh Bellott believed the correspondent was George Lowe of Congleton. George Lowe had been a Sergeant in William Fallowes regiment at the Battle of Worcester, and a close friend of Henry Bradshawe of Marple.
25. Sir William Brereton's petition protesting the election.
26. Bradshawe's brother, Henry Bradshawe of Marple. It appears from this, and a later letter, from Henry to John, that they feared direct communication.
27. Probably George Newton, John Bradshawe's brother-in-law.
28. *Trans., Hist Soc of Lancs and Ches*, vol II, pps 68, 69.
29. See note 5.
30. J. C. Jeaffreson, ed. *Middlesex County Records*, Vol III.
31, *Chronicle of St Monica's*, Dr. Oliver's Recollections.
32 Sir George Scott, O.B.E., *Lucy Walters Wife or Mistress*, (1947), Sir Richard Bulstrode, *Memoirs and Reflections upon the Reign and Government of King Charles I and King Charles II*. Bulstrode thought that Bradshawe's "relatives" had great enthusiam for the Duke of Monmouth later on. "We are told that when during his northern progress in 1682 the Duke of Monmouth

having lately passed up and down the kingdom in a manner which gave much offense to his Majesty; and having at WestChester where the mayor being a Fanatick, and his wife neice to the late Bradshaw, the Great Traitor, his Grace was very well received by them."

CHAPTER FIFTEEN

Bradshawe's Homes

✠

IT HAS BEEN generally assumed that Bradshawe retired to Cheshire during the six Protectorate years. There are, however, no records that indicate he maintained any long-term residence in Cheshire. Clear evidence of his palatial residences in Westminster, Somer Hill near Tonbridge, Walton-on-Thames, and Fonthill-Gifford does exist. As befits a man of his prominence, he would have travelled in grand style between his homes. A story was told about the highway robbery of Bradshawe. Capt. James Hind, the former Royalist scoutmaster who had escaped the king's defeat at Worcester, made an unsuccessful attempt to rob Cromwell, but he had more success when he confronted Bradshawe.

Figure 28. Bradshawe's House in Congleton

"The place where this rencontre happened was upon the road between Sherborne and Shaftesbury. The Serjeant was much in state in a traveling chariot drawn by six horses. Hind rode up to the side of the carriage and demanded the Serjeant's money, who, supposing his name would carry terror with it, told him who he was. Quoth Hind, I fear neither you nor any king-killing villian alive. I have now as much power over you as you lately had over the king, and I should do God and my country good service if I made the same use of it; but live, villian, to suffer the pangs of thine own conscience, till justice shall lay her iron hand upon thee, and require an answer for thy crimes, in a way more proper for such a monster, who art unworthy to die by any hands, but those of the common hangman, and at any other place than Tyburn. Nevertheless, although I spare thy life as a regicide, be assured that unless thou deliverest thy money immediately thou shalt die for thy obstinacy'. Bradshawe began to be sensible that the case was not now with him, as it had been when he sat at Westminster Hall attended by the whole strength of the Parliament. He put his hand in his pocket and pulled out about forty shillings in silver which he presented to the Captain, who swore he would that minute shoot him through the heart if he did not find coin of another specie. The Serjeant at last gave the Captain a purse full of Jacobuses.

Hind having thus got possession of the cash, he made Bradshawe yet wait a considerable time longer, while he made the following eulogium upon money.

'This, sir, is the metal that wins the heart forever. O precious gold, I admire and adore thee as much as either Bradshawe, Pryn, or any other villian of the same stamp who for sake of thee would sell their Redeemer again, were He now upon earth. This is the incomparable medicament which the Republican physicians call the wonder-working plaister. It is truly catholic in operation, and somewhat of a kin to the Jesuit's Powder, but more effectual. The virtues of it are strange and various, it makes justice deaf as well as blind, and it takes out spots of the deepest treason as easily as Castile soap does common stains; it alters men's constitutions in two or three days more than a virtuoso's transfusion of blood can do in seven years. It is a great Alexispharmick, and helps poisonous principles of rebellion, and those that use them. It miraculously exalts and purifies the eyesight and makes traitors behold nothing but innocence in the blackest malefactor. It is a mighty cordial for a declining cause; it helps faction and schism as certainly as the itch is destroyed by butter and brimstone. In a word it makes fools wise men and wise men fools, and both of them knaves. The very colour of this precious balm is bright and dazzling. If it be properly applied to the fist, that is, in a decent manner, and a confidential dose, it infallibly performs all the above-mentioned cures and many others too numerous to be here mentioned.'

Having finished, he pulled out his pistol, and said, 'You and your infernal crew have a long while run on, like Jehu, in a career of blood and impiety, pretending that zeal for the Lord of Hosts has been your only motive. How long you may be suffered to continue in the same course, God only knows. I will, however, for this time stop your race in the literal sense of the words.'

With that he shot the six horses in Bradshawe's chariot and left him minus money and means of continuing his journey."

This alleged robbery must have taken place while Bradshawe was on his way to or from his manor of Fonthill Giffard, Dunworth Hundred, in Wilshire. The manor comprised most of the parish and much land in nearby Tisbury parish and into Somerset. Reverend Watson says that in his time there existed, at Marple, a survey "drawn on vellum, of the manor of Fountain (sic) Gifford, in Wiltshire, part of the possessions of the Right Honourable John Bradshawe, 1658, containing 2,668 acres, 0 rods, 39 perches . . . also a description of the demeanes of the Honour of Summerhill, (Somer Hill in Kent) being a parcel of lands belonging to the Right Honourable and faithful patriot of his country, John Bradshawe, Lord President of the Council of State, Anno Libertatis Anglie Restitutae secundo, Anno Dom: 1650." In the early seventeenth century, the local court for Dunworth Hundred was held at the church in the town of Tisbury. During Bradshawe's lordship, 1651 to 1659, the court was held at Fonthill House.[1] In his will, Bradshawe left £20 to the poor of Fonthill. He also bequeathed £20 to "Palmer the Keeper at Somerhill" and £10 to "Coysh the other Keeper." Provisions were made for Mr. Dowling of Fonthill and his wife, Mr. Legate the minister, Mr. Heysham and his wife, Thomas Shipton "my servant," old Goddard, Joane "my cook," and others.

Figure 29. Somer Hill, Kent

Bradshawe's most unusual residence was the former dean's house attached to Westminster Abbey. At a meeting of the governors of the school and almshouses of Westminster, dated March 23, 1650, it was ordered "That the rooms hereafter mentioned vizt: The parlor and a Chamber going to it, three Chambers above the Parlor, a Study, the Tower Chamber, a Gallery, two Rooms above the Kitchen, a Buttery, a Cellar. a Coal House, a Wood House, the Private Garden betwixt the Cloisters and the House with convenient Passage to them, Part of the late Dean's Stable unlet, and the Coachhouse, now in the possession of the Lord President be Let unto his Lordship for the term of 40 years if he live so long." On April 4, Bradshawe was given additional space: "The Jerusalem Chamber, and Lower and upper Galleries, the two Chambers adjoining with the Garrets over them being all on the West Side of the late Dean's House with a Passage from the hall to the Jerusalem Chamber and the Garden adjoining." In this house, John Bradshawe would die in 1659. Bradshawe immediately set about making repairs and alterations. On April 27, a carpenter was paid to cut a door, tie the roof and floor, and lay a new floor in a room at the very top of the southwest tower of the abbey. A chimney and new fireplace were added to the room,[2] and most amazingly, two rooms made of oak were erected on top of the tower over the new room. It took thirteen loads of oak, fourteen new casements, 143 feet of new glass, and £48 worth of sheet lead to complete the two upper rooms. The rooms were connected by a wooden bridge and surrounded by "a Rale (rail) at the top of the Tower round about the stairs."[3] These wooden rooms were, in all probability, used as Bradshawe's study and library. From there he could look across all London and down on the Parliament. The populace must have looked up in amazement. Dr. George Bate wrote of Bradshawe, "and in the Deanery of Westminister, where for safety's sake he built his study on the top of Westminster Abbey higher than the like was ever seen before, getting as high to Heaven he could whilst he lived as not expecting to come there when he died . . ."[4] Another Royalist pundit said that a church roof "was the nest of such an unclean Bird I have not heard."

Figure 30. The Dean's House at Westminster Abbey

In July, "the Lodgings which Mr. Paye, deceased, formerly had" were added to Bradshawe's lease. Bradshawe seems to have occupied the house for the next two years at little or no charge. Sir William Masham, who succeeded as lord president of the council, Mr. Blagrave, Mr. Gourdon,

Col Purefoy, Mr. Millington, Mr. Lowe, and Sir John Hippersley were appointed a committee to examine Bradshawe's lease and consider "what rent is fit to be set for the said House for time Past and to come and to consider of the charges that the said Lord Bradshawe hath been at." Bradshawe supplied a muniment to be considered by the committee:

That part of the house which is intended to be leased to the Lord Bradshawe contains only a hall or parlor, a gallery, a kitchen I a dining chamber, and withdrawing rooms adjoining to it, the Tower chamber, some three Lodging chambers I a study, with some other odd rooms not worth mentioning, all of which are exceedingly smoky, lie at such a distance as that they have no dependence one upon another; the quiet of them is perpetually disturbed by the Scholars and otherwise, and these rooms being put into very good repair cannot be worth above—per annum. The little house formerly in Mr. Payes holding contains only 4 Smoky rooms, and two closets being placed upon the top of the Cloisters right over against Colonel Humphrey's house. This house of Colonel Humphrey's is far larger and more convenient having Cellarage &c. which the other wants and is now let at £ 8 per annum, so as if his lordship have the like measure that others have, it cannot be valued above £5 yearly.

Figure 31. Remains of the hearth in Bradshawe's room, southwest tower, Westminster Abbey.

The stable holds about 10 horses and 2 coaches and is worth about £10 yearly.

His Lordship hath already disbursed in repairs and building upon the freehold as appears by the bills 218:17:10

And is to bestow in necessary repairs to make it tenantable as appears by the Certificate of Mr. Carter and Mr. Stephens to whom it was referred by this Committee 149:08:07

In all 368:06:05

The house and premises being subject to casualties and repairs cannot for a Lease for 21 years or 2 lives be valued to be worth above 7 years and a half's purchase and 300 £ of the Sum above (and being accounted as paid by way of fine) will at that rate strike off 40 £ a year of rent.

If it be objected the rooms built upon the 2 towers were not necessary but built for pleasure, It will receive this Answer that it was necessary to cover the towers with lead to preserve them and the very lead came to 46 £ as appears in the plummers bill, and the other materials which are left upon the freehold besides workmanship came to at least 40 £ more and the whole work came to 140 £, so as there will be but 54 £ to be deducted out of the 68 £:6s:5d; remaining above the 300 £ before mentioned to be accounted as paid by way of fine.[5]

Figure 32. Bradshawe's Study rooms built on top the southwest tower, Westminster Abbey. Later additions to the tower are shown in dotted lines.

A forty-year lease, dated September 23, 1654, granted Bradshawe the rooms he described along with Paye's house and the house of Col. John Humphreys, who was then deceased. The rent established was £30 per annum. One stipulation was made: Bradshawe was to allow the governors of the school to use the Jerusalem Chamber for their elections. The bills of 1653 and 1654 show that Bradshawe made a new kitchen, a servant's dining room, a gentleman's dining room, and a new staircase.

He also fitted out the "Abbot's Chamber" and the "withdrawing room" next to it as my lady's apartments. There was a charge for a key to two locks for Mr. Rowe and locks for the "Room where the Writing is." Mr. Parnell's room was mentioned. There must have been a large clock because money was spent on "the chamber where the gackwaite (jack-weight) goeth."

John Milton, though now nearly blind, was still in contact with Bradshawe. Emeric Bigot, a French savant, had requested Milton to compare some doubtful passages in a book on the manner of holding Parliament compared with the originals in London. Milton wrote Bigot, March 24, 1658, that he compared the passages:

by reference to the Manuscript in possession of the illustrious Lord Bradshaw,[6] *and also the Cotton Manuscript.*

Cromwell had instituted a second parliamentary chamber, a quasi House of Lords, known as the "Other House," and invited Bulstrode Whitlocke to become a member under the title Viscount Henley. Bradshawe had also been offered elevation to the peerage. He refused. The Other House had been restored to curb some powers of the Commons. Cromwell also set up a special high court against Whitelocke's advice. Bradshaw, as one of the commissioners of the Great Seal, served on this court.

In the middle of summer 1658, Cromwell's health began to deteriorate. By August he was bedridden at Hampton Court. Dr. George Bate and other eminent medical experts attended him. At the beginning of September he died. Whitelocke wrote some were of the opinion that he was poisoned.[7] Dr. George Bate has been named as a suspect poisoner.[8]

Richard Cromwell, Oliver's son, was chosen protector, and a new Parliament was called. All the generals of the army declared their allegiance to the new protector. The new protector reconfirmed Bradshawe's appointment as chancellor of the duchy of Lancaster, December 5.

In the January election for Richard Cromwell's Parliament, the old distribution of just two seats for the county of Chester was restored.

A caucus of Cheshire gentry selected Peter Brooke and Richard Leigh of Lyme. Once again Bradshawe's name was cried up by the popular voice. There was universal support for Richard Leigh, so the contest was between Brooke and Bradshawe for the remaining place. Bradshawe had the support of the sheriff, John Leigh of Booths, who was an old army officer and a longtime supporter of Sir William Brereton. Randle Holme described the election, "the most part of the ancient gentry stood for Mr. Legh of Lyme and Mr. Peter Brooke (.) In opposition of the latter (,) other justices stood for the Judge Jo Bradshaw(e), great Amulation was amongst them, but after three days polling where Brook(e)s carried it, the court was removed to Congleton where Bradshaw(e) did outnumber him, but it was through the sheriff's friendship, for he having take the votes for Bradshaw(e) . . . (text unreadable). adjourn the court, before the contrary parties could come to give their votes . . . attorney Bradshaw[9] made a speech at Congleton wherein he termed Legh a child and Brooke a . . . (sic)."[10]

Sheriff John Leigh's account alleged that Peter Brooke and Thomas Mainwaring had offered threats and abuse at the Chester election, which made it necessary for him to transfer the election to Congleton:

if the sheriff had not upon good discretion forborn to right himself upon the said public affronts there had been great danger of confusion and bloodshed, it being observed that many of the affronters party were weaponed and prepared which by the sheriff's forbearance and care and prudence of Colonel Thomas Croxton Governor of Chester having men at readiness to prevent such inconveniences was happily prevented both at Chester and Congleton . . . That Roger Wilbraham of Nantwich esq coming to give his vote for Serjeant Bradshawe, Mr. Brooke did openly reprove him and in open court checked one William Gandy being a freeholder and passing his vote for the serjeant, telling him it had been more fit for him to have been at home and to have paid his father's debts . . . That Mr. Mainwaring when the sheriff was taking votes at Chester said openly I am sorry you are my kinsman, you are so far from being a gent. & as he was coming from court said to the sheriff in a threatening way, when you are out of your sheriff's office I will talk to you . . . That at the election at Congleton the said Captn Shepley on the stairs of the townhall where the polling then was, asked divers persons who they were for and calling up such as were for Mr. Legh & Mr. Brooke let them pass but kept back such as were for Mr. Serjeant Bradshawe which was likely to have occasioned much quarreling and breach of the peace.[11]

Col. Henry Bradshawe wrote to his brother:

I have not of late troubled you with letters because of your heaviness and the hazard of sending . . . I shall only remind you of one unchristian word which Mr. Peter Brooke spoke in the outter ward of Chester Castle . . . for my neighbor Mr. Richard Leigh was much more civil but did report something of untruths which he pretended came from me . . . whatever they or either of them pretend they are no friends to you or me . . . we stood for God and our Country and he gave good success.

Bradshawe did not attend the first sitting of Parliament on January 27. Because of the dual return, the Committee of Privileges examined Bradshawe and Leigh's claims to represent Cheshire. Bradshawe was reported as duely elected. He agreed to be a commissioner of the Great Seal along with two pronounced Republicans (serjeants-at-law Fountain and Tyrell), but that commission seems to have been temporarily stalled. He took the oath to be true to this Commonwealth without a single person kingship or House of Lords. Bradshawe wrote to someone in Cheshire:

"*I must let you know (whatever the usual practice is or hath been to the contrary), my course hath been, and ever shall be otherwise, for by law elections ought to be unprovided and free, and the freeholders (which term comprehends all the degrees of the county what have votes, for you will not say you have an upper and lower house, Lords and Commons there) are to be left upon the place to make their own choice without being sought unto, or imposed upon by any; and the way of Pre-engaging in a divided, combining manner . . . I cannot well relish that expression of your charging me with concealing me (sic) desires in this elective business, inferring thereby that I should have proclaimed myself beforehand or my desire had been to it, whereas to the former I must tell you, I hold it unlawful as containing a prejudice in it to the subsequent votes of the county which ought to be most united and free.*"[12]

Bradshawe answered the charge that he had received considerable support from the universally hated Quakers in Cheshire, "if they were freeholders and acted as the Law prescribes, why should any be so arbitrary as to exclude them or so simple to be offended at them, this privilege is a high part of their birthright." J. S. Morrill says, "Taken as a whole, this position could be seen as an assault on the whole social and political basis of the gentry. Their right to articulate the county's needs and desires as they saw best would be swept aside . . . If Bradshawe meant what he wrote, and if his views were widely circulated, then the gentry were fighting to preserve their way of life."[13] Bradshawe, Ludlow, Vane, Haselrig, and Scott soon persuaded the fellow MPs to take measures limiting the powers of the protector and the Other House.

On March 28 it was resolved "that is shall be part of this Bill to be brought in to declare the Parliament consists of Two Houses . . . that this House will transact with the persons now sitting in the other House as an House of Parliament during this present Parliament and that it is not hereby intended to exclude such peers as have been faithful to the Parliament from their privileges of being duely summoned to be members of that house." In April a resolution was passed forbidding officers of the army, i.e, the council of officers, to meet without the authority of the protector and both houses. For some time, the council of officers had rankled over the fact that Richard Cromwell had never been in the army yet he retained his father's title of commander-in-chief. Generals Fleetwood, Lambert, and Desborough joined with a group of other officers called the Wallingford House Group to overthrow Tumbledown Dick, the protector. They dismissed the sitting Parliament and recalled the old Rump of the Long Parliament that Oliver Cromwell had dismissed in 1653. Forty-two old members, lead by Speaker Lenthall, triumphantly reentered the Commons. John Bradshawe was out.

John Bradshaw of Congleton, probably the attorney general of Cheshire, died in March, and his will was proved on April 1. He left his estate at Hope in Lancashire to "the honorable John Bradshawe Serjeant-at-Law, Thomas Mawdlesley citizen and grocer of London, and Roger Kent of Congleton for the use of my son Thomas (until he reaches age 24)."[14] At least one of Lord President Bradshawe's dopplegangers was now removed from the scene.

Notes to Chapter Fifteen

1. *P.R.O.*, E317/ Wilts. / 7.
2. The remains of the fireplace still existed in 1998 when I was allowed to visit "Bradshawe's room" through the courtesy of the Clerk of Works at Westminster. The boys of Westminster School have long believed that Bradshawe's ghost can sometimes be seen walking the adjacent triform gallery of the Abbey church.
3. The rooms are depicted in David King's drawing of the South Aspect of the Abbey Church in *Dugdale's Monasticon* (first edition, 1655) vol I, facing pg. 60. The higher elevations of the southwest tower that we see today were not erected until 1740.
4. Dr. George Bate, *The Lives Actions and Executions of the Prime Actors and Principall Contrivers of that horrid murder of our late pious and sacred Sovereigne King Charles the first*, (London, 1661), 534.
5. J. Armitage Robinson, D.O., *The Abbot's House at Westminster*, (Cambridge Univ Press, 1911),
6. Sir Edward Coke (1552-1634), Speaker of the House and Chief Justice of England possessed a rare manuscript copy of Modus *Tenendi Parliamentum—The Manner of Holding Parliaments*. If that copy had come into Bradshaw's hands before 1658, it must have come from Coke's papers. Catherine Drinker Bowen, *The Lion and the Throne*, (Boston, 1956).
7. H. F. McMains, *The Death of Oliver Cromwell*, (Univ of Kentucky Press, 2000).
8. Ibid.
9. This was John Bradshaw, Attorney-General of Cheshire. John Bradshawe the regicide was not present at the election in Congleton.
10. *Harleian Mss 1929*, f. 20; British. Library.
11. John Rylands Library. *Legh of Lyme Mss*, unfoliated filing Box 65,
12. Ibid
13. J.S. Morrill, *Cheshire 1630-1660*, etc, (Oxford Univ Press, 1974),
14. *PCC, 224 Pell, quire 224*, He names his father, Lawrence Bradshaw, and daughters, Penelope and Frances.

CHAPTER SIXTEEN

Death and Resurrection

*How small, of all that human hearts endure,
that part which laws or kings can cause, or cure.*
Samuel Johnson

✠

ALL THE STRUCTURES of Cromwell's Protectorate were quickly swept away by the restored Rump Parliament. General Charles Fleetwood was appointed commander-in-chief of the army. Fleetwood's wife was Cromwell's daughter Bridget, the widow of Henry Ireton. A Committee of Safety was established to administer the government. Side by side with that committee, the Council of State was reconstituted, consisting of thirty-one members. Ten council members were not MPs of the recalled Rump, among whom were Bradshawe, Fairfax, Lambert, and Ashley-Cooper. It appears that Bradshawe briefly resumed his old role as lord president.

All this activity kept Bradshawe from his court circuit and Mr. Ratcliff, recorder of Chester, was deputed by Bradshawe to sit the Easter assizes. Sir Peter Leycester, however, thought Bradshawe was too ill to leave London.

The appointment of commissioner of the Great Seal was again introduced in June. Bradshawe lay desperately ill at Fonthill Giffard in Wiltshire. His letter to Speaker Lenthall relating to the appointment was read to the house on June 9:

Honourable Sir[1]

I have by Mr. Love, a member of the happy Parliament received the House's pleasure touching myself in relation to the Great Seal, wherein as I desire with all humble thankfulness to acknowledge the respect and favour done me in honouring me with such a trust; so I should reckon it a great happiness if I were able immediately to answer the call and personally attend the service, which at present I am labouring under an aguish distemper of about eight months continuance: for recovery whereof (after much physic in vain) according to advice, on all hands (though my fits have not yet left me) to receive benefit and advantage thereby. And further I humbly by Parliament's leave and permission if upon their occasion they shall not in their wisdom think fit otherwise to dispense with me. In the meantime it hath been and is no small addition to my other applications that for want of health, it hath not been in my power according to my heart's earnest desire to be serviceable in my poor measure to the public. But by the help of God when through his goodness my strength shall be restored (of which I dispair not) I shall be most free and willing to serve the Parliament and Commonwealth in any capacity and that through divine assistance with all diligence constancy and faithfulness and to the utmost of my power.

Sir, I judged it my duty to give this account of myself to the House and humbly desire by your hand it may be tendered to them; for whom I daily pray that God would bless all their Counsel and consultations and succeed all their unwearied endeavours for the happy settling and establishment of these lately languishing and now received Commonwealth upon sure and lasting foundations.

Sir I rest and am your humble servant

Jo: Bradshawe
(Fonthi) '11 in Wyltshire . . . in 1659
. . . . scentis Republica primo.

For the Right Honble William Lenthall, Speaker of the Parliament of the Commonwealth of England. These

Consider what it is we ask, and consider whether it be not the same thing we have asserted with our lives and fortune . . . a Free Parliament.

And what a slavery is it to our understandings, that these men that now call themselves a Parliament, should declare it an act of illegality and violence in the late aspiring General Cromwell to dissolve their body in 1653, and not make it the like in the garbling of the whole body of the parliament from four hundred to forty in 1648 ? What is this but to act what they condemn in others A new free Parliament This is our cry.

In this postscript, of all extant correspondence, Bradshawe most clearly states his enduring Republican sympathies.

By July, Bradshawe had recovered some health and returned to London. The Council of State once again assigned him lodgings in Whitehall, and he took his oath of office as keeper of the Great Seal. Illness lingered about him, however, and it seems he was unable to attend sittings of council throughout midsummer. Bulstrode Whitelocke was elected lord president of the Council of State.

Sir George Booth, Bradshawe's fellow MP in the 1654 Parliament, revealed his true Royalist sympathies in July. It is obvious that Bradshawe's challenge to the old gentry of Cheshire had infuriated Booth and his coconspirator Sir Thomas Middleton. Charles II sent Booth a commission, constituting him commander of the king's forces in Cheshire, Lancashire, and North Wales. Booth readily accepted and led the Cheshire rising. He gathered a force of men and captured the town of Chester. Richard Leigh of Lyme had been prepared to join Booth, but he was already imprisoned at York. The Council of State issued a commission, dated August 4, to Col. Henry Bradshawe, on consideration of his past fidelity and good services, to raise a company of volunteer foot and place himself at the head of them as colonel, but before a muster could be arranged, a company of Booth's soldiers attacked Marple Hall. Henry Bradshawe wrote to Booth on the seventh:

For Sir George Booth,
Honoured Sir, The undeserved respect which my late father and his familie have formerly hadd from your late renowned grandfather, and that which I also have experienced from your honor, hath laid such an obligacion upon me and myne as will never by me be forgotten, and I am confident hadd you been acqainted with any designe of any under your command against me, I should not have hadd my unfinished house so rifled, and my estate so carried away, my poor weif, children and familie, so afrighted as they were upon Friday night last by persons

callinge themselves souldiers sent by Holland, as their captain aledged. Sir, I hadd not, nor have I in the least measure advised, acted, or consented up to any thinge against you, or any in your armie, or that hath relation to you, neither was or am privie to any plott contrived, or raisinge of men, either directlie or indirectlie against you, or the cause you have in mind, &c.

Two days later he warned Booth of danger:

For Sir George Booth
I have received certayn intelligence of a considerable armie coming from the Parliament toward our county, and beseech you be pleased to give me leave to intreate you that you would seriouslie consider the cause thereof, of your publike intencions and acctions, and the consequence thereof, and in tyme desist and submitt to the all-seeinge decree and providence of our merciful God. That he alone may be your counsell, guide, and governor, is the hartie praier of, Sir, your thanckful humble servant . . . Be pleased to take notice that our county and Lancashire are the onlie disturbing unsettled ones.

General Lambert was dispatched from London to crush Booth's forces, which he accomplished at Winnington Bridge in late August.

John Bradshawe, though obviously ill, began attending the Council of State. On August 13, an order to deliver and pay to Richard Simpson, treasurer of the navy, the sum of £50,000 was signed by Whitelocke as president, Archibald Johnston, John Dixwell, Henry Vane, H. Morley, Thos Challoner, and John Bradshawe.[2] There is something peculiar about Bradshawe's signature; it is not his familiar, underlined, script. It appears that another hand has signed for him. On the fifteenth, an order to pay out of money collected for the relief of Protestants in Piedmont—£800 toward payment for one thousand coats and breeches provided by Mr. Walton for the soldiers that came from Dunkirk[3]—was signed by Whitelocke (President), Haselrig, Neville, Harrington, and Thomas Scott. Bradshawe's signature is not on this document.

On the twentieth, a similar order, unsigned by Bradshawe, for money out of the Piedmont money was to Lt. Col Clements and John Young: £1,500 pounds for 2,100 tents and 920 beds and mattresses to be delivered in stores of the army and navy.[4] On the twenty-sixth, pay out of such money into public Exchequer of the moiety of the excise of beer, also perry cider and matheglyn (a spiced or medicated form of mead), and from city of London and other places heretofore in farm or out of any money that shall be brought in—£4,000 to Edward Backwell (goldsmith of London) to transport for use in payment of Garrison of Dunkirk and Mardike[5]—John Bradshawe's signature on this document is strong and recognizable as his own hand. On September 1, from money paid by Alderman Viner and Alderman Pack to Mr. Jeffrey Fleetwood—£200 for 1,200 pairs of stockings, 1,200 pair of shoes, and 1,200 shirts contracted by our officers of ordinance and delivered for us (to) soldiers lately returned from Flanders[6]—Sir Henry Vane signed as president and Bradshawe signed in a firm hand.

On September 6, £1,500 was given to Richard Hutchinson, Treasurer of the Navy, for the pay of the sick and maimed soldiers, widows and orphans of the Savoy and Ely House.[7] Vane signed as president and Bradshawe's signature is, again, firm and strong. An order that £100,000 be paid to Richard Hutchinson, Treasurer of the Navy, for the use of the navy, was issued on September 15 and signed by President Vane, John Berners, Henry Neville, Thomas Scott, and Bradshawe. Bradshawe's signature is not his familiar script. It is similar to the hand of Thomas Scott.[8]

At the end of August, Lady Frances Booth had addressed a letter to Bradshawe, which he reported to the council. The council gave order that Bradshawe was to "signify to her that the best course for her husband to find favour is that he and she deal candidly in making full discovery of the enemy's designs, in which Sir George Booth was lately engaged against Parliament."

Seven days later, Lady Booth's messenger delivered to Bradshawe a letter from Lady Booth to Sir Arthur Haselrig, one in cypher from C.R. (King Charles II) to Sir George Booth and other papers, with the first examination of Sir George Booth during the sitting of the council on September 5, 1659.[9]

Thomas Scott was elected president of the council for a fortnight on September 19. Bradshawe, Wariston, Colonel Thompson, Colonel Downes, Haselrig, Harrington, Reynolds, Scott, and Dixwell were added to the Committee for the Fees of the tower. The council ordered that "Bradshawe's report of the orders for regulating the Council" be read at the next sitting.

On October 4, a report was made to the Committee of Safety concerning the list of officers for Guernsey; Thomas Cromwell was listed as an ensign, Increase Mather as the chaplain, and Samuel Bradshaw as the surgeon and commissary officer.[10]

Bradshawe presented a report from the Committee for Examinations in the Earl of Chesterfields case, October 5.

Thomas Scott, as president of the council, signed an order dated October 5 to the keeper of the gatehouse in Westminster *"to receive into your custody the body of Thomas Lodge and him to detain under secure imprisonment upon suspicion of high treason in order for his examination and trial at Law."*[11]

Thomas Lodge of Chipping Camden had been captured in Oxford in September and implicated in the July uprisings. Additional signatures to this document were John Bradshawe, Johnston, Valentine Walton, and Sydenham. This was one of the last documents signed by Bradshawe.

Soon a dispute arose between Parliament and the officers over command of the army. Lambert followed Cromwell's example and dissolved the Parliament and arrested Speaker Lenthall on October 13. Fleetwood, Lambert, Desborough, Sir Henry Vane, Ludlow, and Colonel Bury were appointed a Committee of Safety for all government appointments.

Colonel Sydenham, MP for Dorset, said in council that the army was forced to dissolve Parliament by the call of divine providence. Ludlow says that Lord President Bradshawe, who was present, "tho' by long sickness very weak and much extenuated, yet animated by his ardent zeal and constant affection to the common cause, upon hearing these words, stood up and interrupted him, declaring his abhorrence of that detestable action and telling the Council that being now going to his God, he had not patience to sit there and hear his great name so openly blasphemed and there upon departed to his lodgings and withdrew himself from public employment."[12] Bellot speculated that this took place on the fifteenth, which was the last occasion Bradshawe attended the council. Dr. George Bate wrote from his Royalist point of view:

Lambert turned out the Parliament again; he (Bradshawe) *raves now like one stark mad, slinging out of the room in a fury, and calling them all Traitors, and whilst the Committee of Safety sat, he seeing now all things that would make for the King's interest, goes home and takes to his bed, and never comes abroad more, his wicked body was tortured with many distempers, languishing in much pain and misery,*

Dr. Bate, as the most prominent medical man of the day, probably attended John Bradshawe. If H. F. McMains's speculation that Dr. Bate may have been part of a Royalist plot to poison Cromwell is correct,[13] then Bradshawe's death could be viewed as another possible poisoning.

Henry Bradshawe, Gilbert Gerard, and Thomas Stanley, JPs of Chester, made a presentment to the grand jury at the general court sessions in Knutsford, Cheshire, October 17, that Sir George Booth of Dunham Massey and fifty-five others had voluntarily taken up arms and adhered to the late insurrection. In Lancashire, the home and chapel of old John Bradshaw of Bradshaw Hall was searched for weapons.

On October 27, Henry Champion wrote to Hugh Potter:

Chancery we have not any, because Bradshaw(e), albeit in a dying condition, with a great deal of pity, keeps the seal, and as it is said lays it under his pillow.[14]

Without the Great Seal, the Committee of Safety could not legitimize their ordinances, but they only had to wait. The old Republican was nearly at his end.

Some authorities differ on the date of Bradshawe's death: September 30 or November 18. Whitelocke asserts that he died October 31 of a "quartan ague" which had held him for about a year. It was not an easy death. Often the treatment, with liberal doses of Peruvian bark, mercury and antimony, was worse than the illness. No doubt Dr. George Bate, who violently hated Bradshawe, attended him. Bate had attended Cromwell in his final illness. Ague was a common illness which the people of England blamed on bad air—malaria—although that specific term did not appear until the midseventh century. Two types of ague were identified: tertian ague which appeared in cycles of forty-eight hours and quartan which recurred every seventy-two hours. That could explain Bradshawe's intermittent appearances at the council. Dart[15] gives a Royalist point of view: "That infamous wretch Bradshaw president of the mock court of justice where he impudently insulted and gave sentence of death against his sovereign. He was a dark melancholy miscreant and as well qualified to kill him prince or his father in private as to give judgment in publick. He died in despair i.e. that he should do no more mischief; for in other respects he was infirmally infatuated; his soul went to make its peace the 18th day of Nov 1659, and left his wretched carcass in the Dean's House which was made a present to him for his good services. Thence it was brought to the church and buried the 22nd following. The Restoration following soon after there was no monument for him."

Marchmont Needham's *Mercurius Politicus* for October 30 gives the Parliamentarian point of view, probably written by John Milton: "This day it pleased God here to put a period to the life of the Lord President Bradshaw after a year's lingering under a fierce and most odious Quartan Ague, which in all possibility would not have taken him away yet awhile, had he not by his indefatigable affection toward the Publick affairs and safety in a time of danger wasted himself with extraordinary labors from day to day. For the Commonwealth he always lived and for the sake of the Commonwealth he died so soon. To do right to the Dead when it is now no time to flatter and that I may propound a Noble pattern to our Nation give me leave to say what after ten years observation I know to be true; he was a man of most exemplary piety with no noise or outward ostentation, one that truly feared God and made it the business of his Family to serve him, so that more constant Devotion and Temperance both not seen in any other, A great Patron of Ministers, in his own house and abroad, that were ministers indeed and a true lover of Learned men, yet of none that were either seditious, so that over those whom he once owned whosoever a strict and curious eye; and it is hard to say, whether bounty toward them or abundant charity toward the godly poor were most conspicuous in his Christian practice. For a sound head and heart in things Religious, a rare acute Judgment in the state of things Civil, an even conduct of the administration of State affairs, an eloquent Tongue to inform a Friend or convince an Adversary, a most equal heart and hand in distributing Justice to both, a care of conscience in resolving and courage to execute a resolution, this Nation (I am persuaded) hath seldom seen the like; and it concernth us that remain behind to be earnest followers of his great Example who died the same man that he had lived, always constant to himself, greater than envy, and well-assured of Immortality . . . I cannot but sprinkle a few tears upon the Corpse of my Nobelest Friend and leave the Commonwealth to put on Mourning for so great a loss."[16]

Mercurius Politicus for November 22 reported the day's events, "This afternoon the Funerals of the Lord Bradshawe were performed in a very solemn manner and his Body interred in the Abbey Church, being attended thither from his own house by persons of the greatest honor, now resident in the Town, viz; most part of the Long Parliament, divers members of the Committee of Safety, many Sergeants-at-Law and others of the several Inns of the Court, officers of the Army, several of the aldermen and many of the most eminent citizens of London besides a numerous Traine of other Gentlemen and persons of Quality of all Professions which passed in good order to the Abbey, the whole ceremonie being directed by an Officer at Arms. The Pall was carried up by four judges and four Sergeants-at-Law, viz: The Lord Chief Baron Wilde, the Lord Chancellor Steele, Justice Newdigate, and Baron Thorpe, Sergeant Bernard, Sergeant Littleton, Sergeant Maynard, and Sergeant Crooke.

The chief mourner Henry Bradshawe, Esq. Nephew of the deceased; other mourners were the Lord Terril Nephew of the and the Lord Fountaine, his late Brother-Commissioners of the Great Seale, Mr. Justice Archer, Mr. Solicitor Ellis, Richard Bradshaw, esq, who hath served this Commonwealth many years in the honorable Quality of Resident in Hamburg and been employed in several other publick negotiations with Princes; besides many other persons of quality . . . . The sermon was preached by Mr. John Rowe whose text was taken out of the 57 of Isaiah ver 1 being sufficient he waved (as his manner is) the vain pomp of Funeral Commendations and it was the more fitly done, because an hour was too narrow a compass of time, to comprise the memorials of him, whose services for this Commonwealth are of themselves sufficient to make a complete and noble History."

There is no explanation for the absence of Henry Bradshawe of Marple, brother of the late Lord President. Henry went to law to surrender the role of executor of his brother's will, and the post was assigned to Henry Bradshawe Jr. The will was probated in London on December 16.

Gen. George Monck,[17] governor of Scotland, had been opposed to the army's intervention in Parliament. His belief that the army should be the servants of civilian authority, not the tool of ambitious generals, was not voiced during Cromwell's reign. Now he purged his command of dissidents and led his army south toward London. Lambert mustered an unenthusiastic force to march north.

In Yorkshire, General Fairfax brought out his army in support of Monck. Lambert scurried back in London; the Parliament army had deserted him. Rumors were circulated that Bradshawe's house in Westminster was being prepared for General Monck. Throughout the rest of January, London was filled with rumors. Monck entered London on February 3 where he met Praise-God Barebone at the head of a mob of fanatics. Barebone presented a petition to Parliament for the exclusion of the king and royal family.

Monck countered with a letter chastising Parliament for giving too much attention to Barebone and his mob. Monck restored the Parliament as constituted before Pride's Purge. William Prynne, a great basket-hilted sword at his side, was the first to enter the house. They quickly dissolved themselves. Monck was now fully convinced the restoration of monarchy was inevitable and desirable but said nothing publicly. He committed nothing to paper and secretly sent representatives to speak advice to Charles Stuart in Holland. On April 15, a new Parliament was returned with a Royalist majority. Sir Harbottle Grimston was chosen speaker. Thirteen days later, Sir John Grenville, the king's emissary, presented five letters to Parliament containing the Declaration of Breda and the general pardon. Unanimously the Commons proclaimed that the rule of England lay in the king, Lords, and Commons. Loyal ties immediately began changing as some old Parliamentarians scurried to place themselves under protection of a general pardon. Monck was proclaimed general of the forces of England, Scotland, and Ireland. Charles Stuart began to correspond freely with members of the new Parliament, and on May 8 they proclaimed him King Charles II of England.

Vengeance was now in the hands of the Royalists. A bill of general pardon, indemnity and oblivion was introduced in Parliament on May 9. Everyone in the kingdom was to be pardoned upon application, except those specifically designated to be hanged as traitors and those who would be permanently excluded from holding any office. Of the sixty-seven men who were present at the sentence of Charles I or who signed the death warrant, Cromwell, Bradshawe, Ireton, and Pride were excluded from any pardon and posthumously attained. A bill of attainder involved the loss of all property and a corruption of the blood and rights from or through them to their descendants. On May 15 it was moved that "John Bradshawe deceased, late Sergeant-at-Law, be one of those that shall by Act of Parliament be attained of high treason for the murthering of the late King's Majesty." Twenty-three of the king's judges, though in their graves, were attained.

The Earl of Clarendon said that when the declaration relating to England was debated in the king's council, some thought that too many had been exempted from pardon and it would be sufficient to exempt only Cromwell, Bradshawe, and three or four others.

The old embittered Presbyterian and now member of Parliament for Bath, William Prynne, wanted to extend the death penalty beyond just those who had sat in judgment of King Charles I. Working among the dusty and moldering papers of the early Commonwealth, he searched for damning evidence against his enemies. Although he obtained the thankless post of keeper of the records at the Tower of London, it seems he had little assistance, and he pleaded with the council for a small fire with which to warm his hands in the cold dark rooms at the tower. He complained that his assistants, William Ryley and others, "would not soile their hands, nor indanger their healthes to assist me."

On May 25, General Monck welcomed the Merry Monarch home at Dover. Mr. John Reading, late canon of Canterbury, presented a Bible to the king and delivered a speech of congratulation to him on the shore where he landed.

Reading's speech and Latin verses by *Rich Bradshaw* were printed in pamphlet form.[18] The Latin translates:

> *Upon the most desired return of the Kings most Sacred Majesty at Dover*
> *An humble Sute, or Supplication*
> *For King, and Law, and the whole Nation*
> *The King is Law's life Aristotle cries.*
> *Stopt be the mouth which Royal Law defies.*
> *May Charles the second King, live long and reign,*
> *The Lawes concur at length reviv'd again*
> *Let Protestants rejoyce from bondage free,*
> *Let non-conformists each Exiled be.*
> *Let God Arise, and the King's Enemies*
> *Scattered shall be with their Hypocrisies*
> *The King is living Law*
> *Our King is lively Law, our Nostrils breath,*
> *Light of our Eyes, whose absence worse than death.*
> *Judah's a Lyons Whelp, let us Lambes be,*
> *Since Wolves, and Foxes shamed, Fear, and Free;*
> *Our Shepherd's come, great wonders God hath done,*
> *What was dispis'd is now the head Corner stone*
> *For He the Scepter beareth our Law-Giver*
> *Whose wrath's a Lyon fell to the bad liver*
> *Yet his free Mercy will Him glory bring,*
> *Hence fear ye God, and honour ye the King.*
> *GOD SAVE THE KING.*
>
> *So prayeth the most humble of your Majesties continual Subjects,*
> *Rich. Bradshaw.*

The citizens of York celebrated in a special way. "The effigies of the late tyrant and usurper Oliver Cromwell cloathed in a pink satin suit with that of that base miscreant and unjust judge John Bradshaw(e), habited in a judge's robe, as likewise the hellish Scotch Covenant and the late State's arms, which were erected in the common hall, were all on the same day hung upon a gallows set-up for that purpose in the pavement and at last put into three tar barrels and burnt together with the gallows, in the presence of a thousand citizens in arms and a multitude of other spectators—29th May 1660." Similar demonstrations took place in other cities.

On July 12, the house ordered their sergeant-at-arms to deliver up John Bradshawe's goods. Eighteen of the late king's judges were imprisoned in the tower,[19] twenty were at large,[20] and nineteen would be executed before the year end.[21] John Milton was hidden by Andrew Marvell and other friends who circulated rumors that he was dead.

Thomas Parnell, Bradshawe's old secretary, sued for pardon and soon thereafter fled to Dublin where he had a distinguished career and died in 1685. He was the ancestor of Charles Stewart Parnell. Admiral William Penn would go on to serve with distinction in the king's navy, and his son would become the proprietor of the Quaker Colony of Pennsylvania. Richard Bradshaw, the former Commonwealth resident in Hamburg, served for a while with Penn on the admiralty board before retiring to Pennington in Lancashire. Bulstrode Whitlocke obtained pardon and died in 1675. Dixwell, Whalley, and Goffe escaped to New England where they were protected by local inhabitants and lived out their lives.

In December, Parliament voted to have the bodies of Bradshawe, Cromwell, Ireton, and Pride dragged from their graves in Westminster Abbey, drawn on hurdles to the gallows at Tyburn, and there hanged, beheaded, and buried. On the day of the disinterment, Samuel Pepys was with a certain Mr. Davenport[22] at an alehouse in Fleet Street where they discussed the day's events. *"Which methinks,"* said Pepys, *"do trouble me that men of as great courage as he was, should have dishonour, tho' otherwise he might deserve it."*

James Norfolk, sergeant-at-arms for the House of Commons, began the search for the bodies of Cromwell, Bradshawe, Ireton, and Pride on Saturday, January 26, 1661. Work resumed on Monday, and Cromwell's coffin was located beneath the east end of the middle aisle in Henry the Seventh's Chapel. It is questionable whether Ireton's body was ever found and certain that Thomas Pride's carcass was not found. Cromwell's very rich coffin was brought out of the vault and opened on Monday in the presence of a crowd who paid sixpence each to see the putrid body unwrapped from its lead cocoon. Norfolk let the crowd assume that he had found Ireton. To have done less would have caused trouble. Two coffins were taken out of Westminster Abbey on Monday night and carted to the Red Lion in Holborn. There was no public viewing of the grisly remains, and a guard was mounted. Norfolk may have substituted a body for that of the missing Ireton. He could have brought an unidentified coffin out of the vault in Westminster or could have obtained a body from the body snatchers who illegally supplied London anatomists.

Bradshawe's tomb, being the most recent and therefore easily located, was left until Tuesday. Nevertheless it proved the most difficult as the workmen were overpowered by an awful stench upon opening the grave. It is possible that Bradshawe's body had not been embalmed, although the three-week interval between his death (October 31) and his funeral (November 22) would indicate otherwise. Bradshawe's simple coffin arrived at the Red Lion late on Tuesday.

Early Wednesday morning the three coffins were tied to a hurdle and hauled to Tyburn. Rugge's *Diurnal* recorded the dismal event:

"Jan 30th was kept a very solemn day of fasting and prayer. This morning the carcasses of Cromwell Ireton and Bradshawe (which the day before had been brought from the Red Lion Inn Holborn) were drawn upon a sledge to Tyburn and then taken out of their coffins and in their shrouds hanged by the neck, until the going down of the sun. They were then cut down their heads taken off and their bodies buried in a grave made near the gallows. The coffin in which was the body of Cromwell was a very rich thing, very full of gilded hinges and nails."

Edward Sainthill, a Spanish merchant, recorded another account:

"The 30th Jan being that day 12 years from the death of the King, the odious carcasses of Oliver Cromwell, Major General Ireton and Bradshawe were drawn upon sledges to Tyburn where they were hanged by the neck from morning till four in the afternoon, Cromwell in a green cere cloth, very fresh embalmed. Ireton having been buried very long like a dried rat yet corrupted . . . Bradshawe in his winding sheet, the fingers of his right hand and his nose perished, having wet the sheet through; the rest very perfect, insomuch that I knew his face when the hangman after cutting his head off, held it up. Of his toes, I had five or six in my hand which the apprentices had cut off. Their bodies were thrown into a hole under the gallows in their cere cloths and sheet.

Cromwell had eight cuts (before he was beheaded), Ireton four, being in cere cloths, and their heads were sit up on the south end of Westminster Hall."

John Evelyn, the diarist, reported that thousands of people witnessed the spectacle at Tyburn. Sainthill makes the interesting observation that (apparently) Cromwell and Ireton's heads were more difficult to sever than was Bradshawe's. The bodies of Cromwell and Ireton were wrapped in cerecloth and the cloth impregnated with sticky resin while Bradshawe was in a simple winding sheet. This might indicate that Bradshawe's body was not embalmed.

Pepys relates how on February 5 he saw the heads of Cromwell, Ireton, and Bradshawe set up on the further end of Westminster Hall. The *Kingdomes Intelligencer* for February 5, 1661, reported "The heads of those three notorious regicides Oliver Cromwell, John Bradshaw(e), and Henry Ireton, are set upon poles on the top of (the southern end of) Westminster Hall, by the common Hangman. Bradshaw(e) is placed in the middle (over that part where that monstrous High Court of Justice sat) Cromwell[23] and his son-in-law on (either) side of Bradshaw(e)."

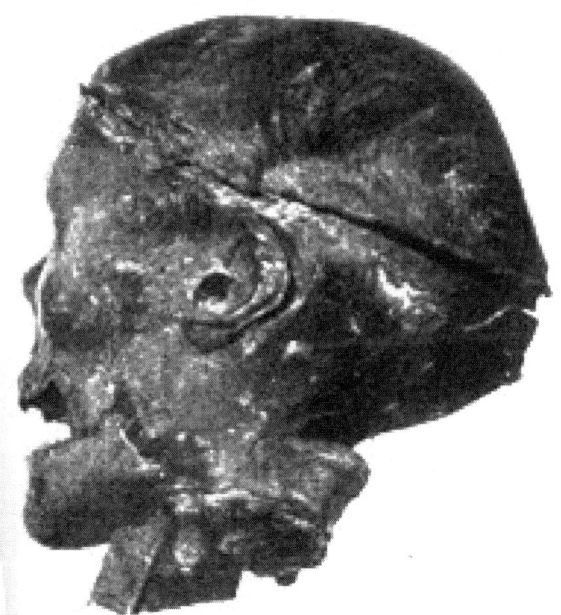

Figure 33. Cromwell's mumified head, photographed in the 19th century

Figure 34. Plaque at Sidney Sussex College, Cambridge, marking the burial of Cromwell's head

Secretary Nichols wrote:

Feb 1, 1661, The Queen and Princess have reached Harve after three days passage. All is quiet. The arch-traitor Cromwell, and two of his choicest instruments, Bradshaw and Ireton, finished the tragedy of their lives in a comic scene at Tyburn: a wonderful example of justice.

The thorough cleansing of Westminster Abbey was undertaken soon after the Restoration. Not only did the memory of John Bradshawe suffer the indignity of having his earthly remains pitched into an unmarked pit, but the remains of Mary Marbury Bradshawe, his wife, suffered the same fate. The king's secretary, Edward Nichols, addressed a letter to the dean and chapter:

It is his Majesty's express pleasure and command that you cause the bodies of the several persons undernamed, which have been unwarrantably interred in Henry the 7th and other chapels and places within the Collegiate Church of Westminster since the year 1641, to be forthwith taken up and buried in some place of the churchyard adjoining the said church, whereof you may not fail; and for so doing this shall be your warrant.

Henry 7 Chapel

Dr. Issac Dorislaus	Coll. Richard Deane
Mrs. Elizabeth Cromwell	Coll. Humphrey Mackworth

Sir Wm Constable	Mrs. Desborough
Anne Fleetwood	Coll. Robert Blake
Coll. John Meldrum	Mr. John Pymme
Mr. Humphrey Salway	Coll. Boscawen
Denis Bond	Mrs. Bradshaw(e)
Mr. Thos. Hardrick	Coll. Edw. Popham
Dr. Twiss	Thomas May
Valentine Strong	Steven Marshall
Mr. Wm Stroud	

All twenty-one of these, including John Bradshawe's wife, Mrs Bradshaw(e), were said to have been buried in one pit dug at the back doors of two prebendal houses, which at that time blocked up the north side of the abbey between the north transept and the west end. John Bathurst Deane, author of *The Life of Richard Deane,* 1870, said that the Dean of Westminster caused, in 1869, the ground to be opened on the spot of the supposed mass grave. He found no evidence of a decent burial such as fragments of coffins and skeletons lying side by side in orderly deposit. Instead he found a confused mass of bones "so mixed together as to suggest an irreverent emptying of coffins into a large common pit."

Notes to Chapter Sixteen

1. Communicated to the *Illustrated London News*, Oct 18 1856
2. *Birch Collection,* Add'l Mss 4197, British Libary #209
3. Ibid. # 214
4. Ibid. # 216
5. Ibid. # 219
6. Ibid. # 221
7. Ibid. # 224
8. Ibid # 227
10. *Cal State Papers, Dom.*
11. Original document auctioned at Bonhams Gallery, London, in 1999.
12. Rev John Watson's Mss., Bodleian Library
13. H. F. McMain, *The Death of Oliver Cromwell.*
14. Appendix of the *3rd Report, Hist. Mss. Commission,* 89; Duke of Northumberland's Mss.
15. *History of Westminster Abbey,* vol 2, 143.
16. *Notes & Queries,* 4th Ser., II, p 138; J. P. Earwaker,.*East Cheshire,* vol II, 71,
17. Gen. George Monck had adhered to the King at the beginning of the Civil Wars and had been imprisoned in the Tower. He joined the Parliamentarians later. He distinguished himself at the Battle of Dunbar. His wife, Anne Clarges, a thorough Royalist, may have had a hand in the Restoration. Rumours said she engaged in the selling of offices and promoting her favorites to the Privy Council. *Continuation of Lord Clarendons Life*; "She was a great mistress of all the low eloquence of abusive rage, and seldom failed to discharge a volley of curses against such as thoroughly provoked her. Nothing is more certain, than that the intrepid commander, who was never afraid of bullets, was often terrified by the fury of his wife." John Aubrey said that Anne was a blacksmith's daughter who had been Monck's seamstress and mistress while he was confined at the Tower. King Charles II elevated Monck to the dignity of 1st Duke of Albermarle.
18. Wing R453; Gerald Maclean ed, *Return of the King; An Anthology of English Poems Commemorating the Restoration of Charles II,* (Electronic Text Center, Univ. of Virginia).
19. Hardress Waller, Wm Heveningham, Issac Pennington, Henry Marten, Gilbert Pennington, Robert Tichburn, Owen Roe, Robert Lilliburne, Henry Smith, Edmund Hervey, John Downes, Vincent Potter, Augustine

Garland, George Fleetwood, Simon Mayne, Thomas Wait, James Temple, and Peter Temple.

20. Wm Saye, John Barkstead, Sir Michael Livesly, Miles Corbett, Thomas Woogan, Mr. Love, Daniel Blagrave, Andrew Boughton, Edward Denby, John Dixwell, Thomas Challoner, John Lisle, Wm Cawley, John Okey, Wm Goffe, John Hewson, Valentine Walton, Edward Whalley, Edmund Ludlow, and Car. Holland. Wm Hewlett was reprieved.

21. Thomas Harrison, head on Westminster Gate and body quarters hung on the gates of the City; John Cook, head on Westminster Hall; Hugh Peters, head on Westminster Hall body quartered; Daniel Axtell, body quartered; Adrian Scroope, body quartered; John Carew, body quartered and given to his brother; Francis Hacker, body given to his son; and Thomas Scott, head on London Bridge, body quartered.

    Before he was executed Thomas Scott made a confession of his espionage activities during the Commonwealth—*Stowe Mss*, fol 185, British Library.—"The affairs of Holland & the war there, were conducted with great advantage by my gaining the Minutes of every Nights debate in their Councils, This was effected by Father Creely's / Capt Holland's emmisaries and by Mr. Bolton and Capt Bishop engaged by L(ord) Bradshawe. I sent Issac Birkenhead to Denmark who gave some intelligence and so did Mr. (Richard) Bradshaw the resident at Hamburgh."

22. Bellot speculated that this might have been Bradshawe's old friend, James Davenport.

23. Cromwell's head was elevated above an ancient tavern on the side the present House of Commons committee rooms of Westminster Hall. It was known as *Paradise* or *Heaven*. At the other end, under the old Exchequer Chamber, was a coffee-house known as *Hell*. Restoration wits joked that this was the nearest Cromwell would come to Heaven. Bradshawe's head was spiked near the center of the Hall, above the spot where the King's trial had taken place. For a full account of Cromwell's head see *Biometrika, Vol 26, No.3 The Portraiture of Oliver Cromwell with Special Reference to the Wilkinson Head*, pp 1-116, Dec 1934.

CHAPTER SEVENTEEN

Remains and Remembrance

When these clay-bodies are in grave, and children stand in place,
This shews we stood for truth and peace
and freedom in our days;
And true born sons we shall appear of England that is our mother,
Gerrard Winstanley,
"A Watch-word to the City and the Armie," 1649

✠

SEVENTEENTH-CENTURY ENGLISH REPUBLICANISM, inspired by elements of classical Greek, Rome, Venice, and Old Testament Israel, contained many diverse points of view. Gerrard Winstanley and the Digger movement urged the formation of a collectivist state guided by inner light. John Lilburne's Levelers wished to widen the male voting franchise beyond just freeholders.

The particular republicanism of John Bradshawe and his small band of like-minded colleagues looked to the future for hopes of progress undisclosed by the past. What also developed was the germ of a stunning idea "That man is actually capable of governing himself."[1] Gerrard Winstanley's radical Digger movement proclaimed "Every single man, Male and Female, is a perfect Creature of himself." "Reason makes a man live moderately and peacefully with all . . . and why? . . . Because this man stands in need of others and others stand in need of him; and therefore makes a man do as he would be done unto." If people would subject themselves to reason, then they need "not run abroad after any Teacher and Ruler."

The definition of "man" as a single person, rather than a society or the family, was relatively new. The word "individual" was first applied to a single human being in 1626.[2] The concept that an individual could decently govern himself without the restraining influence of the bishops, the law courts, and the monarchy would only be developed later.³

Bradshawe's republicanism did not quite stretch to the thought of an unbridled individual governing himself. Down that path lay the excesses of Tudor court and the execution of an unbridled individual monarch. Bradshawe had issued the April 1649 order to disperse Winstanley's Digger colony off of St. George's Hill. Still he could envision the right of a people to organize into a body politic free from external interference. This had flowed from the pre-1649 coordination principle that sovereignty was shared equally by the Lords, Commons, and the king. Supremacy was being claimed for the Commons alone by the time of the king's trial, in fact, supremacy for the "Rump" of the Commons remaining from Pride's Purge. After the king's execution, the new republic rested upon the sovereignty of the Rump and its committees, the verdicts of the high court of justice, the executive ability of Bradshawe's Council of State, and the enforcement of Cromwell's army, all for the commonweal.⁴ Milton maintained, in 1651, the Commonwealth was superior to the monarchy because it could not degenerate into tyranny.⁵ Yet few ordinary people of the day would say that they had exercised any right to organize themselves in this form of a body politic. Winstanley had asked why the civil wars had been fought and the king executed if not "to return into freedom again, without respecting persons, or else what benefit shall the common people have (that have suffered most in these wars) by the victory that is got over the King?" Ever since the defeat of the Royalists at Worcester, it was becoming increasingly obvious that England would be ruled by Parliament or by the army.

Cromwell forcibly dissolved the Parliament before it could reform itself and vote new elections. Bradshawe defended the Rump on principle by telling Cromwell "no power on earth can dissolve them but themselves", even though he had small confidence in them. However soiled the Rump Parliament's reputation had become, Bradshawe preferred to be ruled by them rather than the sword of the army. Bradshawe said if forced to accept that power was to be vested in one man, then King Charles II would be a better man than Oliver Cromwell.

During the Protectorate, Sir Henry Vane, the younger, wrote a pamphlet proposing a republican form of government overseen by a house of representatives, a senate, and a president . . . not unlike the republican form established in the United States of America more than a century later.

After Cromwell's death, Bradshawe openly critized the structure of both the Protectorate Parliaments and the earlier Rump. "A new free Parliament! that is our cry," Bradshawe told Speaker Lenthall in 1659.

The Parliament that Bradshawe so fervently urged could, he believed, fulfill their obligations if free from coercion and threats—threats from the abuse of powerful landowners and local magistrates, threats from the pronouncements of Ecclesiastical courts, threats from the sword of an army, threats from an all-powerful anointed king, or threats from the dictatorship of a Protector. A free Parliament would, instead, fulfill their obligations for the good of the people and the country because it was in their own self-interest and self-preservation as a body to do so. Self-interest would guide ordinary men and they need not be directed by their social superiors. They could govern themselves, and they could govern the country. The very existence of the commonweal depended upon the idea of a responsible self-government under law.

This was radical republican thinking in which neither King Charles nor Oliver Cromwell believed. Bradshawe did. It marked a difference between Bradshawe and Cromwell, the idealistic untiring lawyer versus the firebrand impatient general, responsible self-government versus strict government control of the individual. Vaguely similar conflicts could, I suppose, be found in many later revolutions.

The law, as embodied in the judiciary, had undergone radical change in John Bradshawe's lifetime. The Stuart kings had used the law courts and their judge's chancery, ecclesiastical, common pleas, Star Chamber, eyres of the forest, and King's Bench, as royal hounds to harry nobles and commoners alike. One or two judges had risked royal anger. In the 1638, Ship Money Tax case Mr. Justice Hutton of the Common Pleas declared "the subjects of England are free men, not slaves, free men, not villeins." After the great confrontation with King Charles, the judges maintained a degree of independence and professed themselves the people's watchdog. When the republic of England came apart in 1653, Bradshawe disagreed with Cromwell on the independence of the judiciary and the supremacy of Parliament. Cromwell bullied judges, intimidated juries, and dismissed Parliament. Bradshawe insisted that Cromwell violated the law.

Bradshawe certainly had more experience in law, politics, and government than Cromwell. His climb to the higher echelons of local and national government had taken thirty years from the day he first arrived at Gray's Inn: called to the bar from Gray's Inn at age twenty-five; steward of Glossop Manor at age twenty-seven; mayor of Congleton at age thirty-four; high steward of Congleton at age thirty-seven; judge of the London Sheriff's Court at age thirty-eight; member of the Cheshire county Committee for Assessment at age forty; prosecutor for Parliament's trial of lords Macguire and MacMahon at age forty-two; junior counsel for the Parliament, called to the Grand Company of Ancients in Gray's Inn at age forty-three; counsel-at-law for the Committee of Advance Money at age forty-four; counsel for John Lilburne's case against the House of Lords, Attorney General for Sequestrations and Solicitor General for the Commonwealth, counsel for the state and the merchants against Lord Baltimore, counsel for the Committee to Reform Oxford College, and counsel to prosecute Judge Jenkins at age forty-five; sergeant-at-law, Chief Justice of Chester Flintshire and Wales, and nominee for commissioner of the Great Seal at age forty-six; Lord President of the high court to try King Charles at age forty-seven; lord president of the Council of State at age forty-eight; Chancellor of the Duchy of Lancaster at age forty-eight; MP for Cheshire at age fifty-two; commissioner of the Great Seal at age fifty-six; once again Lord President of the Council of State at age fifty-seven.

Cromwell had much more experience at military matters than Bradshawe. JP for Huntingdon at age twenty-eight to twenty-nine; MP for Huntingdon at age thirty; MP for Cambridge at age forty-one; cavalry commander at age forty-three; lieutenant general at age forty-six; at the fore in the organization of the New Model Army at age forty-seven; commander of the army at age fifty; member of the high court to try King Charles and member of the Council of State at age fifty; conqueror of Irish rebellion at age fifty-one; victor over the Scots at age fifty-two; conqueror of Charles II at Worcester at age fifty-three; dissolved the Parliament at age fifty-four; Lord Protector of England, Scotland and Wales at age fifty-five; refused the title of "king" but retained the right to name his successor at age fifty-eight.

Christopher Hill, writing in the the *Independent*,[6] said "Parliament's victory in the Civil War had been won by arming the lower orders to fight against the old regime: and in the 1640s they began to put forward social and political demands of their own . . . Fear lest the revolution should be pushed too far toward democracy led the men who had defeated Charles I to recall his son in 1660. But he knew, and they knew, that each was dependent on the other. As (Conrad) Russell observes, the Americans and the French celebrate their great revolutions; England's rulers bashed up theirs, although it was the model to which Americans and French revolutionaries looked back. There is no justification for suppressing its memory today."

The postrestoration Royalists were anxious to suppress all memory of the revolution. A kingdomwide search for Bradshawe's papers was instituted. In 1660 and 1661, warrants were sent to the mayor of Bristol ordering the apprehension of George Bishop "who had custody of papers taken by John Bradshawe . . . the better to carryon his execrable designs." Nicholas Bowden of Bowden, Derbyshire, asked for a warrant to seize some law books for himself "confiscateable as being John Bradshawe's" Charles Herne, keeper of the storehouses of the Customs of London, was ordered to deliver to Mr. Bowden seven boxes of books, "supposed to be the goods of Serjeant Bradshawe."[7] As late as 1686, the king was still pursuing George Bishop, "March 8 1686, Whitehall Charles R to the Mayor of Bristol," after stating that George Bishop, city of Bristol, had theretofore had custody of the papers and writings of John Bradshawe "who took divers papers and writings out of the King's Library at Whitehall which could not be recovered." The King ordered the examination of Bishop and a report to Thomas Raymond, keeper and clerk of papers and records of state. Secretary Edward Nichols countersigned.[8]

After the restoration of the monarchy, few people were prepared to stand up for either Republican or Protectorate principles. Among the few was John Cook, who just a few days before his execution wrote to his wife:

We are not traitors, nor murderers, nor fanatics, but true Christian and good commonwealth men, fixed and constant on the principles . . . which the parliament and army declared and engaged for; and to that noble principle of preferring the universality, before a particularity, that we sought the public good and would have enfranchised the people, and secured the welfare of the whole groaning creation, if the nation had not more delighted in servitude than in freedom.

I ask nae ye Whig or Tory
For Commonwealth or Right Divine;
Say, dear to you is England's glory
Then, gie's a hand O' thine.

Notes to Chapter Seventeen

1. John Stevens, *Observations on Government*, (1787), quoted by Joyce Appleby; *The Radical Double-Entendre in the Right to Self-Government in Origins of Anglo-American Radicalism*, 304, (Humanities Press, N.J. and London, 1991), ed. by Margaret Jacob and James Jacob. Stevens' "assertion directly challenged the traditional wisdom that men and women were incapable of self-restraint and that elaborate institutions were required to control human vice."
2. *The Oxford English Dictionary*
3. Joyce Appleby, *The Radical Double-Entendre*; "This belief that human beings (excluding, of course, the distaff side) ought to be autonomous, with the corollary that the authority of family, church and state should be diminished in order to foster this autonomy, was the most radical concept in eighteenth-century Anglo-American thought. It found its fullest political expression when Thomas Jefferson mobilized an opposition movement in the 1790s. In Alexander Hamilton's programme he discerned the re-emergence of traditional forms of power. In articulating that threat Jefferson revealed his break with the classical world of politics. At the same time he showed the political potential in other strains of English thought . . . Acted upon as a truth and an ideal, it entailed radical changes in those institutions which had been created to curb liberty and protect man from himself."
4. *Oxford English Dictionary*, Common weal:—1) common well-being, 1469,—Commonwealth: 1.) public welfare, general good, 2.) the body politic; a state, esp., viewed as a body in which the whole people have a voice or an interest, 1513. 3.) A republic, 1618, 4.) The republican government of England between 1649 and 1660.
5. John Milton, *First Defense of the English People*.
6. *The Independent, London*, (August 27, 1992)
7. *Calendar of State Papers, Dom.*; Oct 1660
8. *Royal Comm on Hist Mss*, Pt I, 5th Rpt, (HMSO, 1876) *Collection of Rev. H. T. Ellacombe*.

APPENDICES

Appendix 1. William Bradshaw of Halton, ...395
Appendix 2. Capt Robert Bradshaw (1565-1628) of Limehouse, Stepney, and Clerkenwell 396
Appendix 3. John Donne, Sir Thomas Egerton, and Charles Bradshaw..398
Appendix 4. Sir Walter Ralegh and Quartermaster Bradshaw........400
Appendix 5. Religion and the Civil Wars 401
Appendix 6. John Bradshaw and Nehemiah Wallington 402
Appendix 7. Job and Joseph Bradshaw of the Massachusetts Bay Company 404
Appendix 8. John Overall and Alexander Nowell, Deans of St Paul's, ...405
Appendix 9. Sir Edward Coke 407
Appendix 10. Bastard Fuedalism) 409
Appendix 11. Nicholas Bradshaw 411
Appendix 12. Robert Bradshaw of Worksop 420
Appendix 13. Bradshaws of Windley and Alderwasley 421
Appendix 14. Germaine Bradshaw and John Curzon of Kedleston 422
Appendix 15. Peter Bradshaw 423
Appendix 16. Anne Bradshaw and Arbella Stuart..........................425
Appendix 17. Thomas Howard, Earl of Arundel and Surrey 427
Appendix 18. The Confusing account of two John Bradshawes of Gray's Inn..................................429

Appendix 1. William Bradshaw of Halton,

The moument brass remains affixed in Halton church to this day. Henry Bradshaw (d; 1553) was the son of William Bradshaw (d; 1537) of Wendover and grandson of William Bradshaw (1419-1477) of Haigh near Wigan, Lancashire. In 1521 he was admitted to the Inner Temple from Barnard's Inn. In 1531 he seems to have been some sort of functionary in the Court of Chancery because he prepared and signed a statement of the suit,—Cade and Other vs Clarke and Others,—which was submitted to Sir Tomas More, Lord Chancellor; *Selden Society*, Volume XXV, *Select cases before the King's Council in the Starr Chamber, A.D. 1509-1544*, pps 184-191 . . . . In 1532 he appeared a plaintiff with Thomas Audley the King's Sergeant-at-Law (Judge at the trial of Sir Thomas More and later Lord Chancellor), Richard Rich (Sir Thomas More's prosecutor), and others in a Feet of Fines for recovery of lands at Stowe in Essex. From 1533 to 1535 he served on the Inner Temple parliament and his signature appears as the first to sign the oldest extant Inner Temple register of 1547. In 1536 he was Reader for the Michelmas term; 1537 auditor of the Inner Temple treasurers accounts; 1540 Solicitor-General to King Henry VIII; assisted in the prosecution of Queen Catherine Howard which resulted in her execution; helped to frame the Act whereby the Colleges, Chantries, and Hospitals, Guilds, and etc. (with the exception of Oxford and Cambridge) in England are granted to the King with all their revenue; June 18, 1545 he was appointed King's Attorney General in succession to William Whorwood where he continued until May 21, 1552; 1547 assisted in framing the King's will; 1548 witnesses King Henry VIII's will in which he receives a bequest; 1552 Chief Baron of the Exchequer to King Edward VI. Bradshaw took the suspected original will of Henry VIII with him and kept it "under seal in the Tally Office." In 1553 he witnessed the will of King Edward and agreed to the succession of Lady Jane Grey. Henry Bradshaw died 27 July 1553. His wife, Joan, survived until 1596 at the manor of Noke. Her monumental brass is still affixed to the wall of tiny church of Noke. In his last will Henry Bradshaw specified his desire that his wife and executors should "promise my daughter Bridgett to marry such gentleman in the county of Lancashire, Derby, or elsewhere as shall be of the name of Bradshaw." At his death Bradshaw was holding lands in Tiddeswell Derbyshire, Orsett Essex, and Wigan Lancashire which was "purchased of my cousin Ralph Bradshaw" (Ralph Bradshaw of Haigh 1480-1554. Mayor of Wigan, heir to his brother Sir Roger d; 1537), other cousins were William d: 1554, and Thomas Bradshaw. This last Thomas was grandfather of Francis and Alexander Bradshaw of High Wycombe;—Cal State Papers 1634, pg 186. Henry Bradshaw also held the revision, by indenture, of the manor of Haigh should his cousins Ralph, Sir Roger, William, and Thomas die without male issue; which they did not. Bradshaw named his old friend Roger Cholmley, Chief Justice of England, as one of his executors.

Appendix 2. Capt Robert Bradshaw (1565-1628) of Limehouse, Stepney, and Clerkenwell

Robert Bradshaw, son of Thomas Bradshaw of Clerkenwell, was Master of Cordell's ship *Centurion* which fought a celebrated five-hour sea battle with Spanish pirates in Straits of Gibralter, April 1591. (Richard Hakluyt, *The English Voyages*), during which Bradshaw's crew of forty-eight men and boys fought off 200 pirates who had grappled four galleys alongside and attempted to climb aboard. "Such was the courage of the Englishmen, that so fast as the Spaniards did come to enter, they gave them such entertainment, that some of than were glad to tumble alive into the Sea, being remedilesse for ever to get up alive." The pirate commander's galley was grappled astern and shot wild fire onto the Centurion, "yet, God be thanked, by the great and diligent foresight of the Master it did no harme at all." Throughout the fight "the 'Trumpet of the Centurion sounded foorth the deadly points of warre . . . on the contrary part, there was no warlike Musicke in the Spainsh Gallies, but onely their whistles of silver, which they sounded foorth to their own contentment." Bradshaw's ship was "shot, spoiled, rent, and battered . . . . very sore, shot through the maine Maste . . . . and 4 of the men of the said shippe (were killed), the one of them being the Masters mate. Ten other persons were hurt, by meanes of splinters which the Spainards shotte: yea in the ende when their provision was almost; spent, they were constrained to shoote at them hammers, and the chaines from their slaves . . . ." On the 15th of Pay 1591 Andrew White, bookseller of London, obtained from the Stationers Company the right to print his copy of The wonderful vyctore obteyned by the

'Centuryon' of London, againste ffyve Spanish gallies, the iiijth of Aprill beinge E(aster) daye 1591. On the same day he also entered a ballad version of the same "vyctorye." Bradshaw joined in the 1591 expedition to the West Indies and Virginia as Master of the ship *Affection* in John Watts's squadron. The efforts of the squadron to seek Roanoke survivors were critized for being poorly organized and more concerned with trade than rescue. They were hampered by foul weather and receding tides in the James River. Bradshaw was a member of the unusual crew of senior captains who were ordered to man the ship *Prince* when it conveyed the Princess Elizabeth and her husband the Count Palantine to the Netherlands, 1613. W.G. Perrin, ed., *Autobiography of Phineas Pett*, 1948, *Navy Rec Soc*, 106-07). Pett said when the ship departed from Queenborough "in the setting of the sails, many seamen being with us that were prime commanders and captains, attending the Lord Admiral and his retinue, had everyone their voice in commanding and countermanding one another, they bred a mere (complete) confusion and put the master (Captain John King) clean besides almost (of out) his senses; so that the fine ship was put on ground at the top of high water, upon the tongue of the spit of sand going into Queenborough . . . . When we saw we were so fast as there was not a hope of getting the ship off that tide, I desired the liberty to sound the place where she sat, which the Lord Admiral easily gave his consent to do. I then calling into the boat with me some of the captains that were masters and mariners, amongst which I chose captain Robert Bradshaw and captain [Michaell Geare for two principal, with others . . . . and finding soft ground . . . . we were satisfied that the ship could take no hurt if she had strength sufficient to bear so massy a weight as she had in her ordnance, victuals, and other things in hold, and her masts and sails above head, with so much company, both of the mariners belonging to the ship and the Lord Admiral's retinue, being not so few in all as 800 Persons; but God be thanked, the ship took no harm at all; . . . . and so with with little difficulty she was heaved afloat into the channel in the morning tide." Bradshaw was an "Elder Brother" and Master of Trinity House in 1622. His first wife (married 1586) was Susan daughter of Thomas Smith of Bacton, Suffolk, and they had three daughters and, perhaps, a son and namesake who died in 1597 at Stepney. His last will and testament (P.C.C. 46 Barrington) makes it clear that he had a second wife "Elizabeth" who survived him.

Appendix 3. John Donne, Sir Thomas Egerton, and Charles Bradshaw

John Donne, the poet, (1573-1631) was a "secretary" of Sir Thomas Egerton, (1540-1617) the great Lord Chancellor in the reigns of Queen Elizabeth I and King James 1. Egerton was a base born son of Sir Richard Egerton (d: 1579) of Ridley in Cheshire and Alice Spark of Bickerton. Both Ridley and Bickerton are near Bunbury and two of the Egertons of Ridley were uncles to Mary Marbury who would become John Bradshawe's wife. Egerton probably spent his childhood at Adlington Hall just a few miles below Marple Hall and Wybersley Hall; he is buried at nearby Dodleston which he had purchased from Thomas Grosvenor. Lord Chancellor Egerton's loyal step-mother, into whose care he came when aged eight or nine, was Anne (da599) daughter of Richard Grosvenor, widow of Sir Thomas Legh of Adlington, and aunt of Thomas Grosvenor (1538-1579) of Eaton who married Anne (d; 1599) daughter of Roger Bradshaw (1518-1589) of Haigh in Lancashire. It is likely he would have been well acquainted with the Bradshaws of Derbyshire, Cheshire, and Lancashire. Edgerton may have assisted Anne Bradshaw's brothers Richard (d; ca 1599) and Thomas to become Sergeants-at-Arms to Queen Elizabeth. Thomas Bradshaw was knighted 25 July 1615 Military Knights of Windsor—St. George's Chapel. Another brother Roger Bradshaw (1564/5-1612) was Cannon of Hereford Cathedral and Chaplain to King James. Egerton was raised a Roman Catholic but converted to Protestantism. He was the first lay Chancellor to have household chaplains. Although not Puritans, they were prominent Calvinist theologians and outstanding preachers, many of whom he sponsored and promoted; John King, John Fenton, John Williams, John Downham, Thomas Ingmethorpe. (*Patronage in Late Renaissance England,* Wm Andrews Clark Library 1983). Both Downham and Igmethorpe were related, by marriage, to the Bradshaw family. Sometime after 1595 Egerton married, as his second wife, the twice widowed daughter of William More (d; 1599) of Loseley House. By this marriage Egerton was brother-in-law to Sir George More, son and heir of William More. William More possessed the refectory of the old dissolved Blackfrairs Monastry in London and his steward, Charles Bradshaw, lived in two upper chambers. In 1576 William More, Esq. and "Charles Bradshaw, yeoman" were defendants in a suit in Chancery brought by William Raye and Margaret his wife respecting houses in Blackfriars.—(R.T.D. Sayles, *Lord Mayors Pageants of the Merchants-Taylors in the 15th, 16th, & 17th Centuries,* 1931); Thomas Rowe, Lord Mayor,1568 "Itm—paide to Charles Bradshaw for making of V J gownes and vj payre of sleves (sic) at xil' pece—vJs." (This could be the same person). Several letters from Charles Bradshaw to More are quoted in the Seventh Report of Historical Manuscripts Commission. In one letter without date, Bradshaw writes "I pray you let Master George understand I have sent him a pair of white shoes . . ." Charles Bradshaw occupied "2 upper rooms or chambers" in Blackfriar's refectory which are specifically mentioned in the indenture when the old building was purchased in 1576 by Richard Farrant for the Children's theatre. This theatre operated until 1584 when once again became a residence. In 1595 James Burbage, father of Shakespeare's fellow actor Richard Burbage, purchased the Blackfriar's refectory and Bradshaw was apparently still in residence there. Burbage intended to install London's first private indoor theatre in the great hall of the old rectory but that plan was delayed and in 1610 Richard assumed full control of his late father's venture. Three years later Shakespeare purchased a house in Blackfriars from Henry Walker, "citizen and Minstrel of London." Walker had purchased the property from Matthew Bacon "a student of Gray's Inn." Abutting the house was an old building called "The King's Wardrobe." This seems to have been merely an investment as Shakespeare immediately leased it; he had previously invested in Burbage's Blackfriar theatre just a couple of hundred yards uphill. *Othello* is said to have been acted in Blackfriar's theatre before 1621 and *Two Noble Kinsmen* at an unknown date. Collier'.s assertion that *Othello* was acted at the Lord Chancellor's house at Harefield near Uxbridge in 1602 was based on one of Collier's many forgeries. A bill of complaint, dated 1615, was addressed in Chancery to Lord Chancellor Egerton by "Wllyam Shakespere, gent" (Jointly with others including Richard Bacon) asking that Egerton compel Matthew Bacon of Gray's Inn to deliver up to them a number of deeds and other papers which had come into Matthew's hands on the recent death of Anne Bacon his mother. Sir Thomas Egerton, having survived his two previous wives, took the Dowager Countess of Derby as his third in 1600. John Donne's years in Egerton's household from 1597 until he secretly married Anne More on Christmas day 1600 were the most productive of Donne's career. Sir George More had been a member of the Inner Temple with Anthony Bradshaw of Duffield in 1576 and succeeded to his father's estates and in 1601. He was enraged when his daughter, without permission, secretly married the poet John Donne. Donne was committed to prison until Lord Chancellor Egerton intervened on his behalf. Sir George More was Lord Lt. of the Tower and had among his prisoners Sir Walter Ralegh, Mary, Countess of Shrewsbury, Arbella Stuart and her lady-in-waiting, Anne Bradshawe, the daughter-in-law of his fellow Anthony Bradshawe. John Donne was created Dean of St. Paul's cathedral in 1621, the year after John Bradshawe, the future regicide, came to Gray's Inn.

Appendix 4. Sir Walter Ralegh and Quartermaster Bradshaw

Sir Walter Ralegh was released from his imprisonment in 1617 and in March set sail for Guiana in the ship *Destiny* accompanied by five or six other ships. The voyage was intended to find a fabled gold mine that King James hoped would solve his money problems. The quarter-master for the fleet was "Mr. Bradshawe." Bradshawe, who is not identified by a given name, was Lieutenant to Captain John Pennington on board the *Starre alias the Jason of London*. The voyage was a disaster and Ralegh's son was killed by the Spanish in Guiana; Ralegh wrote; "God knowes I nevr knewe what sorrow meant till now . . . . my braines are broken, and tis torment to mee to write, and Especially of Miserie." Pennington and Ralegh in the the *Jason & Destiny* returned to Ireland where they hoped to seek sanctuary until they could plead mercy from the King. There was no mercy for Ralegh but he had loyally written the King's Secretary of State recommending "20 or 30 very adventurous gentlemen and of sinyular courage" Mr Bradshawe and others—"to the end that if his Majesty shall have cause to use their service, it may please you to take knowledge of them for very sufficient men" (Ralegh to Sir Ralph Winwood, 21 March 1618) (V.L Harlow, *Ralegh's Last Voyage* Argonaut Press, London, 1932). I suspect, on slim evidence, that "Mr. Bradshawe" was the Captain Richard Bradshaw of the Dorchester Company who had a grant of land in Saco, Maine, as early as 1610. *Cal of State Papers, Colonial Ser. America* 1574-1660, *Colonial Correspondence 1622*, 32-35; Wilbur Spencer, *Pioneers on Maine Rivers*, (Baltimore, 1973). and Henry S. Burrage, *The Beginnings of Colonial Maine*, (1914). Captain John Pennington was briefly imprisoned but went on to a brilliant naval career, rose to the rank of Admiral, and died, a committed Royalist, at Muncaster Lancashire in 1646. He was unmarried and left a legacy to his cousin William Pennington of Muncaster, father-in-law to Sir Roger

Bradshaw (1628-1684), 1st Bt., of Haigh, another committed Royalist. During his lifetime Admiral John Pennington's affairs were managed by Sir Issac Pennington, Puritan Lord Mayor of London, a friend of John Milton, a member of the Council of State with Lord President John Bradshawe, and a signer of King Charles First's Death Warrant. Sir Issac's son, another Issac, became a Quaker and father-in-law of William Penn of Pennsylvania fame. William Penn's aunt was Rachel, wife to Ralph Bradshaw of Pendleton Lancashire. Ralph Bradshaw's brother, John Bradshaw, was at Gray's Inn from 1638. Ralph's cousin, another John Bradshaw, was at Gray's Inn from 1632.

Appendix 5. Religion and the Civil Wars

"Religion certainly played a Part in the English Civil War. Beyond that statement general agreement among historians ceases." For the first two decades of the 1600s Puritanism was loosely defined as refusal to conform to the rites and ceremonies of the established English church, or the presbyterian attitude of rejecting church government by bishops; to suggest that a Puritan was simply one who who championed Calvinist predestination would have been incomprehensible. Non-conformists and even presbyterians were not then considered totally outside the church, just erring members who deserved some latitude. Catholics, Brownists, Anabaptists, The Family of Love, Atheists, and the separatist Pilgrim fathers were considered well outside the pale. There was, in fact, a campaign to altogether ban the use of the term Puritan. John Pym refused to accept "that odious and factious name of Puritans" which opponents were trying to fasten on promoters of a bill for better observance of Sundays during the Parliament of 1621. A belief in Calvinist teaching united the nonconformists and the leaders of the established church until the supremacy of Arminianism was supported and promoted by King Charles after 1625. Advocates of Arminianism, as propounded on the work of the Dutch theologian Arminius, believed that God's universal grace held out the hope of salvation to all People and disagreed with Calvinist teaching that God had divided the whole of mankind into those predestined to Heaven and those predestined for Hell—the Saints and Strangers of the Pilgrim Fathers. After the death of King James in 1625 his successor Charles I made clear his preference for Arminianism: all predestination teaching was forbidden at Cambridge, and a royal proclamation effectively made the Church of England an

Arminian institution. Calvinist opponents were branded *Puritans*. The Bishop of Salisbury summed it up; "Why that should now be esteemed Puritan doctrine, which those held who have done our Church the greatest service in beating down Puritanism, or why men should be restrained from teaching that doctrine hereafter, which hitherto has been generally and publicly maintained, (wiser men perhaps may say) but I cannot understand." Nicholas Tyacke, *Puritanism, Arminisnism, and Counter Revolution,* Sec 2, Pt 4., Conrad Russell, ed. *The Origins of the English Civil War,*

Appendix 6. John Bradshaw and Nehemiah Wallington

Sloane Mss 922, fol 76b; British Library.—Nehemiah Wallington's notes; "A letter from my Cozen John Bradshaw to his grandfather,—Master John Wallington, Concerning the misery and troubles of Rochell—Loving Grandfather dutie and Love remembered . . . I now haveing the opertunity of sending to you by this one Shipp the *Amitie* which onlie is sent to England I thought good to write unto you to Let you understand the paisages of our later designes, which are these briefly on ye XIII of this present my Lord General gave order to shoote a peace of Ordeynance and to put out a penant; in ye fore top mast head to make sign to the leading shipps to way Anchor and to fallon the third time but wee were forced to Lead waie in the Sir Georg and we did linger for the leading Shipps to fall on which att 3/4 flcx:xi came on. but did now as they did the second time shooting of many peeces to small purpose And the tides being at ye lowest after two hours fight came all off againe and nothing doune On the XIX of this month there was called a Councell of Warre and a new way propounded for the attempting of ye enemy which was to gee up side by side by the enemy with men of warre and to send in a maine Shipe to the wall side But God which disposeth all things had otherwise determined of the event for on the XX in the afternoone there came newes that Rochell had surrendered in the morning and that the King had entered with two Regiments of soldiers promising them their conscience their lives their meanes but he would raze theire walls And yt [that] all Frenchmen which were in our Fleete should have 8 days to come in and if they did not come in in yt time to be held as Traytors but as for Monsr. Sabiz and Count Navarre Monsr. sabey his mother and her household he would give them no Quarter There died in this Siege of famine Sixteen of thousand persons the rest induring a world of miserie most of their food being hides, leather and old gloves other provisions which were very scarce att an excessive rate

> A Bushell of wheat at twenty pound
> A pound of bread at twenty shillings
> A quarter of mutton at five pound of money
> A pound of butter at thirty shillings
> An Egge at eight shillings
> An ounce of sugar at two shillings sixpence
> A dried fish at twenty shillings
> A pound of Grapes at twenty shillings
> A pint of Milke at thirty shillings

Also it is reported yt through the famine young Maids of 14 or 16 yeares old did look like old women of a hundred years old This famin was such that poore people would cutt of[f] the Buttocks of dead men as they lay in the church yard unburied All the English that came out looked like Anatanies they lived two months with nothing but Cow hides and Goates skinnes boiled. The dogges. catts. myce and frogges being all spent; And this with a wor.ld of misery besides did they suffer in a hope of our relieving them. Thus much I thought good to let you und erstand The 28 of this month all day and night we had an exceding grate storm that 3 or 4 of our small men being cast away but this day it pleased God to send us a fair winde but our Barge being at Rochel and many Ships not ready wee were constrained to remaine here still, but if the winde continue we shal be at home with all expetie For we have grat want of beare and other provision through the whole fleete most Part of the fleete have drunk water this month I thank God I have had my health all this voyage & I hope I have lost no time in it haveing gott some experience and knowing some hardnes and some pleasure some want & some plenty I have kept a journall of all occurences this voyage which you shall see when I come home if it please God Thus desiring your prayrs to Almighty God for mee and whole fleet with remembrance of my love to my uncle John & his wife. With all my kindred and friends in general I take leave & rest

Your obedient Grand child John Bradshaw
From George Island
Aboard the George XXX October 1628"

Appendix 7. Job and Joseph Bradshaw of the Massachusetts Bay Company

Robert Rich Earl of Warwick and his brother Henry Earl of Holland were major promoters of Puritan colonization. Their names appear in overlapping lists of adventurers, subscribers, and patentees, interested in nearly all New England colonizing schemes. Warwick as titular head, along with his associates Holland, Sir Ferdinado Gorges, and Captain John Mason, controlled The Council for New England. This was an unusual Partnership occasioned by the 1623 merging of Gorges's old Plymouth Company of west country fishermen and fur traders and the new group of Puritan colonizers. Unlike the colonizers, Gorges and Mason were motivated by the lure of profit from seasonal hunting and fishing voyages, not by thoughts of permanent settlement. At the height of the crisis created by mutiny in Plymouth, the assassination of Buckingham, and military defeats, the Council for New England issued a patent to an entity called *The New England company* without Gorges's and Mason's knowledge. The patent, dated 28 March 1628, was so badly framed it infringed on all the land previously allocated to the old Plymouth company, Part of a 1622 grant given Gorges's son, and half the lands that Gorges's Council for New England had given by indenture to John Pierce and the Mayflower pilgrims after they illegally landed there in 1620. When the New England Company discovered the conflicting claims they determined to deal directly with the king, persuading him, if they could, to give them a charter of Incorporation for both land and government, bypassing Gorges and the Council for New England. This was, perhaps, a design of Warwick and his brother Holland who served on the king's Privy Council. Surprisingly, the plan worked and on 4 March 1629 the king issued a charter transforming the New England Company into the Massachusetts Bay Company. There were about 110 investors in the new company including Job and Joseph Bradshaw, beer brewers of London, who served actively in the planning meetings. Joseph Bradshaw (d; 1632-3) was MP for Westminster. Opponents of the Massachusetts Bay Company would later contend the charter was surreptitiously obtained without the knowledge of a majority of the officers of the Council for New England. Gorges did not learn of the Massachusetts Bay Company charter until about the summer of 1631. When told by Gorges to bring in their charter for examination the Bay Company representatives refused, then revealed that it had been removed to the seat of their government in New England and maintained that since their charter was direct from the king's hand they were not subject to Gorges or the Council for New England. In the Massachusetts colony the puritan government leaders were skating Perilously close to civil disobedience when they resolved no man could be freeman unless he were a member of one of the Puritan churches, and that an oath of allegiance was required of freemen, not to the king, but to the Government of the Commonwealth of Massachusetts ! Despite this clear violation of their own charter they successfully defended themselves against Gorges's demands at a hearing before the Privy Council in 1632. In a last act before surrendering authority to Archbishop Laud's anti-puritan Commission for Regulating Plantations in April 1634, the Privy Council issued an order detaining all vessels going to New England until new instructions could be prepared, When issued, Laud I s instructions required all Masters of vessels to see that New England bound passengers took the king' s oath of allegiance and supremacy, and that they attended religious services according to the Church of England book of Common Prayer. It was too late then; England had what would become its most successful colony and the puritans had their own Commonwealth government beyond the king's control.

Appendix 8. John Overall and Alexander Nowell, Deans of St Paul's,

John Overall, D.O., (1560-1619), Dean of St. Paul's in succession to Alexander Nowell. Overall was prolocutor of the Canterbury convocation which drew up the three books of canons and constitutions. After King James's rejection of the books they disappeared from sight for more than eighty years. A copy of the books, in Overall's hand came, after his death, into possession of his secretary John Cosin and from him into the Cosin Library at Durham. John Cosin became a Bishop and during the Civil wars he was resident with King Charles II in Paris and ministered to Charles according to the rites of the Church of England. Bishop Cosin's son, Charles, was converted to Roman Catholicism by Fr. Richard Bradshaw—*D.N.B, Barton, Richard (a.k.a. Bradshaw)*—and entered the English College of Rome in 1652. Bishop Cosin wrote a book in Latin on Transubstantiation which is now very rare. A copy surfaced in the mid-nineteenth century, bearing the signature of Henry Bradshaw, and was submitted. to the Keeper of manuscripts at the British Library for evaluation of the signature. The Keeper's conclusions read in Part; "For the same signature, see *Add. MSS 24845, 24846 ('Reports of cases in the King's Bench, 38 Hen VIII—34 Eliza, '* and *'King's Bench cases, 1—8 Jac I', holographic manuscripts, in French, which may be originals or contemporary copies of Sir Edward Coke's Reports I)*, the first of which also has the signature of John Caley, the antiquary. The signature may be that of Henry Bradshaw, son of Henry Bradshaw, John Bradshaw(e)'s eldest brother. To this nephew Henry, John Bradshaw(e) bequeathed his law library, which remained at Marple Hall, in Cheshire, till 1784, when it was sold by James Edwards,—*D.N.B. James Edwards (1757-1816) of Edwards and Sons, Pall Mall*—bookseller of Halifax,—Omerod's *Cheshire*, III, 408-9 and Nichol's *Literary History*, IV 881.—At this sale it is possible the above volumes may have been acquired by Caley, who was appointed Keeper of the Records in the Augmentation Office in 1787." Another "servant" of Dr. Overall, perhaps a secretary, was Alexander Bradshaw (died 1603) who had been a old servant of Alexander Nowell the previous Dean of St Paul's (see note 34, Chap. One) The original manuscript of the Convocation's first book passed to the Lambeth Library where it was noted by Archbishop Laud. William Sancroft who became Dean of St. Paul's about 1665 was aware of Overall's manuscript and, in 1690, published Overall's manuscript, collated with the Lambeth manuscript, under the title *"Bishop Overall's Convocation Book, MDCVI, concerning the Government of God's Catholick Church and the Kingdoms of the whole world."* Five letters from a John Bradshaw to William Sancroft dated from 1655 to 1665 are preserved in *the Harle Mss 3783; 3784—fol 80 & 218; 3785—fol 41 & 236*. The hand writing is difficult to decipher but one letter, dated June I, 1655 reads in part; "I have received (illegible) yours of December 12th. I confess it to my folly in Part that Rob Beaumont (Beaumont?) makes so light of the (illegible) books. For when I was last in [towne?] Wllym (two words illegible) a number of books I had bought, so without much difficulty (illegible) out (illegible) is my (illegible) what they cost me." In subsequent letters this John Bradshaw, who must have been a clegyman, asks Sancroft for preferment and mentions his wife and family "still at St. Gear. Botolph Lane." He also mentions Mrs. Ann Bradshaw in (illegible) alley, Thamesflood, London.

Appendix 9. Sir Edward Coke

In 1571 Edward Coke (1552-1634) came to reside at Clifford's Inn, London. At that time Roger Bradshaw was "Principal of Clifford's Inn." In November 1572 Coke was enrolled at the Inner Temple where he was joined by Anthony Bradshawe, John Bradshawe of Lye Staffordshire, Baptist Hicks, Roger Manwood, and Roger Downes in the following year—"students of the municipal law in the Inner Temple" as Fuller puts it. He was called to the bar on 20 April 1578, after a period study somewhat shorter than then customary, He was Recorder of Coventry, 1585; Recorder of Norwich, 1586; bencher of the Inner Temple, 1590; Solicitor-General, reader of the Inner Temple, and Recorder of London, 1592; Speaker of the House of Commons, 1592-93; Attorney General, 1593-96/7; Treasurer of the Inner Temple 1596, chief justice of the Common Pleas 1606, chief justice of the King's Bench 1613, and high steward of the University of Cambridge 1614. He came into conflict with Sir Francis Bacon who was warmly supported by Essex, as early as 1593. From the time of his call to the bar he took careful notes of the cases which he heard argued, and in 1600 he began their publication with the first of his "Reports," afterward bringing out ten volumes (volumes xii, and xiii, which deal largely with questions of royal prerogative, were not published in his lifetime) at various dates up to 1615. (See Note 1 above, as regards Judge John Bradshawe's law library). Francis Bacon criticized Coke's "*Reports*";—"Great judges" he said, "are unfit persons to be reporters, for they have either too little leisure or too much authority, as may appear well by . . . those of my Lord Coke . . . ," Coke conducted the prosecution in the trials of James and Richard Bradshaw with their compatriots Steer, Burton, and Bompass for the Oxfordshire Rising, to throw down enclosures, in 1596,—*The Oxfordshire Rising*, John Walter, Univ of Essex, *Past and Present*, No. 107.—The ringleaders were brought to London with "their hands pynnioned and their legs round under the horse bellys and so looked unto as they maie not have Conference one with other in the waie hither." Their pre-trial examinations, headed by Coke, were entrusted to a small but powerful committee of four, including Sir Francis Bacon, who, in violation of English law, had been empowered to employ torture "for the better bowlyinge forth of the truthe." Coke submitted his brevait of the case to Sir Robert Cecil with a recommendation that the ringleaders of the rising be prosecuted for treason under the Statute 13 Elizabeth 1, as levying war against

Queen Elizabeth, rather than on the usual statute 25 Edward III which required the actual levying of war against the crown and a requirement that parliament first be consulted in new cases. The decision to try the conspirators for treason raised important points of legal principle and required some bending of the law. Coke, however, expressed the opinion that there was sufficient evidence to convict the Bradshaws, Steer, Burton and Bompass. In February 1596/7 Richard Bradshaw, Burton, and Bompass were indicted at the Burford assizes. James Bradshaw and Steer are missing from the indictment leading to the speculation that they were already dead from the effects of torture or the hardships of imprisonment. Coke's harsh pursuit of an indictment for levying war against the queen now hit a snag. The Statute 13 Elizabeth I required the offense to be proved by the test any of two witnesses, unless the accused had confessed without violence, but Bradshaw and Burton had been tortured so any confession was invalid. The judges further recognized that the rising had been aborted before any actual "war" had taken place. In mid-April a massed meeting of judges was held to discuss the case,—*The English Reports, lxxix, ep 1227-1228, London, 1900-30*—, and it was generally agreed the mere action of conspiring to rise and arm themselves was high treason since *"rebellion is all the war"* which the ringleaders could make against the queen. Three judges dissented and argued *"that the resistance ought to be with force to the Queen before such acts shall be treason"* citing a statute of Queen Mary which made an assembly to break down enclosures a felony. On 4 June Coke wrote to Cecil urging him to obtain, from Queen Elizabeth, a special commission under which Bradshaw and Bruton could be tried before an Oxfordshire jury at Westminster. Coke had his way; on 7 June the queen issued a special commission to Lord chief justice Sir John Popham, Judge Edward Fenner, Judge Edmund Anderson, and Judge Francis Gawdy. Four days later Richard Bradshaw and Robert Burton were sentenced to be hanged, drawn, and quartered on Enslow Hill, between Woodstock and Kirtlington. Legal commentators, including Coke himself,—*Third Part of the Institutes, 9-10*—, cited Bradshaw and Bruton's case as an important step in development of the law against treason, although some continued to be troubled by Coke's use of the Elizabethan statute, *Historia placitorurn coronae*, i, 132-53, Hales, *Cobbet's Complete Collection of State Trials and Proceedings for High Treason from the Earliest Period to the Present Time*, i, 1421, and vi, 899-906. Coke had prosecuted this early and obscure case with the characteristic vigour which earned his reputation in later and more notable cases. He flung the names of Bradshaw and Bruton in the faces of Essex and Southampton when he conducted their treason trials in 1600. He obtained Sir Walter Raleigh's conviction for treason in the 1603 trial where the presiding Chief Justice Popham extended the Elizabethan statute as it was modified by Statute 1 and 2 Philip and Mary, stating that Ralegh's treason could be proven by the testimony of one witness who did not have to be produced in court. Coke prosecuted the Gunpowder plotters of 1605; Guy Fawkes was tortured. Francis Bacon engineered Coke's downfall in 1616. Chamberlain summed. up the reasons for Coke's removal from the bench; "The common speech is, that four p's have overthrown and put him down—that; is, pride, prohibitions, praemunire, and prerogative." To the very last years of his life Coke was the object of the king's suspicions. In 1631 the king gave orders that on his death his papers should be secured, lest anything prejudicing the prerogative might be published. After Coke's death Sir Francis Windebank came to his house and seized his papers which were held for seven years. In all of Coke's writings he never mentioned feudal law. He did publish *the Compleat Copyholder*, being a learned discourse of the *antiquity and nature of manors and copyholds with all things thereto incident,* in 1630. Compare this with Anthony Bradshawe's writings on the same subject about two decades earlier.

Appendix 10. Bastard Fuedalism

In the fourteenth century the ancient feudal system of *knight's fee* (i.e. military service in exchange for land rent) was breaking down. The start of the Hundred Years War and the scourge of the Black Plague decimated the ranks of fighting men. In the north these events also occasioned a lack of money which was retarding the development of industry and trade. This forced the younger sons of the gentry, as well as the peasants, to turn to the only craft that was paying, at least, food and clothing war. They were retained by their local overlord as soldiers. The Foresters, Woodwards, and Bailiffs from the royal forests of the High Peak and Cheshire swelled the ranks of the English fighting Legions and bound the King, by obligation, to the great Lords of the north and their retainers. Foresters of Fee served their Lord and the King with traditional weapons; bow and arrow, billhook, axe and spear. The northern nobles held sway while simple weapons remained the only weapons of war but with the introduction of artillery, which the northerners lacked money to buy, their supremacy faded. Soon the development of mining and cloth weaving industries robbed them of even their retainers—*The Problem of the North*, R.R. Reid, 1921.—Still suitable men of the right skill and quality, both social and military were not attracted to the new industries. A new kind of servitude was emerging. A good warrior, particularly if he were knight or bannert, could contract himself to a great lord as a companion in arms or at least a well-paid mercenary.—*Bastard Feudalism,* K. B. McFarlane, Inst, Hist, Research, 1945; and *Lancastrian Affinity*, 1361-1399, Simon Walker, 1990—. Edward III's Parliament of 1341 enacted that all Crown officers must swear to keep the two great charters, Magna Carta and the Forest Charter. Edward thought this statute infringed his prerogative and repealed it with a royal proclamation. By 1359 most of the able fighting men of Lancashire, Derbyshire, Staffordshire, and Cheshire were abroad on the King's service. We have records of some of the Lancashire Commissions of Array and Chancery Rolls; Gilbert de Ince (nearly illegible) confirms the aid of "William de Bradshagh and Roger de Bradshagh;" John de Eccleston confirms the aid of "Ric de Bradshagh of Pynynton" and archers "Henr' de Bradshagh, Jno de Bradshagh, Roger fil' Richard de Bradshagh . . ." The Arrays for most other shires are completely illegible. The Chancery confirmed the King's obligation to "William de Bradshawe (who) has the King's bill for £ 114" for food that William supplied—*Chanc. Misc Rolls B20, no 23; Close Roll 33 Edw III, m30.* "16 Sept 1361—protection with 'clause volumus' for one year, for Henry son of Robert Bradshaw going to Ireland on the king's service in the company of the king's son, Lionel, Earl of Ulster . . . the same for Roger and Henry sons of Simon de Bradshaw of Lancaster" (Lionel, Duke of Clarence was declared heir presumptive to the throne in 1385). "Westminster—Pardon for good service in the war in France, Robert de Bradesch(a)gh, in the company of Walter de Mauny (q. v. *D. N. B)* for having robbed Richard del Mar of Barlay at Barlay of 6s 8d and having robbed Thomas Willons of Barlay of 41, wherof he is indicted or appealed and of any consequent outlawry"—*Cal of Pat Rolls, 35 EdIII* (1361) Part I.—For more than four decades it had been accepted practice to arrange for the King to Pardon the domestic crimes committed by retainers bound for service abroad. "October 1399 (dated at Kennington)—Pardon, in consideration of his having gone beyond the seas, to Thomas de Bradshawe of Muleton of Boudon (Bowden, Le. Chapel-en-le-Frith, Derbs), for the rape of Errma late servant of Peter Le Sukere, and goods of the said Peter and his sister, carried away whereof he is indicted and any consequent outlawries on condition that he stand trial if anyone proceed against him (presumably a challenge to trial by combat) for these and find sufficient security to be of good behavior from now and to come to the king whenever he may be called upon, to stay for one year at his wages." In another dated at Byfleet, he is called Thomas del Bradshawe of Chapel in the Frith—*Cal of Pat Rolls, Ed III*, 1338/40, and seven years later (by the testimony of the Earl of Northampton), signed "By Calais—General Pardon, for his good service in the war in France to Thomas de Bradshagh on condition that he not withdraw from the King's service, so long as he shall stay on this side of the seas, without special license"—*Cal of Pat Rolls, 20 Ed III*, Part IV, 1345—48—. Obviously the better the fighting man the more serious the crime that could be pardoned . . . and perhaps the longer the term of foreign service. It could not have been a large step from that to arranging false criminal accusations and no doubt such abuses took place. After 1369 military service is never again given at the supplication of John of Gaunt as a reason for issuing a pardon to one of his retainers. By the later quarter of the century John of Gaunt's retinue in Gascony was almost exclusively paid retainers whose terms of indenture spelled out their agreed compensation and length of service. The feudal host was last called out in 1385.

Appendix 11. Nicholas Bradshaw

John of Gaunt (1340-1399), 4th son of King Edward III, Duke of Lancaster and the most powerful English lord from 1379 until his death, staffed his household with annuitants and his military companies with indentured retainers—*The Lancastrian Affinity, 1361 /1399*, Simon Walker, 1990.—The position and influence gained by John of Gaunt's retainers is notorious. Lords Latimer and Neville the Chamberlain and Steward of the royal household (1376), Sir Thomas Hungerford Speaker of the Commons (1377), and Michael de la Pole Lord Chancellor and 1st Earl of Suffolk, all wore the Duke of Lancaster's collar of SS's, as did the poets Chaucer and Gower.—*John Gaunt*, Armitage-Smith & *Collar of SS*, A. P. Purey-Smith.—Among his lesser retainers Gaunt had a certain John Bradshaw, holding the office of Chief Forester of Duffield Frith from a time earlier than 1371 when Gaunt returned from France—*Duchy of Lancs Mss Bks*, quoted in *VCR of Derbs*.—He gave Bradshaw orders to supply venison out of the forest to his chief steward,

Godfrey Foljambe, and oaks to repair the Derwent river bridge in 1373. This John Bradshaw may be the man who married Cecily daughter of Thomas Foljambe in Chapel-en-le-Frith parish—*Flower's Visitation of Derbs, 1569* and *Norrey's Visitation of 1611-12, Harle Mss* 886, fol 14, & 1093, fol 61b . . . The following November a commission of oyer and terminer at Westminster heard Gaunt's complaint that James the servant of John Bradshaw the younger, John Bradshaw the younger, Thomas de Bradshaw, Nicholas de Brichour (Bradshaw) of Makeney, John de Bradshaw of Le Chapel Parich and William his brother, along with Geoffrey de Redyche and others, broke into Duffield Frith and High Peak Forest where they hunted, felled trees and undergrowth, carried away these and other goods, and assaulted the Duke's men and servants—*Cal Pat Rolls, Edw III, 1370-74,* Vol 15 pg 396. In August 1374 Gaunt obtained pardon for John Bradshaw (who must be the Chief Forester above) "son of Thomas Bradshaw," even though at Longesdon staffs. he took Geoffrey de Redyche (also listed above), a "felon outlawed for rape of Margaret Forester and let him go at his will, knowing that he was outlawed"—*Ibid.* The following month Robert de Swynnerton was appointed Chief Forester in place of John Bradshaw. At a woodmote court, however, held at *Le Cowhouse,* on 21 July 1391, John de Bradshaw is named as Chief Forester of Postern Park and Henry de Bradbourne also appears;—*The Royal Forests of England,* J. Charles Cox, London 1905.—In 1379 Nicholas Bradshaw (d; ca. August 1415) was the subject of a Commission of inquiry headed by Hugh Earl of Stafford. It had been alleged that Nicholas and twenty men including three other Bradshaws (John, Richard, and Henry), "common disturbers of the Peace, were retained by the Abbot of Dieulacresse Abbey at Leek in Staffordshire to "Perpetuate maintenance in his marches and oppress the people," having "lain in wait for them, maimed and killed some and driven others from place to place"—*Cal Pat Rolls Rich II,* 1377-78 pg 362.—At 1380 Easter term Court in Staffordshire Almarica de Warton appeared and appealed for prosecution of Richard and Henry Bradshaw and many more men, who "are those who served the Abbot of Dieulacresse," for the strange killing of John de Warton, her husband. It was alleged that on Saturday after Easter in 1379, in the town of Leek, the assailants laid in wait for Warton, shot him with an arrow, called upon him to surrender, kept him prisoner for four days and then took him to a place called Le Leekmore (the moor of Leek ?) where they cut off his head. None of the accused could be found in Staffordshire. The Court placed the accused *in exigent* as a first step leading to formal outlawry. Inquisitions were held all through 1380-81. The Abbot was accused as an accessory. The defendants then appeared, denied the charges, requested jury trial, and submitted themselves to imprisonment at Marshalsea in London awaiting trial. The Abbot posted surety and was bailed. The Abbot should have been tried in ecclesiastical court but meanwhile the king's agents intruded themselves, sensing that the wealth of the Abbot might be made forfeit to the Crown. The Sheriff of Staffordshire was ordered to elect a new coroner in place of John Galpyn who the King had removed because he was appearing as attorney for the Abbot in another matter. Galpyn was cut down with a sword by Nicholas Whelock of Chester, aided and abetted by William de Gunstone, monk of Tanonwhistle Abbey, and Peter and John Leghe of county Chester. Almarica de Warton failed to appear and prosecute her claim at Easter term court 1382 but the defendants still had to answer the King's suit, of which the said they were not guilty and they were bailed on surety provided by Nicholas Bradshaw and John Bradshaw. Subsequently all the defendants, except Richard Bradshaw, produced King's Pardons or Letters Patent Pardoning them for any felonies committed previous to December 1382. They were released upon finding surety for their good behavior. Richard Bradshaw's case was continued to Michaelmas term 1383 when the jury stated on oath that he was not guilty and awarded him £5 damages from Almarica because she had not pursued her allegation. At the same court Richard brought a plea of conspiracy against a member of the Inquiry Commission and three original jury members, that had alleged the guilt of he and "his brothers." The head of the Inquiry Commission had been Hugh, 2nd Earl of Stafford. In the course of the fourteenth century the Staffords had raised themselves from the ranks of prosperous gentry to the upper reaches of nobility by a fortunate combination of marriage and military prowess. Hugh Stafford served Henry 1st Duke of Lancaster in France prior to 1361. From 1381 Nicholas Bradshawe would be a paid esquire in the retinue of Hugh 2nd Earl of Stafford along with other Staffordshire men—John Huntingdon, William Wildblood, Haminet Pershale, and Thomas Greenway. When he was supposedly giving surety for his brothers bail at Court in Staffordshire his name appears in the roll of men at arms for the Earl Stafford's French campaign of 1381 as "Nicholas Bradshall." The 2nd Earl died in 1386.

Eighteen year-old King Richard III secretly plotted against John of Gaunt, who had been his guardian and Regent. He gathered his favorites around him in London, raised an army, and endeavored to pack Parliament by ordering the local sheriffs to return only the names of royal retainers. The sheriffs refused the King's order. The Judges were asked to rule on the King's acts and they declared that the King was above the Laws. A group of Lords (the Lords Apellant), including John of Gaunt's son (the future King Henry IV) resisted and by threatening to choose another King, forced Richard II to banish his sycophants. King Richard retained Thomas 3rd Earl Stafford "to stay with the king for life" in 1389, and granted custody of his inheritance while still a minor. Nicholas Bradshawe was principal man and receiver-general of the Stafford estates to Thomas 3rd Earl of Stafford. Thomas died in 1392 and an inspeximus and confirmation of Thomas's writings certified that he had made grants to "his esquire Nicholas Bradshawe"—the office of Constable of Caurs Castle for life together with 20 marks for life—the Lordship of the manor of Whisseton in Northamptonshire for life—the Lordship of the manor of Newton Blossomville in Oxfordshire—and a wood called Whissetonwood with all its franchises, liberties, pastures, mills, commons, and "other profits thereto belonging" for the yearly rent of one red rose. The earl's widow, Anne Plantagenet a sister of John of Gaunt and a cousin of the King, was forgiven part of a debt due the King "because she is the king's widow (a confusing phrase meaning she was the king's ward during her widowhood) and of his lineage and also because except for her dower and late husband's goods she has no means of support." An order to give the Countess Anne her dower was approved for the underaged 4th Earl by "Wm Archbishop of Canterbury, Thomas Earl of Warwick, Sir Nicholas de Stafford, and Nicholas Bradshaw, friends of the heir"—*Cal Close Rolls*, 8 Feb 1391—. William Stafford succeeded his late brother as 4th Earl but died four years later, aged 17. Countess Anne received her dower but further assured her position by marrying her late husband's brother Edmund who became the 5th Earl Stafford. Nicholas Bradshawe continued in service of the new Earl. Added to the retinue of Earl Edmund (not earlier than 1395 but before 1403) are the names of Roger Bradshaw (Nicholas's nephew and a former esquire of John of Gaunt) and Thomas Bradshaw—S.H.C., *Wm Salt Soc*, Vol XNicholas Bradshawe became a recipient of an annuity from Henry Bolingbroke, Earl of Derby, before 1398 and, therefore, one of the Bolingbroke's retainers, as was the Earl of Stafford—*Duchy of Lancs*, 28/4/1 ff 9, 10; 42/16 f.lSS. *The Calendar of Papal Registers*

1362-1404—provides the information that indulgences were granted "that the confessor of their choice may grant to" Nicholas Bradshaw, Henry Bolingbroke Earl of Derby (John of Gaunt's son and the future King Henry IV), and Humphrey Stafford . . . "plenary remission at the hour of their death, or (in some cases) plenary remission as often as they please." All the indulgences are dated at St. Peter's Rome, 8 Boniface IX [1396] and were probably obtained at the submission of John Bradshaw "priest of the diocese of Lichfield"—*Ibid 1390*. John Bradshaw "clerk of the diocese of Lichfield" received, from Pope Boniface in 1399, permission that "he shall not be bound to exhibit (to) any legate or commissary or ordinary or official, the letters by which the late Robert (Stretton) bishop of Lichfield granted him, then in minor orders, dispensation to hold the said church (Aughton in Lancashire) provided that he were ordained sub deacon in a year; which letters John, who was before the end of the year ordained sub deacon and afterward priest, has lost."

Nicholas Bradshawe and his brother, Hugh, began to buy up the manor of Milwich near Stone, Staffordshire. Before 1398 Hugh's son, Roger, who had served as esquire to John of Gaunt in Gascony became Lord of the manor of Turnditch in Derbyshire, Rider and Ranger of the Duke's chace of Asshedon, and Master Forester of Asshedon. After John of Gaunt's death in 1399 King Richard banished Henry Bolingboke and busily set about confiscating all Henry's estates in England.

Bradshawe was caught between the two giants. He was an annuitant of Henry but it was his job as King's Escheator of Staffordshire, Hereford, Salop, and the Welsh Marches (a post he had been given in 1397) to seize Henry's manors. The King formed a tight little group of retainers, Sir William Bagot, Nicholas Bradshawe, and Nicholas Bubbwyth "clerk of Chancery," to seize forfeitures, gather money, and keep the peace. Bradshawe was a Commissioner of the Peace for Nohants, Staffs, and Salop . . . a Comnissioner to enquire and certify concerning felling of trees in the King's hay of Teddesle and the forest of Cannock . . . . attorney, with Bagot and Bubbwyth, to handle the affairs of John Burghill, Bishop of Coventry and Lichfield when he went to Ireland.

Henry Bolingbroke, Earl of Derby, Leicester, and Lincoln, and Duke of Hereford, infuriated by King Richard's seizure of his huge inheritance, took his late father's title of Duke of Lancaster and came home from his exile in France. He gathered his allies and prepared to make armed recapture of his lands. Sir Wm. Bagot rushed to warn the King who was then in Ireland. King Richard was forced to surrender to Bolingbroke and, later, abdicate. On September 30, 1399, Parliament elected Bolingbroke to the throne as King Henry IV, the first English King to speak English as his native tongue. At his coronation he proclaimed the crown to be his in right of conquest, descent from Henry III, and the abdication of his predecessor. Godfrey Chaucer, King Henry's uncle, died in the following year.

It was the royal retainers of King Richard that eased the transition for King Henry. He reconfirmed grants of lifetime privilege and took the fealty of Nicholas Bradshawe, William Bagot, and Nicholas Bubbwyth. He granted Pardons to Bradshawe and others for having acquired manors and lands that had been part of his inheritance. He presented Thomas Bradshaw to the Rectory of Newton-Blossanville Oxfordshire, one of the Stafford manors, in 1400 and Nicholas Bradshaw presented John Ward to the same Rectory on 25 July 1400, so Perhaps Thomas Bradshaw died between 1399 and 1400.

All this reordering of the Duke of Lancaster's manors profoundly affected the northern barons and the first to rebel were the Hollands of Lancashire, traditional enemies of the Bradshaws since the Banastre Rebellion of 1320, and sworn enemies of the Staffords since John Holland had brutally slain Ralph Stafford in 1384. In January 1400 a basket, containing the severed head of Thanas Holland Earl of Kent and Duke of Surrey, was sent to King Henry in much the same way that the head of Holland's grandfather had been sent to the Duke of Lancaster some seventy years earlier. The Holland's rebellion was over. King Henry acknowledged the aid of William Bradshaw who had furnished two men-at-arms and thirty archers—*2 Hen IV, B55, no 15* as quoted by Pym Yeatman in *Feudal History of Derbyshire*.—Thomas Holland left a young widow, Joan, who was sister of the slain Ralph Stafford and of Edmund 5th Earl Stafford, Nicholas Bradshawe's new lord. It would be revealing to know the name of the unamed headsman who decapitated Thomas Holland. It was said to have been done by the townspeople of Cirencester.

A Parliament was summoned to Westminster in January 1401 which met and demanded of their new King redress of longstanding grievances before they gave him a supply of money. They also passed the infamous Statue *de heretico canburendo* (for the burning of heretics). The suppression of Lollardy began in earnest and William Lawtre, a parish priest of London, was the first to be roasted alive.

Roger Bradshaw joined London's famous Mayor, Dick Whittington in providing surety for Richard Greneway probably a relation of Thomas

Greneway who had been Nicholas Bradshawe's old companion in arms. Richard Greneway was imprisoned in March 1401 *Cal Close Rolls,. Henry IV.* Whittington agreed to pay the Exchequer £8 for a *collar of SS* (John of Gaunt's livery) that he had mislaid at Easter 1402,—Select *Cases in the Court of King's Bench,* ed. G.O. Sayles, Seldon Soc, vii, 88, 1971, pg 103.—This sounds, suspiciously, as if Roger Bradshaw had handed over his old collar of Livery to Whittington as part of the surety and when Whittington was called to submit surety to the Exchequer he could not find the valuable collar. Roger was M. P. for Derbyshire (1406), M.P. for Staffordshire (1416). Before 1416 he married Elizabeth, widow of William Croweshawe, and one of the four grand-daughter co-heiresses of Sir Hugh Meynill of Hintes and Langley Meynill, Derbs. In 1416 he obtained the manor of Milwich from Hugh, his father, and the estate of the late Nicholas Bradshaw his uncle. It appears that Roger was dead before 1431 when a pardon was granted to Robert Twyford, executor of the will of Roger Bradshaw for "failing to answer Humphrey Earl of Stafford." Roger was succeeded by his son William who, most likely, was the ancestor Robert Bradshaw of Worksop. In 1421 William son of William son of Roger Bradshaw sold all his lands in Milwich to John Aston, and 33 years later Isabel daughter and heir of Thomas Hexstall sold the watermill at Milwich to William Bradshaw—*Wm Salt Soc, New Ser.* Vol III, 1909.

Owen Glendower raised rebellion in Wales and then the Scots invaded the border region. The king was unsuccessful in Wales but Henry Percy Earl of Northumberland defeated the Scots at the battle of Hamildon Hill where he captured Murdoch and Archibald Earl of Douglas. Thomas Bradshaw of Haigh, Lancs, was in Northumberland's garrison at Berwick-on-Tweed—*Cal of Doc Relating to Scotland,* Vol IV.

A Parliament was called at London for January 1402 but it probably was never assembled. A "Great Council" is spoken of, D.N.B.—*Henry IV,* and at that council or Parliament a Commission was granted to Edmund Earl of Stafford, Nicholas Bradshaw, Robert Frauncys . . . and others, to bring to the attention of the king's leiges in Staffordshire that it has always been the king's intention that the common wealth, laws, and customs of the realm should be observed.

Other minor rebellions followed and King Henry appointed Nicholas Bradshaw to suppress the outbreaks in Buckingham and Northamptonshire, 11 May 1402.

Earl Northumberland and his son Harry *Hotspur* thought it time to press the King for rewards. They offered him their Scot prisoners but were incensed at what the King offered in return. they made common cause with the rebellious Owen Glendower and appealed to the northern barons for support. Northumberland wrote to Ellys Bradshaw of the ancient manor of Bradshaw near Bolton seeking his aid but it is uncertain that the aid was forthcoming. Thomas Bradshaw of Haigh did join Northumberland and was not pardoned until 1425. The King called upon Nicholas Bradshaw and Robert Frauncheys to muster forces—*Cal of Pat Rolls.*—The inevitable battle was drawn at Shrewsbury on the 21st of July 1403 and at the end of that bloody day Edmund Earl of Stafford, his brother Hugh, and Hotspur (with an arrow through his eye) all lay dead. Hotspur's body was quartered and the Parts were displayed on poles along the highway back to London. Nicholas Bradshaw survived. William Bradshaw of Westleigh and Blackrod was wounded—*Jour of Chester Architectural, Arch, & Hist Soc*, pt XII, Div I, 1888, pg 353.—Archibald Earl of Douglas was captured by Sir James Harrington and delivered over for safekeeping to Roger Bradshaw, Nicholas Bradshaw's nephew, the following year the Crown paid Roger £ 30 for his charges in keeping Douglas for twenty-seven days—*S.H.C., Wn Salt Soc*, New Ser, Vol XII and *Exch Issue Rolls 1225-1450*.—Two thirds of the of the Stafford estates were handed over to Queen Joan of Navarre, King Henry's second wife, as a part of her dower—*V.C.H., Staffs*. and *Cal of Close Rolls.*—The remaining one-third was held for the infant Stafford heir, Humphrey, future Duke of Buckingham. Nicholas Bradshaw handed over his office of Constable at Caurs castle to William Branshulf, but kept some of his rights in the "south Park of Blechington." Commencing about this time Nicholas began to serve the King at the highest levels. Richard Lord Grey, the King's Chamberlain, nominated Nicholas Bradshaw and Nicholas Bubbwyth, the King's clerk in Chancery, as his attorneys while he was away on the King's business. Bubbwyth was made Keeper of the Privy Seal and Master of the Rolls (1402). Nicholas Bradshaw traveled the countryside on the King's behalf to borrow money from the great barons. When Bubbwyth was made Bishop of London (1406) Nicholas Bradshaw, Henry Bishop of Winchester, Thomas Langley the Chancellor of England, and Thomas Shelford, clerk, were given the trusteeship over money paid by the Dean of St. Paul for the support of the Bishop of London. Bubbwyth became Bishop of Salisbury (1407), Bishop of Bath and Wells (1408) and was one of three English prelates sent to Rome to decide between the three candidates for Pope (1417). He is buried at Wells Cathedral—John Bradley, *Royal Charters & Ltrs Pat Granted to Burgesses of Stafford*, (1899).

Bradshaw was given commission of Oyer and Terminer to enquire into trespasses of John Standish, Thomas Holcroft, and Nicholas Levenson onto the lands of Richard Earl of Warwick. For his loyal service Nicholas Bradshaw, called *the king's esquire*, was given license to hunt in the chase of Whaddon "all the time that it is in the king's hands by reason of the minority of the son and heir of the Earl of March"—*Cal Pat Rolls Hen IV 1408-1413*.—When King Henry IV died in the Jerusalem Chamber of Westminister Abbey (March 1412) his esquire would have been nearby. Young King Henry V had led a rowdy young life but when he came to the throne he counselled his former companions to forego their dissolute ways. He then rewarded them liberally and ordered they stay at least ten miles away from his royal court. He chose a Privy Council of the wisest men and filled his court with men of the best ability and integrity. He made a complete change in the chief officers of Duffield Forest. Sir Philip Leche of Chatsworth was made Master Forester, John Bradshaw was parker of Shottle, and Henry Bradshaw parker of Postern. Richard Leche, knight, and Roger Bradshaw had been knights of the shire for Derby summoned to Parliament in 1406. Henry V renewed the war with France and won a stunning victory over the French at Agincourt where Peter Leche of Chatsworth and his retinue of Derbyshire foresters distinguished themselves. Evidence proves that Nicholas was dead a month or two before the King set sail on his French expedition. Inquisitions P. M. were held in Northampton, Stafford, and Buckinghamshire where it was found that Nicholas died intestate and Roger Bradshagh, aged 50 and more, was his son and heir. Roger and Richard, sons of Richard Bradshaw, were administrators of Nicholas's goods and chattel. A long process of recovering his life-grants began; Indenture dated 30 November 1416 "of demise to the king and his assigns . . . of the castles and manors (a long list)" that had been the King's gift to . . . Bishop of Norwich, duke of York/ Earl of Arundel, Henry Le Scope, Roger Leche," all now deceased, and the manor of Wardington (county Bucks,) which was held for life by Nicholas Bradshaw, "now deceased"—*Cal of Close Rolls, Hen V 1413-1419*.—There as many more such indentures for recovery. In fact they carried on for another eight years, culminating in a final order to the Chancellor of Ireland to give Humphrey Earl of Stafford "all those lands of his heritage wherof Nicholas Bradshagh was tenant for life." The crown continued the previous King's purge of the Lollards and enacted that whoever read the scriptures in English should forfeit their life and goods. Sir John Oldcastle/ nominal leader of the Lollards, was captured by

Lord Powys in Wales and brought to London, hung up by a chain around his belly, and burned alive. Thomas Bradshaw, the coroner of Derby and steward of the Duke of Bedford paid the reward due to the widow of Lord Powys in 1422—*Pell Rec, Issues of the Exchequer, Hen III—Hen VI* & *Cal of Close Rolls, Hen V, 1413-1419*: 1 Dec 1415 & 28 June 1419

Appendix 12. Robert Bradshaw of Worksop

Robert Bradshawe, son of John Bradshaw of Windley and Champeyne (Derbs]), was "clerk of the kitchen" to Francis Talbot the 5th Earl of Shrewsbury in 1538. He is probably the same Robert who held the reversion of the office of keeper, for life, of the Wardrobe of Beds in the King's manor of Woodstock, Oxon, with fees of 4d per day in 1533—*Cal State Papers, Hen VIII.*—From 1527 the 4th Earl and his son Francis, then styled Lord Talbot, had the stewardship of many of the King's manors and castles. The last will, of Robert Bradshawe of Worksop, Notts, dated July 1553 is quoted in—*Lancs & Ches Rec Soc, De Houghton Deeds & Papers, No. 1505;*—He bequeaths to the 5th Earl of Shrewsbury (d; 1560).—"my lorde and master" . . . my best yoke of oxen or my best gelding or moneyworthe, and "beseeching his lordship of his honour that whereas I at any time have not done my true and faithful fine as is my bounden duties was in money or moneyworth that. (he) take & receive all such stuff and implement of household as I have had of him at any time which remains wholly at Worksop . . . to Lady Talbot (Grace daughter of Robert Shakerley of Little Longstone, Derbs, and widow of Francis Carless) my bay filly . . . to John Atkin "my lord's priest at Sheffield" my buckeskin gerkyn furred with white lambe . . . whereas I delivered to my Lady Talbot a standing cup with cover double gilt I will that my brother Thomas's eldest sonne shall have the same cup and cover. Other bequests to Cassandra Fowke, Joyce Fowke, Francis Fowke (a gown furred with "barke of lizards" a "chamlett" jacket, my best hose, my best shirt, and a satin doublet), cousin Elizabeth Lee, Robert Blount, cousin Charles savage; servant "R" [?], servant Harrison, Thomas [Hi)ndreth, Rowland Lowe "my husbandman" Robert French, Humphrey Bennet, John Tyas, "everyone of my servants that dwell with me, all those that worke in wages, every boye in my lords kitchen as well as those remaining in the cuntrey as those beyng here at Coldharber" (Cold-Harbour, Shrewsbury's London house). He left the remainder of his goods to "my brother Pierson" & my brother Thomas whom I make my full executors in witness whereof I have (scribbled?) thys my laste wille with my owne hande." The will is frayed, fragile, and trn in two but retains a fine seal (S 977).—*Lancs & Ches Rec Soc, Vol 88 De Houghton Deeds and Pprs, No. 1506;*—At London, on 23rd October 1566, Matthew [Parker] Archbishop of Canterbury appointed Roger Fowke, "next of kin to Rob. Bradshawe of Worksoppe co. Notts, dec(eased)" to administer Bradshawe's estates. The Fowkes were Robert Bradshawe's nephews; children of his sister Anne and her husband Robert Fowke of Gunstone, Staffs. *Ibid, No. 1229;*—Indenture dated 33 Elizabeth Aug 1 (1591) Richard Houghton of Parkhall grants to John Fleetwood of Penwortham a 30 year lease of the tithes of corn grain & hay in Barton rendering £6 payable to Thomas Barton of Barton or himself, he having granted the tithes to Thomas Barton last July, the revision of the lease of the rectory and tithes of Preston, having belonged to Robert Bradshaghe (sic) of Worksoppe deceased, by deed of the College of Our Blessed Mother of Leycester (Leicester), dated 23 August Henry VIII (1545).

Appendix 13. Bradshaws of Windley and Alderwasley

The Bradshawes of Windley and Alderwasley had been Foresters of Fee in the wards of Postern and Shottle, Duffield Frith, since the time of John of Gaunt. In 1451 Thomas Fawne of Alderwasley granted, for four years, to Thomas Bradshawe and John Briddon, a close (an enclosure of land) in Shining Cliff Wood and one parcel of land called Derwent Field along with 20 loads of firewood to be taken yearly, with warranty against all men. Thomas Fawne's daughter and heiress married Thomas Lowe who thereby gained possession of Alderwasley and. in 1473, demised to Henry Bradshawe the same land called Shining Cliff and Derwent Field in Alderwasley for a term of three years. Fourteen years later Lowe sold to Richard Blackwell, a copyhold tenant of Alderwasley, a parcel of wood within Shining Cliff called Thistle Lee. Anthony Bradshawe of Duffield (b; 1545) married as his first wife, Griselda the daughter of Richard Blackwell (or Blackwall). In 1523 Henry VIII granted the manor of Alderwasley to his standard bearer and gentleman of the bedchamber, Anthony Lowe (d; 15553, who was "one of the fforesters of the fforest of Duffield Frith and the keeping of certaine pasture and wood there called Milhey (Milnhey) ward"—*Alderwasley and the Hurts,* (Vienna, 1909).—By 1581 Alderwasley was no longer reckoned a part of the Forest—*Duffield Forest in the Sixteenth Century, Jour Derbs Arch*

& Nat'l Hist Soc, Vol XXV, (1903).—John Bradshawe of Windley died shortly before 22 May 1523 when an indenture was made between Roger Meynours (Manners), esq, "servant of the king's cellar, of the one part, and Anthony Lowe, gentleman, of the other part, concerning the office of Keeper of the Park of Postern, in the county of Derby, belonging to Henry Bradshawe (d; 1550), eldest son and heir of John Bradshawe, deceased"—*Wooley Charters, III/95.*—John Bradshawe died in possession of half the manor of Windley and all the manor of Champeyne, His wife was Isabella the daughter of Thomas Kinnersley of Loxley, Staffs. His son and heir Henry Bradshawe married Eleanor the daughter of Richard Curzon of Kedleston and left a son and heir named German Bradshawe. About 1530/31 Henry Bradshawe was one of the receivers of contributions made for finding a priest for Alderwasley chapel. Richard Blackwall and Thomas Lowe were the Trustees—J. Charles Cox, *The Churches of Derbyshire,* vol II, 568, (1877).—. John and Isabella's other children were; Robert Bradshawe of Worksop, Notts., Anne who married John Fowkes of Gunstone Staffs., and possibly Thomas another son.

Appendix 14. Germaine Bradshaw and John Curzon of Kedleston

John Curzon (1551-1632) wrote to the Earl of Shrewsbury, from Kedleston 23 Feb 1598, that (Germaine, or German) Bradshaw has told him the contents of (Ralph) Sachervell's letter to (John) Harpur, which has been shown to the Earl. Curzon protested that the proposals contained in the letter would prevent him from meeting his debts, the debts that his late father Francis (b; 1532) owed the Earl, and from conveying his estate to his wife Millicent. *Cal of the Talbot Papers, Derbs Arch Soc, Vol 4,* (1968), 9, 192. John Curzon submitted proposals of his own to Shrewsbury seeking the release from prison of (?) Vernon, who stood bond for the late Francis Curzon, father of John, for debts amounting to £24,000 (a monstrous fortune at that time). Curzon proposed that he would allow Vernon 'the income from the manors of Kedleston, Weston, and Aldwark Grange (Derbs) on condition that certain Curzon relations and pensioners were provided for, and that Curzon himself might enjoy Kedleston House and the gardens and property of Germayne Bradshaw, his cousin—*Cal of the Shrewsbury Papers, Derbs Arch Soc,* Vol 1, 1968, P3 121.—Curzon wrote again in 1604 asking that Shrewsbury use his influence to suppress rumors spread by Thomas Taylor to the effect that the Germayne Bradshaw (fl; 1597/8) had been insane. In 1588

Bradshaw had been judged, by the Court of wards, *to be a fool but not an idiot.*—Bunting, *Chapel-en-le-Frith*. By old common law, the custody of all idiots devolved on the Crown—whenever a man was alleged to have been an idiot from birth, there was issued a writ *de idiota inquirendo*, a Jury was summoned, and if the charge were found to be true the Crown took custody of his lands and all the profits there from, unless someone came forward who had interest enough to procure a grant of the profits for himself. Bradshaw, it was said, conveyed his lands to Curzon in payment of debts. The lands are not readily identified but they must have been substantial because Germayne Bradshaw was the grandson of John Bradshaw (d,1523), Forester-of-fee in Postern park, who had possessed half the manor of Windley and Champagne park (or Champeyne) at his death, and the only son of Henry Bradshaw (1520-1550) eldest son and heir of the previous John. Champagne Park had been disafforested from Duffield Frith and placed in private hands during the reign of Edward I. In November 1330, Henry, Earl of Lancaster, had bestowed Champagne on his *beloved valet* Robert Foucher and Cicely his wife and their heirs. Champagne Park came to the Bradshaw's by marriage of John Bradshaw with a descendant, perhaps the daughter, of Robert Foucher. Germayne Bradshaw's mother was Eleanor the daughter of Richard Curzon of Kedleston Hall; his maternal grandfather was German Pole of Radbourne; his uncle was Robert Bradshawe of Worksopp. Taylor married Eleanor, the only sister of Germayne Bradshaw, and continued to pester Curzon for money. Anthony Bradshawe wrote to Shrewsbury, 25 January 1609, reporting that, Mrs. (Millicent) Curzon's desire that the Earl's bond for payment of her son's money should be renewed in her son's name instead of those of George Curzon and *Bradshawghe. Cal of the Shrewsbury Papers, Derbs Arch Soc*, Vol 1, 1965.

Appendix 15. Peter Bradshaw

The charge was made sometime after the death of Robert Cecil 1st Earl Salisbury; after 1628. An unknown accuser said that in 1606 Salisbury had heard the King wished to bestow a £ 2,000 reward on Sir Thomas Hamilton. Salisbury, as High Treasurer, arranged for Hamilton to accept land of that value and then used his post to find land of the greatest value but smallest rental yield. He joined Peter Bradshawe with Hanilton, pretending that Bradshawe had done some good service to the State, and made Bradshawe the sale patentee of lands worth £ 30,000 but of a annual value of £ 82:19s.:1d. He then told Hamilton the annual value but not the real worth and persuaded Hamillton to accept £500 ready cash for his £ 2000 reward. Afterward he made Bradshawe sell the land for £ 30,000 and give Salisbury the money. The charges were refuted by Salisbury's son as follows; 1.) Salisbury was not High Treasurer at the time alleged, 2.) Bradshawe was merely nominated by Hamilton and had no relation to Salisbury, 3.) the lands were not purchased from Bradshawe but conveyed to others who surrendered them to the crown and Salisbury got them, amongst other things, from the King by a new grant, 4) some years later these lands, supposed to be worth £ 30, 000, were sold for £ 5700, and 5) these very charges had been previously examined by the George Villers, late Duke of Buckingham, who concluded it "not fitt the business should bee further questioned"—*Mss of the Marq of Salisbury*, Vol XXII, p. 248.—This transaction must be a misunderstanding, or perhaps the real truth, of the Southrop manor business of 1605-06. Peter Bradshawe was dead sometime prior to 1630, when his nephew George Bradshawe filed. a Bill of Complaint against Amy, widow of Peter Bradshawe, for money due him as a partner in the Ireland business carried on with his uncle. Amy Bradshawe and Edward her son brought suit in the Privy Council, through her lawyer Richard Miller, for the arrest of Henry O'Brien 5th Earl of Thomond for money due. The Council apparently directed Thomond to pay but he complained that Amy and Edward would not accept his offer of tender until he paid some other debts. Amy, Edward, and Richard Miller were detained from the 2nd June until 11 June 1630. One of the Privy Councilors who judged the matter was Thomas Howard Earl of Arundel and Surrey who appointed John Bradshawe his Steward of Glossop Manor that year.—*Acts of the Privy Council, 1630-1631*, HMSO1964—Amy remarried John Munday before 1632. Evidence of another transaction which was being investigated about 1632; "Secretary Windebank to John Munday. It is the King's pleasure that he deliver to Roger Wood a copy of a warrant to Peter Bradshaw, late husband of Munday's now wife, by Robert, late Earl of Salisbury, whereby Bradshaw was authorized to convey the manors of Snettesham and Southrepps (sic), and rectory of Ilchester, held by him in trust for the Earl,

1. Robert Earl of Salisbury to Peter Bradshaw, warrant directing him to convey the manor of Snettesham, Norfolk, to Sir Henry Cary, to whom the Earl has sold it [1611/12 Mar 4]

2. Peter Bradshaw to Sir Henry Cary, one of the of the gentlemen of the privy Council, release of all right and interest of Peter Bradshaw in the manor of Snettesham (1611/12 Mar 4)"—*Cal State Papers, Chas I, 1632.*

Appendix 16. Anne Bradshaw and Arbella Stuart

Arbella was ill, or acting ill, in order to forestall her removal from Barnet to Durham. Finally her transfer was set for Wednesday, June 5 1611, but on Monday a planned escape was put into action. Somehow Arbella had assembled a £2800 fund, of which £ 1800 came from her aunt Mary, Countess of Shrewsbury. On the Sunday before the scheduled transfer day, one of Seymour's friends had taken rooms on the south bank of the Thames opposite the Tower. The landlady was amazed by the amount of baggage which was deposited in the rooms. There were a great number of servants arriving and departing, and one who might have been Anne Bradshawe, arrived to collect a black wig that had been made by a local Frenchman living near. On Monday Edward Reeves and Anne Bradshaw arrived at the rooms and in a furtive way carried out all the baggage to a hired waterman's boat to be rowed down to Blackwall. The landlady suspected only an elopement and reported nothing. Meanwhile Lady Arbella escaped her house of confinement in Barnet disguised in a man's doublet, black hat, cloak, and rapier; her own hair covered by a black wig. She was accompanied by William Markham. Arbella and Markham walked about a mile and one-half to a sorry inn and there met with Hugh Compton who waited with horses for the next leg of the escape. The stableman at the inn later told how he held the gelding for the person he had noted as of bizarre appearance "yet . . . being astride in unwonted fashion, the stirring of the horse brought blood enough into her face" as she rode off on the fourteen mile trek toward Blackwall. At about six that evening Arbella, Markham, and Compton met with Anne Bradshaw, Edward Reeves, and Edward Kirton at a Thames waterside inn in Blackwall. It was here the group planned to rendezous with Seymour, but he was not there. Seymour was imprisoned in St. Thomas's Tower adjoining Traitor's Gate. The afternoon of Arbella's escape he shut himself in his room and told his barber that he wanted no callers. He then disguised himself in a black wig, beard, and the clothes of a cart boy. He slipped out of his roan and walked out the West Gate behind an empty cart and onto the Tower wharf where he met Edward Rodney who was waiting with a boat. An hour later they were at Blackwall but that was nine o'clock in the evening; three hours late for his rendezvous with Arbella. Arbella had waited as long as she dared. The watermen pointed out that favorable tides were waning. Into one boat went Arbella and Anne Bradshaw with the luggage, and into a second boat went Crompton, Reeves and Makham, leaving a very nervous Kirton and a maid at the inn to await Seymour. At seven-thirty Kirton feared something had gone wrong so he loaded the maid into the third boat and set out as fast as he could row downriver in pursuit of Arbella and the others. The destination of all the escapers "was a French boat anchored about twenty miles downstream, off Leigh." The watermen rowed through the approaching night and as they passed Greenwich Palace where King James was staying the fugitives must have wondered if their escape had yet been discovered. At Gravesend the oarsmen refused to go farther until bribed with double usual payment. At Tilbury they landed ashore to refresh themselves with drink; Arbella and the others huddled in the boats. Traversing the broad estuary of the Thames was treacherous in the best of conditions but against unfavorable tides and through the dark of night must have been harrowing for all. At daybreak there was no sign of the French boat—it was, in fact, eight miles further on. Crompton tried to bribe the captain of an English boat to take them to Calais but the offer was declined. The captain made mental note of the party of travelers; Arbella strangely swathed in a black cloak and displaying "a marvellous fair white hand" when she removed her glove; Reeves about forty and the younger Crompton wearing a black beard, ... Anne Bradshawe in a black hat looking like Moll Cutpurse (the notorious thief of the time) making escape. In spite of his suspicions the captain pointed out the French ship they sought and 'watched them make their way toward her., Arbella wished to await Seymour's arrival. By the time the French captain insisted his boat depart, without Seymour. Another two hours elapsed before Seymour and Rodney arrived at Leigh to find no sign of Arbella, Anne Bradshawe, or the others in their party. Not knowing if Arbella had been captured, Seymour bought passage to Calais on a coal boat. Meanwhile the escape had been discovered in London. When news of the escape reached Greenwich Palace there was an outrageous outburst although Seymour and Arbella were of no serious threat to King James. He was just furious that they had defied him, A proclamation was issued to arrest the two and anyone accompanying them. Admiral Wiilliam

Monson was ordered to search for them at sea. Anyone who was thought to have been remotely responsible for the escape in London or Barnet was immediately imprisoned. No doubt Anthony Bradshawe and his son, Exuperie, were suspected. Shrewsbury was sent for and questioned. Countess Mary, Shrewsbury's wife, was imprisoned at the Tower where she would remain for many years. In the channel Arbella persuaded the French captain to linger in hope of finding Seymour but they were sighted by the English ship *Adventure* of Captain Crocket who was one of Admiral Monson's searching party. Crocket fired thirteen shots across the bow of the Frenchman and then dispatched an armed boarding party to arrest Arbella, Anne Bradshawe, Crompton, Reeves, and Markham. Once Arbella was in custody the search for Seymour was called off and he landed at Ostend having diverted from Calais.

Appendix 17. Thomas Howard, Earl of Arundel and Surrey

Thomas Howard (1585-1646).—In the reign of Queen Elizabeth Thomas Howard's father, Philip Howard (1557-1595) first Earl Arundel and Surrey and. only child of 4th Duke of Norfolk. by his first wife, died in the 'Tower for his Roman catholic faith. Philip Howard "led a life of frivolity previous to 1580 when he entered the temple and withdrew from the frivolities of Court." He was enrolled as a member of the Inner Temple in November 1579. Philip's half-brother Thomas Howard of Walden (created Earl of Suffolk in 1603, d; 1625) was also enrolled. At that same time Anthony Bradshawe of Duffield and John Bradshawe of Lye Staffordshire (both enrolled November 1573), and John Bradshawe of Lancashire "son of Roger Bradshawe—Principal of Clement's Inn" (enrolled November 1577) were members of the Inner Temple. None of these three Bradshaws were, obviously, Lord President John Bradshawe, the Regicide. King James restored Thomas to his father's titles of Arundel and Surrey but kept the family property so that, for some years, he and his mother lived in reduced circumstances, He was first introduced at Court in 1605. Only after his marriage to Shrewsbury's daughter in 1606 did he have sufficient fortune to begin buying back from the king some property, including Arundel House in London (in 1608 for £4, 000). A handsome young man with money to spend on royal property could quickly become a royal favorite of King James and Arundel led an exciting life often appearing as a performer in masques and Jousts at Court. Arundel went abroad, for his health, just a year before Lady

Arbella Stuart's unfortunate marriage. He returned and received the Garter knighthood at Windsor in May 1611, the month before Arbella's flight. For the next four years he and his countess traveled extensively on the continent, returning from Italy two months after Lady Arbella's death. Arundel, like his wife, was a Roman Catholic but on Christmas Day 1615; the same day that his mother-in-law was given a two-day release from the Tower; he entered the king's chapel at Whitehall and took the sacrament to enter the Church of England, much to his mother's horror. He was accused of becoming a protestant out of political necessity, a charge also leveled at, and privately acknowledged by, many of his contemporaries. Arundel however had begun to develop a genuine affinity for the simple and unadorned life; he was soon Known for his austere disposition, plain speech and dress, haughty manner, and a love of etiquette particularly as regards respect due his rank. These were the same qualities that Clarendon found so objectionable in Lord President John Bradshawe. In would be a mistake to assume that Arundel's adopted simplicity meant he shared Bradshawe's Calvinism or that he was, in any way, a puritan. Clarendon said "he did not love the Scots, he did not love the puritans." Nevertheless he visited Ralegh on board the Destiny in 1617, became a member of the Committee for the Plantation in New England whose moving spirits were strongly puritan, was imprisoned for his hostility to Buckingham, and attempted to mediate the debate between Parliament and the king over the Petition of Right in 1628. The House of Lords had, in 1621, committed him to the Tower for harsh words he spoke to Lord Spencer and only King James I s intervention secured his release from the very place where his mother-in-law was still confined. Above all Arundel was a patron of the arts and learning. He formed the first large collection of works of art in England. He brought Hollar from Prague and employed him to make drawings; Oughtred the famous mathematician was his son's tutor; William Francis Junius was his librarian and lived with. the Howard family for thirty years; Sir Robert Cotton, Sir Henry Spellman, Camden, John Evelyn, and John Selden were his friends. He was a comissioner to determine claims to perform the services at the coronation of King Charles in 1625. John Bradshaw, (d:1633) College of Arms Windsor Herald and Deputy Chamberlain of the Exchequer (who was not the same man as Lord President John Bradshawe), would have worked closely with Arundel in determining those claims. John Bradshaw copied, for Arundel, the Norfolk folios out of the Domesday Book which was then in the custody of Bradshaw—Elizabeth M. Hallam, *Domesday Book Through Nine Centuries*, Bradshaw and Arundel were among the 84 persons selected for the first Royal Academy in 1626—*Archaelogia, Soc of Antiquaries*, Vol 32, p9 132. Arundel obtained the dignity of Earl of Suffolk in succession to his uncle.

Appendix 18. The Confusing account of two John Bradshawes of Gray's Inn

William Langton, Hon. Sec. of the Chetham Society in the 1850s, examined the letters of this John Bradshaw and concluded "It is doubtful whether the letter . . . of John Bradshaw to Sir Peter Legh . . . was written by the regicide. The character of the handwriting, though not decisive, rather militates against the supposition . . . There were two John Bradshaw{e) contemporaries at Gray's Inn, the one admitted a student in 1620, the other in 1622; and the original archives of that house having perished, it is not possible to determine with absolute certainty which of these was the future President of the High Court of Justice, or which was the writer of this letter." *Notes & Queries* 2nd Ser. Vol IX, 17 Mar, pg 205. A John Bradshawe was continuing his correspondence with the Legh's of Lyme after old Sir Peter Legh's death (February 17, 1636) Lady Newton, *The House of Lyme*, (1917). On April 13 1636 he wrote to the widower Francis Legh who was living at Lyme while the teen-aged heir, Peter (b: 1624) was at school in Amersham. John Bradshawe proclaims that he is ready "to doe any service for you and the howse of Lyme as there should be occasion. Uppon Saturday next in the afternoone a Great cause stands referred to be heard before the earl of Derby and the Judges betwixt the Companie of Brewers (for whom I am) and the Alehouses and Innes of the Citie, so as I cannot stirre that night. But upon Easter Sunday, after evening prayer, I shall post to Warrington and attend you the next morning where you can please to appoint."

See *Lancs Mss*, vol xxxviii, pp 316-17, *Lancs P.R.O.* for John Bradshawe's letters to Thomas Ireland, lord of Warrington in. Lancashire, on the subject of a dispute between Sir Peter Legh and Thomas Ireland. On September 4th 1637 Bradshawe had something special to report to the house of Lyme, and writes: "As good a Buck as you can procure to be kylled, for I have a sudden and speceyall occasion to use one on behalfe of a ffrynd and my stomach serves me not to make use of any at this tyme but so reall a friend as yourself." He begs Francis Legh to forgive his boldness and, "I know your realitie, am bound to you for your ffavours, and ever tyed to be in your bond of gratitude . . . Your ffriend most assured, most readie to serve you . . . Jo: Bradshawe".

On 7th June 1638, a John Bradshaw was appointed the King's Attorney General for Cheshire and Flintshire; Somerfield Oldfield of Somerfield Hall near Congleton was appointed Chief Sergeant-at-Law. Lady Newton was, in 1917, convinced that this Attorney-General John Bradshawe was the Regicide, but it is certain, today, that he was not. James Croston and Seacombe, *Historic Sites of Lancashire and Cheshire*, pg 472 make the typical mistake of assuming Attorney-General Bradshawe and John Bradshawe the Regicide were the same person. Seacombe says (unaware that there were two John Bradshawe's) that John Bradshawe sought the post of Vice-Chamberlain of Chester in 1638 but lost out to Orlando Bridgeman and that caused animosity between the Bradshawe's of Marple and the Earl of Derby, leading to Derby's execution at the insistence of Henry Bradshaw of Marple. J. P. Earwaker, *The History of the Church and Parish of St. Mary on the Hill,* (Chester, 1898), 29, agreed with William Langton's conclusion and identified the Attorney-General of of Cheshire as "John Bradshawe, of Congleton, Esq . . . . who although bearing the same names as the celebrated John Bradshawe Esq, the Chief Justice of Chester . . . was no relation to him. Much confusion has arisen between these two persons.

INDEX

The letter *n* following a page number denotes a footnote and the number that follows *n* denotes the footnote number.

A

Abd-el-Malik, 74
Act of 1227, *126*
Adams, John, 265
Afflack, James, 301
al-Ayachi, Sidi, 84
Aldersey, Thomas, 39, 41
Aldersey's Bunbury School, 39
al-Manoun, Abdallah, 74
Amboyna, massacre at, 68
Andrews, Eusebuis, 276
Andrews, Peter, 84
anti-Catholic laws, 38
archery, practice of, 33
Areopagitica (Milton), 182
Assize of Woodstock in 1184, *105*
Ayscue, George, 315-16, 318, 320

B

Bacon, Francis, 13, 53, 67, 90, 123, 184
Bagshawe, Dorothy, 28
Barbados, 82n10, 312-15, 320, 327n1
Barebone, Praise-God, 333
Barebone's Parliament, 333
Barlow, Worthington
   Cheshire Biographies, 12
Barnard, John, 276
Barwick, Edward, 258
Barwick, John, 258, 299

Bate, George, 15, 298, 317
   Elenchus, 221
Battle of Agincourt, 25, 33, 44n7
Battle of Naseby, 166
Bayes, John, 315, 320
Beauties of England and Wales (Britton and Brayley), 12
Becket, Thomas, 109
Belasyse, John, 262
Bellairs, Charles, 30
Bellot, Hugh, 12-13, 15
   Memoirs of John Bradshaw, The, 12
Bennett, Richard, 316, 319, 327n5
Bentley, John, 119
Berkley, George, 83
Bertie, Robert, 83
Bess of Hardwick, 103-4, 119-20, 122
Best, Thomas, 85
bill of attainder, 149, 200-201
Biographical Register of Christ's College Cambridge (Peile), 43
Bishop, George, 292, 295, 302, 322, 333
Blake, Robert, 77-78, 321, 323
Bond, Denis, 325
Book of Common Prayer, 147-48, 267
Book of Sports, 53, 61
Booth, George, 173, 185
Bostock, Robert, 175
Boswell, William, 83n15, 282n33

Botham, Black Harry, 109
Bowden Middlescale, 103
Bradshaw, Alexander, 42, 48, 48n27
Bradshaw, Anthony, 59n2
Bradshaw, Anthony (counterfeiter), 279n12
Bradshaw, Edmund, 60n8, 66, 76-79, 160, 313
Bradshaw, Edward, 63n16, 145, 185
Bradshaw, George, 59n2, 196, 209n5, 313
Bradshaw, James, 169n26
Bradshaw, John (attorney general for Cheshire), 19
Bradshaw, John (attorney general for Chester), 333
Bradshaw, John (deputy chamberlain of the Exchequer), 19
Bradshaw, John (master forester of High Peak Forest), 26
Bradshaw, John (master of the science of defense), 19
Bradshaw, John (of Bradshaw in Lancashire), 19, 57, 155, 170, 194, 304
Bradshaw, John (of Congleton), 169, 191n13
Bradshaw, John (of Haigh), 93
Bradshaw, John (of Southolt), 82, 82, 82n11
Bradshaw, John (of Westminister), 81n9, 82, 82
Bradshaw, John (unknown), 19, 43, 142, 145, 168, 327
Bradshaw, Joseph, 132n2
Bradshaw, Laurence, 25, 239
Bradshaw, Lawrence, 169n20
Bradshaw, Nicholas, 25, 101
Bradshaw, Oliver, 33
Bradshaw, Peter, 46n17, 281n22
Bradshaw, Ralph, 33
Bradshaw, Richard (captain of the Dorchester Company), 85n22
Bradshaw, Richard (commonwealth resident in Hamburg), 275, 281n28, 282n37, 284, 310n17

Bradshaw, Richard (convicted of murder in Dublin Castle), 75
Bradshaw, Richard (of Pennington and Aspull), 63n16, 282n36
Bradshaw, Robert, 161
Bradshaw, Roger, 156, 167n6, 170n28
Bradshaw, Roger (chaplain to King James), 25
Bradshaw, Roger (of Haigh), 156
Bradshaw, Samuel, 60n7
Bradshaw, Surehope, 61n8, 79
Bradshaw, William, 25, 45n7, 77, 84n15, 170n28
Bradshawe, Anne, 123
Bradshawe, Anthony, 28, 35, 107, 110-11, 115, 117-19, 122, 131, 133n8, 138n28
Bradshawe, Catherine Winnington, 29
Bradshawe, Edmund, 53
Bradshawe, Ellis, 60n7
Bradshawe, Francis, 59n3, 59n2, 102, 125, 139n32, 168n7
Bradshawe, George, 133n9
Bradshawe, Godfrey, 102-4, 133n8, 134n11
Bradshawe, Henry (Parliamentary colonel), 30, 163, 183, 305-6
Bradshawe, Henry (the elder), 25, 27, 30, 46n18, 49
Bradshawe, Henry (the younger), 25, 27, 29, 39-40, 132, 132n6, 133n9, 167n7
Bradshawe, John (the regicide), 11, 52-53, 59n2, 60n7, 82n11, 90, 95-97, 101, 125-26, 169n24, 172, 191n14, 193-94, 202, 248, 306
  admittance to Gray's Inn, 54-55, 57
  background of, 32
  becoming chief justice, 251
  becoming high steward of Congleton, 144
  becoming steward of Congleton, 143
  birth of, 29
  as the chief executive of the English republic, 254

early education of, 38-39
first unpublished biography of, 12
intervenes for the Earl of Derby's children, 313
as mayor of Congleton, 144
moving to London, 66
nominated as member of Council of States, 251
plans to relieve Cromwell's army at Dunbar, 285
preparing his last will and testament, 324
presiding over the trial of King Charles I, 212, 214, 216, 218-21, 223-26, 228-29
sends two London doctors to care for Cromwell, 298
sentences a man to death for adultery, 306
stamping on his seal for the death warrant of King Charles I, 24
voted as judge of the Sheriff's Court at the Guildhall, 180
Bradshawe, Katherine, 81, 81n9
Bradshawe, Mary Marbury, 39, 55, 222
Bradshawe, Peter, 45n12, 51, 59n4, 118-19, 128, 136n23
Bradshawe, Philip, 60n7
Bradshawe, William, 26-27, 49, 60n5
Bradshawes of Marple, 33, 36, 51
Bradshaw family, 25, 73, 101
Bradshaw-Isherwood, Kathleen, 30
Bramhall, William, 143
Brandon, Richard, 243
Brereton, John, 53, 60n6
Brereton, Peter, 55
Brereton, William (of Ashley), 55
Brereton, William (of Hanforth), 57, 72, 142, 147, 152, 165, 168n14, 174, 184, 201
Brooke, Henry, 144, 304
Brouncker, Henry, 137n25
Bruen, John, 39-41
Burghall, Edward, 41, 197
Butler, Henry, 117-18

C

Calvinism, 38, 42, 49, 87
Cape Cod, 53
Capel, Arthur, 248-50
Carr, Robert, 55
Cavendish, Mary, 104
Cavendish, William, 120
Caviar, 322-23
Cecil, Robert, 59n4, 120-21, 123, 137
Chamberlain, John, 24
Chapel-en-le-Frith, 10, 33-34, 131
Charles, I, 11, 199-200, 214, 283
  burial of, 238-39
  controversial forced loans of, 90
  execution of, 235-36
  trial of, 212, 214, 216, 218-21, 223-26, 228-29
Charles, II, 311
Charter of the Forest, 87, 105, 129, 134-35
Charter of the Forest in 1217, *106*
Cheshire Biographies (Barlow), 12
Clarendon, Lord, 13, 15, 25, 44, 193
  History of the Rebellion, 15, 171
Clay, John, 122
Cobham, Henry Lord, 121
Cokayne, Edward, 117
Coke, Edward, 69, 88, 90, 115, 218
Coke, John, 70, 90
Committee of Examinations, 182, 315
Committee of Parliament, 307
Committee of Safety, 172
Company of Merchant Adventurers, 275
Compton, William, 201
Conference about the Next Succession (Parsons), 37
Congleton, 143
Constable, William, 322
Constitutiones de Foresta, 105
Cook, John, 213, 248, 331
Cooke, Thomas, 292-93
Corey, Giles, 206
Council of State, 253-54, 261-62, 264, 284, 298, 311, 315, 333

attempts at removing from public view all symbols of the Stuart Kings, 258
beginnings of the, 250
election of fifth, 322
election of fourth, 306, 319
election of second, 274
election of third, 295
four momentous decisions of, 251
nominees for members of, 251
powers of, 278n3
recommendations for new design for the Commonwealth's coins, 259
Courteen, William (the elder), 69, 76, 78, 81n10
Courteen, William (the younger), 86n24
cousin, usage of the term, 136n22, 169n16
Crawford, Lawrence, 163
Crompton, Hugh, 123-24
Cromwell, 13-14, 162-66, 198-201, 204-6, 224-25, 261-63, 268, 275-77, 285, 290-95, 297-99, 301-5, 317-20, 322, 324-26, 329-33
Cromwell, Henry, 15, 55
Cromwell, Oliver, 13, 16, 23, 32, 149, 162-66, 199, 205-6, 242-43, 246, 251-52, 267-68, 298-99, 315-20, 324-25, 329-33
  being appointed as commander in chief of the troops in Ireland, 252
  being appointed as general of the army, 277
  being chosen as chancellor of Oxford, 196
  being promoted to lieutenant general, 163
  capturing Edinburgh and besieging the castle, 291-92
  departing for Ireland, 268
  elected as high steward in Gloucester, 305
  falling dangerously ill, 297-98
  forcibly dissolving Parliament, 324-25, 329
  framing his own proposal for peaceful self-dissolution, 331
  idea of self-denial by, 165
  insisting to have an magnificent state funeral for Henry Ireton, 317
  installing his own spy in the council, 320
  moving to Scotland after signing the Treaty of Brenda, 285
Curzon, John, 117

D

Dakin, John, 138n26
Dallison, Charles, 88
Daniel, Peter, 145-46, 167n6
Davenport, Humphrey, 51, 64, 184, 190
Davenport, James, 174
Davenport, Mary Sutton, 180
Davenport, William, 59n3, 141
Davis, John. *See* Dixwell, John
de Lille, Anna Lady, 213
Denby, Edward, 264
D'Ewes, Simonds, 151
Dixwell, John, 20n14, 242
Donne, John, 53
Downes, John, 224, 233
Downham, John, 39, 48n24
Drax, James, 312
Dutton, William, 319

E

East Cheshire (Omerod), 12
Eccleston, Henry, 300-301
Edisbury, John, 197
Edward, II, 101, 230n1, 232n11
Egerton, Ralph, 39
Eikon Basilke, 257, 272
Eikonoklastes (Milton), 272
Elenchus (Bate), 221
Elizabeth, Queen, 52, 68, 200
  after the death of, 121
  real threat to the throne of, 37
Ellis, Henry, 243, 308
England's New Chains Discovered (Lilburne), 260

English East India Company, 68-69
Ensome, Robert, 74
Evans, William, 238

F

Fairfax, Thomas "Black Tom," 162, 165-66, 189
Fawkes, Guy, 205
Fell, Margaret, 63n17, 281n31
Fell, Thomas, 57, 63n17, 80n1, 256
Felton, John, 72
Fielding, William, 202
Finch, John, 72, 130
Fitzherbert, Thomas, 103
Forest Charter, 115, 134
forester
  description of a, 108
  various sorts of, 108
forest law, 33, 105
Fox, George, 57, 63n17, 281n31
Franklin, Benjamin, 17
Freeborn John. *See* Lilburne, John
fundamental law, 89-91
Furnivall, Elizabeth, 308n6, 332

G

Gardiner, Thomas, 148
Garlick, Nicholas, 103
Garnet, Henry, 122
Gerard, Gilbert, 80n1
Gerard, Richard, 38
Gibson, A. Craig, 14, 190
Gittens, Richard, 242
Glossop, manor of, 102, 109
Glover, John, 41
Goldsmith's Grammar School, 39
Gorges, Ferdinado, 71, 82n13, 85n22, 86
Goring, George, 250
Gray's Inn, 49-51, 53
  central features of the teaching method in, 54
  moot courts in, 54
  street fights with gentlemen from Lincoln's Inn with gentlemen from, 55

Green, George Smith, 205-6
  Oliver Cromwell an Historical Play, 205
Greene, Richard, 144-45
gunpowder plot, 38, 139

H

Halford, Henry, 239
Halford, Henry St. John, 241
Halley, George, 125
Hamilton, James, 248
Hardwick Hall, 120
Harley, Robert, 195, 259
Harrison, John, 74-75
Harrison, Thomas, 199, 251
Harvard College, 308n1
Harvey, Christopher, 41
Haselrig, Arthur, 245, 307
Health's Sickness (Prynne), 91
Heath, Robert, 83n15
Henry, V, 25, 135n18
Henry, VIII, 33, 102, 115, 127
Herbert, Edward, 169n25
Herbert, Phillip, 196, 278n5
Herbert, William, 129
Hercy, John, 118-19
Hewlett, William Hulett, 242
Hibbert, Thomas, 28-29, 45n13
Hickes, John, 231n6
Hill, Christopher, 13, 16, 107, 135
Hind, Capt. James, highway robbery of Bradshawe, 305
Hinde, William, 40-41
History of the Rebellion (Clarendon), 15, 171
Histriomastix (Prynne), 93, 95
Hixon, Humphrey, 96
Holland, Earl, 129
Holles, Denzil, 24, 164-65
Homacheros, 84n16
Hooke, Francis, 75
Hotham, John, 155
House of Commons, 25, 53, 172, 182, 187, 196, 198-99
  success of parliamentary party of, 25
  voting to establish unicameral power, 250

House of Lords, 246, 250-51
House of Lyme, The (Newton), 56
Howard, Thomas, 82n11
Hue and Cry after Sir Arthur Haselrig (Lilburne), 261
Hyde, Edward. *See* Clarendon, Lord
Hyde, Henry, 297

I

Impeachment of Cromwell and Ireton, The (Lilburne), 260
Ireton, Henry, 201, 251
    funeral of, 317

J

James, I, 37, 51-53, 69, 88, 121, 205, 232
    dissolving the parliament, 53
    execution of Catholics under the rule of, 37-38
    fondness for hunting of, 128
    patronizing lawful recreations and honest exercises, 61n11
    on the sale of baronetages to gentlemen, 24
Jefferson, Thomas, 17
Jennyson, Archbishop, 243
John of Gaunt, 35
Jones, John, 38
Jones, Michael, 267-68, 281n28
Jones, Ralph, 243
Judges of England, The (Foss), 12

K

Kelsey, Sean, 9, 278n2, 327n8, 331
Kirton, Edward, 124

L

Lambert (major general), 332-33
Lancashire, 62n12, 100, 156, 161, 173
Laud, William, 92-93, 96, 149, 165
Legh, Peter, 142, 167n7
Leighton, Alexander, 92
    Looking Glass of the Holy War, The, 92
    Zion's Plea, 92

Lenthall, William, 202, 256, 261-62, 329-30
Lilburne, John, 23, 96, 182-83, 249, 269
    England's New Chains Discovered, 260
    Hue and Cry after Sir Arthur Haselrig, 261
    Impeachment of Cromwell and Ireton, The, 260
    Truth's Victory Over Tyrants, 270
Lilburne, Robert, 249, 303
Lincoln's Inn, 55-56
Lisle, Alice, 231n6
Lisle, John, 231n6
Little John, 36
Little Parliament. *See* Barebone's Parliament
Lives of the Chief Justices (Campbell), 12
Long Parliament, 24, 38, 148, 150, 330
Looking Glass of the Holy War, The (Leighton), 92
Love, Christopher, 301
Ludlam, Robert, 103

M

Maddock, John, 74
Magna Carta, 87, 106, 129, 134-35, 150
Manchester, 158-59, 161, 163, 265
Manwaring, Roger, 90-91
Manwood, John, 116
Manwood, Roger, 116
Mare Clausum (Selden), 321
Marple Hall, 27, 31
Marshall, Earl, 106
Marten, George, 314-15
Marten, Henry, 74-75, 319
Marvell, Andrew, 319
Mary, Countess (wife of the Earl of Shrewsbury), 123, 125
Mason, Francis, 313
Mason, John, 75, 86
Mason, Luke, 39
massacre at Jamestown, 57
Mathew, Peter, 74
May, Humphrey, 64

Memoirs of John Bradshaw, The (Bellot), 12
"Memoirs of the Family of Bradshaw of Marple in Cheshire" (Watson), 12
Mercurius Pragmaticus, 259, 271
Mercurius Scoticus, 303
Michelson, John, 151
Militia Ordinance, 154-55, 159
Milton, John, 247, 252, 264, 309n14, 319
  Areopagitica, 182
  Eikonoklastes, 272
  Tenure of Kings and Magistrates, The, 252
minstrels, 34
Modyford, Thomas, 318
Mohammedism, forced conversion to, 74
Mompesson, Giles, 67
monopolies, 66
Moreton, William, 142, 168n14
Morton, Thomas, 41
Moyer, Laurence, 14

N

Needham, Marchmont, 271, 321
Neville, Archbishop, 39
Newman, Samuel, 38
New Model Army, 24, 165, 188, 324
Newton, Lady, 56, 62
  House of Lyme, The, 56
Newton, Thomas, 80n5
Nicholas Bacon, 136n19
Nichols, Edward, 293
Noble, Mark, 20, 242
Nowell, Alexander, 42
Noy, William, 126
Nutt, A. Y., 242

O

Oliver Cromwell an Historical Play (Green), 205
Osbaldestone, Richard, 65
Overton, Richard, 247
Owen, John, 248, 250

P

Pack, Michael, 315, 318
Pamela's prayer, 272
Parnell, Thomas, 146, 169n17, 252, 324
Parsons, Robert, 37
  Conference about the Next Succession, 37
patriot, usage of the term, 91
Peile, John, 43, 62, 62n16
  Biographical Register of Christ's College Cambridge, 43
peine forte et dure. *See* pressing to death
Pell, Thomas, 322
Penn, Giles, 77
Pennington, Issac, 169n26
Pennington, John, 71, 82n13
Percy, Henry, 57
Peter, Hugh, 216, 249, 255, 263-64
Pocahontas, 53, 61n10
polarchy, usage of the term, 87
Pope, Mary, 222
Porter, Endymion, 69, 81n9
Pott, Walter, 39
Presbyterian, 46n20
pressing to death, 205-6
Price, John, 80n5
Prideaux, Edmund, 269
Prideaux, Edward, 295
Proctor, Richard, 180
Prynne, William, 79, 91, 93, 167n2, 182, 262
  Health's Sickness, 91
  Histriomastix, 93, 95
  Unloveliness of Lovelocks, The, 91
Purbeck Temple, 206
Puritan, definition of, 47n21
Pym, John, 90-91, 141, 148, 150, 152, 162, 201

R

Ralegh, Walter, 52, 60n6, 66-67, 80n6, 137n23
Randolph, Ambroise, 252, 282n33
Responsio ad Edictum Elizabethae, 37
Rich, Henry, 250

Rich, Robert, 52, 73, 250, 284
Richard, II, 232n11
River Dee seaport, 143
Robin Hood, 35-36, 105
Robinson, Luke, 252
Rolfe, John, 57, 61n10
Rosworm, Johann, 159, 265-66
Rous, Francis, 90, 195
Rowe, Samuel, 252
Rump Parliament, 246
Russell, Elizabeth, 279n19
Ryley, William, 321

S

Sallee, 73-74, 84n16
Savage, John, 144, 158
Savile, Thomas, 147
Say, William, 202
Scott, Thomas, 252-53, 282n34, 292-93
Sealed Knot, 262
Selden, John, 47, 90, 195
   Mare Clausum, 321
Self-Denying Ordinance, 165, 184, 246
Selleck, David, 333
Seymour, Edward, 25, 138n30
Seymour, William, 120, 122-24
Shaa, Edmond, 39
Shallcrosse, Edmund, 179
Shipton, Samuel, 179
Simpson, Richard, 103
Skeffington, Richard, 185
Skippon, Philip, 304
social elevation, 24
Somer Hill. *See* Summerhill
sovereign power, 87, 91
Sparke, Michael, 92
Stafford, Anne, 102
Stanley, Anne, 333
Stanley, James, 155, 306
Stanley family, 27
Star Chamber, 92, 94-95
Steele, Anthony, 248
Steele, William, 180, 185, 210n15
Stelfox, William, 313
St. John, J. A., 16

St. John, Oliver, 200, 251
Strangeways, Major, 206
Strangwayes, John, 151
Stratford, Hugh, 106
Stuart, Arbella, 53, 61n9, 119-23, 137n23, 138n29
Stuart, Charles. *See* Charles I
Summerhill, 265, 280n20
Sydenham, Edward, 130
Sydney, Algernon, 204

T

Talbot, Francis, 102
Talbot, George, 102, 119
Talbot, Gilbert, 104
Temple, John, 74
Tenure of Kings and Magistrates, The (Milton), 252
Thompson, Martyn P., 89
Thurloe, John, 274, 320
Tomkinson, Christopher, 185
torture, 205
Touchet, Mervin, 93
Trevor-Roper, Hugh R., 72
Tropham, Thomas, 238
Truth's Victory Over Tyrants (Lilburne), 270
Tutbury Fair, 34
Tutbury Honor, 34

U

Unloveliness of Lovelocks, The (Prynne), 91

V

Vane, Henry, 162, 330
Vassall, Samuel, 83n15
Venn, John, 152, 161
Villiers, Edward, 67
Villiers, George, 67, 69-71, 83n13, 85n18, 85n22
   assassination of, 64, 67, 69-71, 73-74, 81, 82, 83, 83n13, 85n18, 142, 305

W

Wainwright, James, 299, 308n4
Walkenden, Robert, 42
Walker, William, 242
Walrond, Humphrey, 312
Warburton, Peter, 269
Watson, John, 12, 280
    "Memoirs of the Family of Bradshaw of Marple in Cheshire," 12
Wells, Bernard, 32
West Indies, 73, 305, 312
Wharton, Philip, 157
Whiitaker, Alexander, 61n10
Whitelocke, Bulstrode, 47n20, 198, 200, 250, 275, 282n34, 307, 322
Widdrington, Thomas, 200, 250
Wilde, John, 152, 200
Williams, John, 265
Willoughby, Francis, 312-14, 318, 320
Wilson, Mary, 275
Wingate, Roger, 84
Winnington, John, 180
Winslow, Edward, 314, 316
Winstanley, Gerrard, 247, 253
Winwood, Ralph, 124
Wood, Antony, 15, 91, 209
Wright, Peter, 312
Wright, Robert, 14
Wright, William, 317
Wyberslegh Hall, 27

Y

Yale, Elihu, 273
Yelverton, Henry, 67, 81n7
Young, Henry, 74

Z

Zidan, Mulay, 76, 84, 84n16
Zion's Plea (Leighton), 92